Lecture Notes in Computer Science 12345

More information about this subseries at http://www.springer.com/series/7408

Wolfgang Ahrendt · Bernhard Beckert ·
Richard Bubel · Reiner Hähnle ·
Mattias Ulbrich (Eds.)

Deductive
Software Verification:
Future Perspectives

Reflections on the Occasion of 20 Years of KeY

 Springer

Editors
Wolfgang Ahrendt ⓘ
Chalmers University of Technology
Gothenburg, Sweden

Bernhard Beckert ⓘ
Karlsruhe Institute of Technology
Karlsruhe, Germany

Richard Bubel
Technical University of Darmstadt
Darmstadt, Germany

Reiner Hähnle ⓘ
Technical University of Darmstadt
Darmstadt, Germany

Mattias Ulbrich ⓘ
Karlsruhe Institute of Technology
Karlsruhe, Germany

ISSN 0302-9743   ISSN 1611-3349   (electronic)
Lecture Notes in Computer Science
ISBN 978-3-030-64353-9   ISBN 978-3-030-64354-6   (eBook)
https://doi.org/10.1007/978-3-030-64354-6

LNCS Sublibrary: SL2 – Programming and Software Engineering

This Springer imprint is published by the registered company Springer Nature Switzerland AG
The registered company address is: Gewerbestrasse 11, 6330 Cham, Switzerland

Preface

A little more than 20 years ago, a group of researchers started out with what became the KeY project. Back then, KeY was one of the early efforts in an emerging community, whose common agenda was to transform deductive verification methods from a largely theoretical endeavor, mostly applied to academic (class room) examples, to techniques and tools that enable effective verification of software developed in widely used programming languages and paradigms, for realistic applications. Indeed, the theoretical underpinnings that had evolved in the 30 years before that, since the late 60s, were vital for the success for this new movement. But the new focus also came with new scientific challenges.

Today, we can say that the more applied focus of the last two decades in deductive verification required not only strong efforts in efficiency and usability of verification tools, but also extensive further development on the theory side. In short, to become more practical, we needed more theory, and continue to do so. To master the concepts in contemporary languages, paradigms, and scenarios (aliasing, exceptions, concurrency, communication, reuse, extendability, dynamic configuration, to name a few), the community had to find new ways to precisely model and efficiently process these phenomena and artifacts, with a focus on applicability and usability. For a more comprehensive exposition of these developments, we refer to "Deductive Software Verification: From Pen-and-Paper Proofs to Industrial Tools" by Reiner Hähnle and Marieke Huisman.[1]

During the deductive verification journey in the past 20 years, the KeY project was only one "means of transport", but a steady one, with strong links to other actors in the community. Therefore, we took the 20 year anniversary of KeY as an opportunity to invite researchers, inside and outside of the project, to contribute to a book capturing some state-of-the-art developments in the field. We feel very lucky that so many of our peers responded. The result is a book whose chapters identify and address some of the latest challenges of deductive software verification. It captures aspects of verification tool development, the integration of different verification techniques, efficiency and usability of verification methods, novel contracts for specification and verification, and history.

Part I, "History," contains a single chapter: "A Short History of KeY." Peter H. Schmitt gives an overview of the beginning and first decade of the project. This is not merely interesting for readers with a special interest in KeY. Instead, it is a rare glimpse into and a reflection on the turns, successes, and also failures, which a long term research project experienced, when coming into being and growing from there, in particular in a (then) new landscape.

---

[1] In *Computing and Software Science: State of the Art and Perspectives*, Bernhard Steffen and Gerard Woeginger (Eds.), LNCS 10000, Springer 2019.

Part II, "Verification Tools," starts with a chapter[2] which also takes a historical viewpoint. It offers a retrospective on the development of the KeYmaera family of provers for hybrid system verification. The second chapter[3] of this part focuses on performance bottlenecks, and their improvement, in the context of the VerCors tool for the verification of parallel programs. Altogether, this part demonstrates the importance of implementation considerations for the impact of verification methods.

Part III focuses on a central technique of deductive verification and, therefore, of this book: *Contracts*. This concept is the cornerstone of modularity, and thus essential in rendering deductive verification scalable. The chapters introduce behavioral contracts for cooperative scheduling[4], propagate the usage of abstract contracts for feature evolution and feature interaction[5], and discuss constraint-based contract inference[6]. Another chapter addresses a long-standing issue in the verification of concurrent applications, by moving from explicit to implicit dynamic frames.[7] The final chapter[8] in this part discusses deductive verification in a very new application area, called smart contracts. Even if smart contracts are rather programs than specification contracts, they realize – and enforce – a contract between the users who chose to engage with it.

It is mandatory for a book on contemporary deductive software verification to include feasibility and usability aspects, which Part IV focuses on. The field has grown out of the analysis of toy examples and is now looking at complex properties of real-world programs. The first chapter[9] provides a tutorial for the challenging verification of the linked list data structure in the Java Collection Framework. The second chapter[10] describes a long term, collaborative challenge named VerifyThis, which calls upon the verification community to verify aspects of realistic software over a longer period, with the ultimate goal to facilitate the application of formal analysis in the software development process. The third chapter[11] presents suggestions to improve usability and user guidance in interactive deductive verification.

Finally, Part V discusses two instances of integration of verification techniques. First, it presents an integration of static and dynamic analysis applied to the classical security problem of noninterference.[12] Second, it presents a novel integration of partial

---

[2] "A Retrospective on Developing Hybrid System Provers in the KeYmaera Family," by Mitsch and Platzer.

[3] "Improving Performance of the VerCors Program Verifier," by Mulder et al.

[4] "Behavioral Contracts for Cooperative Scheduling," by Kamburjan et al.

[5] "Using Abstract Contracts for Verifying Evolving Features and Their Interactions," by Knüppel et al.

[6] "Constraint-based Contract Inference for Deductive Verification," by Alshnakat et al.

[7] "From Explicit to Implicit Dynamic Frames in Concurrent Reasoning for Java," by Mostowski.

[8] "Formal Analysis of Smart Contracts: Applying the KeY System," by Ahrendt et al.

[9] "A Tutorial on Verifying LinkedList using KeY," by Hiep et al.

[10] "VerifyThis! – The Collaborative Long-term Challenge," by Huisman et al.

[11] "Usability Recommendations for User Guidance in Deductive Program Verification," by Grebing and Ulbrich.

[12] "Integration of Static and Dynamic Analysis Techniques for Checking Noninterference," by Beckert et al.

order reduction (an optimization principle hugely successful in model checking) with symbolic execution (which lies at the heart of KeY style deductive verification).[13]

We thank all authors for accepting our invitation and putting a lot of effort into producing the high-quality content we are proud to present here. With this book, we hope to provide the community with insights into recent and latest developments in important subareas of contemporary deductive software verification.

For many years Alfred Hofmann, who retired in 2019, handled the KeY-related LNCS volumes at Springer, including the present one. The editors and the whole KeY team would like to express their gratitude for his constant support, always smooth communication, and many constructive suggestions.

July 2020

Wolfgang Ahrendt
Bernhard Beckert
Richard Bubel
Reiner Hähnle
Mattias Ulbrich

---

[13] "SymPaths: Symbolic Execution Meets Partial Order Reduction," by De Boer et al.

Organization

Editors

Wolfgang Ahrendt	Chalmers University of Technology, Sweden
Bernhard Beckert	Karlsruhe Institute of Technology (KIT), Germany
Richard Bubel	Technische Universität Darmstadt, Germany
Reiner Hähnle	Technische Universität Darmstadt, Germany
Mattias Ulbrich	Karlsruhe Institute of Technology (KIT), Germany

Reviewers

Marcello Bonsangue	Leiden University, The Netherlands
Frank S. de Boer	Centrum Wiskunde & Informatica, The Netherlands
Stijn de Gouw	The Open University, The Netherlands
Crystal Chang Din	University of Oslo, Norway
Sarah Grebing	Karlsruhe Institute of Technology (KIT), Germany
Dilian Gurov	KTH Royal Institute of Technology, Sweden
Mihai Herda	Karlsruhe Institute of Technology (KIT), Germany
Hans-Dieter A. Hiep	Centrum Wiskunde & Informatica, The Netherlands
Marieke Huisman	University of Twente, The Netherlands
Einar Broch Johnsen	University of Oslo, Norway
Sebastiaan Joosten	Dartmouth College, USA
Eduard Kamburjan	Technische Universität Darmstadt, Germany
Michael Kirsten	Karlsruhe Institute of Technology (KIT), Germany
Alexander Knüppel	Technische Universität Braunschweig, Germany
Stefan Mitsch	Carnegie Mellon University, USA
Wojciech Mostowski	Halmstad University, Sweden
Henk Mulder	University of Twente, The Netherlands
André Platzer	Carnegie Mellon University, USA
Violet Ka I Pun	Western Norway University of Applied Sciences, Norway
Philipp Rümmer	Uppsala University, Sweden
Ina Schaefer	Technische Universität Braunschweig, Germany
Jonas Schiffl	Karlsruhe Institute of Technology (KIT), Germany
Peter Schmitt	Karlsruhe Institute of Technology (KIT), Germany
Silvia Lizeth Tapia Tarifa	University of Oslo, Norway
Thomas Thüm	Ulm University, Germany
Lars Tveito	University of Oslo, Norway

Contents

Integration of Verification Techniques

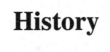

History

A Short History of KeY

Peter H. Schmitt[(✉)]

Department of Informatics, Karlsruhe Institute of Technology (KIT),
Am Fasanengarten 5, 76131 Karlsruhe, Germany
pschmitt@ira.uka.de

Abstract. This paper describes the story of the first nine years of the KeY project, its original goals, the people involved, its setbacks, but also its occasional failures and blind alleys. It is deliberately written in a more personal style, but tries to meet scientific standards of correctness and completeness.

1 The Beginning

The KeY project was conceived on May 14, 1997 in the Abbaye des Prémontrés in Pont-à-Mousson at the 6th Tableaux Conference. Reiner Hähnle and I and a bottle of red wine retreated in the evening into a quiet and cosy nook of the spectacular conference venue to generate ideas for a NEW project. We were both ready for new challenges. Reiner had just completed his *Habilitation*. The nationwide focus project on automated deduction (DFG Schwerpunktprogramm "Deduktion") would come to an end in June 1997 after six successful years. The main results were collected in the monumental book project [13] filling 1250 pages and Wolfgang Bibel published a condensed report [12]. The bulk of research was directed towards theorem proving and theorem provers per se. Applications were seen as the ultimate goal, however, and first steps into applications in mathematics and into software engineering were taken. The examples of applications in software engineering reported in [13] were at very abstract levels. Not a single line of code of an imperative programming language was inspected. That was pretty much the state of the art worldwide. Thus the general direction of follow-up projects was predictable: move deductive support closer to the everyday production of software. But that left open a wide range of choices.

Reiner wrote a three-page summary of our brainstorming session the next day (classified, perhaps tongue-in-cheek, "Confidential"). A first rough idea was to develop a methodology and to build a tool for deductive support early on in the specification phase of software systems. The term *verification* occurred only once in the notes and only in a negative context: We then proposed not to aim for full formal verification but rather for some kind of validation. Considering the lofty goals of the KeY project to come, that was a pussy footed beginning. On the other hand one might view this as a prophetic foresight. In the survey paper [10] on formal verification published 17 years later we find the following sentences:

© Springer Nature Switzerland AG 2020
W. Ahrendt et al. (Eds.): Deductive Software Verification, LNCS 12345, pp. 3–18, 2020.
https://doi.org/10.1007/978-3-030-64354-6_1

In the past decade, it has become increasingly clear that full functional verification is an elusive goal for almost all application scenarios.
Not verification but specification is the real bottleneck in functional verification.

The focus of this paper is on the first two KeY project proposals, thus covering the years from 1997 to 2006. Occasionally, when it fits into the story, I will include more recent episodes and events. In general, however, many important later developments of the KeY system are not touched upon. It remains the task of the next KeY chronographer to address such topics as counterexample generation, symbolic debugging, concurrency, the specification language ABS, and new application areas such as electronic voting and some more. I also want to emphasize that I will not gauge what has been achieved till 2006 against the present state of the art in automated deduction. If you want, you can do this on your own after reading the excellent exposition [30].

It is perhaps the greatest joy of looking back that one can find answers to questions like: How well did we anticipate the future developments? Have we put our project on the right track? Where have we failed? Which successes were just serendipitous? This will be done on the following pages in a more anecdotal than systematic way.

2   The First KeY Project Proposals

That first brainstorming night in Pont-à-Mousson was followed by many joint meetings of my research team with Wolfram Menzel's, trying to decide on the details of the research project. Wolfram Menzel had been a professor in the Computer Science Department at the University of Karlsruhe from year one (1972). His group had just implemented the first version of the program verification system KIV (Karlsruhe Interactive Verifier). I remember very scrupulous and lengthy discussions at these meetings; we left no stone un-turned. Finally, Reiner Hähnle, Wolfram Menzel, and I submitted a proposal to the DFG funding agency on the 16th of December, 1997 under the title, 'Integrierter Deduktiver Software-Entwurf' (Integrated deductive software design). Though we could only ask for funding for a period of three years, we defined milestones for a total duration of six years, making it clear that we would after three years submit an extension proposal. It was approved on the 2nd of November in 1998. DFG would fund three researcher positions for two years, with a third year dependent on submission of a positive progress report.

The extension proposal was submitted on 9 July, 2001 by Bernhard Beckert and me.[1] In the end, everything went well and we received funds for three researchers for six years. The project continued till October 2006, due to not being able to fill all open positions immediately. The shortage of qualified candidates in the field of formal methods was a continuing problem at the time. DFG was very generous in this respect. It did not, of course, increase the amount

---

[1] Reiner had moved to Gothenburg in January of 2000.

of money, but it did extend the time to spend it. In 2003, Bernhard accepted a junior professor position at the University of Koblenz, and DFG graciously allowed subcontracting to him there.

To tell the truth, the original proposal was not accepted by DFG. The reviewers acknowledged the excellent standing of all three proposers in the area of mathematical logic and automated deduction, but they questioned our experience in software engineering. They were also concerned that we would develop a marvelous system that would have little practical value. An important professional principle is never to get angry with a negative review. The raised concerns were not totally without foundation, but they did not take us by surprise. Through personal contacts we had gained insight into how some companies produce software. Telekom AG in Darmstadt and FUN Kommunikationssysteme in Karlsruhe were happy to write letters of support for us. On the academic side, many professors in software engineering thought that program verification people tended to sail to sea in a sieve. They did not care a fig for formal methods. We are grateful to professor Jürgen Ebert from the University of Koblenz, who had run a couple of Meta-CASE tool applications with industrial partners and agreed to act as a mentor on this topic. Our response to the DFG covered little more than one page but it cleared the way to final acceptance.

On the afternoon of 3 June, 1998 I was on my way to Kiel to attend a mathematical meeting. On the train I ran into a colleague from my previous life as a mathematical logician. That morning there had been a terrible train accident close to the community of Eschede. The ICE 884 train had derailed, killing 101 people and severely injuring 88. This blocked the way to our destination, and the train was redirected through village stations that probably had never seen an express train before. We were hours behind schedule. The restaurant car had long run out of supplies and in this extreme situation my colleague confided to me that he had been a reviewer of our proposal, and that he was responsible for the temporary rejection. We still got on friendly with each other, though at that time it was not clear that our project proposal would be accepted in the end.

Both proposals—1997 and 2001—were structured into four major goals. Here are the original section headings in German with English translation:

1. Erweiterung der Entwurfsumgebung
   Extending the design platform
2. Erzeugung von Beweisverpflichtungen
   Generating proof obligations
3. Integriertes Deduktionssystem
   Integrated deduction system
4. Verifikation von Programmen für Chipkarten und Erweiterung auf volles Java oder zweite Fallstudie
   Verification of programs on chip cards and extension to full Java or second case study.

The first publication of the KeY project [32] was a condensed report of the first proposal.

3 The KeY Project Running

The four subsections here correspond to the projects goals as stated at the end of the previous section and in the order given there.

3.1 The CASE Tool

True to the longterm goal of transferring formal methods from academic research into industrial use, we proposed an integrated development environment (IDE) to be used in practice. IDEs at that time were called CASE tools (Computer Aided/Assisted Software Engineering) or even better Meta-CASE tools. *Meta* in this context meant that the tool could be instantiated to accommodate a wide range of different design methodologies. We thought that would make it possible to extend the tool easily with features for deductive verification. We looked at half a dozen of possible candidates for a Meta-CASE tool and installed some of them. In the end, we stuck with Borland Together Control Center. Borland is now a subsidiary of micro focus and the Together product is still on the market [14]. In 2001 we could report that a first version of the integration of KeY into Borland Together Control Center was operational.

After two years, the KeY project was at a critical crossroads. In the technical report [2] we find the line:

> We concentrate on object-oriented analysis and design methods (OOAD), because of their key role in today's software practice.

The question was: Do we not only use a CASE tool but also commit ourselves to a specific OOAD methodology? In [2] we explained how we thought software could be developed within the KeY system:

> In the KeY approach, a hierarchical module concept with sub-modules supports the structuring of large models. The modules in a system model form a tree with respect to the sub-module relation. Besides sub-modules and other model components, a module contains the refinement relations between components that describe the same part of the modeled system in two consecutive levels of refinement. The verification problem associated with a module is to show that these refinements are correct. The refinement relations must be provided by the user; typically, they include a signature mapping.

At the end of this iterative and incremental process a Java program was to be written. This plan was not realized, and I believe that to have been a fortunate turn of events. In the 2001 funding proposal there is no mentioning of OOAD. But we still hung on to the idea that program development and program verification should start with a UML model, with the understanding expressed by the following quote from [20, page 13]:

> The UML is a modeling language, not a method. The UML has no notion of process, which is an important part of a method.

It was of course clear to everybody (including us!) that UML models could never be precise enough to serve as a basis for formal program verification. We concentrated our efforts on making UML models more precise by adding OCL (Object Constraint Language) constraints. An OCL parser, provided by the team of Heinrich Hußmann, then at TU Dresden (since 2003 at LMU), had been integrated into our CASE tool. That still left open the question, how—if at all—would a program developer add OCL? Reiner came up with a fantastic idea: Program developers loved design patterns, i.e., reusable solutions, to commonly occurring problems. We added schematic OCL constraints to design patterns. When using these extended patterns, programmers would add OCL constraints without even noticing it [6].

Considerable time and energy went into supporting the development of OCL. The doctoral thesis of Thomas Baar [5] investigated ways to describe the semantics of OCL-type specification languages. We participated in the international UML conferences 2003 (San Fransisco) and 2004 (Lisbon), getting involved in organizing the OCL workshops at these events.[2]

But the demise of OCL in the KeY universe had already begun in 2001. In the second proposal, investigations were planned into JML (Java Modeling Language) as an alternative specification language. We were unsatisfied with imprecise documentation and annoyed by the in-transparent management of OCL by the Object Management Group (OMG). Our criticism and suggestions went unanswered. We could not even find out if they had been sent to the right people. More importantly, we noticed that many requirements that we wanted to express could not be formalized in OCL: frame and depends-on information of methods, loop invariants, loop termination conditions, etc. I cannot put a date on it, but we eventually dropped OCL in favor of JML. This not only meant that we exchanged one specification language for another; it also meant that we gave up support of early modeling stages. KeY had become a verifier for Java programs.

The OCL workshops are still alive and kicking. The 19th International Workshop on OCL and Textual Modeling will be part of the MODELS conference in Munich in September 2019, organized by Achim D. Brucker from the University of Exeter and Thomas Baar, still on the committee [41]. The minutes [15] of an unofficial meeting of the leading OCL activists in 2013 in Aachen shows, however, that OCL is still riddled with the same problems we encountered when we left, including

- Should OCL be executable?
- What is the semantics of _. allInstances ()?
- Termination conditions for recursive definitions.
- Four-valued logic.

Documentation seems to be much better now [43].

---

[2] The Lisbon conference was the last UML conference; from 2005 on the series was called *MODELS*.

3.2   Proof Obligations

Inititally, verification would start with a UML/OCL model. The requirements specified in this model should be translated into formulas of Dynamic Logic, the logic of KeY's theorem prover—see Sect. 3.3 below. The 1997 proposal envisaged that generation of proof obligations would go through two stages: First, from UML/OCL to a high level specification language with clear semantics, and then from there to Dynamic Logic or directly to first-order logic. As candidates for the high level specification language we chose Yuri Gurevich's Abstract State Machines (ASM) and Abstract Machine Notation (AMN), the specification language of the B-tool. Why this detour? We would need a formal semantics of UML/OCL. This would be accomplished—indirectly—by translation into ASM or AMN, which had established a reputation for formalizing semantics for all kind of things. In addition, Wolfgang Ahrendt, who was one of the first three researchers hired for the KeY project, had gained great expertise with verification based on ASMs through the WAM case study done with the KIV system [50] and through the one year project *Design and Verification Environment for Dynamic Algebras* (Dynamic Algebra was the original name for ASM). These ideas have never been turned into reality. After abandoning UML/OCL modeling there simply was no need for them anymore.

In the beginning we boldly proposed half a dozen proof obligations that we wanted to address: precondition implies postcondition, properties of data types, simplification and consistency of specifications, correctness of refinement, temporal properties. Frame conditions were not on the list, i.e., specifications that given locations are not changed by a method. We discovered only much later that the verification of frame conditions was not just a nice way to make specifications more concise, but essential for tackling larger programs. This also brought to our attention that our semantics of Java did not explicitly model the heap. We did not think that this was a problem and devised our intellectually demanding, theoretically impressive version of frame verification introducing the concept of *non-rigid symbols*. In the accompanying paper we wrote:

> Compared with an explicit modeling of stack and heap, using non-rigid symbols achieves a higher level of abstraction, which improves readability and helps with handling aliasing.

Nobody believed us. The paper was submitted on three different occasions and always rejected with the rather condescending advice that the right way to solve our problem was to model the heap explicitly. In the end we published the paper as a technical report, [19], and added the heap to KeY's Java semantics.

In the first KeY project proposal we mentioned in passing that we would also verify information flow properties, for example that personal data stored on a Java Card could only be read by authorized users. As early as 2003 Reiner and co-authors showed how to encode information flow in Dynamic Logic, see [16] and the later paper [17]. The approach pioneered in [16] was later dubbed *the self-composition approach* by Gilles Barthe [7] and [17] became the standard reference for it. Both papers contained only a few small examples done with KeY.

In his dissertation in 2014, Christoph Scheben [49] also based his implementation in KeY on the self-composition approach, but his goal was to make it workable for larger Java programs. He extended JML with contracts for the flexible specification of information flow properties. In 2018 Simon Greiner presented a general framework for non-interference in component-based systems [26]. These are early instances of a new topic in formal methods research: verification of relational properties. This phrase refers to properties addressing more than one function call. I find it fascinating to witness new research directions in the making. Starting from investigating two runs of one piece of program code with different initial variables assignments, moving on to relate runs of different pieces of program code, and then to the investigation of programs addressing more than one heap. The latter has been implemented in the KeY system by Wojciech Mostowski. He used it to model transaction rollback in Java Card [3, Chapter 10]. More details can be found in [42].

The KeY project was exceptional for using Dynamic Logic, but also for being the only major verification system that does not use an intermediate language. Many program verifiers translate the source program plus specifications into an intermediate low level language. *Boogie* (previously called BoogiePL) [40] and *WhyML*, the intermediate language for the Why3 platform [58], are popular choices. Verification conditions in first-order logic are then generated from the Boogie program. Through the language constructs *assume* and *assert*, specifications are a genuine part of the Boogie program. The advantages of this setup are that the second part can be used without any changes for different source languages or different releases of the same. There is no principle obstacle for a verifier based on Dynamic Logic to employ the intermediate language approach, as has been demonstrated by Mattias Ulbrich's dissertation [55]. But I suspect that relying on Dynamic Logic makes it less likely to follow the intermediate language line. Adopting this line is still an open discussion within the KeY community.

In 2001 the concepts of a Dynamic Logic for Java, which we called JavaDL, were ready, the infrastructure—data types and Java parser—and a prover for first-order logic in place. Implementation of the program verifier could begin. And not too soon. In the first proposal we had prided ourselves on being among the first to propose verification of runnable Java code. In the 2001 proposal we had to list five projects competing in the formalization of a Java semantics for various forms of automated reasoning. These are the references available to us at the time:

- Arndt Poetzsch-Heffter and Peter Müller developed a Hoare logic for a, rather small, subset of Java [44,45].
- Tobias Nipkow and David von Oheimb gave an axiomatic semantics for a sublanguage of Java via embedding in Isabelle/HOL [57].

- The LOOP project at the university of Nijmegen had started under the direction of Bart Jacobs [35,56]. Marieke Huisman was working on her PhD *Java program verification in Higher-order logic with PVS and Isabelle* [34].
- The KIV system had moved to the University of Augsburg and Wolfgang Reif and his team had realized a Dynamic Logic formalization of Java Card [53].
- Robert Stärk presented a formalization of the Java Virtual Machine using Abstract State Machines [52].

We had hopped on the right bandwagon at the right time.

I do not remember when it happened, but is was certainly well before 2001 that a concept was adopted that turned out to be very useful: *taclets* [9]. This format for writing rules for an automated theorem prover had been developed and prototypically implemented by Elmar Habermalz in his dissertation [27] under the tongue twisting name *schematic theory specific rules (STSR)*. It enabled formalizing the logical content of a rule and the pragmatic information on how to use it. Elmar Habermalz had already generated from a given STSR a first-order formula that formalized its correctness. This was also implemented for our taclets, but rarely used at first. It is now used regularly to prove correctness of newly added rules on the basis of a minimal set of axioms.

Generation of counter examples or counter models had not been mentioned in the first proposal but surfaced during the first three years of the project and was included in the second proposal. The local efforts lead to Wolfgang Ahrendt's dissertation [1]. On the international stage Reiner established contacts to Ryuzo Hasegawa on the basis of his work on *model generation theorem provers* [21,28]. In hindsight this was a (probably necessary!) detour. The end user of the KeY system is not so much interested in why a logical claim cannot be proved. Those who are interested will today find answers from the SMT solvers. The end user is really interested in what is wrong with his program. This led to the generation of test cases, as described in Chapter 12 of in the 2016 KeY book [3].

The progress report of the first phase of the KeY project proudly presented the extension of JavaDL by the new modality 'throughout'. In classical Dynamic Logic one could only express that some property holds true after termination of a program, provided the precondition is true at program start. With the new modality one could express that some property holds true during the whole program execution, provided the precondition is true at program start. That this extension required comparatively small effort is a striking example of the advantages of Dynamic Logic. See Subsection 9.4 of the first KeY book [11] for more details. It should be noted that the 'throughout' modality is absolutely necessary for the specification of Java Card programs. Normal program execution requires that power supply should at no time be interrupted nor should the card be removed from the reader. Otherwise special recovery mechanisms must be triggered.

User interfaces are often seen as the orphan child of verification system development. Designing and implementing them does not lead to publications in serious research journals. To counter this tendency the workshop User Interfaces for Theorem Provers, UITP, was brought to life in 1995. In the KeY project we eventually realized that it would not suffice to rely only on the user interface of a CASE tool, and so we started to build our own. The result was—and I believe still is—one of the most user friendly interfaces to a program verification system, with syntax highlighting, navigation in proofs, suggestions of next steps, and drag-and-drop actions. Martin Giese's presentation of the KeY GUI at the 2003 UITP workshop is available at [25].

One exceptionally unique endeavor not a task in the DFG proposal and not funded by DFG money came about through Reiner's personal connections. Together with Aarne Ranta he designed and prototypically implemented an authoring tool, based on the Grammatical Framework [46], that would assist the user in writing specifications simultaneously in OCL and in English [31]. A comprehensive account can be found in the dissertation [38] of Kristofer Johannisson, who also did the bulk of the work.

In light of the progress in natural language technology, I thought it important that this type of research be continued and was very pleased to see that it was. In addition to a careful explanation of the general methodology, the paper [47] lists similar applications of the Grammatical Framework. Even better, a very successful commercial project with the *altran* company has just been completed, translating Z specifications into English in the context of avionic software development subject to the software safety certification standard DO-178C.

3.3   The Deductive System

The third goal of the 1997 proposal was titled *integrated deduction system*. The interactive approach that had been used in the KIV (Karlsruhe Interactive Verifier) was to be integrated with the fully automatic approach used in the $_3T^AP$ system, that had been developed in my group financed by an IBM contract. At the time, the combination of these two types of automated reasoning received much attention in the scientific community; we joined in with [4]. The relevance of this issue for the KeY project was, however, overstated. The deductive component that was implemented in the end for KeY simply was an interactive verifier automating as much as possible, no rocket science behind it. There was another meaning behind the term *integrated deduction system*. We proposed to integrate other reasoning methods and explicitly named (1) model checking, (2) binary decision diagrams, (3) SAT solvers, and (4) special decision procedures. As far as the first three methods are concerned, I still believe that they can be part of a software verification system, though I am not so sure of a deduction system integrating them. Item (4), on the other hand, has been fully realized in KeY by the integration of SMT (Satisfiability modulo theories) solvers.

Implementing Dynamic Logic was unusual, surprisingly so. It had been developed by Vaughan Pratt as early as 1974 and made known to a wider audience by the revised version in David Harel's PhD thesis [33]. Werner Stephan, the principal *mover* in the early days of the KIV system [29], was the first to employ this logic in a program verification system. Reiner had been a research assistant with Werner Stephan's group since late 1985 and programmed the first lines of the system. That experience led Reiner to argue that we should continue to use Dynamic Logic in the KeY system. I had almost no experience with implementation of a program verification system and would have adopted this decision anyway. I had delved into Dynamic Logic myself—on a very theoretical level, publishing a paper on the computational complexity of a fragment of Dynamic Logic, [51]—and was enthusiastic about it. It has worked well so far, and I fancy it will do so in the future, but KIV, KeY, and André Platzer's KeYmaera theorem prover for hybrid systems are the only current verification systems using Dynamic Logic.

At that time, symbolic execution as a verification paradigm fitted so well with dynamic logic that we did not consider alternative paradigms such as the generation of first-order verification conditions.

There is a story to be told about the paper [51] mentioned above. In 1985, the section on mathematical logic at the mathematical institute, University of Freiburg organized a small, low-key meeting on logic in computer science. The invited speakers were Amir Pnueli and David Harel. My paper had also been accepted. I still worked for IBM and had little time to prepare my talk. So I ended up scribbling overhead projector slides outside while the speaker before me was delivering his presentation. When I heard the applause in the lecture hall I shuffled together what slides I had finished, went inside and started my talk. At the end I was very much relieved that everything had gone well. But then David Harel stood up and remarked that my result could not be true, because it contradicted Lindström's theorem. "Oh, too bad, I will try to find out what went wrong," was all I could answer. The official reception for the meeting was scheduled for the evening the same day. By then I had figured out what had gone wrong. Over a glass of champagne I told David Harel that my logic was not closed under negation, so Lindström's theorem did not apply. He apologized, and, as he was on the editorial board of the journal *Information and Control* (from 1987 on, *Information and Computation*), suggested that I submit the paper there, which I did.

Besides the decision on the logic we had to decide on a specific reasoning calculus. Given the previous work in the group there was no discussion: It had to be a a tableau calculus. But which flavor? Bernhard had in his doctoral thesis [8] presented a grande tour d'horizon of possible variations, extensions, combinations of tableau calculi. In the beginning we settled on implementing a tableau calculus with free variables, which we sometimes also called meta variables. This was probably inspired by the research in the focus project on automated deduction that predated the KeY project. The simplest way to make use of universal formulas was to find a suitable ground term t in the proof developed so far and replace a universal formula $\forall x \phi(x)$ by $\phi(t)$. We looked down on people using this cheap solution. We would replace $\forall x \phi(x)$ by $\phi(x)$ with x a fresh variable and would decide later on clever substitutions for x. That is no easy task. You could find a substitution that closes the current proof branch only to discover later that it prevented the closure of the next pending branch. So you want to backtrack and try another substitution. From our experiences with the $_3T^AP$ prover, which was implemented in PROLOG and heavily depended on backtracking, it was mandatory to avoid backtracking. This implied in particular that the calculus had to be proof confluent: Any proof attempt of a true statement can be completed to a full proof. The final proof might contain a bulk of useless intermediate steps, but it would never be necessary to revert to a previous state. Pruning and simplification techniques that violated proof confluence thus had to be avoided. Martin Giese created a number of clever and scientifically brilliant ideas in his dissertation [23]; see also [22] and [24]. In the long run, however, it became clear that this approach was too complicated. For example, an existential quantifier had to be replaced by a Skolem function instead of a mere Skolem constant, and unification algorithms had to be employed. The calculus presented by Martin Giese in the first KeY book [11] no longer used free variables.

In 2001 the KeY theorem prover was ready to prove formulas without programs to our great satisfaction. The system was shown as a tool demo at the FME conference (Formal Methods Europe) in Berlin from 12–16 March, 2001. Even years after this you could find one or two taclets in KeY's taclet base adorned by comment, *This is a hack for the tool demo. To be removed later.*

3.4 Case Studies

In the 1997 proposal we listed three arguments for the choice of Java Card programs as case studies: (1) The programs are small; (2) They avoid complicated language constructs such as real numbers, object cloning or threads; and (we hoped!) (3) Java Cards would be the next big success story in digital industry.

Our hopes were realized, but not quite in the way we expected. Java Card is very much alive. Oracle released version 3.1 in January 2019. 20 billion Java Cards had been sold by 2016, the year of the 20th anniversary of the Java Card Forum, the most influential industry association of companies in the smart card business [48]. Java Card is often found in SIM cards and passports—for example, in the Dutch passport. Blank Java Cards are still sold, and there are open source software projects that support them, for example [37]. But this is not well known. Also, multi-application capability, the initial hype of Java Cards, is not enabled or not allowed on these cards.

Interestingly, arguments (1) and (2) still stand. In that respect, version 3.1 is not much different from version 2.1, with which we started.

The formalization of Java Card semantics [11, Chapter 9] and the verification of Java Card programs [3, Chapter 10] done by Wojciech Mostowski are among the best achievements of KeY verification.

Since I had previously mentioned the LOOP project, it seems appropriate to also refer to the EU-funded "VerifiCard" project, in which the LOOP tool played an important role. For KeY, verification of Java Card programs was a case study, "VerifCard" focussed exclusively on this topic. Unfortunately, the short paper [36], reviewing the general background of the project and its overall goals, is all that can now be found. If you today go to the former project website http://www.verificard.org/, you are redirected to an online marketing & advertising magazine.

In the 2001 proposal the verification of Java Card programs was complemented by the plan to verify general Java library programs, more specifically programs from the Java Collection Framework. One of the most visible successes of the KeY system occurred in 2017 with the formal analysis of TimSort, the main sorting algorithm provided by the Java standard library and by many other programming frameworks. While attempting to verify TimSort, a bug that led to an ArrayOutOfBoundsException for certain inputs was discovered. The fix was made without losing measurable performance, and the KeY system formally proved that the fix is correct and that the bug no longer persists. More detail can be found at the blog [54] or in the paper [18].

4   Synopsis

On the long term goal of the KeY project to transfer deductive verification methods from academic research into industrial use we have made great progress, and the results will most likely contribute to the social need for dependable software. The picture I have in mind is that of a distant mountain top that I want to climb. I can see intermediate hills that I will have to cross, but the valleys are hidden. I do not know how many there will be, how steep they are, nor what rivers will have to be bridged. In the scientific landscape there are, unfortunately, no hiking maps, so it is small wonder that we grossly underestimated the difficulties lying ahead. In the progress report for the first KeY project, we stated that we had taken an essential step towards our long-term goal by integrating a rudimentary version of our system into a CASE tool. Looking back on our hike, it is now clear that we had barely left base camp.

Underestimating the difficulty of an approach is not a big issue, as long as you keep walking. More concerning is that the plan to start verification at the level of UML diagrams did not pan out. There is a general lesson to be learned from this: Do not commit yourself to the hypes of software development processes and tools. They come and go too quickly. Who would have thought that *Eclipse* would so soon be overshadowed by *IntelliJ*? That does not mean that one should ignore these processes and tools, but one should encapsulate the core functionalities of a verification system from its application layer.

The decision to limit programs to be verified to the Java Card subset of Java was a good one. All of the programming constructs that we thought to be too complicated to cover in the first go are not part of Java Card. On the other hand, all constructs in Java Card were within our reach. Atomicity of transactions was a challenge but, as indicated, could be effectively solved. Also, Java Card offered exciting case studies.

We would have saved considerable time and effort had we used ground instantiations for universal quantifiers at the outset instead of taking the free variable detour. But this was not a fool's errand. The outcome was far from obvious when we started; it could have gone either way. Indeed, it is the task of scientific research to provide answers when it is not clear which tools will be most useful.

We did very well over the years in what nowadays is called *networking*. For any topic we tackled, we tried to get into close contact with other researchers on the same or related topics. Starting in 2002 we organized annual meetings, which we called KeY symposia, to foster communication among the project team. It spread to Karlsruhe, Gothenburg, later to Koblenz, and still later to Darmstadt. With very few exceptions we invited external guests to the symposia. They would get an unvarnished view of what was going on inside the KeY project, and we profited from their feedback. For a list of all KeY symposia, see [39]. The KeY symposium in Manigod in 2019 celebrated the 20th anniversary of the KeY project. It was much like an international workshop, with a number of external guests, most of them contributing to the present volume.

I am very proud of the role I played within the KeY project, and it is a great pleasure to see it celebrate its 20th anniversary.

Good Luck and a successful future!

Acknowledgments. Many thanks go to Reiner Hähnle for his valuable and comprehensive comments on a first draft. I am much indebted to Wojciech Mostowski for filling me in with the recent developments of Java Card. Bernhard Beckert discovered numerous smaller mistakes and suggested a more systematic coverage of the dissertations written within the KeY context. Marieke Huisman corrected my false account on the funding of the LOOP project; She also made me add further explanations where the original text could only be understood by the inner circle of the KeY project. Jonas Schiffl helped me with his painstaking scrutiny of spelling and punctuation. It was a great pleasure that Erik Rosenthal agreed to improve style and clarity of the original text.

References

1. Ahrendt, W.: Deduktive Fehlersuche in abstrakten Datentypen. Ph.D. thesis, Karlsruhe Institute of Technology, Germany (2001)
2. Ahrendt, W., et al.: The KeY approach: integrating object oriented design and formal verification. Technical report 2000/4, University of Karlsruhe, Department of Computer Science, January 2000
3. Ahrendt, W., Beckert, B., Bubel, R., Hähnle, R., Schmitt, P.H., Ulbrich, M. (eds.): Deductive Software Verification - The KeY Book - From Theory to Practice. Lecture Notes in Computer Science, vol. 10001. Springer, Heidelberg (2016)
4. Ahrendt, W., et al.: Integration of automated and interactive theorem proving. In: Bibel, W., Schmitt, P. (eds.) Automated Deduction – A Basis for Applications, volume I, 3. Kluwer (1998)
5. Baar, T.: Über die Semantikbeschreibung OCL-artiger Sprachen. Ph.D. thesis, Karlsruhe Institute of Technology (2003)
6. Baar, T., Hähnle, R., Sattler, T., Schmitt, P.H.: Entwurfsmustergesteuerte Erzeugung von OCL-Constraints. In: Mehlhorn, K., Snelting, G. (eds.) Informatik 2000, pp. 389–404. Springer, Heidelberg (2000). https://doi.org/10.1007/978-3-642-58322-3_30
7. Barthe, G., D'Argenio, P.R., Rezk, T.: Secure information flow by self-composition. In: 17th IEEE Computer Security Foundations Workshop, (CSFW-17 2004), 28–30 June 2004, Pacific Grove, CA, USA, pp. 100–114. IEEE Computer Society (2004)
8. Beckert, B.: Integration und Uniformierung von Methoden des tableaubasierten Theorembeweisens. Ph.D. thesis, Karlsruhe Institute of Technology (1998)

9. Beckert, B., Giese, M., Habermalz, E., Hähnle, R., Roth, A., Rümmer, P., Schlager, S.: Taclets: a new paradigm for constructing interactive theorem provers. Revista de la Real Academia de Ciencias Exactas, Físicas y Naturales, Serie A: Matemáticas **98**(1), 17–53 (2004). Special Issue on Symbolic Computation in Logic and Artificial Intelligence
10. Beckert, B., Hähnle, R.: Reasoning and verification: State of the art and current trends. IEEE Intell. Syst. **29**(1), 20–29 (2014)
11. Beckert, B., Hähnle, R., Schmitt, P.H. (eds.): Verification of Object-Oriented Software. The KeY Approach. LNCS (LNAI), vol. 4334. Springer, Heidelberg (2007). https://doi.org/10.1007/978-3-540-69061-0
12. Bibel, W.: DFG-Schwerpunktprogramm "Deduktion". KI **12**(4), 38–40 (1998)
13. Bibel, W., Schmitt, P.H. (eds.) Automated Deduction - A Basis for Applications. Vol. I. Foundations - Calculi and Methods. Vol II. Systems and Implementation Techniques. Vol. III. Applications, vols. 8, 9, 10 of Applied Logic Series. Kluwer Academic Publishers (1998)
14. Borland. Together Control Center. https://www.microfocus.com/de-de/products/together/overview
15. Brucker, A.D., et al.: Report on the Aachen OCL meeting (2013). http://ceur-ws.org/Vol-1092/aachen.pdf
16. Darvas, A., Hähnle, R., Sands, D.: A theorem proving approach to analysis of secure information flow. In: Gorrieri, R. (ed.) Workshop on Issues in the Theory of Security, WITS. IFIP WG 1.7, ACM SIGPLAN and GI FoMSESS (2003)
17. Darvas, Á., Hähnle, R., Sands, D.: A theorem proving approach to analysis of secure information flow. In: Hutter, D., Ullmann, M. (eds.) SPC 2005. LNCS, vol. 3450, pp. 193–209. Springer, Heidelberg (2005). https://doi.org/10.1007/978-3-540-32004-3_20
18. de Gouw, S., de Boer, F.S., Bubel, R., Hähnle, R., Rot, J., Steinhöfel, D.: Verifying Openjdk's sort method for generic collections. J. Autom. Reason. **62**(1), 93–126 (2017)
19. Engel, C., Roth, A., Schmitt, P.H., Weiß, B.: Verification of modifies clauses in dynamic logic with non-rigid functions. Technical report 2009-9, Department of Informatics, Karlsruhe Institute of Technology (2009)
20. Fowler, M., Scott, K.: UML konzentriert - die Standardobjektmodellierungssprache anwenden: mit neuester Version UML 1.1. Addison-Wesley-Longman (1998)
21. Fujita, H., Hasegawa, R.: A model generation theorem prover in KL1 using a ramified -stack algorithm. In: Furukawa, K. (ed.) Proceedings of the Eighth International Conference on Logic Programming, Paris, France, 24–28 June 1991, pp. 535–548. MIT Press (1991)
22. Giese, M.: Incremental closure of free variable tableaux. In: Goré, R., Leitsch, A., Nipkow, T. (eds.) IJCAR 2001. LNCS, vol. 2083, pp. 545–560. Springer, Heidelberg (2001). https://doi.org/10.1007/3-540-45744-5_46
23. Giese, M.: Proof search without backtracking for free variable tableaux. Ph.D. thesis, Karlsruhe Institute of Technology, Germany (2002)
24. Giese, M.: Simplification rules for constrained formula tableaux. In: Cialdea Mayer, M., Pirri, F. (eds.) TABLEAUX 2003. LNCS (LNAI), vol. 2796, pp. 65–80. Springer, Heidelberg (2003). https://doi.org/10.1007/978-3-540-45206-5_8
25. Giese, M.: Taclets and the key prover. Electr. Notes Theor. Comput. Sci. **103**, 67–79 (2004)
26. Greiner, S.: A framework for non-interference in component-based systems. Ph.D. thesis, Karlsruhe Institute of Technology, April 2018

27. Habermalz, E.: Ein dynamisches automatisierbares interaktives Kalkül für schematische theoriespezifische Regeln. Ph.D. thesis, Karlsruhe Institute of Technology, Germany (2001)

28. Hähnle, R., Hasegawa, R., Shirai, Y.: Model generation theorem proving with finite interval constraints. In: Lloyd, J., et al. (eds.) CL 2000. LNCS (LNAI), vol. 1861, pp. 285–299. Springer, Heidelberg (2000). https://doi.org/10.1007/3-540-44957-4_19

29. Hähnle, R., Heisel, M., Reif, W., Stephan, W.: An interactive verification system based on dynamic logic. In: Siekmann, J.H. (ed.) CADE 1986. LNCS, vol. 230, pp. 306–315. Springer, Heidelberg (1986). https://doi.org/10.1007/3-540-16780-3_99

30. Hähnle, R., Huisman, M.: Deductive software verification: from pen-and-paper proofs to industrial tools. In: Steffen, B., Woeginger, G. (eds.) Computing and Software Science. LNCS, vol. 10000, pp. 345–373. Springer, Cham (2019). https://doi.org/10.1007/978-3-319-91908-9_18

31. Hähnle, R., Johannisson, K., Ranta, A.: An authoring tool for informal and formal requirements specifications. In: Kutsche, R.-D., Weber, H. (eds.) FASE 2002. LNCS, vol. 2306, pp. 233–248. Springer, Heidelberg (2002). https://doi.org/10.1007/3-540-45923-5_16

32. Hähnle, R., Menzel, W., Schmitt, P.H.: Integrierter deduktiver Software-Entwurf. KI **98**(4), 40–41 (1998). In German

33. Harel, D.: First-Order Dynamic Logic. Lecture Notes in Computer Science, vol. 68. Springer, Heidelberg (1979). https://doi.org/10.1007/3-540-09237-4

34. Huisman, M.: Reasoning about Java programs in higher order logic using PVS and Isabelle. IPA dissertation series, vol. 3, IPA (2001)

35. Huisman, M., Jacobs, B.: Java program verification via a Hoare logic with abrupt termination. In: Maibaum, T. (ed.) FASE 2000. LNCS, vol. 1783, pp. 284–303. Springer, Heidelberg (2000). https://doi.org/10.1007/3-540-46428-X_20

36. Jacobs, B., Meijer, H., Poll, E.: Verificard: a European project for smart card verification. Newslett. Dutch Assoc. Theor. Comput. Sci. **2001**, 32–38 (2001)

37. Javacard pro, open source smart card specialist

38. Johannisson, K.: Formal and informal software specifications. Ph.D. thesis, Department of Computing Science, Chalmers University of Technology and Gothenburg University (2005)

39. List of key symposia. https://www.key-project.org/key-symposium

40. Le Goues, C., Leino, K.R.M., Moskal, M.: The boogie verification debugger (tool paper). In: Barthe, G., Pardo, A., Schneider, G. (eds.) SEFM 2011. LNCS, vol. 7041, pp. 407–414. Springer, Heidelberg (2011). https://doi.org/10.1007/978-3-642-24690-6_28

41. MODELS. 19th International Workshop in OCL and Textual Modeling. https://oclworkshop.github.io/2019/cfp.html

42. Mostowski, W.: A case study in formal verification using multiple explicit heaps. In: Beyer, D., Boreale, M. (eds.) FMOODS/FORTE -2013. LNCS, vol. 7892, pp. 20–34. Springer, Heidelberg (2013). https://doi.org/10.1007/978-3-642-38592-6_3

43. OMG. About the object constraint language specification version 2.4, February 2014. https://www.omg.org/spec/OCL

44. Poetzsch-Heffter, A., Müller, P.: Logical foundations for typed object-oriented languages. In: Gries, D., de Roever, W.P. (eds.) Programming Concepts and Methods, IFIP TC2/WG2.2,2.3 International Conference on Programming Concepts and Methods (PROCOMET 1998), Shelter Island, New York, USA, 8–12 June 1998. IFIP Conference Proceedings, vol. 125, pp. 404–423. Chapman & Hall (1998)

45. Poetzsch-Heffter, A., Müller, P.: A programming logic for sequential Java. In: Swierstra, S.D. (ed.) ESOP 1999. LNCS, vol. 1576, pp. 162–176. Springer, Heidelberg (1999). https://doi.org/10.1007/3-540-49099-X_11
46. Ranta, A.: Grammatical Framework: Programming with Multilingual Grammars. CSLI Publications, Stanford (2011). 1-57586, ISBN-10: 1-57586-626-9 (Paper)-627-7 (Cloth)
47. Ranta, A.: Translating between language and logic: what is easy and what is difficult. In: Bjørner, N., Sofronie-Stokkermans, V. (eds.) CADE 2011. LNCS (LNAI), vol. 6803, pp. 5–25. Springer, Heidelberg (2011). https://doi.org/10.1007/978-3-642-22438-6_3
48. The impact of java card technology yesterday and tomorrow: Safran identity & security celebrates 20 years with the java card forum. Press Release (2016)
49. Scheben, C.: Program-level specification and deductive verification of security properties. Ph.D. thesis, Karlsruhe Institute of Technology (2014)
50. Schellhorn, G., Ahrendt, W.: Reasoning about abstract state machines: the WAM case study. J. UCS **3**(4), 377–413 (1997)
51. Schmitt, P.H.: Diamond formulas: a fragment of dynamic logic with recursively enumerable validity problem. Inf. Control **61**(2), 147–158 (1984)
52. Stärk, R.F., Schmid, J., Börger, E.: Java and the Java Virtual Machine: Definition, Verification, Validation. Springer, Heidelberg (2001). https://doi.org/10.1007/978-3-642-59495-3
53. Stenzel, K.: Verification of java card programs. Technical report 2001-5, Institut für Informatik, Universität Augsburg (2001)
54. http://www.envisage-project.eu/proving-android-java-and-python-sorting-algorithm-is-broken-and-how-to-fix-it/
55. Ulbrich, M.: Dynamic logic for an intermediate language: verification, interaction and refinement. Ph.D. thesis, Karlsruhe Institute of Technology, June 2013
56. van den Berg, J., Huisman, M., Jacobs, B., Poll, E.: A type-theoretic memory model for verification of sequential Java programs. In: Bert, D., Choppy, C., Mosses, P.D. (eds.) WADT 1999. LNCS, vol. 1827, pp. 1–21. Springer, Heidelberg (2000). https://doi.org/10.1007/978-3-540-44616-3_1
57. von Oheimb, D., Nipkow, T.: Machine-checking the Java specification: proving type-safety. In: Alves-Foss, J. (ed.) Formal Syntax and Semantics of Java. LNCS, vol. 1523, pp. 119–156. Springer, Heidelberg (1999). https://doi.org/10.1007/3-540-48737-9_4
58. The Why3 platform. http://why3.lri.fr/

Verification Tools

A Retrospective on Developing Hybrid System Provers in the KeYmaera Family
A Tale of Three Provers

Stefan Mitsch$^{(\boxtimes)}$ and André Platzer

Computer Science Department, Carnegie Mellon University, Pittsburgh, USA
{smitsch,aplatzer}@cs.cmu.edu

Abstract. This chapter provides a retrospective on the developments of three theorem provers for hybrid systems. While all three theorem provers implement closely related logics of the family of differential dynamic logic, they pursue fundamentally different styles of theorem prover implementations. Since the three provers KeYmaera, KeYmaeraD, and KeYmaera X share a common core logic, yet no line of code, and differ vastly in prover implementation technology, their logical proximity yet technical distance enables us to draw conclusions about the various advantages and disadvantages of different prover implementation styles for different purposes, which we hope are of generalizable interest.

Keywords: History of formal methods · Theorem provers · Differential dynamic logic · Hybrid systems

1 Introduction

Hybrid systems verification is demanding, because the joint discrete and continuous dynamics of hybrid systems bring about significant challenges that merit nothing less than the best support in formal verification. The two primary approaches for hybrid systems verification are model checking based on set-valued search through their state space [3,15,18] and theorem proving based on deductive proofs decomposing the system [45,51].

While a few prior approaches defined parts of hybrid systems in other provers, KeYmaera [56] was the first dedicated theorem prover for hybrid systems. This chapter takes a retrospective on the development of the KeYmaera family of provers for hybrid systems. This is one of the few occasions where the same logic (with only slight variations) has been implemented as theorem provers in widely different styles, enabling us to draw conclusions about the respective advantages and downsides about the different prover implementation styles. With KeYmaera

This material is based upon work supported by the Air Force Office of Scientific Research under grant number FA9550-16-1-0288 and FA9550-18-1-0120. Any opinions, finding, and conclusion or recommendations expressed in this material are those of the author(s) and do not necessarily reflect the views of the United States Air Force.

W. Ahrendt et al. (Eds.): Deductive Software Verification, LNCS 12345, pp. 21–64, 2020.
https://doi.org/10.1007/978-3-030-64354-6_2

[56] first released on 2007-11-02, KeYmaeraD [62] first released on 2011-10-29, and KeYmaera X [20] first released on 2015-04-18, this chapter is reflecting on experience with more than 12 years of KeYmaera implementation and usage.

The name KeYmaera is a pun on *Chimera*, a hybrid monster from Classical Greek mythology. As the name suggests, KeYmaera is based on the prover [1], which is a dedicated theorem prover for dynamic logic for Java programs covered in many other chapters of this book. Even if that common code basis with KeY was limited to the original KeYmaera prover, the name stuck with its subsequent clean-slate implementations of KeYmaeraD and KeYmaera X.

The third time's the charm, but a lot can be learned about the relative advantages and disadvantages from the different prover designs that may help make informed tradeoffs in other projects for other purposes. KeYmaera is built as a sequent calculus prover for differential dynamic logic [43] making ample use of the taclet mechanism [5] that KeY offers to concisely write proof rule schemata with side conditions and schema variable matching conditions that are checked by Java code. KeYmaeraD is built as a sequent calculus prover for (quantified [46]) differential dynamic logic [43] by directly implementing its rule schemata in the host language Scala. Finally, KeYmaera X is built as a uniform substitution calculus prover for differential dynamic logic [50] whose axioms and proof rules are concrete formulas or pairs of formulas and need no schemata. In addition to their different rule application mechanisms do all three provers reach fundamentally different decisions for their style of basic proof data structures. The experience with the implications of these different prover implementation styles enables us to draw conclusions that we hope to be of generalizable interest.

2 Differential Dynamic Logic and Its Proofs in a Nutshell

Differential dynamic logic (dL) [43,45,48,50,51,59] supports specification and verification of hybrid systems written in a programming language. Differential dynamic logic provides a direct syntactic representation of hybrid systems along with logical formulas that express properties of their behavior. Polynomials can be used as terms and, with sufficient care about avoiding divisions by zero [10], also rational functions etc. The syntax of *hybrid programs* (HP) is described by the following grammar where α, β are hybrid programs, x is a variable and $e, f(x)$ are terms, Q is a logical formula:

$$\alpha, \beta ::= x := e \mid ?Q \mid x' = f(x) \,\&\, Q \mid \alpha \cup \beta \mid \alpha; \beta \mid \alpha^*$$

Assignments $x := e$ and tests $?Q$ (to abort execution and discard the run if Q is not true) are as usual. Differential equations $x' = f(x) \,\&\, Q$ can be followed along a solution of $x' = f(x)$ for any amount of time as long as the evolution domain constraint Q is true at every moment along the solution. Nondeterministic choice $\alpha \cup \beta$ runs either α or β, sequential composition $\alpha; \beta$ first runs α and then β, and nondeterministic repetition α^* runs α any natural number of times.

For example, the dynamics depicted in Fig. 1 is modeled with the differential equation system $x'=x^2yz$, $y'=z$, where x determines the magnitude of repulsive ($x \leq 0$) or attraction force ($x \geq 0$) to the center, y determines the position in the force field, and z controls how quickly to follow the flow (the system stops when $z = 0$). The hybrid program in (1) repeatedly chooses nondeterministically between $z := 0$ to stop flow, or $z := y$ to amplify y in the differential equation:

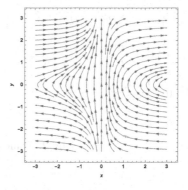

Fig. 1. Flow of differential equation $x'=x^2yz$, $y'=z$ for $z = 1$

$$((z := 0 \cup z := y); \underbrace{\{x'=x^2yz, y'=z\}})^* \quad (1)$$
$$\underbrace{}_{\text{stop flow}} \underbrace{}_{\text{amplify}} \underbrace{\phantom{\{x'=x^2yz, y'=z\}}}_{\text{ODE, see Fig. 1}}$$

It is important that the right-hand sides of assignments are not simply substituted into the ODE in all cases, since a wrong substitution $z := y$ results in a vastly different ODE $x' = x^2y^2, y' = y$. The assignments $z := 0$ and $z := y$ in (1) pick values for z: z is either 0 or equal to the value of y at the time of the assignment (in this case, equal to the value of y at the beginning of the ODE). Also, the value of z in this example stays constant throughout the ODE, since there is no z' and so implicitly $z' = 0$.

The formulas of dL describe properties of hybrid programs. *Formulas of differential dynamic logic* are described by the following grammar where P, Q are formulas, $e, \tilde{e}$ are terms, x is a variable and α is a hybrid program:

$$P, Q ::= e \geq \tilde{e} \mid \neg P \mid P \wedge Q \mid P \vee Q \mid P \to Q \mid P \leftrightarrow Q \mid \forall x\, P \mid \exists x\, P \mid [\alpha]P \mid \langle\alpha\rangle P$$

The operators of first-order real arithmetic are as usual with quantifiers ranging over the reals. For any HP α and dL formula P is $[\alpha]P$ true in a state iff P is true after all ways of running α. Dually, $\langle\alpha\rangle P$ is true in a state iff P is true after at least one way of running α. The former is particularly useful for stating safety properties while the latter is useful for stating liveness properties, but their mixed use is powerful as well. The semantics and axiomatization of dL are described elsewhere [43,45,47,48,50,51,59]. For this chapter, it suffices to understand dL informally and remember, e.g., that dL formula $P \to [\alpha]Q$ is valid (true in all states) iff the postcondition formula Q holds after all runs of hybrid program α that start in initial states satisfying assumption formula P.

For example, the conjecture that $x \geq 0$ always remains true after running the program (1) if $x \geq 0$ was true before is expressed in dL formula (2):

$$\overbrace{}^{\text{all runs of hybrid program } \alpha}$$
$$\underbrace{x \geq 0}_{\text{assumption formula } P} \to [((z := 0 \cup z := y); \{x'=x^2yz, y'=z\})^*] \underbrace{x \geq 0}_{\text{postcondition formula } Q} \quad (2)$$

The dL sequent calculus [43,45,51] works with *sequents* of the form $\Gamma \vdash \Delta$ for a finite set of formulas Γ (*antecedent*) and a finite set of formulas Δ (*succedent*).

$$([:=]) \; [x := e]p(x) \leftrightarrow p(e)$$

$$([\cup]) \; [\alpha \cup \beta]P \leftrightarrow [\alpha]P \wedge [\beta]P$$

$$([;]) \; [\alpha;\beta]P \leftrightarrow [\alpha][\beta]P$$

$$([\cup]R) \; \frac{\Gamma \vdash [\alpha]\phi, \Delta \quad \Gamma \vdash [\beta]\phi, \Delta}{\Gamma \vdash [\alpha \cup \beta]\phi, \Delta}$$

$$(\text{loop}) \; \frac{\Gamma \vdash J, \Delta \quad J \vdash [\alpha]J \quad J \vdash P}{\Gamma \vdash [\alpha^*]P, \Delta}$$

$$([\cup]L) \; \frac{\Gamma, [\alpha]\phi, [\beta]\phi \vdash \Delta}{\Gamma, [\alpha \cup \beta]\phi \vdash \Delta}$$

$$(\text{dI}) \; \frac{\Gamma \vdash F, \Delta \quad Q \vdash [x':=f(x)](F)'}{\Gamma \vdash [x' = f(x) \,\&\, Q]F, \Delta}$$

Fig. 2. Some dL axioms and proof rules

The meaning of sequent $\Gamma \vdash \Delta$ is that of dL formula $(\bigwedge_{P \in \Gamma} P) \rightarrow (\bigvee_{Q \in \Delta} Q)$. All assumptions are listed in Γ, the set of alternatives to prove are in Δ.

Some typical axioms and proof rules of dL are listed in Fig. 2. The axiom $[\cup]$, for example, expresses that any formula of the form $[\alpha \cup \beta]P$ is equivalent to the corresponding conjunction $[\alpha]P \wedge [\beta]P$. The proof rules $[\cup]R$ and $[\cup]L$ provide corresponding decompositions of $[\alpha \cup \beta]P$ into $[\alpha]P$ as well as $[\beta]P$ when $[\alpha \cup \beta]P$ is a succedent formula on the right or an antecedent formula on the left in sequent calculus, respectively. The $[\cup]R$ rule is easiest to understand without Δ, but whenever Δ is true, the conclusion is true whether or not $[\alpha \cup \beta]P$ is. The loop proof rule expresses that for proving the conclusion $\Gamma \vdash [\alpha^*]P, \Delta$ below the rule bar it suffices to pick an invariant formula J and show that J is initially true or Δ (left premise above rule bar), that J remains true after any run of the loop body α (middle premise), and that J implies the desired postcondition P (right premise). The differential invariant proof rule dI expresses that F is always true after a differential equation $x' = f(x) \,\&\, Q$ if it is true initially (left premise) and its differential $(F)'$ is true when Q is after assigning the right-hand side $f(x)$ of the differential equation to its left-hand side x' (right premise). The differential formula $(F)'$ intuitively expresses that F locally remains true when following the differential equation $x' = f(x)$. Rule dI makes it possible to prove properties of ODEs without having to solve them [59].

Figure 3 illustrates how these axioms and proof rules are used in a sequent proof of the dL formula (2). In a sequent proof, the conclusion (below the horizontal bar) follows from the premises (above the bar), justified by the axiom or proof rule annotated to the left of the bar. The first step at the bottom of Fig. 3 ($\rightarrow$R) makes the left-hand side of the implication available as assumption. Next, the loop rule splits the proof into three subgoals: the left premise (base case) and the right premise (use case) close, because their succedent holds by antecedent assumption, the middle premise (induction step) details are listed in Fig. 3a.

In the proof of the middle premise (induction step), after splitting the sequential composition by axiom $[;]$, the nondeterministic choice axiom ($[\cup]$) splits the proof into two separate modalities. The $[:=]$ axiom applied to the assignment $z := 0$ simply replaces the occurrences of z with 0. In the second assignment ($z := y$), however, the right-hand side cannot simply replace the left-hand side, since it is bound in the subsequent differential equation; therefore, we split off this branch using $\wedge$R and omit further steps, but will return to the discussion of

$$\wedge R \cfrac{\cfrac{\cfrac{*}{x \geq 0 \vdash x \geq 0} \qquad [:=]\cfrac{\cfrac{*}{\vdash 0 \geq 0}}{\vdash [x' := x^2 y \cdot 0][y' := 0]x' \geq 0}}{\text{dI} \cfrac{}{x \geq 0 \vdash [\{x'=x^2 y \cdot 0,\, y'=0\}]x \geq 0}} \quad \cdots}{x \geq 0 \vdash \quad [\{x'=x^2 y \cdot 0,\, y'=0\}]x \geq 0}$$

$$[:=]\cfrac{x \geq 0 \vdash \quad [z := y][\{x'=x^2 yz,\, y'=z\}]x \geq 0}{x \geq 0 \vdash \quad [z := 0][\{x'=x^2 yz,\, y'=z\}]x \geq 0}$$

$$[\cup]\cfrac{\wedge [z := y][\{x'=x^2 yz,\, y'=z\}]x \geq 0}{x \geq 0 \vdash [(z := 0 \cup z := y)][\{x'=x^2 yz,\, y'=z\}]x \geq 0}$$

$$[;]\cfrac{}{x \geq 0 \vdash [(z := 0 \cup z := y);\ \{x'=x^2 yz,\, y'=z\}]x \geq 0}$$

(a) Proof of middle premise of rule loop (induction step)

$$\rightarrow R \cfrac{\text{loop} \cfrac{\cfrac{*}{x \geq 0 \vdash x \geq 0} \qquad \text{Induction step (3a)} \qquad \cfrac{*}{x \geq 0 \vdash x \geq 0}}{x \geq 0 \vdash [((z := 0 \cup z := y);\ \{x'=x^2 yz,\, y'=z\})^*]x \geq 0}}{\vdash x \geq 0 \rightarrow [((z := 0 \cup z := y);\ \{x'=x^2 yz,\, y'=z\})^*]x \geq 0}$$

Fig. 3. Sequent proof of dL formula (2)

such assignments in later sections. Now the differential equation shape fits the dI rule: the resulting left branch shows that invariant $x \geq 0$ is true initially, while the right branch shows that the differential $(x \geq 0)'$, which expands to $x' \geq 0$, is true after assigning the right-hand sides of the differential equation.

The provers, KeYmaera 3, KeYmaeraD, and KeYmaera X differ fundamentally in terms of how they implement the dL proof calculus, which also manifests in differences in the concrete mechanics of such sequent proofs, as will be shown below. Only KeYmaera X uses axioms such as [∪] while KeYmaera 3 and KeYmaeraD implement sequent calculus rules similar to [∪]R,[∪]L instead. KeYmaera 3 provides a proof rule schema mechanism in which the rules are implemented while KeYmaeraD implements sequent calculus proof rules directly using the pattern matching variables of the language it is implemented in. A full list of axioms and proof rules of dL is provided elsewhere [43,45,50,51,59].

3   KeYmaera 3 – A Big Prover With a Big Heart

The KeYmaera 3 theorem prover[1] [56] implements the original sequent calculus of differential dynamic logic for hybrid systems [42,43,45] in a mix of Java and some Scala by extending the KeY prover, a prover for Java programs.

Design Principles. The rationale behind the design of KeYmaera is that the quickest way of getting a theorem prover for hybrid systems working is to build it on top of another successful prover. As a dynamic logic prover with a well-established prover infrastructure and sophisticated user interface, the KeY prover

---

[1]   KeYmaera versions 1–3 are available at http://symbolaris.com/info/KeYmaera. html.

[1,2,6] is the canonical choice. On the highest level of abstraction, the design of KeYmaera needed the programming language Java within dynamic logic modalities of KeY to be replaced by hybrid programs. Of course, semantical changes required a move from the arithmetic over integers and object-oriented data types that are dominant in Java programs to the arithmetic over reals for hybrid systems instead. But the hope was that KeY's rule application mechanism with taclets (lightweight, soundness-critical tactics that can invoke soundness-critical code, see [5]) and propositional/first-order logic calculus automation could be retained, and all the considerable effort that went into the nontrivial user interface design of KeY could be reused directly for hybrid systems.

Implementation Realities. For KeYmaera 3, the dL sequent calculus rule [∪]R for programs starting with a nondeterministic choice would be written as:

$$([\cup]R) \ \frac{\vdash [\alpha]\phi \quad \vdash [\beta]\phi}{\vdash [\alpha \cup \beta]\phi}$$

KeY provides *taclets* [5], which combine proof rules describing what syntactic element is replaced by which other transformed element with grouping into proof rule priorities. The [∪]R rule is implemented in KeYmaera 3 as a taclet:

```
1 box_choice_right {
2   \find (==> \modality{#boxtr}#dl ++ #dl2\endmodality(post))
3   \replacewith (==> \modality{#boxtr}#dl\endmodality(post));
4   \replacewith (==> \modality{#boxtr}#dl2\endmodality(post))
5   \heuristics (simplify_prog)
6   \displayname "[++] choice"
7 };
```

Taclet `box_choice_right` uses \find to search for a succedent formula (as indicated by the occurrence in the right-hand side of the sequent turnstyle ⊢ rendered as ==> in ASCII) with a [·]-type modality whose top-level program is of a nondeterministic choice form #dl ∪ #dl2 (where ∪ is rendered as ++ in ASCII, and #dl and #dl2 are hybrid programs) and any formula post as a postcondition, see Line 2. Each such occurrence will be replaced with two premises in which the corresponding active formula is, instead, replaced by the same [·]-type modality and the same postcondition formula that matched post in \find and with the hybrid program that matched #dl as the hybrid program on the first premise (Line 3) and with the hybrid program that matched #dl2 as the hybrid program on the second premise (Line 4), respectively. The declaration \heuristics (simplify_prog) in Line 5 assigns the use of this taclet to the group simplify_prog that the proof strategy uses with higher priority than expensive proof rules. The \displayname in Line 6 shows what name is used for the rule on the user interface. The presence of the schema variable character # highlights that an internal matching algorithm will be run in Java to check that what occurs in place of #dl actually is a hybrid program and what occurs in place of #boxtr actually is a box-type modality, etc. There is a second taclet that handles nondeterministic choices in box modalities in the antecedent, and two more taclets that handle nondeterministic choices in diamond modalities.

The proof strategy mechanism that KeYmaera 3 inherits from KeY computes the priorities of the heuristic groups of all taclets after instantiating them to the formulas at hand and checking for their applicability. It favors the use of high priority taclet uses over lower priority taclets. For fair rule selection, lower priority taclets gain priority over time if they have been applicable to the same formula in a goal for a long time. When selecting preexisting heuristic groups such as simplify_prog, taclets will immediately be used by the automatic proof strategy with the priority associated to that heuristic group. That makes it easy to add simple proof rules to the proof automation. More advanced proof strategies that conditionally use proof rules or use proof rules in succession are much more difficult to encode with priorities. To understand where succession of proof rules comes in, think of an assumption $\forall x\,(x = e \rightarrow \phi)$ where the quantifier first wants to be instantiated to e and then the resulting equality is subsequently rewritten. Those cases need new strategy features implemented in Java that add or subtract cost for the applicability of a rule as a function of the state of the proof to make it cheaper for proof strategies to apply the taclets in the intended order. For example with a strategy feature that gives equality rewriting a low cost if the proof tree has previously instantiated a universal quantifier of an implicational formula conditioned on an equation for the quantified formula. Disproving formulas by exhaustion of rule applications is not feasible with such an approach because many different orderings of applicable proof rules would have to be considered, so extraneous mechanisms for disproving are required [63].

Successes. The hope of enabling a quick implementation for hybrid systems theorem proving by building it on top of KeY was largely met. KeY's user interface also proved to be extremely valuable to quickly get visual feedback on what proof search was doing or where rule applications went wrong. KeY's taclet mechanism provides a mechanism to quickly capture proof rules and proof strategy hints simultaneously in a single place. This makes it easy to add rules to the prover that are automatically applied by proof search with simple customization of the priority with which a rule group is used. The direct implementation style of the taclet application mechanism also makes it reasonably fast. With moderate effort this leads to a hybrid systems prover that is able to prove moderate-complexity problems with user-provided invariants and solvable differential equations. More sophisticated problems needed more sophisticated invasive changes to the prover to become scalable, but starting from KeY certainly got KeYmaera 3 a leg up.

By design, KeY manages a single proof tree on which a single proof strategy sequentially executes proof rules at a leaf whose premises will be added as children; KeYmaera inherits this proof management. This explicit proof data structure can be displayed directly in the user interface and makes it possible to traverse the proof tree if a proof strategy feature wants to understand the structure of the proof to determine the priority of a possible taclet application. In fact, traversal of the proof tree is often crucial to strategically coordinate taclet uses with one another, because, besides rule cost and heuristic caches, the proof tree is the only means of communication from one taclet application to another.

After major revisions and additions to the proof strategies with conditional proof rule application and sequencing, as well as means of conducting separate hypothetical proofs and caching, it was possible to achieve significant proof automation in KeYmaera 3, including fixedpoint-based invariant generation [54].

KeYmaera provides a pragmatic combination of built-in proof automation and click-based user interaction. The underlying KeY prover manages a single proof and makes it possible to interrupt proof automation at any intermediate stage. That way, users can complement deficiencies of proof automation by inspecting how far automation got, then backtracking to some intermediate proof step before the automation went off the rails, help by selective manual interaction, and then yield control to proof automation again. Anecdotally, this capability was one of the most admired features beyond the full automation that KeYmaera provided. The downside is that novice users, amid the overwhelmingly large number of automatically created proof obligations, often loose track of the remaining proof effort and how it relates to the original proof goal, and whether it would be better to undo automatic proof steps to limit excessive branching.

Challenges. More challenging than anticipated was the correct rendition of differential dynamic logic sequent calculus rules as taclets. Taclets provide flexibility and apply rules in more general scenarios without having to explicitly state them. This makes it significantly easier to write taclets. But one of the unintended consequences of that taclet application mechanism is precisely that rules can be applied in settings that are more general than what one might have had in mind. What is useful for locally sound proof rules such as $[\cup]R$ can easily create soundness problems for complicated rules. The taclet for $[\cup]R$ can be used even in scenarios that were not explicitly programmed in, for example under update contexts. Thanks to KeY's taclet application mechanism, the rule $[\cup]R$ can automatically be applied in a more general style in any additional sequent context $\Gamma \vdash \Delta$ with any finite set $\mathcal{U}$ of parallel assignments (called *update* [2,7,43]) that later simultaneously change the values of the affected variables:

$$[\cup]R\frac{\Gamma \vdash \mathcal{U}[\alpha]\phi, \Delta \quad \Gamma \vdash \mathcal{U}[\beta]\phi, \Delta}{\Gamma \vdash \mathcal{U}[\alpha \cup \beta]\phi, \Delta}$$

But the taclet application mechanism can quickly cause unsoundness for complicated rules such as loop invariants when the taclet implementor does not explicitly consider all possible generalizations. A loop invariant proof rule for nondeterministic repetitions in KeYmaera 3 could be phrased, e.g., as:

$$(\text{loopR}_{\ell})\frac{\vdash J \quad J \vdash \phi \quad J \vdash [\alpha]J}{\vdash [\alpha^*]\phi}$$

But it would be entirely incorrect if the taclet application mechanism also wraps rule loopR$_{\ell}$ into a sequent or update context:

$$\text{loopR}_\xi \frac{\Gamma \vdash \mathcal{U}J, \Delta \quad \Gamma, \mathcal{U}J \vdash \mathcal{U}\phi, \Delta \quad \Gamma, \mathcal{U}J \vdash \mathcal{U}[\alpha]J, \Delta}{\Gamma \vdash \mathcal{U}[\alpha^*]\phi, \Delta}$$

Every single occurrence of Γ or Δ or $\mathcal{U}$ in the second or third premise causes unsoundness, so such generalization needs to be prevented at all cost!

Due to its more delicate nature, the loop invariant rule needs more care when phrased as a taclet to avoid inadvertent taclet generalization like loopR$_\xi$ above:

```
1  loop_inv_box_quan {
2    \find (==> \modality{#boxtr}#dl*\endmodality(post))
3    "Invariant Initially Valid":
4      \replacewith (==> inv);
5    "Use Case":
6      \replacewith (==> #UnivCl(\[#dl\]true, inv->post, false));
7    "Body Preserves Invariant":
8      \replacewith (==> #UnivCl(
9        \[#dl\]true,
10       inv -> \modality{#boxtr}#dl\endmodality(inv),
11       true))
12   \heuristics (loop_invariant, loop_invariant_proposal)
13   \onlyRigidFunctions
14   \displayname "ind loop invariant"
15 };
```

This taclet implements the loop invariant rule loop with generalization resilience:

$$(ind') \frac{\vdash \phi \quad \vdash \forall^\alpha(\psi \to [\alpha]\psi) \quad \vdash \forall^\alpha(\psi \to \phi)}{\vdash [\alpha^*]\phi}$$

The universal closure operator $\forall^\alpha$ forms the universal closure $\forall x_1 \ldots \forall x_n$ where $x_1, \ldots, x_n$ are all variables bound/written to by the hybrid program α. The #UnivCl meta operator[2] in Lines 6 and 8 (abbreviating #dlUniversalClosure) is implemented in 788 complex lines of Java and computes the inverse transitive closure of the operators of the variable dependencies of the modality passed in as its first argument over the formula passed in as its second argument and optimizes some of those dependencies depending on the third argument. The two alternative names used in the \heuristics group in Line 12 are arbitrary but used as hooks in the priority-based proof strategy implementation to trigger the use of the best rules under the present circumstances. The meta operators that introduce universal closures are crucial to make the implicit taclet generalizations sound when they wrap the rule into a sequent or update context $\Gamma, \Delta, \mathcal{U}$:

$$ind' \frac{\Gamma \vdash \mathcal{U}J, \Delta \quad \Gamma \vdash \mathcal{U}\forall^\alpha(J \to \phi), \Delta \quad \Gamma \vdash \mathcal{U}\forall^\alpha(J \to [\alpha]J), \Delta}{\Gamma \vdash \mathcal{U}[\alpha^*]\phi, \Delta}$$

---

[2] The meta operator introduces $\forall X \, [x := X]$, because KeY and KeYmaera distinguish categories of variables. They do not allow quantification over program variables x and do not allow assignment to logical variables X, so a mix with both is needed.

Any changes in update $\mathcal{U}$ to bound variables of α will be overwritten by the universal quantifiers of the closure $\forall^\alpha$. Likewise any assumptions about the initial state that reside in Γ, Δ will become obsolete by the quantifiers of $\forall^\alpha$. A downside of this approach is the abundance of irrelevant formulas it leaves around in Γ, Δ. This also makes the proof steps harder to trace except for expert users. Finally, the `\onlyRigidFunctions` constraint in Line 13 triggers a search through the matched formulas to check no assignable function symbols occur, which would render the usage of the taclet unsound.

The differential invariants proof rule dI of Fig. 2 is implemented as a taclet:

```
1  diffind {
2    \find (==> \[#normODE\]post)
3    \varcond (\isFirstOrderFormula(post))
4    "Invariant Initially Valid":
5      \replacewith (#InvPart(\[#normODE\]post) ==> post);
6    "ODE Preserves Invariant":
7      \replacewith (==> #UnivCl(
8        \[#normODE\]true,
9        #DiffInd(\[#normODE\]post),
10       false))
11   \heuristics (invariant_diff, diff_rule)
12   \onlyRigidFunctions
13   \displayname "DI differential invariant"
14 };
```

Upon each use of this taclet, the metaoperator `#InvPart` in Line 5 triggers a computation to extract the invariant from the differential equation, whose schema variable `#normODE` has a matching algorithm to check that the concrete differential equation is given in normalized form (so a list of equations with the only derivatives occurring once as an isolated variable on the left-hand side and a single formula without derivatives as evolution domain constraint). The meta operator `#UnivCl` for universal closure that was already used in the loop taclet is important for soundness also in the differential invariants taclet, which additionally uses a meta operator `#DiffInd` in Line 9 for computing the differential invariant condition for the postcondition `post` as a function of the differential equation matched by `#normODE` [44,45]. The presence of the `\varcond` in Line 3 additionally indicates that a meta operator will be run before using the taclet to check that the postcondition `post` is a first-order logic formula. Almost all of the insights behind differential invariants in KeYmaera are provided in the opaque implementation of the meta operators. The meta operators for the `diffind` taclet are implemented in 2413 lines of Java and Scala code.

Assignments can be handled very easily with taclets in KeYmaera but the main reason is that they are immediately converted to updates `{#dlx:=#dle}` who have their own built-in application algorithm called update simplifier:

```
1  assignment_to_update_right {
2    \find (==> \modality{#allmodal}#dlx:=#dle\endmodality(post))
3    \replacewith (==> {#dlx:=#dle} post)
```

```
4    \heuristics(simplify_prog)
5    \displayname ":= assign"
6  };
```

While the taclets give a general idea of the way how a proof rule is applied, most of their more subtle soundness-critical aspects are hidden in the Java implementation of their corresponding schema matching and meta operators.

Modest modifications of the automatic proof search strategy that derives from assigning taclets to strategy groups are easy by changing the priority with which the strategy group of a taclet is being applied. More involved changes of proof search procedures cannot be encoded well with rule priorities but need major invasive changes to KeYmaera's proof strategies. Fixedpoint-based invariant search procedures [54] required multiple proofs to be formed and quickly discarded if unsuccessful, which is counter to the sequential intention of proof search within a proof tree in KeYmaera. Every time the proof search strategy needs to decide whether to apply, say, an invariant proof rule with a member J_1 of a stream of generated invariants, it would start a new *hypothetical proof* in the background to see if that proof with that invariant candidate J_1 would succeed. And if it does succeed, the prover discards the entire hypothetical proof (hence the name) and commits to making the first proof step with that invariant J_1, otherwise it tries a hypothetical proof with another invariant candidate J_2.

The downside of such a sequential emulation of parallel proof exploration in KeYmaera's sequential proof engine is the large number of repeated steps. This is especially true when nested loops and differential equations occur in more complex hybrid systems, so that an entire nested chain of proofs needs to be finished and then discarded to commit to the first proof step; most of the discarded steps need to be repeated later at the next important turn of the proof. Performance mitigation includes a cache that remembers successful and unsuccessful proof attempts of propositionally similar questions at choice points to better guide proof search in the future or in later nested hypothetical proofs.

KeYmaera implements a complete deduction modulo theories approach using free variables and Skolemization with invertible quantifiers and real quantifier elimination [43]. This approach is instrumental for handling complicated modality/quantifier nestings and automatically enables sound quantifier shifts while preventing unsound quantifier rearrangements. The downside is that this requires a proof-global proof rule for real existential quantifiers over modal formulas.

Both full automation and click-based user interaction are great for novice users exploring medium complexity problems. More difficult problems come with more substantial challenges that are more likely out of reach for fully automatic proof strategies yet too tedious to click through manually.

Another challenge with the design of KeYmaera is the absence of proof tactics or proof scripts and the fact that all attempts of adding them rendered them soundness-critical. It is simple to choose from among KeYmaera's predefined proof strategies but so hard to add custom proof automation that only three people succeeded. Even conceptually simple customizations such as noncanonical decompositions inside out are hard to implement but can have a huge impact on keeping the branching factor down to save millions of proofs steps [60, 61].

Explicit storage of the proof tree with all proof steps makes it easy to inspect and navigate what was done. Likewise exhaustive applicability checks for taclets at every proof step make it convenient for users to determine which proof rules make sense to try. Both decisions are adverse for large proofs with large formulas, which causes nontrivial memory pressure and wastes an enormous amount of time with identifying at every step which rules are applicable where and how and at what cost. These effects accumulate so that KeYmaera 3 may need an hour per proof step in larger proofs. Storing the full proof tree also requires a lot of reproving effort when loading a (full or partial) proof, often taking a few hours on complex case studies. This is an example where different prover design choices are needed depending on the expected size of proofs.

The biggest downside of the KeYmaera prover design is that its general infrastructure and proof mechanisms come at the cost of leading to quite a large soundness-critical prover kernel. While this kernel is isolated from the rest of the prover, its taclet infrastructure, schematic matching mechanisms, and built-in operators not only give the kernel a very central flavor in the entire prover implementation but also lead to its roughly 136k lines of soundness-critical code written in a mix of mostly Java and some Scala as well as more than 2000 taclets.

Outcomes. Major case studies verified in KeYmaera include safety of a roundabout aircraft collision avoidance system [55], safety, controllability, reactivity and liveness of the European Train Control System ETCS [57], adaptive cruise control systems for cars [28], robot obstacle avoidance scenarios [32], basic safety for the Next-generation Airborne Collision Avoidance System ACAS X [23], and an adversarial robotic factory automation scenario [61]. KeYmaera is embedded into the hybrid systems modeling environment Sphinx [34], which provides UML-style graphical and textual modeling of hybrid programs, and interacts with KeYmaera to discharge proof obligations in dL.

These case studies confirm that differential dynamic logic is versatile for verifying even complicated hybrid systems. They reassure that KeYmaera has solid automation capabilities and makes it possible to interactively verify complicated systems out of reach for automation. What they also confirm is the nuisance of repetitive interaction that users face when working on complicated applications far out of reach for the small selection of automatic proof strategies that ship with KeYmaera. Especially model changes require tedious repetitions of interactive proofs. KeYmaera proofs store every proof step in detail, so are not a very practical source when redoing proofs making verification results hard to modify.

Other takeaways include the loss of traceability for non-experts caused by the additional quantifiers, updates, and static-single-assignment variable renaming that KeYmaera introduces to make local taclet applications sound. Inexperienced users easily get lost in the proof tree and fail to exercise appropriate branching control, which significantly increases verification complexity. Even experienced users may get lost in the details of a complete proof tree with all steps while missing contextual knowledge when projecting out intermediate proof steps.

What Else KeYmaera 3 Offers. Beyond the scope for this chapter is the fact that KeYmaera 3 also implements the extensions of differential-algebraic dynamic logic with differential algebraic equations [44], differential temporal dynamic logic with safety throughout [45], differential dynamic game logic that adds separate game constructs on top of dL [61], and was finally also extended to implement quantified differential dynamic logic for distributed hybrid systems [46]. KeYmaera links to a large number of real arithmetic decision procedures and even has a built-in implementation for simple real arithmetic [58]. The implementation of differential temporal dynamic logic is particularly parsimonious in KeYmaera 3 as, e.g., the `#boxtr` schema variable used in taclet `box_choice_right` can match on either dL's box modality or the throughout modality of differential temporal dynamic logic. One taclet implements two rules.

4   KeYmaeraD – An Experiment in Distributed Theorem Proving With Direct Control

The KeYmaeraD hybrid systems theorem prover[3] [62] is a bare-bones prover with a direct rendition of the differential dynamic logic sequent calculus [43] (with extensions for distributed hybrid systems [46]) in Scala.

Design Principles. Beyond supporting *distributed* hybrid systems, KeYmaeraD was designed with the primary motivation of overcoming inherent scalability limits caused by the sequential prover design of KeYmaera 3. Rather than having a single proof tree explored sequentially as in KeYmaera 3, KeYmaeraD supports a more general AND/OR proof tree where some nodes are AND-branching (all subgoals need to be proved, it suffices to disprove one) and other nodes are OR-branching (one subgoal needs to be proved, or all need to be disproved). In order to favor execution speed and retain a lightweight implementation, KeYmaeraD does not provide a rule application mechanism such as KeYmaera 3 taclets but entirely relies on the pattern matching capabilities of the host language (Scala). KeYmaeraD supports a built-in computation unit abstraction that is used to decide which part of the *parallel* AND/OR proof tree to explore next. In terms of user interaction, KeYmaeraD provides basic AND/OR proof tree rendering with minimalistic goal printing and interaction with the Scala REPL for rule and tactic application, but does not provide other UI infrastructure like KeYmaera 3 and KeYmaera X to filter rules by applicability or to suggest proof steps.

Successes. KeYmaeraD allows direct programming of proofs in the Scala host language and provides ways of combining them with simple tactic combinators in Scala. Its tactic library captures direct proof rule application but does not implement a sophisticated tactic library combining inferences to achieve higher-level reasoning. The AND/OR proof tree of KeYmaeraD emphasizes parallel

---

[3] KeYmaeraD is available at http://symbolaris.com/info/KeYmaeraD.html.

proof search to explore different proof options, which provides significant opportunities for quickly discovering proofs. For example, KeYmaeraD can efficiently construct proofs for a given list of loop invariants in parallel. This is a very powerful mechanism for medium complexity examples where the computational demand does not significantly exceed the computational resources. The direct implementation in a host language ensures low computational cost per rule application. KeYmaeraD is also the first ever prover for distributed hybrid systems.

Challenges. The biggest downside of KeYmaeraD's prover design is its inflexible rule application, limited to top-level sequent calculus uses. Where KeYmaera 3 is sometimes overly permissive, KeYmaeraD is overly narrow-minded in its proof rules and only supports one style of proofs. For example, it would be impossible to avoid exponential blowups that some proofs face unless working inside out [37,61]. While Scala gives a lot of flexibility, the downside is that proofs can only be conducted by programming them in Scala or typing them into a command line in Scala's read-eval-print-loop (REPL), both of which require expert knowledge about the prover's internal implementation details. The simplistic user interface only renders the proof tree and expects REPL commands to apply proof rules with a `goto` command to select the proof tree node, thereby making it comparably hard for novices to get started. Since everything is implemented explicitly in Scala, it is easy to change the prover, but KeYmaeraD does not provide sufficient soundness protection because users can create arbitrary new proof rules in any arbitrary part of the code or they could annotate incorrect solutions of differential equations that KeYmaeraD will use without checking.

Implementation Realities. KeYmaeraD implements the $[\cup]\wedge L, [\cup]\wedge R$ sequent calculus proof rule schemata (see below) in Scala as a function mapping a sequent to a list of sequents:

```scala
val choose = new ProofRule("choose") {
  def apply(p: Position) = sq => {
    val fm = lookup(p, sq)
    fm match {
      case Modality(Box, Choose(h1, h2), phi) =>
        val fm1 = Modality(Box, h1, phi)
        val fm2 = Modality(Box, h2, phi)
        val sq1 = replace(p, sq, Binop(And, fm1, fm2))
        Some((List(sq1),Nil))
      case _ => None
    }
  }
}
```

Rule `choose` Line 3 uses `lookup` to access the sequent `sq` at position `p`, and then matches on the shape of that formula. Extension of the rule to make it applicable in other contexts or to other shapes with additional match cases is

soundness-critical. This code implements the following sequent calculus proof
rule schemata:

$$([\cup]\wedge L) \; \frac{\Gamma, [\alpha]\phi \wedge [\beta]\phi \vdash \Delta}{\Gamma, [\alpha \cup \beta]\phi \vdash \Delta} \qquad ([\cup]\wedge R) \; \frac{\Gamma \vdash [\alpha]\phi \wedge [\beta]\phi, \Delta}{\Gamma \vdash [\alpha \cup \beta]\phi, \Delta}$$

The loop rule of Fig. 2 is implemented in 61 LOC as a function from the
invariant formula to a proof rule, listing how the rule applies in a sequent:

```
1  val loopInduction : Formula => ProofRule =
2  inv => new ProofRule("loopInduction[" + inv + "]") {
3    def apply(pos: Position) = sq => (pos, sq) match {
4      case (RightP(n), Sequent(sig, c, s)) =>
5        val fm = lookup(pos, sq)
6        val initial = replace(pos, sq, inv)
7        fm match {
8          case Modality(Box,Loop(hp, True, inv_hints), phi) =>
9            val inductionstep =
10             Sequent(sig, List(inv),
11                             List(Modality(Box, hp, inv)))
12           val closestep =
13             Sequent(sig, List(inv), List(phi))
14           Some((List(initial, inductionstep, closestep), Nil))
15         case _ => None
16       }
17       .... /* elided lines for diamond modality */
18     case _ => None
19   }
20 }
```

This `loopInduction` rule discards all context in Lines 10–13 to avoid universal closures, which simplifies the implementation considerably but requires
users to tediously retain any information needed from the context as part of the
loop invariant, which is brittle when editing models. This decision makes loop
invariant generation more challenging (not implemented in KeYmaeraD).

KeYmaeraD does not implement differential induction dI of Fig. 2 as a separate proof rule, but instead provides that functionality combined with differential
cuts [45,48,59] as a `diffStrengthen` rule that augments the evolution domain
constraint of a differential equation with a condition `inv`:

```
1  val diffStrengthen : Formula => ProofRule =
2  inv => new ProofRule("diffStrengthen[" + inv + "]") {
3    def apply(pos: Position) = sq => (pos, sq) match {
4      case (RightP(n), Sequent(sig, c, s)) =>
5        val fm = lookup(pos, sq)
6        fm match {
7          case Modality(Box, Evolve(ode,h,inv_hints,sol), p) =>
8            val (ind_asm, ind_cons) = if (Prover.openSet(inv))
9                (List(inv, h),
10               setClosure(totalDeriv(None, ode, inv)))
```

```
11            else (List(h), totalDeriv(None, ode, inv))
12          val inv_hints1 = inv_hints.filter(inv != _)
13          val fm1 = Modality(Box,
14                           Evolve(ode,
15                                  Binop(And, h, inv),
16                                  inv_hints1,
17                                  sol),
18                    p)
19          val iv = Sequent(sig, h::c, List(inv))
20          val ind = Sequent(sig, ind_asm, List(ind_cons))
21          val str = replace(pos, sq, fm1)
22          Some((List(iv, ind, str), Nil))
23        case _ => None
24      }
25    case _ => None
26  }
27 }
```

This code implements the following sequent calculus proof rules, where $Cl(P)$ is the approximate topological closure of P and P_x^θ substitutes term θ for variable x in P:

$$(\text{dSc}) \ \frac{\Gamma, Q \vdash J, \Delta \quad Q \vdash (J)'^{f(x)}_{x'} \quad \Gamma \vdash [x' = f(x) \,\&\, Q \wedge J]F, \Delta}{\Gamma \vdash [x' = f(x) \,\&\, Q]F, \Delta} \quad (\text{J closed})$$

$$(\text{dSo}) \ \frac{\Gamma, Q \vdash J, \Delta \quad Q, J \vdash Cl((J)')^{f(x)}_{x'} \quad \Gamma \vdash [x' = f(x) \,\&\, Q \wedge J]F, \Delta}{\Gamma \vdash [x' = f(x) \,\&\, Q]F, \Delta} \quad (\text{J open})$$

The diffStrengthen rule distinguishes between open and closed invariants (Lines 8–11): open differential invariants [45] can assume the invariant in the assumptions ind_asm during their inductive proof, on closed invariants only the evolution domain h is assumed in ind_asm in the induction step, because it would be unsound to assume inv [45]. The main implementation in Prover.totalDeriv computes the differential invariant condition ind_cons for inv as a function of the differential equation ode and amounts to an extra 1500 lines of Scala code. The result of the diffStrengthen rule are three subgoals (Lines 19–22): the invariant inv must hold initially from the evolution domain constraint h and context c; its differential invariant condition ind_cons must be preserved from the assumptions ind_asm; then inv can strengthen the evolution domain constraint h in the augmented differential equation (Lines 13–18).

Assignments [:=] are implemented in Scala by turning them into equations:

```
1 val assign = new ProofRule("assign") {
2    def apply(p: Position) = sq => {
3      val Sequent(sig, c, s) = sq
4      val fm = lookup(p, sq)
5      fm match {
6        case Modality(_, Assign(vs), phi) =>
7          var phi1 = phi;
8          var sig1 = sig;
9          var c1 = c;
10         for(v <- vs) v match {
```

```
11      case (Fn(vr, Nil), tm) =>
12        val vr1 = Prover.uniqify(vr);
13        phi1 = Prover.renameFn(vr, vr1, phi1);
14        sig1 = sig.get(vr) match {
15          case Some(sg) => sig1.+((vr1, sg))
16          case _        => sig1
17        }
18        val fm1 = Atom(R("=", List(Fn(vr1, Nil), tm)));
19        c1 = c1 ++ List(fm1);
20        ... /* case (Fn(vr, List(arg)), tm) elided */
21      }
22      val sq1 = replace(p, Sequent(sig1, c1, s), phi1)
23      Some((List(sq1), Nil))
24
25    case _ => None
26  }
27  }
28 }
```

This code implements the following sequent calculus proof rule, where y is fresh in the sequent and P_x^y is P with all occurrences of x renamed to y:

$$([:=]\text{eq}) \quad \frac{\Gamma, y = e \vdash P_x^y, \Delta}{\Gamma \vdash [x := e]P, \Delta} \quad (y \text{ fresh})$$

Rule `assign` does not attempt any simplification (e.g., substitution), but chooses to always rename and introduce equations. It obtains a fresh variable `vr1` with `Prover.uniqify` (Line 12) and then uses `Prover.renameFn` (Line 13) to rename `vr` to `vr1` in the postcondition `phi`. The effect of the assignment is collected as an equation in the context (Lines 18–19), and the signatures of the sequent are updated to include the fresh variable (Lines 14–17).

While the challenge of KeYmaeraD's loop rule is that it discards all information from the context, the challenge of KeYmaeraD's `assign` is the opposite: it retains all assumptions, even assumptions that have become irrelevant or, if substituted, would lead to significantly simpler assumptions. For example, on

$$x = y \vdash [x := x + 1][x := 2x][x := x - 2]x = 2y$$

repeated application of rule `assign` results in

$$x = y, x_0 = x + 1, x_1 = 2x_0, x_2 = x_1 - 2 \vdash x_2 = 2y$$

instead of the simpler $x = y \vdash 2(x + 1) - 2 = 2y$ of [:=] substitution of Fig. 2. Retaining such old versions of variables has a significant impact on the practical performance of real arithmetic [45, Sect. 5.3.2], where just one formula can be the difference between termination within a second and no answer within a day.

Outcomes. The prover KeYmaeraD is an interesting experiment to see what happens when directly implementing a prover to address the shortcomings of

KeYmaera 3, embracing parallel proof search, and generalizing it to distributed hybrid systems. KeYmaeraD is useful for experts familiar with its implementation detail and enables proofs of distributed hybrid systems out of reach for all other verification tools (except later versions of KeYmaera 3). But KeYmaeraD never attracted a sustainable user base. Its blessing of *enabling* low-level control of parallel proof search was simultaneously its curse of *requiring* low-level control to benefit from parallel exploration while simultaneously requiring low-level attention to the logical transformation of formulas. This includes the need for explicit augmentation of invariants with assumptions about constants and tracking of static-single-assignment-renamings of variable generations. But KeYmaeraD is useful for experts who appreciate direct control of proofs close to bare metal.

Statistics. KeYmaeraD comes with 38 built-in proof rules, some of which implement multiple modality cases at once (e.g. `choose`). The statistics give a ballpark estimate even if they are not quite comparable with other provers because KeYmaeraD has only partial support for differential equations and $\langle \cdot \rangle$ modalities and $\exists$ quantifiers, and does not yet provide invariant generation or proof storage.

What Else KeYmaeraD Offers. Most significantly, KeYmaeraD also implements quantified differential dynamic logic QdL for *distributed* hybrid systems [46]. While no interesting hybrid systems were verified with KeYmaeraD, its primary applications use *distributed* hybrid systems technology. KeYmaeraD was used to verify disc-type collision avoidance maneuvers for arbitrarily many aircraft in QdL [29] as well as safety of a surgical robot controller obeying arbitrarily many operating boundaries [25], which are out of scope for all other tools. Since KeYmaeraD is not based on KeY, it did not inherit KeY's automatic proof strategy support and also requires manual instantiation of quantifiers. That is why, ironically, a subsequent implementation of part of the distributed hybrid systems logic QdL in the original KeYmaera 3 prover was more practical.

5   KeYmaera X – An aXiomatic Tactical Theorem Prover With a Small Microkernel

The clean-slate KeYmaera X theorem prover for hybrid systems [20] is a direct implementation of the differential dynamic logic uniform substitution proof calculus [50], complemented by built-in propositional sequent calculus rules for performance reasons, and is implemented in Scala. The uniform substitution style has a significantly simplifying impact on the overall prover design and substantially simplifies soundness arguments thanks to the resulting minimal kernel.

Design Principles. The most important goal in the design of KeYmaera X is its systematic attention to a small-core LCF [30] design, identifying the minimal essential building blocks of a sound hybrid systems prover. An explicit goal of

KeYmaera X is to identify a minimal axiomatic prover core (*prover μkernel*) based upon which a hybrid systems prover can be built easily that is guaranteed to be sound if the μkernel is sound. The crucial ingredient to enable this is dL's uniform substitution calculus [50], which made it possible to avoid proof rule schemata and axiom schemata entirely. Unlike in KeYmaeraD, conceptual simplicity was *not* obtained at the expense of flexibility. Unlike KeYmaera 3, no schematic rule application mechanism such as taclets was used. Uniform substitutions enable a significantly more flexible proof calculus than what KeYmaera 3 had to offer, although never at the expense of soundness. Another goal of the KeYmaera X prover was to increase modularity by having separate responsibilities, e.g., separate modules for prover μ kernel, tactic language, tactic libraries, persistence layer, communication layer, web user interface, that are each mostly isolated from one another and, thus, easier to modify or replace separately. For user interaction purposes, KeYmaera X strives for close mnemonic analogy with textbooks, favors proof step result simplicity over internal reasoning simplicity, and presents internal automation steps on demand rather than mixed with user-initiated steps.

Uniform Substitution. The uniform substitution proof rule [50], originally due to Church for first-order logic [14, §35,40], says that if a formula ϕ has a proof, then the result $\sigma(\phi)$ of substituting terms for function symbols, formulas for predicate symbols, hybrid programs for program constant symbols, and context formulas for quantifier symbols, according to uniform substitution σ is proved:

$$(\text{US}) \ \frac{\phi}{\sigma(\phi)}$$

The big deal about uniform substitution is that it makes superfluous all schemata and instantiation mechanisms such as taclets and schema variable implementations of KeYmaera 3 and host-language matching code of KeYmaeraD. The soundness-critical part of the implementation of the nondeterministic choice axiom [∪], for example, reduces literally to just providing one concrete dL formula:

$$[a \cup b]P \leftrightarrow [a]P \wedge [b]P$$

This axiom is an ordinary concrete dL formula in which a, b are program constant symbols and P is a nullary quantifier symbol (P can also be thought of as a predicate symbol $p(\bar{x})$ with the vector $\bar{x}$ of all variables as arguments). If a particular instance of this axiom is needed during a proof, all a tactic needs to do is ask rule US to generate an appropriate instance, e.g., with the uniform substitution $\sigma = \{a \mapsto x := x + 1, b \mapsto x' = x, P \mapsto x \geq 0\}$ as follows:

$$\text{US} \frac{[a \cup b]P \leftrightarrow [a]P \wedge [b]P}{[x := x + 1 \cup x' = x]\, x \geq 0 \leftrightarrow [x := x + 1]\, x \geq 0 \wedge [x' = x]\, x \geq 0}$$

In KeYmaera X, rule US is mostly used backwards from conclusion to its premise by identifying which substitution σ reduces $\sigma(\phi)$ to a known or easier formula. Unification outside the soundness-critical μkernel finds the appropriate uniform substitution σ required for a desired inference step (e.g., after matching $[x := x + 1 \cup x' = x] x \geq 0$ against $[a \cup b]P$). The same uniform substitution proof rule US resolves, e.g., all the subtleties with the use of assignment axioms where the admissibility conditions of US [50,51] adequately prevent unsound reasoning. Uniform substitution enables reasoning in context [50], which make uniformly substituted axioms significantly more versatile and flexible than, e.g., the automatic context generalizations of KeYmaera 3, while always rigorously maintaining soundness of such generalizations.

Implementation Realities. Thanks to uniform substitutions, the implementation of axioms in KeYmaera X reduces to providing a direct copy of the dL formula of the axiom given in plain text in the KeYmaera X prover μkernel:

```
1 Axiom "[++] choice"
2   [a;++b;]p(||) <-> [a;]p(||) & [b;]p(||)
3 End.
4 Axiom "[:=] assign"
5   [x:=f();]p(x) <-> p(f())
6 End.
7 Axiom "[:=] assign equality"
8   [x:=f();]p(||) <-> \forall x (x=f() -> p(||))
9 End.
```

These are direct ASCII renditions of the $[\cup]$ choice axiom and the $[:=]$ assignment axiom. The ++ symbol is ASCII for $\cup$ and the notation p(||) indicates that p is a nullary quantifier symbol (predicational) instead of a nullary predicate symbol as in p(). This is all there is to the soundness-critical part in the prover μkernel of the implementation of those axioms, because uniform substitution is available in the μkernel to soundly put concrete terms in for the function symbol f(), put concrete formulas in for the predicate symbol p(.) of its argument (.) or for the predicational symbol p(||), and put concrete hybrid systems in for the program symbols a; and b;. Thanks to unification outside the soundness-critical μkernel, using such axioms is easily done with a tactic that instructs the unifier to unify with and use the appropriate axiom at the position where it will be applied to:[4]

```
val choiceb = useAt("[++] choice")
```

Tactics get more complicated when different circumstances require different proofs, e.g., assignments sometimes need renaming to avoid conflicts. But tactics are not soundness-critical, so the μkernel is isolated from such complications:

```
1 @Tactic("[:=]", conclusion = "__[x:=e]p(x)__<->p(e)")
2 val assignb = anon by { w =>
```

---

[4] Besides unification, the implementation of the generic useAt tactic identifies the (blue) key of an axiom to unify with and generically handles, e.g., equivalence transformations and implicational assumptions that arise during the use of the axiom.

```
 3    useAt("[:=] assign")(w)
 4  | useAt("[:=] self assign")(w)
 5  | asgnEq(w)
 6 }
 7 @Tactic(
 8    names = "[:=]=",
 9    premises =    "G, x=e |- P, D",
10    //     [:=]=   -------------------
11    conclusion = "G |- [x:=e]P, D",
12    displayLevel = "all"
13  )
14 val asgnEq = anon by ((w, seq) => seq.sub(w) match {
15 case Some(Box(Assign(x, t), p)) =>
16   val y = freshNamedSymbol(x, seq)
17   boundRenaming(x, y)(w) &
18   useAt("[:=] assign equality")(w) &
19   uniformRenaming(y, x) &
20   (if (w.isTopLevel&&w.isSucc) allR(w) & implyR(w) else ident)
21 })
```

The **assignb** tactic combines axioms and tactics with the | combinator to try succinct axioms first and fall back to more complicated tactics only when necessary: it first tries axiom [:=] with **useAt("[:=] assign")(w)** for its succinct result if it is applicable; upon failure, the tactic tries to resolve self-assignments of the form $x := x$, and finally, it applies the generic **asgnEq** tactic that is applicable to any assignment in any context. The **@Tactic** annotations provide naming and rendering information for registering and displaying tactics.

Axioms that are only sound for hybrid systems but not hybrid games use the clunky notation a{|^@|}; to indicate that a; cannot mention the game duality operator ^{d} rendered as ^@ in ASCII so a; is a program not a game symbol:

```
1 Axiom "I induction"
2   p(||)&[{a{|^@|};}*](p(||)->[a{|^@|};]p(||))->[{a{|^@|};}*]p(||)
3 End.
```

Thanks to the syntactic internalization of differential operators in differential dynamic logic [50], the implementation of differential invariants is quite simple:

```
1 Axiom "DI differential invariance"
2   ([{c&q(||)}]p(||) <-> [?q(||);]p(||))
3               <- (q(||)->[{c&q(||)}]((p(||))'))
4 End.
```

A few similarly simple further axioms are needed to, then, remove the resulting differential operator from p(||)', e.g., for distributing differentials over ∧:

```
1 Axiom "&' derive and"
2   (p(||) & q(||))' <-> (p(||))' & (q(||))'
3 End.
```

But the entire construction is syntactic within the logic dL itself [50] instead of as a soundness-critical algorithm implementing a built-in metaoperator #DiffInd with a Java program as in KeYmaera 3 or a Scala program as in KeYmaeraD.

Successes. Probably the biggest success of the KeYmaera X design is how well it has managed to keep the size and complexity of its soundness-critical prover μkernel at only about 2000 lines of code that are mostly straightforward. That makes it much easier to check whether a change could damage the prover, because *i)* soundness is rarely the issue, as code in the μkernel rarely changes, *ii)* completeness is usually the worst that may be affected in most changes, which is more easily noticed with testing (if something no longer proves that did) compared to soundness-critical changes (nobody notices if something suddenly would prove that should not), and *iii)* many changes are monotonic additions that add new tactics whose presence, by design, cannot damage the functioning of the rest of the prover. It is liberating to advance provers under such a design that encourages fast-paced development and teams. The result is a significantly more flexible proof calculus that is able to apply axioms in any binding context inside formulas, checked for soundness by uniform substitution (whereas KeYmaera and KeYmaeraD are restricted to reasoning at top-level operators).

Another major success of the KeYmaera X prover is its versatile user interface [36], which makes the use of the prover transparent compared to the theory. In a nutshell, formal proofs and proof rules can be read and understood equally on paper and in the prover without requiring a shift in perspective.[5] One indication that this design was successful is the fact that undergraduate students are able to learn how to use KeYmaera X in a course [51] well enough even if almost all of them have not had any prior exposure to logic or cyber-physical systems. Contributing in no small part to the successful design of the KeYmaera X user interface is its modular design separate from all the rest of the prover, enabling easier experimentation and complete rewrites.

The modular code base of KeYmaera X is fairly resilient to change. Beyond the intended points of change, it was possible to swap out axioms to prove hybrid games [52], swap out uniform substitution application mechanisms [53], swap out unification, swap out central proof data structures and proof storage, change how formulas in sequents are indexed, and swap out the entire tactic framework.

KeYmaera X has sufficiently modular automatic proof tactics that make it easy to benefit from automatic invariant generators for continuous dynamics such as Pegasus [64]. It is also comparably easy to maintain alternative proof automation tactics in harmonious coexistence, e.g., when it is not clear ahead of time which approach or which combination of approaches will work best.

---

[5] Ironically, minor notational differences still exist as concessions to ASCII and curly-brace language notation, but major changes such as different proof notations, updates or static-single-assignment-renamed versions of variables are avoided.

Challenges. Its focus on soundness makes it comparably easy to spot soundness bugs in KeYmaera X, because its μkernel is short and structurally simple, and because all else gets caught when trying to draw incorrect inferences (e.g., incorrect tactics). But the same cannot be said for performance and completeness bugs. Because KeYmaera X, for performance reasons, does not memorize its proof steps and only reports problems if a proof step was unsound, it is hard to notice where tactics found proofs in unnecessarily complicated yet sound ways. For example, when a tactic goes in circles a few times before successfully completing a correct proof, then it is much harder to notice the wasted effort.

Tactic implementation often needs to trade off performance, completeness, and comprehensibility, because it is not only inherently difficult to enumerate all the sound ways of applying axioms in diverse contexts (which is exactly the benefit of using uniform substitution), but also inherently difficult to decide what of that context information should be kept for completeness and which facts to discard to increase comprehensibility and scale. These considerations show up in tactic implementation for KeYmaera X with a performance and completeness impact. But the same challenges surface in KeYmaera and KeYmaeraD where, however, they furthermore cause a soundness impact! For example, consider the following axiom for differential weakening, which allows us to prove postcondition p(||) from the evolution domain constraint q(||) of an ODE {c&q(||)}.

```
1 Axiom "DW differential weakening"
2   [{c&q(||)}]p(||) <-> ([{c&q(||)}](q(||)->p(||)))
3 End.
```

Axiom DW differential weakening by itself does not make the question much easier, since the differential equation {c&q(||)} is still around even after applying the axiom from left to right. In order to make progress in the proof, a tactic will need to combine axiom DW differential weakening with techniques to abstract the modality away, for example by using axiom V vacuous or rule G, as put into operation in the example in Fig. 4.

```
1 Axiom "V vacuous"
2   p() -> [a{|^@|};]p()
3 End.
```

$$(G) \ \frac{\vdash \phi}{\vdash [\alpha]\phi}$$

$$\dfrac{\dfrac{*}{\vdash \forall x \, (x \geq 0 \to x \geq 0)}^{\mathrm{QE}}}{\dfrac{\vdash [x' = 2 \,\&\, x \geq 0]\forall x \, (x \geq 0 \to x \geq 0)}{\dfrac{\vdash [x' = 2 \,\&\, x \geq 0](x \geq 0 \to x \geq 0)}{\vdash [x' = 2 \,\&\, x \geq 0]x \geq 0}^{\mathrm{DW}}}^{\forall^\alpha}}^{\mathrm{V}}$$

$$\dfrac{\dfrac{\bullet}{\dfrac{*}{\vdash x \geq 0 \to x \geq 0}^{\mathrm{QE}}}}{\dfrac{\vdash [x' = 2 \,\&\, x \geq 0](x \geq 0 \to x \geq 0)}{\vdash [x' = 2 \,\&\, x \geq 0]x \geq 0}^{\mathrm{DW}}}^{\mathrm{G}}$$

(a) Abstraction with axiom V vacuous   (b) Abstraction with rule G

Fig. 4. Tactic alternatives for differential weakening by vacuity or generalization

In this example, the proof in Fig. 4b is more concise than Fig. 4a and gives a less surprising result without universal quantifiers. Why may we still want to use the proof technique in Fig. 4a? Consider $x_0 \geq 1 \vdash [x' = 2 \;\&\; x \geq x_0]x \geq 0$, where it is important to retain the initial assumption $x_0 \geq 1$ (rule G is only applicable in an empty context, so would discard assumption $x_0 \geq 1$ by weakening). Many conjectures are best served (for users and automation) by concise reasoning that leaves less clutter around, but for completeness it becomes necessary to retain certain facts. A prover has to decide what is appropriate in which situation.

Learning from the successes of KeYmaeraD, initial attempts on a tactic framework for KeYmaera X emphasized concurrent and speculative tactic execution in the spirit of modern processor designs for performance reasons. Relying only on aggressively concurrent execution turns out to be a misguided idea during development, because, even with sound proofs, concurrent execution makes it near impossible to debug where and why tactics are failing if there is no reliable way of triggering the same failure in the same order again. The current sequential tactic framework entirely dismisses all aspirations for concurrent execution (except when using explicit parallel tactic combinators), and is significantly more successful in practice.

For modularity reasons, KeYmaera X has a tactic interpreter that runs a tactic on a sequent to completion returning the remaining open premises (if any, else the sequent is proved). This design results in a clear separation of concerns compared to the rest of the prover. But, unlike in KeYmaera 3, it is difficult to meaningfully interrupt an automatic proof in the middle and then help out interactively. This is related to the fact that, other than an exhaustive list of all individual proof steps, there is no reliable way to record the resulting proof, because there is no guarantee that interrupting the automatic tactic after the same amount of time or the same number of inferences in the future will result in the same remaining open premises. To mitigate, KeYmaera X provides ways of running tactics in exploratory mode, whether the tactic completes successfully or not, and a second tactic interpreter records and exposes internal proof steps.

The reliance of the KeYmaera X user interface on a web browser makes it much easier to distribute proof development to multiple users and provides browser-powered rendering capabilities. But it requires dealing with the acute idiosyncracies of browser dependencies, unreliability of JavaScript and its libraries.

Outcomes. Fairly subtle properties of major complicated systems have been successfully verified with KeYmaera X, including the Next-generation Airborne Collision Avoidance Systems ACAS X [24], obstacle avoidance [33] and waypoint navigation [13] for ground robots, and air pressure brakes for trains [31]. The syntactic rendition of proofs as tactics in KeYmaera X was also exploited to enable provably safe reinforcement learning in cyber-physical systems [21], as well as tactical verification of component-based hybrid systems models [40]. ModelPlex [37] crucially exploits the axiomatic approach of KeYmaera X that enables in-context reasoning and avoids splitting ModelPlex proofs into multiple branches, so that all runtime conditions are collected in a single proof goal. The first implementation of ModelPlex in KeYmaera [35] with its restriction to top-level rules branches heavily, which requires a soundness-critical step of collecting and factoring all open branches from an unfinished proof. The strict separation of generating invariants, sfolutions of differential equations, and other proof hints, from tactically checking them enables KeYmaera X to include numeric and other potentially unsound methods (e.g., for generating barrier certificates) into its invariant generation framework Pegasus [64] for nonlinear ODEs.

These case studies confirm the advanced scale at which differential dynamic logic proving helps make hybrid systems correct even for fairly complex applications with very subtle properties. The use of tactics in the Bellerophon tactic language of KeYmaera X [19] played a big role in proving them. When beyond the reach of full automation, proof tactics are significantly easier to rerun, modify, and check compared to point-and-click interactive proofs. The comparably fast-paced development with a small μkernel underneath a large library of tactics also makes it easier to advance proof automation, including automation of complete differential equation invariant proving [59]. The curse of improving proof automation, however, is that tactics may have to be adapted when more of a proof completes fully automatically and the remaining formulas change.

The ARCH competition [38] highlights significant improvements for full automation of continuous dynamics from KeYmaera to KeYmaera X, but also that the tactics in KeYmaera X, while more automatic, still lose efficiency compared to the proof search and checking procedures of KeYmaera. The benefit of separating proof automation in tactics from the μkernel manifests in performance and automation improvements between KeYmaera X versions: proof automation in KeYmaera X improved [38] to the level of scripted proving reported a year earlier [39], and additional scripted functionality became available.

Statistics. Besides uniform substitution, renaming, and propositional sequent calculus rules with Skolemization, the KeYmaera X μkernel provides 5 axiomatic proof rules with concrete dL formulas and 54 concrete dL formulas as axioms. A large number of tactics (about 400) are built on top of this μkernel and are, thus, not soundness-critical.

What Else KeYmaera X Offers. Beyond serving as a hybrid systems theorem prover, KeYmaera X implements differential game logic for hybrid games [49], which, quite unlike the case of games added to KeYmaera 3 [61], required only a minor change. This is an example illustrating why the axiomatic approach makes it significantly easier to soundly change the capabilities of a prover. The axiomatic approach is also beneficial to obtain formal guarantees about the prover μkernel itself [11], and serves as the basis for transforming hybrid systems proofs to verified machine code through the compilation pipeline VeriPhy [12].

6   Comparison of Underlying Reasoning Principles

In this section, we compare how differences in the underlying reasoning principles result in differences in the concrete mechanics of conducting sequent proofs and differences in the code base organization.

Implementation Comparison by Example. We discuss assignments, loops, and differential equations as illustrative examples of the implementation choices across KeYmaera, KeYmaeraD, and KeYmaera X.

Assignments. Assignments, even though seemingly simple at first glance, become tricky depending on the binding structure of the *imperative* programs that follow. Let us briefly recap how handling assignments differs across provers:

– KeYmaera turns all assignments into updates, but delegates the soundness-critical task of how to apply these updates to the update simplifier and leads to soundness-critical decisions of invisibly leaving updates around all taclets;
– KeYmaeraD opts for the always-safe choice of introducing universal quantifiers and turning all assignments into extra equations, but this results in a plethora of similar symbols and equation chains that can (i) be confusing for users, (ii) be exceedingly challenging for real arithmetic solvers, and (iii) increase the complexity of identifying loop invariants and ODE invariants;
– KeYmaera X exploits the safety net of the underlying uniform substitution algorithm: its tactic replaces the free occurrences of the assigned variable, and only if the prover kernel rejects this[6], falls back to introducing equations.

The following example illustrates the difference in the behavior between KeYmaera (**K3** for short below), KeYmaeraD (**KD**), and KeYmaera X (**KX**):

$$x = 1 \vdash \{x := x + 1\}[?x \geq 1]x \geq 0 \quad \textbf{K3 (update)}$$

$$x = 1, x_1 = x + 1 \vdash [?x_1 \geq 1]x_1 \geq 0 \quad \textbf{KD (equation)}$$

$$\frac{x = 1 \vdash [?x + 1 \geq 1]x + 1 \geq 0 \quad \textbf{KX (substitution)}}{[:=]\, x = 1 \vdash [x := x + 1][?x \geq 1]x \geq 0}$$

In this example, the assigned variable x occurs free but not bound in the formula $[?x \geq 1]x \geq 0$ following the assignment and so can be substituted. Despite this, KeYmaera and KeYmaeraD stick to their fixed behavior of introducing updates and equations, respectively. KeYmaera X uses a substitution in the above example, and adapts its behavior appropriately using free and (must)bound variables from the static semantics of dL [50]. The wide variety in the examples below of how to best handle assignments in sound ways explains why that is best decided outside the soundness-critical prover core.

---

[6] Earlier implementations of the KeYmaera X assignment tactic attempted to syntactically analyze the formula to decide which axiom to use, which is essentially the task of the update simplifier in KeYmaera. This approach turned out to be too error-prone, unless the tactic exactly mimics the uniform substitution algorithm.

Must-bound not free: After the assignment, the assigned variable is definitely bound but not free, so the assignment has no effect:

$$[:=] \frac{\vdash [x := 3]x \geq 3}{\vdash [x := 2][x := 3]x \geq 3}$$

Free and must-bound: After the assignment, the assigned variable is free and definitely bound, so all free occurrences can be substituted:

$$[:=] \frac{\vdash [x := 2 + 1]x \geq 3}{\vdash [x := 2][x := x + 1]x \geq 3}$$

Free and maybe-bound: The assigned variable is bound on some but not all paths of all runs of the program, so not all free occurrences are replaceable and therefore KeYmaera X introduces an equation (for traceability KeYmacra X retains original names for the "most recent" variable and renames old versions in the context; higher index indicates more recent history):

$$[:=] \frac{x_0 = 1, x = 2 \vdash [\{x' = x\}]x \geq 2}{x = 1 \vdash [x := 2][\{x' = x\}]x \geq 2}$$

Free and must-bound before maybe-bound: The assigned variable is definitely bound again later, so the free occurrences can be replaced:

$$[:=] \frac{\vdash [x := 2 + 1 \cup x := 3][(x := x + 1)^*]x \geq 3}{\vdash [x := 2][x := x + 1 \cup x := 3][(x := x + 1)^*]x \geq 3}$$

In context substitutable: The assignment occurs in the context of a formula and substitution is applicable:

$$[:=] \frac{\vdash [\{x' = -x^2\}](x + 1)^2 \geq 2}{\vdash [\{x' = -x^2\}][x := x + 1]x^2 \geq 2}$$

In context not substitutable: The assignment occurs in the context of a formula but substitution is not applicable because the assigned variable is maybe bound later:

$$[:=] \frac{\vdash [(x := x + 1)^*]\forall x\, (x = 2 \rightarrow [\{x' = 3\}]x \geq 2)}{\vdash [(x := x + 1)^*][x := 2][\{x' = 3\}]x \geq 2}$$

Right-hand side may be bound: The right-hand side of the assignment cannot simply be substituted in because it is maybe bound on some paths:

$$[:=] \frac{y < 0, x = y^2 \vdash [y := -x \cup \{y' = x\}]y < 0}{y < 0 \vdash [x := y^2][y := -x \cup \{y' = x\}]y < 0}$$

Note that a must-bound occurrence before any maybe bound occurrences again enables plain substitution, as shown below:

$$[:=] \frac{y < 0 \vdash [x := y^2 + 1][y := -x \cup \{y' = x\}]y < 0}{y < 0 \vdash [x := y^2][x := x + 1][y := -x \cup \{y' = x\}]y < 0}$$

The benefits and drawbacks of implementations are summarized in Table 1.

Table 1. Assignment comparison

	Pros	Cons
KeYmaera	Common proof step result (updates)	Complexity hidden in critical update simplifier, affects other taclets
KeYmaeraD	Common proof step result (equations)	Creates distracting equations and Skolem symbols (challenging for users and QE and invariants)
KeYmaera X	Favors simplicity, creates variables and quantifiers only when necessary, works in context	Less easily predictable proof step result makes automated follow-up tactics challenging

Loop Induction. Loop induction showcases how the specific implementations in the provers result in different demands on user intervention afterwards. KeYmaera favors completeness and retains all context in the taclet but requires users to discard unwanted assumptions (distracting users and arithmetic procedures [45]). KeYmaeraD implements the obvious sound rule of removing all context but requires users to explicitly retain any desired assumptions in the loop invariant (which needs fragile adaptations when the model or proof changes). The KeYmaera X tactic attempts to strike a balance between the two in the usual cases, requiring users to retain extra assumptions in unusual cases. KeYmaera X tactics enable additional features, such as referring to the state at the beginning of the loop with the special function symbol *old*. The example in Fig. 5 illustrates the differences in loop induction implementations (the loop invariant $x \geq 1$ for KeYmaeraD needs to be augmented with the additional constant fact $\ldots \wedge b > 0$). Completeness of the loop tactic is more challenging than for assignment, since it has to transform sequents into the shapes expected by the axioms used internally. An early version of the tactic lost constant facts when they were not isolated or when they were "hidden" in negated form in the succedent (e.g., lost $b > 0$ in a sequent $x = 1 \wedge b > 0 \vdash [(x := x + 1/b)^*]x \geq 1$). The current tactic applies α-rules first to attempt isolating constant facts, so it still loses information, e.g., when nested inside $(x \geq 1 \wedge b > 0) \vee (x \geq 4 \wedge -b < 0)$. The benefits and drawbacks of implementations are summarized in Table 2.

Differential Induction. Similar to loop induction, KeYmaera favors completeness and retains all context. KeYmaeraD implements differential invariants not as a separate rule, but integrated with differential cuts in a single "differential strengthen" rule. KeYmaera X is closer to KeYmaera, but automatically closes the resulting goals if not explicitly asked to stop at an intermediate result. The

K3 $x = 1, b > 0 \vdash x \geq 1$

KD $x = 1, b > 0 \vdash x \geq 1 \wedge b > 0$

KX $x = 1, b > 0 \vdash x \geq 1$

(a) Base case

K3 $x = 1, b > 0 \vdash \forall x \, (x \geq 1 \rightarrow x \geq 0)$

KD $x \geq 1 \wedge b > 0 \vdash x \geq 0$

KX $b > 0, x \geq 1 \vdash x \geq 0$

(b) Use case

K3 $x = 1, b > 0 \vdash \forall x \, (x \geq 1 \rightarrow [x := x + 1/b]x \geq 1)$

KD $x \geq 1 \wedge b > 0 \vdash [x := x + 1/b](x \geq 1 \wedge b > 0)$

KX $b > 0, x \geq 1 \vdash [x := x + 1/b]x > 1$

(c) Induction step

$$\text{loop} \frac{\text{Base case (5a)} \quad \text{Use case (5b)} \quad \text{Induction step (5c)}}{x = 1, b > 0 \vdash [(x := x + 1/b)^*]x \geq 0}$$

Fig. 5. Difference in loop induction: KeYmaera (**K3**), KeYmaeraD (**KD**), and KeYmaera X (**KX**)

Table 2. Loop induction comparison

	Pros	Cons
KeYmaera	Fast one step rule, common proof step result (keeps full context, universal closure for soundness)	Universal closure with new names, needs manual removal of undesired assumptions, hard to extend features (careful: soundness)
KeYmaeraD	Fast one step rule, common proof step result (discards context)	Needs manual action to retain necessary assumptions, bad for invariant generation, hard to extend features (careful: soundness)
KeYmaera X	Less user intervention in the usual cases, easily extensible (e.g., *old* terms for ghosts)	Completeness is challenging in unusual cases, users may not immediately be able to help since usual cases work on their own

following example illustrates the difference between the differential induction implementations ($\checkmark$ indicates when goals are closed automatically).

$$\text{(init)} \qquad\qquad\qquad \text{(step)}$$

K3 $x^2 + y^2 = 1 \vdash x^2 + y^2 = 1 \qquad x^2 + y^2 = 1 \vdash \forall x \, \forall y \, (2xy + 2y(-x) = 0)$

KD $x^2 + y^2 = 1 \vdash x^2 + y^2 = 1 \qquad\qquad\qquad \vdash 2xy + 2y(-x) = 0$

KX $x^2 + y^2 = 1 \vdash x^2 + y^2 = 1 \checkmark \quad x_0^2 + y_0^2 = 1 \vdash [x' := y][y' := -x]2xx' + 2yy' = 0 \checkmark$

$$\text{DI} \frac{}{x^2 + y^2 = 1 \vdash [x' = y, y' = -x]x^2 + y^2 = 1}$$

Solving ODEs. The intuitively (but not computationally!) easiest way of proving a property of a differential equation $[x' = f(x) \,\&\, Q]P$ is to replace it with a property of its solution [43,48,50] with a universal quantifier for all times $t \geq 0$. When $y(t)$ is the solution over time t of the above differential equation (and other side conditions hold [43,48,50]), then $[x' = f(x) \,\&\, Q]P$ is equivalent to:

$$\forall t {\geq} 0 \left((\forall 0 {\leq} s {\leq} t \, [x := y(s)]Q) \to [x := y(t)]P \right)$$

The inner quantifier checks that the evolution domain constraint Q was true at every intermediate time s. It would be correct to prove $[x' = f(x) \,\&\, Q]P$ by proving a formula that merely assumes that Q was true at the end time t:

$$\forall t {\geq} 0 \left([x := y(t)]Q \to [x := y(t)]P \right)$$

Often it is more efficient to just consider the endpoint, but sometimes completeness requires the presence of the assumption about all intermediate times s. That is why all three provers implement both versions. Of course, either reasoning principle is only correct when the side conditions hold [43,43,48], most importantly that $y(t)$ actually is a solution of the differential equation (system) $x' = f(x)$ and satisfies the symbolic initial value $y(0) = x$.

　　KeYmaera trusts the differential equation solver of Mathematica or the Orbital[7] library to produce correct solutions (the conversions and taclet infrastructure are about 2k lines of code). KeYmaeraD trusts its builtin integrator and linear algebra tools (about 1k lines of code), or the user to annotate the correct solution of the differential equation with @solution in the model. KeYmaera X implements differential equation solving purely by proofs in tactics (about 1.5k lines of code) based on one axiom for solving constant differential equations [50]:

```
1 Axiom "DS& differential equation solution"
2   [{x'=c()&q(x)}]p(|x'|) <-> \forall t (t>=0 ->
3   \forall s (0<=s&s<=t->q(x+c()*s)) -> [x:=x+c()*t;]p(|x'|))
4 End.
```

Code Structure and Soundness-Critical Proof Infrastructure. Figure 6 summarizes the code base of the KeYmaera family provers, structured as follows:

> **Kernel** core data structures and soundness-critical rules, parsing and printing, as well as interfacing and interaction with external tools for arithmetic;
> **Tactics** proof primitives, and framework support for automation and scripting;
> **UI** non-critical user-facing infrastructure and proof presentation.

KeYmaera (Fig. 6a). The KeY core provides data structures to represent sequent proofs, express logics and specification languages, as well as soundness-critical

---

[7] The Orbital library is a Java library providing object-oriented representations and algorithms for logic, mathematics, and computer science.

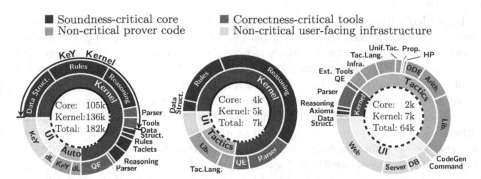

(a) KeYmaera: extends ex- (b) KeYmaeraD: direct (c) KeYmaera X: small uniform
isting dynamic logic prover impl. in host language substitution core (tactic exten-
KeY (extensions critical)   (extensions critical)   sions non-critical)

Fig. 6. Source code structure (black/solid arc: soundness-critical core, dark gray/dot-
ted arc: correctness-critical tools, medium gray/dashed arc: non-critical prover code,
light gray/dashed arc: non-critical user-facing infrastructure),

support for taclet implementation and soundness-critical reasoning infrastructure to conduct proofs and analyze cases. The KeYmaera core extends the KeY
core with data structures for dL, dL rules and taclets (see Table 3 for details), as
well as reasoning support for dL (formula analysis, computing transition models
of hybrid programs, and image computation). The KeY and KeYmaera parsers
are not strictly soundness-critical, since proofs are rerun from scratch from
pretty-printed input models. KeYmaera interfaces with numerous external tools
for flexible QE support, which results in a considerably larger QE package than
KeYmaeraD and KeYmaera X. The taclet mechanism registers taclets with proof
automation strategies, as well as with UI elements (taclets appear automatically
in context menus, and create dialog boxes and input elements).

KeYmaeraD (Fig. 6b). The KeYmaeraD core includes data structures to represent the dL syntax, sequents, proof trees, and rationals. Differential dynamic
logic is implemented entirely with soundness-critical builtin rules (for details see
Table 3), with reasoning support to apply rules, simplify arithmetic, schedule
reasoning jobs, and propagate results through the proof tree. The KeYmaeraD
parser is not strictly soundness-critical, since proofs cannot be stored, but are
always run from scratch. The QE package is restricted to Mathematica. The tactic language provides basic combinators and maps dL operators to builtin rules;
the library contains a selection of basic automation procedures (e.g., exhaustively
apply α/β-rules, hybrid program simplifications). The UI renders the proof tree
directly to a scrollable Java JTree but does not allow interaction with the proof.

KeYmaera X (Fig. 6c). The KeYmaera X core includes data structures for the
syntax, nonschematic axioms and rules (see Table 3) together with managing
sequents, and core reasoning functionality to compute static semantics, uniform
substitution, and renaming. Its parser is not strictly soundness-critical, since it is

safeguarded with cryptographic checksums (or print-reparse-checks) on storage and users can inspect printed outputs. The QE functionality provides transformations to and from data structures of external solvers and the interaction with those solvers. The tactics framework includes additional external non-critical tools for invariant generation, simplification, and counterexample generation. It provides non-critical but convenient proof infrastructure, such as unification, expression traversal, combined renaming and substitution. The tactic language allows users to compose/write new tactics and provides tactic interpreters, ways to store tactic results as lemmas, and to interface with external tools. Noteworthy tactics packages are Unif. Tac. to apply axioms by unification, Prop. for propositional reasoning, HP for hybrid programs, ODE for substantial differential equations proof automation, and Arith. for arithmetic, equality rewriting, quantifier instantiation/Skolemization, interval arithmetic, and simplification. The tactic library bundles those with a library of lemmas derived from the core axioms, and provides additional reasoning styles, such as ModelPlex [37], component-based proofs, and invariant provers for loop/ODE invariant search.

Comparison of Core Taclets, Rules, and Axioms. Table 3 compares the size of the core dedicated to expressing differential dynamic logic: KeYmaera taclets are slightly more verbose[8] than KeYmaeraD host-language rule implementations and KeYmaera X axioms[9]. The most noteworthy difference in the code structure is how soundness-critical code is scattered across the code base. Both KeYmaera and KeYmaeraD have soundness-critical code in the core as well as in the tactics, while, overall, only about a third of their

Table 3. Core size LOC: KeYmaera taclets, KeYmaeraD rules, KeYmaera X axioms

	K3	KD	KX
Propositional	140	257	212
HP	1202	352	55
ODE	322	241	122
Arithmetic	1033	103	0

KeYmaera: +39k LOC rule code

code bases are non-critical. KeYmaera X, in contrast, confines soundness-critical code entirely to the core data structures, uniform substitution, bound renaming, and the small set of builtin rules. The provers differ in their proof manipulation: in KeYmaera the proof tree data structure keeps track of proof steps and open goals, in KeYmaeraD the tactic framework with its proof tree is responsible for correctly combining proof steps into a proof, whereas in KeYmaera X only the core can manipulate proof objects and a proof is obtained by transforming the original proof object containing the conjecture into one with an empty list of subgoals. KeYmaera X, thus, is the only LCF-style prover among the three.

Code Size. In terms of overall size, KeYmaeraD has by far the smallest overall code base, but, as a bare-bones prover, comes without the convenient user interfaces and proof support and automation of KeYmaera and KeYmaera X. More

---

[8] The main taclet code complexity, however, is hidden in the soundness-critical implementation code that is backing the taclets.

[9] KeYmaera X, in addition to axioms, uses host-language rule implementations for propositional rules, which are included in the count.

importantly, however, KeYmaera X comes with the smallest and least complex soundness-critical core, which has direct consequences for the trustworthiness and the extensibility of the prover. Extension of KeYmaera requires adding new soundness-critical taclets and taclet support code, and registering those with the taclet application mechanism. It is often impossible to extend KeYmaera without making changes to soundness-critical code. Extension of KeYmaeraD typically requires adding new soundness-critical rules in the prover core in the host language, while the primary purpose of the tactics framework is to express problem-specific proof scripts; tactic registration is only necessary to add tactics to automation, since proofs are expressed in the host language. Extension of KeYmaera X typically requires adding new tactics, and registering those with tactic automation if they should be used automatically; new soundness-critical axioms are only necessary when extending the underlying logic. Another note-worthy difference is in the sizes of QE packages: KeYmaera dedicates consider-able code size to interfacing with numerous external tools; KeYmaeraD focuses on only Mathematica; KeYmaera X interfaces with Z3 and Mathematica, but its architecture of reproving inputs of external tools also enables separating critical QE calls from non-critical invariant and counterexample generation.

Summary. The code bases differ considerably in their size, the way they sep-arate soundness-critical from non-critical reasoning, and the way they support extension; the total size of KeYmaeraD may be small enough to justify the use of soundness-critical builtin rules, but with increasing size at or beyond the size of KeYmaera, it becomes increasingly difficult to justify the correctness of extensions. Separation in the style of KeYmaera X enables extensibility and courageous automation in tactics. The considerable amount of code that both KeYmaera and KeYmaera X dedicate to the user interface and proof support results in quite different user interaction experience, as discussed next.

7   User Interaction

The presentation of sequent proofs on limited screen estate is challenging, and the design choices of which information to readily emphasize and which information to make available on request considerably influence the user interaction.

KeYmaera. For user interaction, KeYmaera emphasizes the tree structure of sequent proofs and internal automation steps when presenting proof obligations. Proof obligations and formulas are rendered almost in ASCII syntax, see Fig. 7.

Users perform proofs by interacting exclusively on the top-level operators by selecting proof steps from a context menu. A proof tree is beneficial for displaying the history and source of proof obligations (which steps produced a certain subgoal), but can be challenging to immediately spot the open proof obligations, especially those resulting from automation. In KeYmaera, proof automation adds its internal steps to the proof tree, which is useful to interact with automation, learn doing proofs by observing proof automation on simple examples, but can be hard for users to map with their interaction (a single click produces many steps, where did automation start, which subgoals were there already, which ones are new). Except for experienced users, it's also hard to map nodes in the tree to the input formula and statements in the input program, which, however, is vital information for users to understand the open goal when their input is required. The results of intermediate and internal steps are non-persistent, which makes step-by-step interaction faster but loading and continuing unfinished proofs slow (all proof steps need to be redone on load). Table 4 summarizes the benefits and drawbacks of the KeYmaera proof tree presentation, its top-level interaction, and its presentation of automation internals.

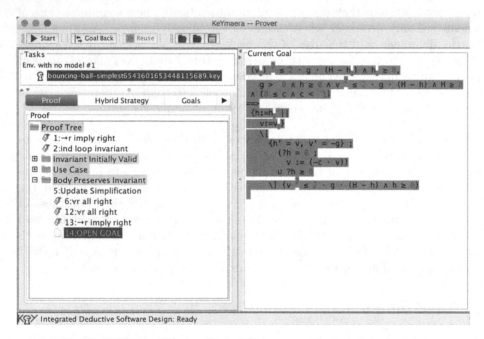

Fig. 7. KeYmaera UI: proof tree left, sequent of selected node right

KeYmaera D. Proofs in KeYmaeraD are explicitly programmed in Scala, either as a Scala program or in Scala's native read-evaluate-print loop and displayed as a listed tree in its user interface (Fig. 8). In dL, proof steps primarily manipulate programs and formulas, but branch only occasionally; rendering such deep trees verbatim may waste screen estate and require cumbersome horizontal and vertical scrolling simultaneously to navigate a proof. KeYmaeraD comes with a small library of base tactics corresponding to each proof rule and provides tactic combinators to express proof alternatives, repeat proof steps, compose proof steps, branch the proof, or try rule applications. Expert users can leverage the full

Table 4. KeYmaera user interaction summary

	Pros	Cons
Proof tree	History and source of proof obligations obvious	Dissimilar to textbook proofs, spotting open obligations after automation challenging
Top-level interaction	Next proof step often obvious, unclear if on formula or update	Duplicate proof effort after branching
Automation internals	Learn proving by observing, more robust on replay	Challenging to undo
Automation settings	Fine-grained automation steering	Settings are part of proof and lost if different per branch
Non-persistent intermediate steps	Faster on performing steps	Slow on proof loading

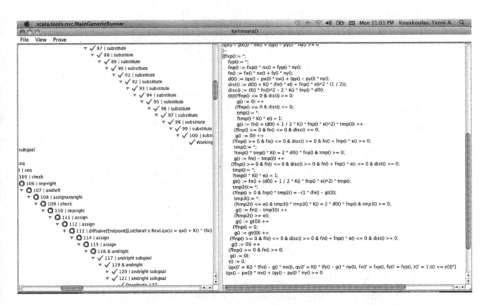

Fig. 8. KeYmaeraD UI: proof tree left, sequent of selected node right

flexibility of the programming language and its development tools when implementing proofs and tactics, but novice users get little help for getting started. Table 5 summarizes the benefits and drawbacks of implementing proofs in a host language on an AND/OR tree with only top-level user interaction in sequents.

Table 5. KeYmaeraD user interaction summary

	Pros	Cons
Proofs in host language	Flexible, readily available development tools	Hard for novice users
AND/OR proof tree	Explore alternatives, history obvious	Dissimilar to textbook sequent proofs, spotting open goal combinations challenging
Top-level interaction	Next proof step often obvious	Duplicate proof effort after branching

Fig. 9. KeYmaera X UI: Proof menu, open goals in tabs with full sequent proof deduction, proof hints and help in context menu, recorded tactic at the bottom

KeYmaera X. KeYmaera X emphasizes open proof tasks and close mnemonic analogy with textbooks and user inputs both in its presentation as a HTML rendering of sequent proofs and in its user interaction, see Fig. 9. The client-side JavaScript-based web UI enables flexibility in rendering proofs and is operating-system independent, but at the cost of additional data structure serialization (not necessary in a native UI integrated with the prover) and handling browser idiosyncrasies. The user interface design strives for a familiar look-and-feel with tutoring for novice users, flexibility to accommodate various user preferences in reasoning styles, traceability of internal automation steps, and experimentation with custom proof strategies [36]. The internal steps of automation and tactics are hidden from users and expanded only on demand. Open goals are represented in tabs on the UI, which, in contrast to a proof tree, emphasizes the remaining proof agenda. Each tab shows an open goal as the topmost sequent, and renders the history of proof steps as deduction paths from the proof tree root to that open goal, and so the proof tree is implicit (for expert users, however, an explicit proof tree can be beneficial to inspect the structure of the proof [22]). Tab headings present an opportunity to highlight short summaries about the open goal and the proof history, but require careful ordering and—just like nodes in a proof tree—need visual cues to guide user attention (e.g., draw attention to tabs with counterexamples). Users perform proof steps at any level even in the context of other formulas and programs, which helps reduce duplicate proof effort for experienced users. Flexible reasoning at any level may help users follow their natural thought process but may make it harder to discover all applicable proof steps (which is tackled with redundant information about proof steps in context menus, proof menus, proof hints, and searchable lists of all available tactics). The implementation of in-context proof step application and custom user proof search strategies crucially requires the safety net of uniform substitution, since it is otherwise challenging to anticipate all potential tactic uses and safeguard them to ensure only sound syntactic transformations in sound contexts. Table 6 summarizes the benefits and drawbacks of focusing on presenting proof obligations in favor of a proof tree, sequent proof rendering, interaction anywhere, and persistent intermediate steps.

8 Related Work

The development history from LCF to Isabelle/HOL is explained by Paulson *et al.* [41] with insights into the design choices and evolution of proof requirements that drove the development of the tool ecosystem.

The literature [68, 69] compares provers in terms of their library size, logic strength, and automation on mathematical problems (with references for several other prover comparisons between Isabelle/Coq/NuPRL/HOL/ALF/PVS). A qualitative comparison of the Isabelle, Theorema, Mizar, and Hets/CASL/TPTP theorem provers [26] highlights user-facing differences in expressiveness, efficiency, proof development and management, library coverage, documentation, comprehensibility, and trustworthiness. Comparisons of the Mizar and Isar proof languages [67] focus on a technical perspective and user experience.

Of complementary interest is the comparison of performance and number of problems solved in theorem prover competitions [4, 65] and hybrid systems tool competitions [17]. While those are valuable from a utilitarian perspective, we argue that bigger insights are to be had from looking inside the box to understand the technical consequences of prover design decisions and, more importantly, how one best enables prover performance while preventing to accidentally "solve" a

Table 6. KeYmaera X user interaction summary

	Pros	Cons
Proof obligations	Focus on proof tasks	Proof history only shown after mouse click
Sequent proof rendering	Close to textbook sequent proofs	Separate HTML rendering
Explicit on-demand automation internals	Presentation corresponds with user interaction	Recomputes internal steps, tactic changes may fail replay
Interaction anywhere	Reduce proof effort duplication, follow natural thought process, beneficial for efficiency and responsiveness	Hard to anticipate all potential uses of tactics, discoverability (menu, proof hints, context menu)
Persistent intermediate steps	Fast on proof loading	Slower on step-by-step interaction

problem incorrectly due to a soundness mistake in the implementation. Arguably the biggest level of soundness assurance can be had from formal verification of the prover, which is possible [11] thanks to the simplicity of the uniform substitution calculus of dL. While solving all soundness challenges in principle, this does not yet lead to a high-performance prover kernel implementation in practice.

9   Takeaway Messages

Advantages of KeYmaera 3 Implementation Approach: very easy to get started with minimal effort (in large part due to the KeY prover basis) and without much thought about what goes where, taclets minimize the need to separate a rule from strategic advice on how to apply it. A gigantic advantage, although specific to the particular KeY basis, is that prover development gets proof visualization and interaction features from day one, which is an immensely helpful debugging aid for rule implementations, proof automation, and the conduct of case studies. The ability to interrupt proof automation and roll it back partially before interacting and handing off to automation again also leads to fairly powerful proof capabilities for experts at the expense of a loss in robustness and traceability compared to the modular tactical proofs of KeYmaera X. Advanced proof strategies or proof scripts, however, also become prohibitively complicated.

Advantages of KeYmaeraD Implementation Approach: extremely transparent with all details in one place about what happens. A downside is that there is virtually no isolation of soundness-critical core versus the rest of the prover.

Adding automation or writing proofs requires detailed knowledge of the internal prover implementation details. KeYmaeraD was successful in terms of its parallel distributed proof search. The reason why the curse of concurrency was significantly less of an issue for KeYmaeraD than KeYmaera X is that KeYmaeraD does not optimize what reasoning to use for which formula, but only ever has one reasoning style for every connective. This hints at a tradeoff that parallel proofs become pleasant only when the individual subproofs become suboptimal and when sufficient computing resources for a simultaneous exploration of all options are available. This comparison is not exhaustive, however, because KeYmaeraD does not provide complex tactics such as differential equation solving [50], differential invariant axiomatization [59], or proof-based invariant generation [54].

Advantages of KeYmaeraX Implementation Approach: the simplicity of LCF-style prover μkernels makes it obvious to see what soundness depends on and what the overall correctness argument is. The resulting prover architecture is modular, thereby separating responsibilities such as the uniform substitution mechanism, axiom indices, unification algorithm, tactics, UI rendering. It is easier to get modularity just right in KeYmaera X. While we believe this to be a general phenomenon in μkernel provers, this success story is slightly modulated by the fact that the third prover design was informed by the prior successes and complications of KeYmaera 3 and KeYmaeraD. The KeYmaera X approach also makes it easier to advance automatic proof principles by adding tactics, which are, by design, noncritical and open to experimentation and incremental development. Examples of such tactics implemented in KeYmaera X and extended incrementally include ModelPlex [37], component-based verification [40], an axiomatic differential equation solver [50], and ODE automation [59,66].

Advice for Future Provers: With the benefit of hindsight, we provide a list of the most impactful decisions and words of advice for future prover designs that can be summarized as justifying that simplicity always wins in the end. The soundness and simplicity of uniform substitution provers cause significant benefits throughout the prover. Immediately invest in common infrastructure such as unification algorithms to simplify tactical implementations down to the essentials and make them robust to change. Invest in proof tree visualization early, because that is an essential debugging aid *during* development. The time spent to develop simple initial proof visualizations is significantly less than the time that their presence saves during prover development. The comparison of KeYmaeraD versus KeYmaera X is an instance of the *bon mot* that premature optimization is the root of all evil, although, admittedly, KeYmaera X still has not achieved anywhere near the distributed proving performance of KeYmaeraD (on the limited continuous dynamics that KeYmaeraD supports). The comparison of all provers clearly indicates that the downstream effects of favoring speed over soundness are self-defeating in the long run. There is a never-ending tension between the desire to build provers in theoretically well-designed elegant programming languages compared to mainstream programming languages. Implementing provers in the former gives more elegant and robust provers, but the frequent lack of libraries requires tedious manual programming effort for data storage, web communication, parsing, IDE integration etc., that are peripheral to core proving.

The most fundamental difference between the three provers comes down to the explicit embrace (KeYmaera 3) or implicit inclusion (KeYmaeraD) of proof rule schemata with side conditions versus the strict adherence to nonschematic axioms or rules without side conditions thanks to uniform substitution (KeYmaera X). Working with schemata makes it easy to add a new reasoning principle but also easy to cause soundness mistakes because a proof rule schema always applies except for an explicit list of exception conditions. This automatic generalization is most easily observed in KeYmaera 3 taclets but also holds for KeYmaeraD's native code implementations of proof rule schemata. Working with nonschematic axioms is better at avoiding soundness glitches by making both syntactic dependencies and generalizations explicit and easier to implement. But working with nonschematic axioms still makes it easy to cause completeness mistakes. Subtle occurrence patterns can make tactics fail to prove provable formulas. Since complicated interaction patterns then manifest as completeness bugs instead of as soundness bugs, they cause less harm and are more easily identified with a failing proof than with a successful proof of an untrue formula.

Acknowledgements. The authors thank Brandon Bohrer and the chapter reviewers for helpful feedback on this article.

References

1. Ahrendt, W., et al.: The KeY tool. Softw. Syst. Model. **4**(1), 32–54 (2005). https://doi.org/10.1007/s10270-004-0058-x
2. Ahrendt, W., Beckert, B., Bubel, R., Hähnle, R., Schmitt, P.H., Ulbrich, M. (eds.): Deductive Software Verification - The KeY Book. LNCS, vol. 10001. Springer, Cham (2016). https://doi.org/10.1007/978-3-319-49812-6
3. Alur, R., et al.: The algorithmic analysis of hybrid systems. Theor. Comput. Sci. **138**(1), 3–34 (1995). https://doi.org/10.1016/0304-3975(94)00202-T
4. Bartocci, E., et al.: TOOLympics 2019: an overview of competitions in formal methods. In: Beyer, D., Huisman, M., Kordon, F., Steffen, B. (eds.) TACAS 2019. LNCS, vol. 11429, pp. 3–24. Springer, Cham (2019). https://doi.org/10.1007/978-3-030-17502-3_1
5. Beckert, B., et al.: Taclets: a new paradigm for constructing interactive theorem provers. Revista de la Real Academia de Ciencias Exactas, Físicas y Naturales, Serie A: Matemáticas (RACSAM) **98**(1) (2004)
6. Beckert, B., Hähnle, R., Schmitt, P.H. (eds.): Verification of Object-Oriented Software: The KeY Approach. LNCS, vol. 4334. Springer, Heidelberg (2007). https://doi.org/10.1007/978-3-540-69061-0
7. Beckert, B., Platzer, A.: Dynamic logic with non-rigid functions. In: Furbach, U., Shankar, N. (eds.) IJCAR 2006. LNCS (LNAI), vol. 4130, pp. 266–280. Springer, Heidelberg (2006). https://doi.org/10.1007/11814771_23

8. ter Beek, M.H., McIver, A., Oliveira, J.N. (eds.): FM 2019. LNCS, vol. 11800. Springer, Cham (2019). https://doi.org/10.1007/978-3-030-30942-8

9. Belta, C., Ivancic, F. (eds.): Hybrid Systems: Computation and Control (part of CPS Week 2013), HSCC 2013, Philadelphia, PA, USA, 8–13 April 2013. ACM, New York (2013)

10. Bohrer, B., Fernandez, M., Platzer, A.: dL$_\iota$: definite descriptions in differential dynamic logic. In: Fontaine [16], pp. 94–110. https://doi.org/10.1007/978-3-030-29436-6_6

11. Bohrer, B., Rahli, V., Vukotic, I., Völp, M., Platzer, A.: Formally verified differential dynamic logic. In: Bertot, Y., Vafeiadis, V. (eds.) Certified Programs and Proofs - 6th ACM SIGPLAN Conference, CPP 2017, Paris, France, 16–17 January 2017, pp. 208–221. ACM, New York (2017). https://doi.org/10.1145/3018610.3018616

12. Bohrer, B., Tan, Y.K., Mitsch, S., Myreen, M.O., Platzer, A.: VeriPhy: verified controller executables from verified cyber-physical system models. In: Grossman, D. (ed.) Proceedings of the 39th ACM SIGPLAN Conference on Programming Language Design and Implementation, PLDI 2018, pp. 617–630. ACM (2018). https://doi.org/10.1145/3192366.3192406

13. Bohrer, B., Tan, Y.K., Mitsch, S., Sogokon, A., Platzer, A.: A formal safety net for waypoint following in ground robots. IEEE Robot. Autom. Lett. 4(3), 2910–2917 (2019). https://doi.org/10.1109/LRA.2019.2923099

14. Church, A.: Introduction to Mathematical Logic. Princeton University Press, Princeton (1956)

15. Doyen, L., Frehse, G., Pappas, G.J., Platzer, A.: Verification of hybrid systems. In: Clarke, E., Henzinger, T., Veith, H., Bloem, R. (eds.) Handbook of Model Checking, pp. 1047–1110. Springer, Cham (2018). https://doi.org/10.1007/978-3-319-10575-8_30

16. Fontaine, P. (ed.): CADE 2019. LNCS (LNAI), vol. 11716. Springer, Cham (2019). https://doi.org/10.1007/978-3-030-29436-6

17. Frehse, G., Althoff, M. (eds.): ARCH19. 6th International Workshop on Applied Verification of Continuous and Hybrid Systemsi, part of CPS-IoT Week 2019, Montreal, QC, Canada, 15 April 2019, EPiC Series in Computing, vol. 61. EasyChair (2019)

18. Frehse, G., et al.: SpaceEx: scalable verification of hybrid systems. In: Gopalakrishnan, G., Qadeer, S. (eds.) CAV 2011. LNCS, vol. 6806, pp. 379–395. Springer, Heidelberg (2011). https://doi.org/10.1007/978-3-642-22110-1_30

19. Fulton, N., Mitsch, S., Bohrer, B., Platzer, A.: Bellerophon: tactical theorem proving for hybrid systems. In: Ayala-Rincón, M., Muñoz, C.A. (eds.) ITP 2017. LNCS, vol. 10499, pp. 207–224. Springer, Cham (2017). https://doi.org/10.1007/978-3-319-66107-0_14

20. Fulton, N., Mitsch, S., Quesel, J.-D., Völp, M., Platzer, A.: KeYmaera X: an axiomatic tactical theorem prover for hybrid systems. In: Felty, A.P., Middeldorp, A. (eds.) CADE 2015. LNCS (LNAI), vol. 9195, pp. 527–538. Springer, Cham (2015). https://doi.org/10.1007/978-3-319-21401-6_36

21. Fulton, N., Platzer, A.: Verifiably safe off-model reinforcement learning. In: Vojnar, T., Zhang, L. (eds.) TACAS 2019. LNCS, vol. 11427, pp. 413–430. Springer, Cham (2019). https://doi.org/10.1007/978-3-030-17462-0_28

22. Grebing, S.: User interaction in deductive interactive program verification. Ph.D. thesis, Karlsruhe Institute of Technology, Germany (2019). https://nbn-resolving.org/urn:nbn:de:101:1-2019103003584227760922

23. Jeannin, J.-B., et al.: A formally verified hybrid system for the next-generation airborne collision avoidance system. In: Baier, C., Tinelli, C. (eds.) TACAS 2015. LNCS, vol. 9035, pp. 21–36. Springer, Heidelberg (2015). https://doi.org/10.1007/978-3-662-46681-0_2

24. Jeannin, J., et al.: A formally verified hybrid system for safe advisories in the next-generation airborne collision avoidance system. STTT **19**(6), 717–741 (2017). https://doi.org/10.1007/s10009-016-0434-1

25. Kouskoulas, Y., Renshaw, D.W., Platzer, A., Kazanzides, P.: Certifying the safe design of a virtual fixture control algorithm for a surgical robot. In: Belta and Ivancic [9], pp. 263–272. https://doi.org/10.1145/2461328.2461369

26. Lange, C., et al.: A qualitative comparison of the suitability of four theorem provers for basic auction theory. In: Carette, J., Aspinall, D., Lange, C., Sojka, P., Windsteiger, W. (eds.) CICM 2013. LNCS (LNAI), vol. 7961, pp. 200–215. Springer, Heidelberg (2013). https://doi.org/10.1007/978-3-642-39320-4_13

27. 2012 27th Annual IEEE Symposium on Logic in Computer Science (LICS), Los Alamitos. IEEE (2012)

28. Loos, S.M., Platzer, A., Nistor, L.: Adaptive cruise control: hybrid, distributed, and now formally verified. In: Butler, M., Schulte, W. (eds.) FM 2011. LNCS, vol. 6664, pp. 42–56. Springer, Heidelberg (2011). https://doi.org/10.1007/978-3-642-21437-0_6

29. Loos, S.M., Renshaw, D.W., Platzer, A.: Formal verification of distributed aircraft controllers. In: Belta and Ivancic [9], pp. 125–130. https://doi.org/10.1145/2461328.2461350

30. Milner, R.: Logic for computable functions: description of a machine implementation. Technical report, Stanford University, Stanford, CA, USA (1972)

31. Mitsch, S., Gario, M., Budnik, C.J., Golm, M., Platzer, A.: Formal verification of train control with air pressure brakes. In: Fantechi, A., Lecomte, T., Romanovsky, A. (eds.) RSSRail, pp. 173–191. Springer, Cham (2017). https://doi.org/10.1007/978-3-319-68499-4_12

32. Mitsch, S., Ghorbal, K., Platzer, A.: On provably safe obstacle avoidance for autonomous robotic ground vehicles. In: Newman, P., Fox, D., Hsu, D. (eds.) Robotics: Science and Systems (2013)

33. Mitsch, S., Ghorbal, K., Vogelbacher, D., Platzer, A.: Formal verification of obstacle avoidance and navigation of ground robots. Int. J. Robot. Res. **36**(12), 1312–1340 (2017). https://doi.org/10.1177/0278364917733549

34. Mitsch, S., Passmore, G.O., Platzer, A.: Collaborative verification-driven engineering of hybrid systems. Math. Comput. Sci. **8**(1), 71–97 (2014). https://doi.org/10.1007/s11786-014-0176-y

35. Mitsch, S., Platzer, A.: ModelPlex: verified runtime validation of verified cyberphysical system models. In: Bonakdarpour, B., Smolka, S.A. (eds.) RV 2014. LNCS, vol. 8734, pp. 199–214. Springer, Cham (2014). https://doi.org/10.1007/978-3-319-11164-3_17

36. Mitsch, S., Platzer, A.: The KeYmaera X proof IDE: concepts on usability in hybrid systems theorem proving. In: Dubois, C., Masci, P., Méry, D. (eds.) 3rd Workshop on Formal Integrated Development Environment. EPTCS, vol. 240, pp. 67–81 (2016). https://doi.org/10.4204/EPTCS.240.5

37. Mitsch, S., Platzer, A.: ModelPlex: verified runtime validation of verified cyberphysical system models. Form. Methods Syst. Des. **49**(1–2), 33–74 (2016). https://doi.org/10.1007/s10703-016-0241-z. Special issue of selected papers from RV'14

38. Mitsch, S., Sogokon, A., Tan, Y.K., Jin, X., Zhan, B., Wang, S., Zhan, N.: ARCH-COMP19 category report: hybrid systems theorem proving. In: Frehse and Althoff [17], pp. 141–161

39. Mitsch, S., et al.: ARCH-COMP18 category report: hybrid systems theorem proving. In: ARCH18. 5th International Workshop on Applied Verification of Continuous and Hybrid Systems, ARCH@ADHS 2018, Oxford, UK, 13 July 2018, pp. 110–127 (2018). http://www.easychair.org/publications/paper/tNN2

40. Müller, A., Mitsch, S., Retschitzegger, W., Schwinger, W., Platzer, A.: Tactical contract composition for hybrid system component verification. STTT 20(6), 615–643 (2018). https://doi.org/10.1007/s10009-018-0502-9. Special issue for selected papers from FASE 2017

41. Paulson, L.C., Nipkow, T., Wenzel, M.: From LCF to Isabelle/HOL. Formal Asp. Comput. 31(6), 675–698 (2019). https://doi.org/10.1007/s00165-019-00492-1

42. Platzer, A.: Differential dynamic logic for verifying parametric hybrid systems. In: Olivetti, N. (ed.) TABLEAUX 2007. LNCS (LNAI), vol. 4548, pp. 216–232. Springer, Heidelberg (2007). https://doi.org/10.1007/978-3-540-73099-6_17

43. Platzer, A.: Differential dynamic logic for hybrid systems. J. Autom. Reas. 41(2), 143–189 (2008). https://doi.org/10.1007/s10817-008-9103-8

44. Platzer, A.: Differential-algebraic dynamic logic for differential-algebraic programs. J. Log. Comput. 20(1), 309–352 (2010). https://doi.org/10.1093/logcom/exn070

45. Platzer, A.: Logical Analysis of Hybrid Systems: Proving Theorems for Complex Dynamics. Springer, Heidelberg (2010). https://doi.org/10.1007/978-3-642-14509-4. http://www.springer.com/978-3-642-14508-7

46. Platzer, A.: A complete axiomatization of quantified differential dynamic logic for distributed hybrid systems. Log. Meth. Comput. Sci. 8(4:17), 1–44 (2012). https://doi.org/10.2168/LMCS-8(4:17)2012. Special issue for selected papers from CSL'10

47. Platzer, A.: The complete proof theory of hybrid systems. In: LICS [27], pp. 541–550. https://doi.org/10.1109/LICS.2012.64

48. Platzer, A.: Logics of dynamical systems. In: LICS [27], pp. 13–24. https://doi.org/10.1109/LICS.2012.13

49. Platzer, A.: Differential game logic. ACM Trans. Comput. Log. 17(1), 1:1–1:51 (2015). https://doi.org/10.1145/2817824

50. Platzer, A.: A complete uniform substitution calculus for differential dynamic logic. J. Autom. Reas. 59(2), 219–265 (2017). https://doi.org/10.1007/s10817-016-9385-1

51. Platzer, A.: Logical Foundations of Cyber-Physical Systems. Springer, Cham (2018). https://doi.org/10.1007/978-3-319-63588-0. http://www.springer.com/978-3-319-63587-3

52. Platzer, A.: Uniform substitution for differential game logic. In: Galmiche, D., Schulz, S., Sebastiani, R. (eds.) IJCAR 2018. LNCS (LNAI), vol. 10900, pp. 211–227. Springer, Cham (2018). https://doi.org/10.1007/978-3-319-94205-6_15

53. Platzer, A.: Uniform substitution at one fell swoop. In: Fontaine [16], pp. 425–441. https://doi.org/10.1007/978-3-030-29436-6_25

54. Platzer, A., Clarke, E.M.: Computing differential invariants of hybrid systems as fixedpoints. Form. Methods Syst. Des. 35(1), 98–120 (2009). https://doi.org/10.1007/s10703-009-0079-8. Special issue for selected papers from CAV'08

55. Platzer, A., Clarke, E.M.: Formal verification of curved flight collision avoidance maneuvers: a case study. In: Cavalcanti, A., Dams, D.R. (eds.) FM 2009. LNCS, vol. 5850, pp. 547–562. Springer, Heidelberg (2009). https://doi.org/10.1007/978-3-642-05089-3_35

56. Platzer, A., Quesel, J.-D.: KeYmaera: a hybrid theorem prover for hybrid systems (system description). In: Armando, A., Baumgartner, P., Dowek, G. (eds.) IJCAR 2008. LNCS (LNAI), vol. 5195, pp. 171–178. Springer, Heidelberg (2008). https://doi.org/10.1007/978-3-540-71070-7_15

57. Platzer, A., Quesel, J.-D.: European train control system: a case study in formal verification. In: Breitman, K., Cavalcanti, A. (eds.) ICFEM 2009. LNCS, vol. 5885, pp. 246–265. Springer, Heidelberg (2009). https://doi.org/10.1007/978-3-642-10373-5_13

58. Platzer, A., Quesel, J.-D., Rümmer, P.: Real world verification. In: Schmidt, R.A. (ed.) CADE 2009. LNCS (LNAI), vol. 5663, pp. 485–501. Springer, Heidelberg (2009). https://doi.org/10.1007/978-3-642-02959-2_35

59. Platzer, A., Tan, Y.K.: Differential equation invariance axiomatization. J. ACM **67**(1), 6:1–6:66 (2020). https://doi.org/10.1145/3380825

60. Quesel, J.D.: Similarity, logic, and games - bridging modeling layers of hybrid systems. Ph.D. thesis, Department of Computing Science, University of Oldenburg (2013)

61. Quesel, J.-D., Platzer, A.: Playing hybrid games with KeYmaera. In: Gramlich, B., Miller, D., Sattler, U. (eds.) IJCAR 2012. LNCS (LNAI), vol. 7364, pp. 439–453. Springer, Heidelberg (2012). https://doi.org/10.1007/978-3-642-31365-3_34

62. Renshaw, D.W., Loos, S.M., Platzer, A.: Distributed theorem proving for distributed hybrid systems. In: Qin, S., Qiu, Z. (eds.) ICFEM 2011. LNCS, vol. 6991, pp. 356–371. Springer, Heidelberg (2011). https://doi.org/10.1007/978-3-642-24559-6_25

63. Rümmer, P., Shah, M.A.: Proving programs incorrect using a sequent calculus for java dynamic logic. In: Gurevich, Y., Meyer, B. (eds.) TAP 2007. LNCS, vol. 4454, pp. 41–60. Springer, Heidelberg (2007). https://doi.org/10.1007/978-3-540-73770-4_3

64. Sogokon, A., Mitsch, S., Tan, Y.K., Cordwell, K., Platzer, A.: Pegasus: a framework for sound continuous invariant generation. In: ter Beek et al. [8], pp. 138–157. https://doi.org/10.1007/978-3-030-30942-8_10

65. Sutcliffe, G., Benzmüller, C., Brown, C.E., Theiss, F.: Progress in the development of automated theorem proving for higher-order logic. In: Schmidt, R.A. (ed.) CADE 2009. LNCS (LNAI), vol. 5663, pp. 116–130. Springer, Heidelberg (2009). https://doi.org/10.1007/978-3-642-02959-2_8

66. Tan, Y.K., Platzer, A.: An axiomatic approach to liveness for differential equations. In: ter Beek et al. [8], pp. 371–388. https://doi.org/10.1007/978-3-030-30942-8_23

67. Wenzel, M., Wiedijk, F.: A comparison of Mizar and Isar. J. Autom. Reasoning **29**(3–4), 389–411 (2002). https://doi.org/10.1023/A:1021935419355

68. Wiedijk, F.: Comparing mathematical provers. In: Asperti, A., Buchberger, B., Davenport, J.H. (eds.) MKM 2003. LNCS, vol. 2594, pp. 188–202. Springer, Heidelberg (2003). https://doi.org/10.1007/3-540-36469-2_15

69. Wiedijk, F. (ed.): The Seventeen Provers of the World. LNCS (LNAI), vol. 3600. Springer, Heidelberg (2006). https://doi.org/10.1007/11542384

Improving Performance of the VerCors Program Verifier

Henk Mulder[1], Marieke Huisman[1(✉)] [ID], and Sebastiaan Joosten[2] [ID]

[1] University of Twente, Enschede, The Netherlands
hmulder88@gmail.com, m.huisman@utwente.nl
[2] Dartmouth College, Hanover, NH, USA
Sebastiaan.Joosten@dartmouth.edu

Abstract. As program verification tools are becoming more powerful, and are used on larger programs, their performance also becomes more and more important. In this paper we investigate performance bottlenecks in the VerCors program verifier. Moreover, we also discuss two solutions to the identified performance bottlenecks: an improved encoding of arrays, as well as a technique to automatically generate trigger expressions to guide the underlying prover when reasoning about quantifiers. For both solutions we measure the effect on the performance. We see that the new encoding vastly reduces the verification time of certain programs, while other programs keep showing comparable times. This effect remains when moving to newer backends for VerCors.

1 Introduction

Program verification has been an active research area for many years now [9]. In particular, many program verification tools have been developed for many years (e.g., KeY [1], VeriFast [10,11], and Dafny [13] have all been developed for more than 10 years). In this paper we focus on the VerCors verifier, which focuses in particular on the verification of concurrent and distributed software, and has been under development since 2011 [2–5]. It is being developed with the ultimate goal to make verification usable for developers that are not necessarily formal method experts, but to reach this goal, still substantial work is needed.

As program verification tools are becoming more powerful and are used to verify larger programs, their performance also becomes more and more a crucial factor. In particular if we want non-developers to be end-users of the verification tools, a good performance and reaction time is essential for acceptance of the technology (in addition to many other aspects, such as the amount of specifications that have to be written, understandability of error messages etc.).

In this paper we discuss work that we did to improve the performance of VerCors. VerCors is developed as a front-end for Viper [16], which is an intermediate verification language framework that understands access permissions. VerCors

---

S. Joosten—Work done while at the University of Twente.

W. Ahrendt et al. (Eds.): Deductive Software Verification, LNCS 12345, pp. 65–82, 2020.
https://doi.org/10.1007/978-3-030-64354-6_3

encodes annotated programs written in a high-level programming language into Viper; Viper then uses symbolic execution to generate proof obligations, which are passed on to Z3 [7]. Note that because VerCors uses Viper as an intermediate representation, all that we can do to improve the performance is to change the Viper encodings; we never generate Z3 specifications directly.

We first describe how we identified the main performance bottlenecks in VerCors, and then we describe our solutions to these problems. In particular, we identify that (1) the encoding of arrays into Viper, and (2) the use of quantifier expressions in specifications without triggers to inform Viper on how to guide its underlying prover[1], were two of the main performance bottlenecks. To address these issues we developed a new array encoding, which also was more suitable to reason about multi-dimensional arrays, and took advantage of several recently developed features in Viper, such as the support for nested quantifiers over access permissions [16]. Furthermore, we implemented a technique to automatically generate triggers during the transformation from VerCors to Viper.

Of course, the contributions of this paper are mainly VerCors-specific, as we focused on improving the performance of VerCors. However, we believe that also some general lessons can be extracted from our experiences. In particular, we have developed a simple way to count subexpressions that help identify performance bottlenecks, which would be reusable for other program verification tools as well. Furthermore, most verifiers deal with arrays and quantifiers in some way, so we believe that also the lessons learned will be useful for other tool developers.

The remainder of this paper is organised as follows. Section 2 gives a high-level overview of the VerCors architecture. Section 3 discusses how we identified performance bottlenecks. Section 4 presents the old and new array encoding and evaluates their performance. Section 5 discusses how we automatically generate triggers to guide the verification of quantified expressions, which is then also evaluated experimentally. Finally, Sects. 6 and 7 discuss related work and conclude. More details about the work described in this paper, as well as more extensive performance comparisons, are available in the Master's thesis of the first author [15].

2 Background: VerCors Implementation

VerCors currently verifies programs written in multiple concurrent programming paradigms, such as heterogeneous concurrency (C and Java), and homogeneous concurrency (OpenCL) [5]. In addition, it can also reason about compiler directives as used in deterministic parallelism (OpenMP).

VerCors uses a specification language based on the Java Modeling Language (JML) [6] extended with separation logic-specific notations [17]. Programs are annotated with pre- and postconditions that specify its intended behaviour, and the tool checks whether the implementation respects the annotations. For

---

[1] Triggers are a widely-used technique to give hints about the instantiation of quantifiers to an automatic prover.

detailed information about the VerCors specification language we refer to the
VerCors website at http://www.utwente.nl/vercors.

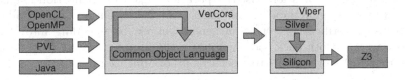

Fig. 1. Architecture of the VerCors tool set

VerCors is built as a transforming compiler for specified code: it transforms
programs in one of the VerCors input languages into an input language for
a back-end verifier (currently Viper [16]). Figure 1 outlines the overall VerCors
architecture. This architecture is set up to make it easier to create new (language)
front-ends, to experiment with other transformations, and to use new back-end
verifiers.

VerCors has front-end parsers for (concurrent) Java and C, for programs
with OpenMP compiler directives and for OpenCL kernels. These parsers are
extended with parsers for the specification language as used in VerCors. Further, there is a parser for the PVL language: the internal VerCors prototyping
language. Each parser parses the annotated source program and produces an
abstract syntax tree (AST) in the Common Object Language (COL). The AST
of the COL language consists of nodes that represent the various concurrency
abstractions that are supported by VerCors.

Transformations on the AST rewrite it to a tree that consists of nodes that
can easily be mapped to the language that is used in the chosen back-end verifier. Two techniques are used to transform the AST. First of all, visitor patterns
are used to replace a high level abstraction node by a semantically equivalent
structure of simpler nodes. These transformations replace language constructs
by their definitions, such as the flattening of expressions into a list of commands
according their execution order. Second, a collection of standard rewrite rules
is provided for rewriting into equivalent expressions, for example to make verification easier. To ensure that these transformations preserve the semantics,
these transformations are taken as input from a separate file, making it easier
to review and validate them, a process currently done by hand. It also makes it
easy to extend the set of transformations. Every transformation is defined in its
own *compiler pass*. The passes are referenced by a name, which makes it easier
to reuse transformations, and to develop transformations for different back-end
verifiers with other (syntactical) requirements.

The back-end verifier is then used to verify the transformed program. Viper
programs, written in the input language Silver, are symbolically executed using
Silicon. The resulting first-order proof obligations are then given to Z3. To map
possible errors back to the original source program, VerCors keeps track of where

each node in the AST originated from. The only back-end that is currently supported is Viper [16], which is a intermediate verification language infrastructure that supports access permissions. This makes it highly suitable as a back-end for tools that use (permission-based) separation logic as specification language. Viper has two reasoning modes: one using symbolic execution (named Silicon) and one using verification condition generation via an encoding into Boogie (named Carbon). Both back-ends in Viper make use of the SMT (satisfiability modulo theories) solver Z3 [7] to discharge proof obligations.

3   Analysis of Performance Bottlenecks

In order to improve the performance of the VerCors verifier, we must first understand where the tool lacks performance. Therefore we talked with users and developers, both of VerCors and Viper, and we collected programs that were slow to verify. In particular, we interviewed all the PhD students in Twente that use and develop VerCors, and asked them for particularly slow programs. Their answers also included programs obtained from their experiences with supervising individual students on verification projects. In addition, we also interviewed one of the main Viper developers, who explained about the performance bottlenecks they had observed in Viper. Even though this group is limited in size, we believe that their answers are representative for the problems, in particular because they also included experiences from student projects.

We then compared the runtimes of the programs to the elements of VerCors that these programs use. We count the use of VerCors features by counting subexpressions in the AST, through a modification of the VerCors tool. As an example, consider the following expression, which specifies that all elements in the array named input are zero:

```
(\forall int i;
    0 <= i && i < input.length; input[i] == 0);
```

We count the following subexpressions (13 in total):

- expr.BindingExpression:Forall (1)
- expr.constant.ConstantExpression (2)
- expr.NameExpression (4)
- expr.OperatorExpression:LT (1)
- expr.OperatorExpression:LTE (1)
- expr.OperatorExpression:And (1)
- expr.OperatorExpression:Length (1)
- expr.OperatorExpression:Subscript (1)
- expr.OperatorExpression:EQ (1)

We used this to inspect many of the programs in our standard example set. This way of measuring performance allows us to see if certain VerCors features indeed correlate with slow runtimes. VerCors users have stated that arrays, sets, bags (both datatypes for specification), barriers (a synchronisation primitive), and quantifiers can yield slow performance. The Viper developers have also pointed to quantifiers as a likely bottleneck for performance.

Our use of programs for confirming performance bottlenecks is highly biased, for the following reasons:

- The sample size for many constructions is very small. Many VerCors constructions are tested by one or several unit tests in the example directory, and these unit tests are often their only use. Verification of such small instances is typically trivial, and hence the verification time for those constructions might not be representative.
- The programs we collected are biased towards constructions that have good performance. VerCors users are sometimes forced to make verification times faster for pragmatic reasons, and only the versions that are among the fastest will end up in our example set.
- The VerCors users who were asked to identify bottlenecks also created many of the programs. Thus, when we use those programs to confirm potential bottlenecks, we use a biased sample.

We nevertheless compared the performance of our programs to the VerCors features in it. Our experiments suggest that arrays and forall quantifiers are indeed bad for performance. For the other constructs, e.g. sets, bags, barriers, and the existential quantifier, there were not enough programs to confirm or deny this.

In the remainder of this paper we show the effects on overall performance when changing how arrays and forall quantifiers are treated. As certain programs indeed showed substantial speedups due to this change, we will conclude that at least in those programs, arrays and forall quantifiers have been bottlenecks.

4   Array Encoding

As discussed above, our verification time analysis indicated that the treatment of arrays was one of the potential performance bottlenecks. Therefore we changed the encoding of arrays into Viper. This section first briefly describes the old encoding, and then explains how a better encoding helps to improve the verification times.

4.1   Old Array Encoding

In the original array encoding, the parsing phase transforms all Java, C and PVL arrays into COL arrays. COL arrays are then transformed into Viper, using the Viper built-in notion of sequences. First of all, every sequence is wrapped by an Option type. This enables reasoning about both initialized and uninitialized arrays: OptionNone models an uninitialized array (e.g. a C array pointing to NULL or a Java or PVL array being null), while OptionSome contains the initialized array. In order to reason about permissions to elements in the array, the

```
input != VCTNone() && (|getVCTOption1(input)| == N
   && (forall i: Int, j: Int :: true
      && (0 <= i && i < |getVCTOption1(input)|
         && 0 <= j && j < |getVCTOption1(input)|
         && getVCTOption1(input)[i] ==
            getVCTOption1(input)[j])
      ==> i == j))
```

Listing 1. Viper encoding of \array(input, N).

inner type of the array is wrapped in a Cell type. Eventually this Cell type is transformed into a reference to a field in Viper, which allows us to reason about permissions on this field. These steps are summarised in Fig. 2.

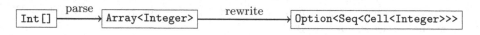

Fig. 2. Steps of the old array encoding

Multi-dimensional arrays (arrays of arrays) are flattened into a one-dimensional array. In addition, a function is generated, which is used to calculate the index of the element in the flattened array that corresponds to the element of the multi-dimensional array. This flattening was necessary because previous versions of Viper did not allow nested quantifications, or quantification with multiple variables, for permissions. However, it also made the verification more complex, because the function to compute the index in the flattened array is non-linear, and reasoning about non-linear functions is undecidable and not well-supported by Z3.

As mentioned above, verification of arrays was identified as a performance bottleneck. Our investigations and discussions with the Viper developers indicated that this was in particular due to the predicate that we used to specify *injectivity* of the array encoding. By construction, arrays in Java and C are injective, thus every element in the array is different from all other elements in the array (every slot is a distinct block of memory). If we encode arrays as a sequence of references, this in not necessarily the case, since a sequence can look like e.g. xs = 0X4, 0X4, 0X8, ..., where the first two elements are references to the same block of memory. Therefore Ver-Cors contains predicates to specify that an array (or matrix) is valid (keywords: \array(<name>, <dim>) and \matrix(<name>, <dim1>, <dim2>)), where valid means that the array or matrix is not null, has the specified dimensions and all slots are different. With the old encoding, the predicate \array(input, N) was encoded in Viper as shown in Listing 1 (with a similar encoding for \matrix(<name>, <dim1>, <dim2>)).

The problem is that Z3 has difficulties reasoning about the quantified expressions. Typically, provers allow the user to provide triggers to guide the proving process [8], in particular providing hints about how to instantiate quantifiers. In Viper, if no triggers are specified, it will try to infer suitable triggers (VerCors does not support triggers in the input language, since additional transformations on the AST may render the triggers unsuitable). For this function, in the body of the quantified expression there are two array accesses: for the element at index i and for the element at index j. Therefore Viper infers two triggers for this expression (matching on the access to element i and on the access of element j). As a result, during the proving process for every element of the array two instances of the expression are created, thereby creating a possible quadratic blowup of relations that the prover has to maintain, and this causes verification to become slow.

4.2   New Array Encoding

To improve support for the verification of multi-dimensional arrays, and to avoid the performance bottleneck of reasoning about array injectivity, we develop a new encoding of arrays.

First of all, as in the more recent versions of Viper it is possible to use universal quantifiers for expressions with multiple quantified variables, it is no longer required to flatten multi-dimensional arrays. Thus, also the non-linear function to calculate the index into the flattened array is no longer required, if we encode multi-dimensional arrays directly as multi-dimensional sequences.

To model the injectivity of arrays, we created the domain encoding in Listing 2. In this encoding every element of an array is modeled by the loc function, which combines a VCTArray object with an index. The domain is parameterized with the CT type as the type for the elements in the array. In the cases where we want to reason about permissions on elements in the array, this can be a reference to a field, but it can also be any other type as defined in the resulting Viper program. The functions first and second are used to retrieve the VCTArray object and the index from an array element. These functions are only used internally by the axiom all_diff. In the all_diff axiom, the relation between on one side the VCTArray plus an index, and on the other side the corresponding element in the array is made explicit for all elements in the array, thereby encoding injectivity of the array. Note that the axiom all_diff has only one trigger (loc(a, i)), rather than the two triggers that were inferred in the old array encoding to specify injectivity. Further there is a function alen, which models the length of the array.

As multi-dimensional arrays are no longer flattened, we now also have to consider the encoding of the inner arrays within a multi-dimensional array. For simplicity, we will explain this in terms of a 2-dimensional matrix, using the term row to refer to an inner array within the matrix[2]. Just as in the old encoding

---

[2] The implemented encoding works for arbitrary multi-dimensional arrays.

```
1  domain VCTArray[CT] {
2     function loc(a: VCTArray[CT], i: Int): CT
3     function alen(a: VCTArray[CT]): Int
4     function first(r: CT): VCTArray[CT]
5     function second(r: CT): Int
6
7     axiom all_diff {
8        forall a: VCTArray[CT], i: Int :: { loc(a,i) }
9           first(loc(a,i)) == a && second(loc(a,i)) == i
10    }
11
12    axiom len_nonneg {
13       forall a: VCTArray[CT] :: { alen(a) }
14          alen(a) >= 0
15    }
16  }
```

Listing 2. Viper domain for new array encoding

we wrap the outer array (matrix) in an Option type, to be able to reason about Java arrays being null or C arrays pointing to NULL. For the inner arrays (rows) there is a choice to be made. For Java the rows could also be null. In C there are variants where rows can be NULL (the matrix is a list of pointers to rows), and variants where rows can not be NULL (the matrix is flattened to a single array during compilation). In order to make a simple and uniform translation into Viper, the choice was made to always wrap rows in Option types in the COL language. This allows to capture both the different kinds of C arrays, as well as Java arrays within the same language construct. It is future work to investigate if we can fine-tune this encoding: with the current approach we loose some information about the original array in the source language.

As we do not see the necessity to reason about permissions or values of entire rows in a matrix, the rows are not wrapped in a Cell type. However, the inner types of the rows are being wrapped in a Cell type, which makes it possible to reason about permissions to the elements of the matrix. Figure 3 summarises the transformation steps for a 2-dimensional matrix.

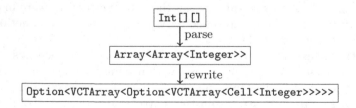

Fig. 3. Steps of the new encoding for a 2-dimensional matrix

With this new encoding, it is no longer required to explicitly specify injectivity for valid arrays and matrices, as this is implicitly encoded by the `all_diff` axiom in the `VCTArray` domain (Listing 2). Thus the Viper function that encodes the valid array property now only states that the reference is non-null and that the array has the specified length. For a valid matrix a non-null condition is generated for the outer array, together with the condition that the matrix has the specified number of rows. Additionally, for every row in the matrix it generates a non-null constraint and a condition that the row has the specified number of cells (columns). Notice that if we would have wrapped the rows in Cell types as well, then Viper could no longer deduce that all rows are different, since each row would now be encoded as a reference to a field with an `Option<VCTArray <Cell<Integer>>>` type, so that two elements of the outer array of the matrix could point to the same referenced field.

4.3 Experiments

In order to measure the effect on performance of verification using the new array encoding, a set of programs has been selected from the VerCors example repository. This set of programs contain all the different concurrency abstractions and data types that are supported by VerCors and for which programs are available. Thereby it is possible to see if the new array encoding might also have unforeseen effects on the verification of other program or specification constructs. In the experiment each example is verified 5 times, and the mean time is used to compare results for the different versions of the tool.

4.4 Results

Because of updates to VerCors and updates to the Viper back-end, several versions have been compared. We indicate the Viper version by a number, and when we have used the new array encoding this is indicated by a suffix -a. This gives the following versions:

- `Vct1`: Version of the tool for which all the programs verify. Used as a base-line for the experiment.
- `Vct2`: Version of the tool with an updated version of the Viper back-end. Required to make use of nested quantification for multi-dimensional arrays.
- `Vct2-a`: Version `Vct2` with the new array encoding.
- `Vct3`: Updated version of VerCors with a later update to the Viper back-end, with the old array encoding.
- `Vct3-a`: Version `Vct3` with the new array encoding.

Table 1 shows the results of our experiment to compare the verification times using the old array encoding and using the new array encoding. The new array encoding is based on version `Vct2` of the tool. However, due to a non-linear calculation that was needed in the old array encoding to calculate the new index in a flattened array for a multi-dimensional array, it was no longer possible to verify some programs with multi-dimensional arrays with this version of the tool. We also show results for an earlier version of the tool, version `Vct1`, in which all benchmarks verify.

Table 1. Comparing total verification times (in ms) of `Vct1`, `Vct2` and `Vct2-a`. Sorted by relative speedup from `Vct2` to `Vct2-a`.

File	Vct1	Vct2	Vct2-a
case-studies/prefixsum-drf.pvl	193286	–	50141
carp/histogram-submatrix.c	19579	–	17664
verifythis2018/challenge2.pvl	21709	–	–
carp/summation-kernel-1.pvl	24320	18896	16817
manual/option.pvl	6798	8876	8364
waitnotify/Queue.pvl	5441	7518	7116
type-casts/TypeExample1.java	5261	7151	6776
basic/CollectionTest.pvl	5047	7570	7308
witnesses/TreeWandSilver.java	33340	32210	31800
layers/LFQHist.java	13597	15113	15111
arrays/DutchNationalFlag.pvl	10799	13019	13024
futures/TestFuture.pvl	6824	8401	8656
floats/TestFloat.java	15827	15542	16393
openmp/add-spec-simd.c	14440	14127	16136
openmp/addvec2.pvl	12822	13312	16037
floats/TestHist.java	21423	17862	22361

Using the new array encoding we can see that we are now able to verify the `case-studies/prefixsum-drf.pvl` and the `carp/histogram-submatrix.c` again. Further we see that the `case-studies/prefixsum-drf.pvl` example is almost four times faster to verify, from version `Vct1` to version `Vct2-a`. This is the example that was pointed out by users to be slow to verify, and in which the experts identified the array encoding as being a possible performance bottleneck. The `verifythis2018/challenge2.pvl` example no longer verifies in version `Vct2` and `Vct2-a` of the tool. Upon closer inspection, this is not related to the array encoding, but to a bug in the Viper backend in verifying a loop-invariant: the same program would sometimes verify and sometimes fail. We think that optimizations for sequences in Viper may explain the degradation in performance for the `floats/TestHist.java` and `openmp/addvec2.pvl` programs, since in the new array encoding we no longer make use of sequences. Future work may be to investigate if we can apply possible similar optimizations as for sequences to our array encoding.

In Table 2 we compare results from version `Vct2` to version `Vct3` and `Vct3-a`, which are later versions of VerCors with an update to the Viper back-end.

Table 2. Comparing total verification times (in ms) of Vct2, Vct3 and Vct3-a. Sorted by relative speedup from Vct3 to Vct3-a.

File	Vct2	Vct3	Vct3-a
case-studies/prefixsum-drf.pvl	–	–	98715
carp/histogram-submatrix.c	–	–	18095
floats/TestFloat.java	15542	–	–
carp/summation-kernel-1.pvl	18896	19694	18934
manual/option.pvl	8876	10275	10103
basic/CollectionTest.pvl	7570	8483	8391
waitnotify/Queue.pvl	7518	8283	8197
type-casts/TypeExample1.java	7151	8022	8068
witnesses/TreeWandSilver.java	32210	29072	29334
arrays/DutchNationalFlag.pvl	13019	13887	14036
futures/TestFuture.pvl	8401	9568	9741
layers/LFQHist.java	15113	16130	16481
openmp/add-spec-simd.c	14127	15514	18842
openmp/addvec2.pvl	13312	14673	18530
floats/TestHist.java	17862	20226	34278

Overall we see a performance decrease after the Viper update. With the new version of Viper used in Vct3 and Vct3-a, we can no longer unambiguously claim that the new array encoding improved the performance. While there are two benchmarks that only work when the new array encoding is used, there are also some benchmarks that clearly become slower under the new encoding. Overall, this Viper update has degraded performance.

Furthermore, the floats/TestFloat.java example no longer verifies in version Vct3 and Vct3-a. Verification of this example does not terminate due to a matching loop in a quantified expression in the specification. Matchings for quantifier instantiations in general influence verification performance. We look at this in detail in Sect. 5.

5   Trigger Generation

As mentioned earlier, VerCors has no support for triggers in the input language. The main reason for this is that VerCors rewrites the AST, and could thereby invalidate triggers. For instance, to encode parallel blocks, VerCors generates new quantifiers, and these quantified variables are not covered by the triggers that were in the input program. Thus VerCors relies mainly on Vipers capability of inferring triggers. However, to improve the situation, we have to investigate if during the transformation we could generate some triggers explicitly, and if this would improve performance.

```
1  class Subscripts {
2    invariant (\forall int i; 0<=i && i<|s|/2; s[i] == s[2*i
       ]);
3    void fun(seq<int> s);
4  }
```

Listing 3. Function specification with complex index expression.

Quantifiers in Z3 are instantiated via a mechanism called triggers [8]. The idea is to associate every quantified expression with a trigger set. We focus on the case that a quantified expression like $\forall x.E(x)$ (and its associated trigger set) becomes a positive literal in Z3's procedure. When this happens, Z3 can introduce values for x, say $c_1, \ldots, c_n$, and add $E(c_1), \ldots, E(c_n)$ to the set of positive literals. The trigger set helps Z3 to determine which values for x to use. A trigger is an expression with the meaning: if this expression is unifiable with a ground term that occurs in any literal, use that ground term to instantiate x. A trigger set is a set of such expressions.

5.1   Rewriting Complex Index Expressions

In the general case, a quantified expression can have multiple variables: $Q x_1, \ldots, x_N, E$. In order to generate triggers for Viper, which passes them down to Z3, we have to make sure that they adhere to the restrictions that Viper imposes on triggers (see [18] for more information on these restrictions):

- All quantified variables occur in the trigger set.
- Each trigger contains a quantified variable.
- Each trigger contains a function symbol: a single quantified variable by itself is not a valid trigger.
- The trigger expression does not contain any arithmetical operator (like addition on integers).
- Triggers do not contain accessibility predicates, i.e. you are not allowed to use permission expressions in your triggers.

This can be challenging, because data structures that are often used in combination with quantified expressions are arrays or sequences. However, we cannot generate triggers of the form input[i+1], since the index part of the expression uses the + operator, and this is not allowed by Viper. Thus, as a first step, we developed a rewriting procedure to rewrite index expressions in the allowed format.

To illustrate this rewriting procedure, consider Listing 3.

In this example the forall quantifier specifies that for all elements in the first half of the sequence, the element at the position twice as far from the start should have the same value. In this example there are two candidate trigger expressions: s[i] and s[2*i]. This is not a valid trigger set, since the second expression contains the arithmetic operator *. To eliminate the multiplication,

we use rewriting to (1) introduce a fresh quantifier variable u1, (2) replace the 2*
i expression in the body of the expression with the new variable, and (3) add an
equality to the range expression of the quantifier, stating that the new variable
should be equal to 2*i. This results in the following expression.

(\forall int i,int u1; 0<=i && i<|s|/2 && u1==2*i; s[i]==s[u1])

This gives us the candidate triggers s[i] and s[u1], which adhere to the
Viper restrictions on triggers.

One point of consideration is the effect of the complexity that we add to the
quantifier expression by adding a quantified variable. The extra variable adds
a dimension to the domain of the quantifier, which could make it even harder
for the SMT solver to find the right instances to discharge a proof. We believe,
however, that the SMT solver can easily discharge the added equality in the
selection of the quantifier (in our example the equality u1 == 2*i), and that
the positive effect of being able to generate an appropriate trigger will outweigh
the costs of the added complexity. Another way in which we add complexity,
is that by adding an extra trigger (in this case for s[2*i]), more clauses are
added. This is typically a desired additional complexity, as it enables us to prove
more properties (Z3 applies the clause in more situations), but it has a potential
to backfire by causing time-outs. Our experiments show that this is the case,
and that there are programs where rewriting helps the prover, whereas in other
programs rewriting causes the verification to fail.

5.2 Generating Triggers

After eliminating complex index expressions, we can try to generate trigger sets
for universal quantifiers at the end of the rewriting phase (as this ensures that
the generated triggers will not be invalidated by other transformations). Both
the range and the body of the quantifier expression are trigger candidates. From
these subexpressions we identify all trigger candidates: expressions that mention
at least one of the quantified variables, have some sort of structure (thus not the
variable itself) and do not contain an accessibility predicate. We then generate
the powerset of all trigger candidates, and from this select all sets that mention
all quantified variables.

We chose to consider all possible valid combinations of trigger expressions,
to make sure that we do not inadvertently block necessary quantifier instantiations. The intuition is that these triggers still contain more abstractions (e.g.
domain encodings used by VerCors) than triggers that would be inferred by
Viper. Thereby our triggers are more specific and cause less spurious quantifier
instantiations in the SMT solver. It is future work to investigate if some mini-
malisations are possible. However, our experiences are that starting with the full
powerset does not have a significant overhead.

5.3   Experiments

We used the same set of programs as in Sect. 4.3 to compare verification times using the rewriting and trigger generation techniques discussed in this section. Version Vct3-a is the version of VerCors in which all the aforementioned techniques are implemented. This version already makes use of the new array encoding as introduced in the previous section. Using a command line option, we can enable rewriting of complex indexes and the generation of triggers separately. For each configuration the programs have been verified 5 times, and the mean verification times are shown in the table.

5.4   Results

Table 3 shows the verification times for our experiments. Column Vct3-a shows the verification times without rewriting index expressions, and without trigger generation. In column Vct3-a-t1 only trigger generation is enabled. In column Vct3-a-t2 only rewriting complex index expressions is enabled and in the column Vct3-a-t3 both the rewriting of complex index expressions and trigger generation are enabled.

Table 3. Comparing total verification times (in ms) for version Vct3-a, with and without triggers. Sorted by relative speedup from Vct3-a to Vct3-a-t3.

File	Vct3-a	Vct3-a-t1	Vct3-a-t2	Vct3-a-t3
floats/TestFloat.java	–	32693	–	34219
openmp/add-spec-simd.c	18842	19329	–	–
openmp/addvec2.pvl	18530	19629	–	–
floats/TestHist.java	34278	24412	31877	23122
case-studies/prefixsum-drf.pvl	98715	96133	68190	69797
arrays/DutchNationalFlag.pvl	14036	14153	14673	13975
manual/option.pvl	10103	10266	11123	10072
type-casts/TypeExample1.java	8068	7993	8002	8081
futures/TestFuture.pvl	9741	9880	9708	9819
layers/LFQHist.java	16481	16457	16662	16657
carp/histogram-submatrix.c	18095	18380	18058	18324
basic/CollectionTest.pvl	8391	8289	8394	8500
carp/summation-kernel-1.pvl	18934	19517	21016	19222
waitnotify/Queue.pvl	8197	8190	8304	8351
witnesses/TreeWandSilver.java	29334	29502	30290	30001

There are a couple of things we can see from the results. Without triggers floats/TestFloat.java does not verify. Verification for this program runs indefinitely due to a matching loop in the back-end SMT solver. By generating triggers for the quantified expressions in this program, the matching loop is broken and the tool is able to verify it. Verification of `floats/TestHist.java` is nearly 30% faster if triggers are generated. For the other results in the `Vct3-a-t1` column we see minimal differences in verification times, because we can not generate valid trigger sets for the quantified expressions in these programs. If we enable the rewriting of complex indexes, we see that the `openmp/add-spec-simd.c` and `openmp/addvec2.pvl` programs fail to verify. This is caused by the added complexity introduced by adding quantified variables for complex index expressions. For `case-studies/prefixsum-drf.pvl` we see that only rewriting complex index expressions already has a positive effect on the verification time. Combining the two techniques show positive results for 3 of the 15 programs, but cause 2 programs to fail. Thus the use of triggers show a positive effect on performance. However, transformations that are needed to enable trigger generation can have negative side-effects. Therefore future work could focus on how to rewrite quantified expressions in a way that enables trigger generation, without adding too much complexity.

6 Related Work

The work in this paper is focused very specifically on the performance of program verification with VerCors. However, if we look more broadly, we can see various studies that investigate and compare the performance of different verification techniques, as discussed below. To the best of our knowledge, there are no other reports that analyse specifically which parts of an annotated program have most impact on the performance of the program verifier.

Kassios et al. compared the performance of verification using symbolic execution with the performance of verification condition generation-based verification [12]. Their work compares different technique to obtain the necessary first-order proof obligations, whereas we compare the performance effect of different Viper encodings for the same source program.

Leino et al. identify matching loops in quantified expressions as a significant contributor to instabilities in performance and user experience in program verification [14]. They propose to move trigger logic away from the SMT solver and into the high level verifier. In particular, they present three techniques for trigger selection that they then implemented in the Dafny verifier: quantifier splitting, trigger sharing and matching loop detection. In our work, we have also investigated ways to generate suitable triggers at a higher level. Our results also show a performance benefit, but still requires more investigation to understand all possible consequences.

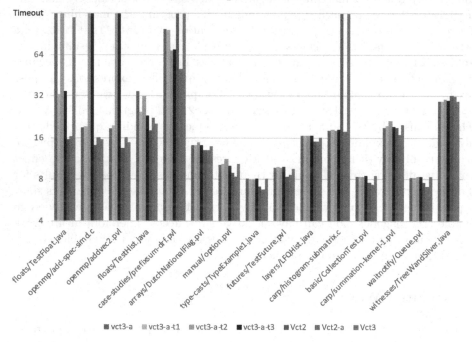

Fig. 4. Summary of Tables 1, 2, and 3

7   Conclusions

In this paper we have discussed two techniques to improve the run-time performance of the VerCors program verifier: changing the encoding of arrays, and changing the way triggers are generated. This gives a good speedup on some programs from our standard example set, but on many programs, the run-time hardly changes. A summary of the measurements presented in this paper is given in Fig. 4. However, our benchmarks come from a set of programs that were selected to work well with the version of VerCors that does not have the improvements described in this paper. We therefore believe that the changes, which do help in some cases, will have a large positive impact on the practical use of VerCors. In particular, as our new encoding is simpler because of the implicit injectivity, we expect that in the future we might have to add less auxiliary lemmas about the bounds on array index expressions. Moreover, we should also stress that the new array encoding also enabled an easier encoding of the various kinds of (multi-dimensional) arrays one finds in Java and C. As future work, we plan to further fine-tune our improvements to further improve the performance of VerCors.

Acknowledgements. The work in this paper has been supported by the NWO VICI project Mercedes (project nr. 639.023.710).

References

1. Ahrendt, W., Beckert, B., Bubel, R., Hähnle, R., Schmitt, P.H., Ulbrich, M.: Deductive Software Verification - The KeY Book. LNCS, vol. 10001. Springer, Heidelberg (2016)
2. Amighi, A., Blom, S., Huisman, M., Zaharieva-Stojanovski, M.: The VerCors project: setting up basecamp. In: Programming Languages Meets Program Verification (PLPV 2012), pp. 71–82 (2012)
3. Amighi, A., Blom, S., Darabi, S., Huisman, M., Mostowski, W., Zaharieva-Stojanovski, M.: Verification of concurrent systems with VerCors. In: Bernardo, M., Damiani, F., Hähnle, R., Johnsen, E.B., Schaefer, I. (eds.) SFM 2014. LNCS, vol. 8483, pp. 172–216. Springer, Cham (2014). https://doi.org/10.1007/978-3-319-07317-0_5
4. Blom, S., Huisman, M.: The VerCors tool for verification of concurrent programs. In: Jones, C., Pihlajasaari, P., Sun, J. (eds.) FM 2014. LNCS, vol. 8442, pp. 127–131. Springer, Cham (2014). https://doi.org/10.1007/978-3-319-06410-9_9
5. Blom, S., Darabi, S., Huisman, M., Oortwijn, W.: The VerCors tool set: verification of parallel and concurrent software. In: Polikarpova, N., Schneider, S. (eds.) IFM 2017. LNCS, vol. 10510, pp. 102–110. Springer, Cham (2017). https://doi.org/10.1007/978-3-319-66845-1_7
6. Burdy, L., et al.: An overview of JML tools and applications. Int. J. Softw. Tools Technol. Transf. **7**(3), 212–232 (2005)
7. de Moura, L., Bjørner, N.: Z3: an efficient SMT solver. In: Ramakrishnan, C.R., Rehof, J. (eds.) TACAS 2008. LNCS, vol. 4963, pp. 337–340. Springer, Heidelberg (2008). https://doi.org/10.1007/978-3-540-78800-3_24
8. Detlefs, D., Nelson, G., Saxe, J.B.: Simplify: a theorem prover for program checking. J. ACM **52**(3), 365–473 (2005)
9. Hähnle, R., Huisman, M.: Deductive software verification: from pen-and-paper proofs to industrial tools. In: Steffen, B., Woeginger, G. (eds.) Computing and Software Science. LNCS, vol. 10000, pp. 345–373. Springer, Cham (2019). https://doi.org/10.1007/978-3-319-91908-9_18
10. Jacobs, B., Piessens, F.: The VeriFast program verifier. Technical report CW520, Katholieke Universiteit Leuven (2008)
11. Jacobs, B., Smans, J., Piessens, F.: Solving the VerifyThis 2012 challenges with VeriFast. Int. J. Softw. Tools Technol. Transfer **17**(6), 659–676 (2015)
12. Kassios, I.T., Müller, P., Schwerhoff, M.: Comparing verification condition generation with symbolic execution: an experience report. In: Joshi, R., Müller, P., Podelski, A. (eds.) VSTTE 2012. LNCS, vol. 7152, pp. 196–208. Springer, Heidelberg (2012). https://doi.org/10.1007/978-3-642-27705-4_16
13. Leino, K.R.M.: Dafny: an automatic program verifier for functional correctness. In: Clarke, E.M., Voronkov, A. (eds.) LPAR 2010. LNCS (LNAI), vol. 6355, pp. 348–370. Springer, Heidelberg (2010). https://doi.org/10.1007/978-3-642-17511-4_20
14. Leino, K.R.M., Pit-Claudel, C.: Trigger selection strategies to stabilize program verifiers. In: Chaudhuri, S., Farzan, A. (eds.) CAV 2016. LNCS, vol. 9779, pp. 361–381. Springer, Cham (2016). https://doi.org/10.1007/978-3-319-41528-4_20

15. Mulder, H.: Performance of program verification with VerCors. Master's thesis, University of Twente (2019)
16. Müller, P., Schwerhoff, M., Summers, A.J.: Viper: a verification infrastructure for permission-based reasoning. In: Jobstmann, B., Leino, K.R.M. (eds.) VMCAI 2016. LNCS, vol. 9583, pp. 41–62. Springer, Heidelberg (2016). https://doi.org/10.1007/978-3-662-49122-5_2
17. Reynolds, J.C.: Separation logic: a logic for shared mutable data structures. In: Proceedings of 17th Annual IEEE Symposium on Logic in Computer Science, pp. 55–74. IEEE (2002)
18. Viper tutorial. Accessed 09 Apr 2020

Contracts

Behavioral Contracts for Cooperative Scheduling

Eduard Kamburjan[1]([✉])[ID], Crystal Chang Din[2][ID], Reiner Hähnle[1][ID], and Einar Broch Johnsen[2][ID]

[1] Department of Computer Science, Technische Universität Darmstadt, Darmstadt, Germany
{kamburjan,haehnle}@cs.tu-darmstadt.de
[2] Department of Informatics, University of Oslo, Oslo, Norway
{crystald,einarj}@ifi.uio.no

Abstract. Formal specification of multi-threaded programs is notoriously hard, because thread execution may be preempted at any point. In contrast, abstract concurrency models such as actors seriously restrict concurrency to obtain race-free programs. Languages with *cooperative scheduling* occupy a middle ground between these extremes by explicit scheduling points. We introduce *cooperative contracts*, a contract-based specification approach designed for cooperative scheduling. It permits to specify complex concurrent behavior succinctly. Cooperative contracts are formalized as behavioral contracts in a compositional behavioral program logic in which they can be formally verified.

1 Introduction

Specification contracts for methods are *the* pivotal concept that makes deductive verification of non-trivial programs feasible [32]. The main idea is simple: the behavior of each method of a program is described (precisely or approximately) by a declarative contract, consisting of (i) logical formulas characterizing its pre- and poststates and (ii) a set of memory locations that limit the method's frame (assignable locations). This allows a deductive verification system to replace a method call with a declarative description obtained from its contract. Verification of a large program is thus broken down into tasks of manageable size that consist in verifying that each method satisfies its contract. Formal specification languages based on contracts exist, for example, for the industrial languages Java [50] and C [11].

The contract-based approach works well for *sequential* programs and is supported in industrial-strength verification tools [4,39,49,51], but it is notoriously difficult to specify *concurrent* programs. The reason is that in the sequential case specification and execution are based on the same unit of computation: a method. In standard concurrency models (such as in C, Java, or Scala) this is not the case: method execution can be interrupted ("preempted") at any time by another method with a possibly overlapping frame. To combat the myriad of

© Springer Nature Switzerland AG 2020
W. Ahrendt et al. (Eds.): Deductive Software Verification, LNCS 12345, pp. 85–121, 2020.
https://doi.org/10.1007/978-3-030-64354-6_4

possible interleavings with accordingly complex data races, it becomes necessary to encode program-wide assumptions about permitted scheduling sequences into method contracts. This in turn leads to contracts becoming bulky, hard to write, and even harder to understand, because their local nature is lost [12].

An extreme solution to this problem is to restrict the permitted form of concurrency radically, as in actor-based, distributed programming [8], where methods are executed atomically and concurrency only occurs among actors with disjoint heaps. In this setting, behavior—like in the sequential case—can be completely specified at the level of interfaces, typically in terms of behavioral invariants jointly maintained by an object's methods [22,27]. However, this restricted concurrency enforces that systems are modeled and specified at a high level of abstraction, essentially as protocols. It precludes realistic modeling of concurrent behavior, such as waiting for results computed asynchronously on the same processor and heap.

Cooperative scheduling, as realized in *active object* (AO) languages [21], occupies a middle ground between preemption and full distribution. It is based on an actor-*like* model of concurrency [3] and *futures* to handle return values from asynchronous calls [10,18,22,29,33,53,60]. Programs voluntarily and in a *syntactically explicit* manner suspend their execution, such that a required result may be provided by another task: Method activations on the same processor and heap *cooperate* to achieve a common goal. The crucial point is that code locations where suspension may occur are explicitly marked and *only* at those locations preemption may occur. At the same time, *strong encapsulation* is enforced: an object may only access its own fields. In consequence, data races can only occur between tasks executing on the same object.

It was demonstrated in several case studies that cooperative scheduling permits realistic modeling of concurrent behavior of industrial software, allowing, for example, precise runtime prediction [6,52] or the exhibition of performance bugs [59]. A still open problem is *deductive verification* of non-trivial programs with cooperative concurrency. The research question is: *Is there a generalization of sequential specification contracts to the cooperative setting that permits succinct, intelligible specifications and a compositional calculus for deductive verification?* In this paper we give an affirmative answer. We define a specification language called *behavioral contracts for cooperative scheduling*, "cooperative contracts" in short, that addresses fundamental problems encountered when generalizing sequential to cooperative concurrent behavior:

1. Due to strong object encapsulation, the specification of interfaces and of implementations diverges. The latter know implementation aspects that the former have no access to.
2. In the time gap between method invocation and activation or between a method's termination and reading the returned result, as well as at suspension points, it is possible that different tasks on the same object interleave. It must be possible to specify *locally* at such points which tasks can be relied upon to have finished and which might overlap.

3. As futures can be passed around as parameters and thus may be read in arbitrary code locations, it is not possible to determine statically the method that computes a future's value. Again, this information must be specified.

In addition, cooperative contracts must permit to specify frames, similar to sequential contracts.

The second main contribution of this paper is a program logic in which active object programs together with their specification can be expressed. The third contribution is a compositional deductive verification system that permits to formally prove the validity of logically rendered contracts. That calculus is sound relative to a formal semantics which is supplied as well.

To present our framework we need to fix a concrete AO language. We chose a subset[1] of ABS ("abstract behavioral specification") [40], because it has a stable and well-maintained ecosystem and its sequential fragment is similar to Java so that cooperative contracts can be presented as an extension of JML [50].

The following section introduces and explains the usage of cooperative contracts by way of a case study: we formally specify a concurrent publisher-subscriber model with dynamic allocation of proxy servers. Section 3 formally defines syntax and semantics of our active object language. Section 4 defines *behavioral program logic* (BPL) [42], a first-order dynamic logic that can represent active object programs together with their behavioral specification. Cooperative contracts are then rendered in BPL, the details are given in Sect. 5. We close with related work (Sect. 6) and a conclusion (Sect. 7).

The main ideas for specification and verification with cooperative contracts were first presented in [47]. Their encoding into BPL was first explored in [44]. The present account is rewritten from scratch. The publisher-subscriber case study is completely new, as is the formal semantics of the active object language. In contrast to the prior publications, frames are added and handled uniformly with method contracts. The program logic and, as a result the deductive verification system and the proof sketches, is simplified in contrast to both prior publications.

2   Cooperative Contracts for Active Objects

We introduce the main concepts of the active object (AO) language ABS [2,40] as well as the methodology of our specification framework by way of a case study.

2.1   Case Study

Consider a publisher–subscriber model, where clients may subscribe to a service, while the service object is responsible for generating news and publishes each news update to the subscribing clients. To avoid bottlenecks when publishing, the service delegates publishing to a chain of proxy objects, where each proxy handles a bounded number of clients, as illustrated in Fig. 1.

---

[1] The restriction to a subset is purely for presentation purposes. A forthcoming implementation will support full ABS.

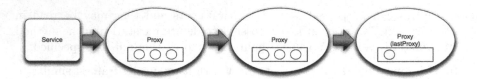

Fig. 1. A publisher-subscriber model with proxies handling at most three clients each

The interfaces and implementations of service and proxies are shown in Fig. 2. The ABS code is fully executable and the complete model is found at `abs-models.org`. The `publish()` method of the `Proxy` class takes advantage of asynchronous method calls with futures: a proxy object first initiates publication down the chain of proxies via asynchronous, recursive calls on the `nextProxy` pointer, before it retrieves the news item `ns` and forwards that to its client list. If the current proxy object is the last in the chain, then the next news production cycle is initiated via a call to the `produce()` method of `Service`.

On the other hand, the recursive call in `add()` of `Proxy` is blocking: We use `r = o.m()` as a shorthand for `Fut<T> fut = o!m(); r = fut.get`. This is harmless since the implementation of `add()` does not deadlock and terminates after at most `limit` many calls.

Among several relevant properties one would like to specify for the `publish()` method are that the future passed to it is not null and that all clients of the current proxy object received the news update upon termination. In the following we illustrate that such properties can be easily and succinctly stated in our framework.

Recall that in the AO language ABS a task cannot be preempted, unless it is at a suspension point. The latter is marked explicitly by an **await** statement. Hence, the code between method activation, **await** statements, and method termination, respectively, runs uninterrupted. We speak of *atomic segments*. The scope of each atomic segment has a unique name, which is specified by the annotation [atom: ''name''] at the **await** statement that closes it. The syntactic end of a method declares an implicit atomic segment whose name defaults to the method name. Therefore, a method without **await** statement has exactly one atomic segment named after the method. In addition, `sync` labels identify statements, where the value of a future is read. For example, the `publish()` method can be annotated as follows:

```
Unit publish(Fut<NewsI> fut) {
  NewsI ns = null;
  if (nextProxy != null) {
    nextProxy!publish(fut);
  }
  [sync: "getNews"]          ns = fut.get;
  [atom: "notifyClients"] await this!toClients(ns);
  if (nextProxy == null) {
    service!produce();
  }
}
```

```
1  interface ServiceI {
2    Unit setup(Int lm, ProducerI prod);
3    Unit subscribe(ClientI cl);
4    Unit produce();
5  }
6
7  class Service implements ServiceI {
8    ProducerI producer = null;
9    ProxyI proxy = null;
10   ProxyI lastProxy = null;
11   Int limit = 0;
12
13   Unit setup(Int lm, ProducerI prod) {
14     limit = lm;
15     producer = prod;
16     proxy = new Proxy();
17     proxy.setup(lm, this);
18     lastProxy = proxy;
19     this!produce();
20   }
21
22   Unit subscribe(ClientI cl) {
23     lastProxy = lastProxy.add(cl);
24   }
25
26   Unit produce() {
27     Fut<NewsI> f_news =
28       producer!detectNews();
29     await f_news?;
30     proxy!publish(f_news);
31   }
32 }
33
34 interface ProxyI {
35   Unit setup(Int lm, ServiceI s);
36   ProxyI add(ClientI cl);
37   Unit publish(Fut<NewsI> fut);
38 }
39
40 class Proxy implements ProxyI {
41   Int limit = 0;
42   List<ClientI> myClients = Nil;
43   ProxyI nextProxy = null;
44   ServiceI service = null;
```

```
45   Unit setup(Int lm, ServiceI s) {
46     limit = lm;
47     service = s;
48   }
49
50   ProxyI add(ClientI cl) {
51     ProxyI lastProxy = this;
52     if (length(myClients) < limit) {
53       myClients = append(myClients, cl);
54     } else {
55       if (nextProxy == null) {
56         nextProxy = new Proxy();
57         nextProxy.setup(limit, service);
58       }
59       lastProxy = nextProxy.add(cl);
60     }
61     return lastProxy;
62   }
63
64   Unit publish(Fut<NewsI> fut) {
65     NewsI ns = null;
66     if (nextProxy != null) {
67       nextProxy!publish(fut);
68     }
69     ns = fut.get;
70     await this!toClients(ns);
71     if (nextProxy == null) {
72       service!produce();
73     }
74   }
75
76   Unit toClients(NewsI ns) {
77     Int cnt = 0;
78     while (cnt < length(myClients)) {
79       ClientI cl = nth(myClients, cnt);
80       cl!signal(ns);
81       cnt = cnt + 1;
82     }
83   }
84 }
```

Fig. 2. Implementation of service and proxy interfaces and classes

2.2 Specifying State in an Asynchronous Setting

During the time gap between method invocation and activation, method parameters stay invariant (they are immutable in ABS), but the object's heap (value
of fields) may change. This motivates to split the precondition of asynchronous
method contracts into an interface part relating to method parameters and an
implementation part that specifies heap values. The *parameter precondition* is
guaranteed by the caller who knows the appropriate synchronization pattern. It
is part of the callee's interface declaration and exposed to clients. (For param-
eterless methods the parameter precondition is True and can be omitted.) Vice
versa, the *callee* guarantees the heap precondition. This is so, because only the
callee's implementation has sufficient knowledge of the internal state, Therefore,
the heap precondition is declared in the class implementing an interface and not

exposed to clients. Preconditions follow JML [50] convention and are marked by the *requires* keyword.

Postconditions (keyword *ensures*) work analogously. Like in JML, postconditions are evaluated in the poststate of a method. To access the value of a field at *activation* time of a method, the keyword \old is used.

In addition, like in JML, the implementation contract of a method specifies its *assignable* heap locations. This specifies either a set of memory locations or the shortcuts \nothing, \everything with obvious semantics. It is advisable to specify assignable locations, because their (safe) default is \everything.

Example 1. Parameters of `Proxy.setup()` must fulfill the precondition that the capacity `lm` of a proxy is larger than zero and the service object `s` is not null. The heap precondition expresses that field `limit` is zero and `service` is null. The heap postcondition expresses that after termination of `setup()` the value of `limit` is larger than zero and `service` is not null.

```
interface ProxyI {
  /*@ requires lm > 0 & s !=
  null @*/
  Unit setup(Int lm, ServiceI s)
  ;
}
```

```
class Proxy implements ProxyI {
  /*@ requires limit == 0 && service == null;
    ensures  limit > 0   && service != null;
    assignable {limit, service}; @*/
  Unit setup(Int lm, ServiceI s) {
    limit = lm;
    service = s;
  }
}
```

2.3   Concurrency Context

A caller must fulfill the callee's parameter precondition, but the most recently completed process running on the callee object establishes its heap precondition. In other words, whether the callee's heap precondition holds, depends on the postconditions of the (atomic segments of) methods that run concurrently or that have just terminated. To express this, one specifies the *concurrency context* of a method, in addition to its *memory context* given by the heap precondition. The concurrency context is part of the interface contract and consists of two *context sets*, i.e. sets of atomic segment names:

- *succeeds*: Each atomic segment in this set must *ensure* the heap precondition when it terminates and at least one of them must have run before the specified method starts execution.
- *overlaps*: Each atomic segment in this set must *preserve* the heap precondition. Between the termination of the last atomic segment from *succeeds* and the start of the execution of the specified atomic segment, only atomic segments from *overlaps* are allowed to run.

Context sets are part of the interface specification, but a class may extend context sets with private atomic segment names and methods. It is the obligation of that class to ensure that private methods do not disrupt correct call sequences from the outside. From an analysis point of view, private methods are no different than public ones. Observe that context sets represent global information unavailable when a method is analyzed in isolation. If context sets are not specified in the code, they default to the set of *all* atomic segments in the class, whence the heap precondition degenerates into a class invariant and must be guaranteed by each process at each suspension point [26].

Method implementation contracts need to know their expected context, but the global protocol at the object level can be specified and exposed in a separate coordination language, such as session types [37]. This enforces a separation of concerns in specifications: method contracts are local and specify a single method and its context; the coordination language specifies a global view on the whole protocol. Of course, local method contracts and global protocols expressed with session types [45,46] must be proven consistent. Context sets can also be verified by static analysis once the whole program is available, see Sect. 2.6 for an example.

Example 2. Consider the interface and implementation specification of add() in Fig. 3. The heap precondition of add() is established by setup() which it must succeed. Between setup() and (re-)activation of add() only add() or publish() may run. This is expressed by the specified context sets (recall that method names label the final atomic segment of a method body).

The heap postcondition specifies that add() may increase the length of field myClients, but it will never exceed limit. It preserves the contents of myClients. If the limit was not reached at the beginning of method execution, then client

```
interface ProxyI {
    /*@ requires cl != null;
        succeeds {setup};
        overlaps {add, publish} @*/
    ProxyI add(ClientI cl);
}

class Proxy implements ProxyI {
    /*@ requires limit > 0 && len(myClients) <= limit && service != null;
        ensures 0 < len(myClients) && len(myClients) >= len(\old(myClients)) &&
            ∀ ClientI c; hasElement(\old{myClients}, c); hasElement(myClients, c) &&
            (len(\old(myClients)) < limit -> hasElement(myClients, cl)) &&
            (len(\old(myClients)) == limit -> len(myClients) == len(\old(myClients)));
        overlaps {notifyClients, toClients};
        assignable {myClients, nextProxy} @*/
    ProxyI add(ClientI cl) {
        ProxyI lastProxy = this;
        if (length(myClients) < limit){
            myClients = append(myClients, cl);
        } else {
            if (nextProxy == null) {
                nextProxy = new Proxy();
                nextProxy.setup(limit, service);
            }
            lastProxy = nextProxy.add(cl);
        }
        return lastProxy;
    }
}
```

Fig. 3. Interface and implementation of add() in proxy

cl is indeed in `myClients` upon method termination. In addition, we extend the context set of the interface specification with atomic segment `notifyClients` in the `publish()` method and the private method `toClients()` which also may interleave with `add()`.

The specified concurrency context is used to *enrich* existing method contracts: the heap precondition of a method specified with context sets is implicitly *propagated* to the postcondition of all atomic segments it *succeeds* as well as to pre- *and* postconditions of all atomic segments it *overlaps* with.

Example 3. Continuing Example 2, after propagation, contracts of `setup()`, `add ()` and `toClients()` are as follows[2] (redundant expressions not shown, for example, *limit > 0 && service != null* in `add()`'s postcondition are preserved from its precondition, because of the *assignable* clause):

```
/*@ ensures <as before> && len(myClients)<=limit @*/
Unit setup(Int lm, ServiceI s) { ... }
/*@ ensures <as before> && len(myClients)<=limit @*/
ProxyI add(ClientI cl) { ... }
/*@ requires <as before> && limit > 0 && len(myClients) <= limit && service != null;
      ensures <as before> && limit > 0 && len(myClients) <= limit && service != null
  @*/
Unit toClients(NewsI ns) { ... }
```

2.4   Resolve Contracts

Consider the **get** statement in Line 69 of Fig. 2. It is important to be able to prove properties about its resolved future, for example, `ns != null`. Such a property can be ensured by the postcondition of the method that computed the future, but (like in the example) it is not obvious which methods that could be. For this reason we attach a *resolve contract* to each **get** statement. It consists simply of the keyword *resolvedby*, followed by the set of methods that resolve its future.

The client accessing a future might not be its creator, so properties of method parameters and class fields in the postcondition of the method associated to the future should be hidden. The heap postcondition of a method may contain properties of fields, parameters and results upon termination. We abstract that postcondition into a postcondition for the corresponding method at the interface level, which only reads the result at the client side. In analogy to the split of precondition the latter is called *interface postcondition*. Only if the call context is known, the heap postcondition may be used in addition to the interface postcondition.

Example 4. The **get** statement in Line 69 of Fig. 2 is resolved by `Producer.detectNews()`, the resolve contract is displayed in Fig. 4. Assuming that the interface postcondition of `Producer.detectNews()` contains *result != null*, we can ensure that `ns != null` holds at this point.

---

[2] The specifications of `publish()` and `notifyClients` are shown in the next subsection in connection with specification of suspension points.

2.5   Suspension Contracts

Each **await** statement introduces a scheduling point, where task execution may be suspended and possibly interleaved. From a local perspective, an **await** statement is a *suspension point* where information about heap memory is lost. This is similar to heap preconditions and can be addressed in the same manner: By specifying what is guaranteed at release of control, what can be assumed upon reactivation, and who has the obligation to guarantee the heap property. Accordingly, each suspension point is annotated by a *suspension contract* containing the *same* elements as a method contract: An *ensures* clause for the condition that is guaranteed upon suspension, a *requires* clause for the condition that must hold upon reactivation[3], a *succeeds* context set for the atomic segments that must have run before reactivation and an *overlaps* context set for atomic segments whose execution may interleave. The *assignable* clause always relates to the atomic segment whose suspension contract it is part of.

Example 5. In Fig. 4 we specify the behavior of the suspension point at the **await** statement ''notifyClients'': Upon suspension, the news **ns** passed to toClients() must not be null which can be derived from the resolve contract (see Sect. 2.4). During suspension, only methods add(), publish() can interleave. By adding the method toClients() to the succeeds set, we ensure that the news will have been delivered to the clients upon reactivation.

```
interface ProxyI {
   /*@ requires fut != null;
        succeeds {setup};
        overlaps {add, publish} @*/
   Unit publish(Fut<NewsI> fut);
}

class Proxy implements ProxyI {
   /*@ ensures   len(myClients) <= limit ;
        assignable \nothing; @*/
   Unit publish(Fut<NewsI> fut) {
      NewsI ns = null;
      if (nextProxy != null) { nextProxy!publish(fut); }
      /*@ resolvedby {Producer.detectNews}; @*/
      [sync: "getNews"] ns = fut.get;
      /*@ ensures ns != null &&   len(myClients) <= limit ;
           requires this.service != null;
           succeeds {toClients};
           overlaps {add, publish};
           assignable \nothing; @*/
      [atom: "notifyClients"] await this!toClients(ns);
      if (nextProxy == null) { service!produce(); }
   }
}
```

Fig. 4. Suspension and resolve contracts of publish() in proxy

---

[3] The execution pattern is *inverse* to method execution: on suspension execution stops and is later reactivated. Therefore, it is intuitive to specify *ensures* *before* *requires*. Observe that the *ensures* clause of the top-level method contract specifies the final state upon method termination, i.e. the postcondition of the final atomic segment.

Propagation from context sets into pre- and postconditions of suspension contracts is analogous to the procedure for method contracts. Figure 4 highlights the propagated specification for `publish()` from the heap precondition of `add()`. The name "`publish`" represents the *final* atomic segment of the `publish()` method, so the postcondition of `publish()` is also the postcondition of that atomic segment. After propagation, the contracts express that both atomic blocks preserve the heap precondition of `add()`.

2.6 Service Composition

The specification above is modular in the following sense: To prove that a method adheres to the pre- and postcondition of its own contract and respects the pre- and postconditions of called methods, it is sufficient to analyze its owner class.

However, the correctness of context sets in the cooperation contracts clearly depends on the sequence in which methods are called by client classes. In other words, to verify that a program respects all context sets, requires global, system-wide information. This constitutes a separation of concerns between functional specification (state) and non-functional specification (call sequence). That makes it possible to decompose concurrent system verification into two phases: In the first phase, deductive verification [23] is used to *locally* show that each individual method implements its pre- and postconditions correctly. In the second phase, a *global* light-weight, fully automatic dependence analysis [7] is used to approximate possible call sequences. This approach has two advantages: first, the global analysis need not be done by expensive deduction; second, it is often possible to reuse contracts: if a method is changed with only local effects it is sufficient to re-prove its contract and re-run the dependence analysis. The proofs of all other method contracts remain unchanged.

The dependence analysis of context sets is detailed in the technical report [48]; we only give an example for rejected and accepted call sequences here.

Example 6. Consider the code fragments interacting with a `Proxy` instance p given below (use **await** o!m(); as shorthand for **Fut<T>** f = o!m(); **await** f?;). The left fragment fails to verify the context sets specified above: even though called after `setup()`, `publish()` can be executed first due to reordering, failing its *succeeds* clause. The right fragment verifies, because of the **await** guard and the fact that `publish()` is included in its *overlaps* context set.

```
p!setup(3,s);
p!publish(f);
```

```
await p!setup(3,s);
p!publish(f1);
p!publish(f2);
```

3 Active Object Programs

We define formally the simple active object language Async, based on ABS [40], first the syntax, then the formal semantics.

3.1 Syntax

The Async syntax is shown in Fig. 5. The language has been informally explained with an extensive example in the previous section, so we keep this brief and focus on language features related to communication and synchronization—other features are standard.

Objects communicate by asynchronous method calls, written $e!m(\bar{e})$, with an associated future f. A future's value can be accessed by the statement $x = f$.get once it is resolved, i.e. when the task associated with f terminated. Futures can be shared among objects. Field access between different objects is indirect through (getter/setter) method calls, amounting to strong encapsulation. Cooperative scheduling is realized as follows: at most one process is active on an object at any time and all scheduling points are *explicit* in the code using **await** statements. Execution inside atomic segments is sequential and cannot be preempted. For the set Exp of pure expressions we assume the valuation function to be known, where $e \in$ Exp is a value of Exp. We assume programs are well-typed.

$$
\begin{array}{ll}
\mathsf{P} ::= \bar{\mathsf{I}}\ \bar{\mathsf{C}}\ \{\overline{T\ x = e};\mathsf{s}\} & \mathsf{s} \quad ::= x = rhs \mid \mathsf{skip} \\
\mathsf{I} \ ::= \mathsf{interface}\ \mathsf{I}\ \{\bar{\mathsf{S}}\} & \quad\quad \mid \big[\mathsf{sync} : \text{``string''}\big]x = e.\mathsf{get} \\
\mathsf{C} ::= \mathsf{class}\ \mathsf{C}(\overline{T\ x})\ \{\overline{\mathsf{M}\ T\ x = e}\} & \quad\quad \mid \big[\mathsf{atom} : \text{``string''}\big]\ \mathsf{await}\ \mathsf{g} \\
\mathsf{M} ::= \mathsf{S}\{\overline{T\ x = e};\bar{\mathsf{s}};\mathsf{return}\ e\} & \quad\quad \mid\ \mathsf{if}\,(e)\,\{\bar{\mathsf{s}}\}\,\mathsf{else}\,\{\bar{\mathsf{s}}\}\mid \mathsf{while}\,(e)\,\{\bar{\mathsf{s}}\} \\
\mathsf{S} \ ::= T\ \mathsf{m}(\overline{T\ x}) & rhs ::= e!m(\bar{e}) \mid e \mid \mathsf{new}\ \mathsf{C}(\bar{e}) \\
\mathsf{x} \ ::= \mathsf{v} \mid \mathsf{this}.\mathtt{f} & \mathsf{g} \quad ::= e \mid e?
\end{array}
$$

Fig. 5. Syntax of the Async language

Compared to ABS, Async features optional **atom** annotations for atomic segments as discussed in Sect. 2. A *synchronize* annotation **sync** associates a label with each assignment which has a **get** right-hand side. We assume all names to be unique in a program.

3.2 Trace Semantics

We define a layered denotational semantics for Async, inspired by locally abstract globally concrete (LAGC) trace semantics [25]. The purpose of the *local* layer is to associate with each initial state and each Async statement a *set* of traces that record not only each possible evolution of computation states, but also synchronization events (call, suspension, future resolution, etc.). A set of traces is needed, because, locally, the value of, for example, a resolved future cannot be known. The global layer combines for a given program the local traces into all possible traces such that the involved events and states correspond to a permitted task interleaving in Async. Main advantages of this semantics include (a) a modular separation between sequential and concurrent execution and (b) close correspondence to the rules of the verification calculus for Async.

States and Traces. Let Object and Future denote the sets of possible object and future identifiers in the semantics, with values o and f, respectively. Let Var denote the set of program variables (fields, local variables), Val the set of expression values $\mathtt{v}$ in Async and State the states, i.e., the mappings from Var to Val. Traces combine states $\sigma \in$ State with the following events, which capture synchronization and communication between active objects:

$$ev(\bar{e}) ::= \mathsf{invEv}(o_1, o_2, f, \mathtt{m}, \bar{\mathtt{v}}) \qquad | \; \mathsf{invREv}(o_1, o_2, f, \mathtt{m}, \bar{\mathtt{v}})$$
$$| \; \mathsf{futEv}(o, f, \mathtt{m}, \mathtt{v}) \qquad | \; \mathsf{futREv}(o, f, \mathtt{v}, i)$$
$$| \; \mathsf{suspBoolEv}(o, f, \mathtt{m}, i) \quad | \; \mathsf{reacBoolEv}(o, f, \mathtt{m}, i)$$
$$| \; \mathsf{suspFutEv}(o, f, \mathtt{m}, f', i) \; | \; \mathsf{reacFutEv}(o, f, \mathtt{m}, f', i) \; \cdot$$
$$| \; \mathsf{blkEv}(o) \qquad | \; \mathsf{blkREv}(o)$$
$$| \; \mathsf{newEv}(o_1, o_2, C, \bar{\mathtt{v}})$$

Most events are organized as duals above, with one pair in each line. The event $\mathsf{invEv}(o_1, o_2, f, \mathtt{m}, \bar{\mathtt{v}})$ captures the asynchronous invocation of a method by an object o_1 to a method $\mathtt{m}$ of object o_2 with actual parameters $\bar{\mathtt{v}}$; the future f is the identifier of the future to which the return value from the method will be sent. The dual event $\mathsf{invREv}(o_1, o_2, f, \mathtt{m}, \bar{\mathtt{v}})$ represents the activation of the called method. The event $\mathsf{futEv}(o, f, \mathtt{m}, \mathtt{v})$ captures the resolution of the future with identifier f; here, o is the called object, $\mathtt{m}$ the called method and $\mathtt{v}$ the return value from the call which is passed to the future f. The dual event $\mathsf{futREv}(o, f, \mathtt{v}, i)$ represents the synchronization on this future by object o; note that i here captures the sync *annotation* on get-statements. The event $\mathsf{suspBoolEv}(o, f, \mathtt{m}, i)$ captures the suspension of the active method $\mathtt{m}$ identified by the future f in object o on a Boolean condition; i captures the atom *annotation* on await-statements. The dual event $\mathsf{reacBoolEv}(o, f, \mathtt{m}, i)$ represents the scheduling (or reactivation) of the method after suspension. Similarly, event $\mathsf{suspFutEv}(o, f, \mathtt{m}, f', i)$ captures suspension while waiting for a future f' to be resolved, with the dual event $\mathsf{reacFutEv}(o, f, \mathtt{m}, f', i)$. The event $\mathsf{newEv}(o_1, o_2, C, \bar{\mathtt{v}})$ captures the creation by an object o_1 of a new object o_2 of class C with actual parameters $\bar{\mathtt{v}}$.

The semantics ultimately maps programs into sets of traces over states and events, but in the local layer synchronization points are not yet resolved. For this reason, *local* traces may contain the symbol ⨟ which indicates points where interleaving or blocking can take place. Accordingly, we define another pair of events $\mathsf{blkEv}(o)$ and $\mathsf{blkREv}(o)$ to capture the blocking of an object o at a get-statement while *global* interleaving happens.

Definition 1 (Traces, Local Traces). *Let $\sigma \in$ State be a mapping from variables to values and $ev(\bar{e})$ be an event. A* trace τ *is defined by the following productions:*

$$\tau ::= \varepsilon \mid \tau \curvearrowright t$$
$$t ::= \sigma \mid ev(\bar{e})$$

A local trace π *is defined by the following production:*

$$\pi ::= \tau \mid \tau \mathbin{⨟} \pi$$

Here, ε denotes the empty trace. We only consider finite traces in this work. Let $\langle \sigma \rangle$ denote the *singleton trace* $\varepsilon \frown \sigma$. *Concatenation* of two traces τ_1, τ_2 is written as $\tau_1 \cdot \tau_2$ and only defined when τ_1 is finite. The final state of a non-empty, finite trace τ is obtained by $\mathrm{last}(\tau)$, and the first state of a non-empty trace τ is $\mathrm{first}(\tau)$; we lift these operations to local traces π in the obvious manner.

Since we use (local) traces to give a semantics to compound program statements, it is convenient to have an operator on (local) traces that reflects sequential composition. The technical issue it solves is as follows: Assume that τ_1 is a trace of a statement s_1 and τ_2 a trace of another statement s_2. To obtain the trace corresponding to the sequential composition of s_1, s_2, the last state of τ_1 and the first state of τ_2 must be identical, but the resulting trace should not contain a repeated state. This motivates the *semantic chop* operator $\ast\!\ast$ on local traces (inspired by [54]):

Definition 2 (Chop on Traces). *Let τ_1, τ_2 be non-empty traces, π_1, π_2 non-empty local traces and assume that τ_1, π, π_1 are finite. The semantic chop on traces is defined inductively as follows:*

$$\tau_1 \ast\!\ast \tau_2 = \tau_1 \cdot \tau' \text{ where } \mathrm{last}(\tau_1) = \sigma, \ \tau_2 = \langle \sigma \rangle \cdot \tau'$$
$$(\pi \mathbin{\mathring{,}} \tau_1) \ast\!\ast \tau_2 = \pi \mathbin{\mathring{,}} (\tau_1 \ast\!\ast \tau_2)$$
$$(\pi_1 \mathbin{\mathring{,}} \tau_1) \ast\!\ast (\tau_2 \mathbin{\mathring{,}} \pi_2) = ((\pi_1 \mathbin{\mathring{,}} \tau_1) \ast\!\ast \tau_2) \mathbin{\mathring{,}} \pi_2$$

Local Semantics. We define the semantics of methods bottom-up, starting with individual statements, by a validation function $\mathrm{val}_{\mathsf{X},\mathsf{m},f,\sigma}(s)$ that returns a set of the possible traces when executing a statement s on the current object X, where the future f is associated with the current instance of method m, starting in initial state σ. We assume that a standard valuation function $\mathrm{val}_{\mathsf{X},\mathsf{m},f,\sigma}(e)$ for side effect-free expressions e is given. Let the function $\widehat{C}(C, o, \overline{\mathsf{v}})$ return the initial state of an object o of class C with constructor parameters $\overline{\mathsf{v}}$, let $\widehat{M}(C, \mathsf{m}, \overline{\mathsf{v}})$ the initial local state of a method m of class C with actual parameters $\overline{\mathsf{v}}$, and $M(C, \mathsf{m})$ the body of a method m of class C.

The local trace semantics for statements is given in Fig. 6. The semantics of **skip** in state σ is the singleton trace $\langle \sigma \rangle$. An assignment results in a trace with two states where the latter updates σ with the new binding for the assigned variable. Conditionals and **while**-loops introduce two sets of local traces depending on whether the condition evaluates to true or false; here, only one of these sets can be non-empty.

Object creation introduces an event to reflect the creation of the new object and extends the state with the fields of the new object. We don't know the object identifier o in the local semantics, hence it ranges over Object. Asynchronous method calls introduce an event to reflect method invocation, where f' ranges over Future, and **return** introduces a future resolution event into the trace.

The trace corresponding to the **get**-statement introduces a future reaction event and assigns the return value v to the corresponding variable. Since the value v fetched from the future is unknown, the traces range over the possible value for v. Observe that the fields of the object and the local variables of the

$\mathrm{val}_{\mathsf{X},\mathsf{m},f,\sigma}(\mathsf{skip}) = \{\langle\sigma\rangle\}$

$\mathrm{val}_{\mathsf{X},\mathsf{m},f,\sigma}(x = e) = \{\langle\sigma\rangle \curvearrowright \sigma[x \mapsto \mathrm{val}_{\mathsf{X},\mathsf{m},f,\sigma}(e)]\}$

$\mathrm{val}_{\mathsf{X},\mathsf{m},f,\sigma}(\mathsf{if}\,(e)\,\{s_1\}\,\mathsf{else}\,\{s_2\})$
$\quad = \{\pi \in \mathrm{val}_{\mathsf{X},\mathsf{m},f,\sigma}(s_1) \mid \mathrm{val}_{\mathsf{X},\mathsf{m},f,\sigma}(e)\} \cup \{\pi \in \mathrm{val}_{\mathsf{X},\mathsf{m},f,\sigma}(s_2) \mid \neg\mathrm{val}_{\mathsf{X},\mathsf{m},f,\sigma}(e)\}$

$\mathrm{val}_{\mathsf{X},\mathsf{m},f,\sigma}(\mathsf{while}\,(e)\,\{s\})$
$\quad = \{\langle\sigma\rangle \mid \neg\mathrm{val}_{\mathsf{X},\mathsf{m},f,\sigma}(e)\} \cup \{\pi \in \mathrm{val}_{\mathsf{X},\mathsf{m},f,\sigma}(\bar{s}; \mathsf{while}\,(e)\,\{s\}) \mid \mathrm{val}_{\mathsf{X},\mathsf{m},f,\sigma}(e)\}$

$\mathrm{val}_{\mathsf{X},\mathsf{m},f,\sigma}(x = \mathsf{new}\,\mathsf{C}(\bar{e}))$
$\quad = \{\langle\sigma\rangle \curvearrowright \mathsf{newEv}(\mathsf{X}, o, C, \bar{v}') \curvearrowright \sigma \circ \widehat{C}(C, o, \bar{v}') \mid o \in \mathsf{Object} \wedge \bar{v}' = \mathrm{val}_{\mathsf{X},\mathsf{m},f,\sigma}(\bar{e})\}$

$\mathrm{val}_{\mathsf{X},\mathsf{m},f,\sigma}(x = e!\mathsf{m}(\bar{e}))$
$\quad = \{\langle\sigma\rangle \curvearrowright \mathsf{invEv}(\mathsf{X}, \mathrm{val}_{\mathsf{X},\mathsf{m},f,\sigma}(e), f', \mathsf{m}, \mathrm{val}_{\mathsf{X},\mathsf{m},f,\sigma}(\bar{e})) \curvearrowright \sigma[x \mapsto f'] \mid f' \in \mathsf{Future}\}$

$\mathrm{val}_{\mathsf{X},\mathsf{m},f,\sigma}(\mathsf{return}\,e) = \{\langle\sigma\rangle \curvearrowright \mathsf{futEv}(\mathsf{X}, f, \mathsf{m}, \mathrm{val}_{\mathsf{X},\mathsf{m},f,\sigma}(e)) \curvearrowright \sigma\}$

$\mathrm{val}_{\mathsf{X},\mathsf{m},f,\sigma}(\big[\mathsf{sync} : \text{``}i\text{''}\big]\,x = e.\mathsf{get})$
$\quad = \{\langle\sigma\rangle \curvearrowright \mathsf{blkEv}(\mathsf{X}) \curvearrowright \sigma \,\fatsemi$
$\quad\quad \langle\sigma'\rangle \curvearrowright \mathsf{blkREv}(\mathsf{X}) \curvearrowright \sigma' \curvearrowright \mathsf{futREv}(\mathsf{X}, \mathrm{val}_{\mathsf{X},\mathsf{m},f,\sigma'}(e), v, i) \curvearrowright \sigma'[x \mapsto v]$
$\quad\quad \mid v \in \mathsf{Val} \wedge \sigma' \in \mathsf{State} \wedge \forall \mathsf{X}.x \cdot \sigma(\mathsf{X}.x) = \sigma'(\mathsf{X}.x) \wedge \forall f.x \cdot \sigma(f.x) = \sigma'(f.x)\}$

$\mathrm{val}_{\mathsf{X},\mathsf{m},f,\sigma}(\big[\mathsf{atom} : \text{``}i\text{''}\big]\,\mathsf{await}\,e)$
$\quad = \{\langle\sigma\rangle \curvearrowright \mathsf{suspBoolEv}(\mathsf{X}, f, \mathsf{m}, i) \curvearrowright \sigma \,\fatsemi\, \langle\sigma'\rangle \curvearrowright \mathsf{reacBoolEv}(\mathsf{X}, f, \mathsf{m}, i) \curvearrowright \sigma'$
$\quad\quad \mid \sigma' \in \mathsf{State} \wedge \forall f.x \cdot \sigma(f.x) = \sigma'(f.x) \wedge \mathrm{val}_{\mathsf{X},\mathsf{m},f,\sigma'}(e)\}$

$\mathrm{val}_{\mathsf{X},\mathsf{m},f,\sigma}(\big[\mathsf{atom} : \text{``}i\text{''}\big]\,\mathsf{await}\,e?)$
$\quad = \{\langle\sigma\rangle \curvearrowright \mathsf{suspFutEv}(\mathsf{X}, f, \mathsf{m}, f', i) \curvearrowright \sigma \,\fatsemi\, \langle\sigma'\rangle \curvearrowright \mathsf{reacFutEv}(\mathsf{X}, f, \mathsf{m}, f', i) \curvearrowright \sigma'$
$\quad\quad \mid \sigma' \in \mathsf{State} \wedge \forall f.x \cdot \sigma(f.x) = \sigma'(f.x) \wedge f' = \mathrm{val}_{\mathsf{X},\mathsf{m},f,\sigma}(e)\}$

$\mathrm{val}_{\mathsf{X},\mathsf{m},f,\sigma}(C.\mathsf{m})$
$\quad = \{(\langle\sigma\rangle \curvearrowright \mathsf{invREv}(\mathsf{X}', \mathsf{X}, f, \mathsf{m}, \bar{v}) \curvearrowright \sigma) \ast\!\ast\, \pi$
$\quad\quad \mid \mathsf{X}' \in \mathsf{Object} \wedge \bar{v} \in \overline{\mathsf{Val}} \wedge \pi \in \mathrm{val}_{\mathsf{X},\mathsf{m},f,\sigma\circ\widehat{M}(\mathsf{m},f,\bar{v})}(M(C,\mathsf{m}))\}$

$\mathrm{val}_{\mathsf{X},\mathsf{m},f,\sigma}(s_1; s_2) = \{\pi_1 \ast\!\ast\, \pi_2 \mid \pi_1 \in \mathrm{val}_{\mathsf{X},\mathsf{m},f,\sigma}(s_1) \wedge \pi_2 \in \mathrm{val}_{\mathsf{X},\mathsf{m},f,\mathrm{last}(\pi_1)}(s_2)\}$

Fig. 6. Local trace semantics for Async.

method are unchanged when the statement is executed but that the state may otherwise change, reflecting that **get** is blocking on the object until it can execute, but other objects may execute in the meantime. We use $o.x$ to denote a field x of object o and likewise $f.x$ to denote a local variable of the method identified by the future f. In the semantics of the **await** e statement, the local traces are split between the suspension and reactivation events, with the corresponding state change to $\sigma' \in \mathsf{State}$; here, local variables are unchanged between these events, reflecting that the process is suspended. The condition $\mathrm{val}_{\mathsf{X},\mathsf{m},f,\sigma'}(e)$ expresses that the guard must hold in state σ' for the process to be rescheduled. The **await** $e?$ statement has a similar semantics, but the condition for reactivating the process will be captured in the well-formedness condition on traces.

The semantics of a method m of class C is given by an invocation reaction event for that method, composed with the semantics of its method body (in the state extended with the local variables). The calling object X' cannot be known and ranges over Object. Sequential composition is directly captured by the semantic chop operator.

Initial Configuration and Global Semantics. For a given program Pr in Async with main block $\{T_1 \; x_1 = e_2, \ldots, T_n \; x_n = e_n; s\}$, let $classes(Pr)$ denote the set of class names in Pr, $methods(C)$ the set of method names declared in class C and $\sigma_{main} \in$ State a mapping from the program variables $x_1, \ldots, x_n$ to some concrete (default) values of the corresponding types $T_1, \ldots, T_n$. For a future $f \in$ Future, define the possible local traces of a program Pr to compute f by the following set:

$$traces(f, Pr) = \{\pi \mid \pi \in val_{o,m,f,\sigma}(C.m) \wedge o \in \text{Object} \wedge \sigma \in \text{State}$$
$$\wedge \; C \in classes(Pr) \wedge m \in methods(C)\}$$

Let $\mathcal{T}$ denote a set of sets of local traces. One such set is the set of all possible local trace sets for any future for a program Pr, defined by

$$\mathcal{T}_{Pr} = \{traces(f, Pr) \mid f \in \text{Future}\}$$
$$\cup \{val_{o_{main}, m_{main}, f_{main}, \sigma_{main}}(x_1 = e_1; \ldots; x_n = e_n; s)\} \; .$$

The *initial configuration* of a program Pr is defined as the pair $\langle \sigma_{main} \rangle, \mathcal{T}_{Pr}$.

Let sh denote a *global trace*, i.e. a trace without synchronization markers "$\S$". Global traces are produced by a transition system on configurations $sh, \mathcal{T}$ by means of the following rule:

$$(\text{GLOBAL}) \quad \frac{\tau \S \pi \in \Omega \qquad \Omega \in \mathcal{T} \qquad last(sh) = first(\tau)}{sh, \mathcal{T} \to sh \underline{**} \tau, \mathcal{T}'} \quad \frac{wf(sh \underline{**} \tau) \qquad \Omega' = \{\pi' \mid \tau \S \pi' \in \Omega\} \qquad \mathcal{T}' = (\mathcal{T} \setminus \Omega) \cup \Omega'}{}$$

The intuition behind rule (GLOBAL) is that only a local trace that happens to match the last state of the global trace sh can be selected to extend sh. The selection applies to the first segment of the local trace, after which all possible successor segments from $traces(f, Pr)$ are kept and all other possibilities for f are rejected in $\mathcal{T}'$. Whereas trace semantics for active objects which take a *local* perspective [5,24] require the composition rule to enforce that local variables remain invariant over processor release points, our work takes a *global* perspective by letting the local trace sets range over all possible states. As a consequence, trace composition in (GLOBAL) can be captured directly by the semantic chop operator, which matches the states when composing two traces.

In addition to this matching on states, only those local traces can be selected that conform to the well-formedness predicate $wf(sh \underline{**} \tau)$ over traces. Well-formedness imposes constraints on the ordering of events, expressing legal scheduling and synchronization during execution. For a global trace sh, let

Objects(*sh*) and *Futures*(*sh*) denote the sets of objects and futures that are introduced by the events reflecting object creation and asynchronous method calls in the semantics (including o_{main} and f_{main}). Let $sh|_f$ denote the projection of *sh* to the trace of events involving the process with future f. Let $sh|_o$ denote the projection of *sh* to the trace of events of object o and sh *ew* *ev* that *ev* is the final event occurring in *sh* ("ends with"). These functions all have straightforward inductive definitions. The well-formedness predicate $wf(sh)$ itself is defined inductively in Fig. 7. We abbreviate existentially quantified variables whose value is irrelevant with "_". One can assume a trace to end with an event, because the states after the last event in a trace do not affect well-formedness.

$wf(\sigma_{main}) = true$

$wf(sh \frown \mathsf{invEv}(o_1, o_2, f, \mathtt{m}, \bar{e})) = \{o_1, o_2\} \subseteq Objects(sh) \wedge f \notin Futures(sh) \wedge wf(sh)$

$wf(sh \frown \mathsf{invREv}(o_1, o_2, f, \mathtt{m}, \bar{e})) = sh|_f\ ew\ \mathsf{invEv}(o_1, o_2, f, \mathtt{m}, \bar{e}) \wedge wf(sh)$

$wf(sh \frown \mathsf{futEv}(o_2, f, \mathtt{m}, e)) = \mathsf{invREv}(\_, o_2, f, \mathtt{m}, \_) \in sh$
　　$\wedge\ \mathsf{futEv}(o_2, f, \mathtt{m}, \_) \notin sh \wedge wf(sh)$

$wf(sh \frown \mathsf{futREv}(\_, f, e, \_)) = \mathsf{futEv}(\_, f, \_, e) \in sh \wedge wf(sh)$

$wf(sh \frown \mathsf{suspBoolEv}(o_2, f, \mathtt{m}, i)) = sh|_f\ ew\ ev$
　　$\wedge\ ev \in \{\mathsf{invREv}(\_, o_2, f, \mathtt{m}, \_), \mathsf{reacBoolEv}(o_2, f, \mathtt{m}, \_), \mathsf{reacFutEv}(o_2, f, \mathtt{m}, \_, \_)\}$
　　$\wedge\ wf(sh)$

$wf(sh \frown \mathsf{reacBoolEv}(o, f, \mathtt{m}, i)) = sh|_f\ ew\ \mathsf{suspBoolEv}(o, f, \mathtt{m}, i) \wedge wf(sh)$

$wf(sh \frown \mathsf{suspFutEv}(o_2, f, \mathtt{m}, f', i)) = sh|_f\ ew\ ev$
　　$\wedge\ ev \in \{\mathsf{invREv}(\_, o_2, f, \mathtt{m}, \_), \mathsf{reacBoolEv}(o_2, f, \mathtt{m}, \_), \mathsf{reacFutEv}(o_2, f, \mathtt{m}, \_, \_)\}$
　　$\wedge\ wf(sh)$

$wf(sh \frown \mathsf{reacFutEv}(o_2, f, \mathtt{m}, f', i)) =$
　　$\mathsf{futEv}(\_, f', \_, \_) \in sh \wedge sh|_f\ ew\ \mathsf{suspFutEv}(o_2, f, \mathtt{m}, f', i) \wedge wf(sh)$

$wf(sh \frown \mathsf{blkREv}(o)) = sh|_o\ ew\ \mathsf{blkEv}(o) \wedge wf(sh)$

$wf(sh \frown \mathsf{newEv}(o_1, o_2, C, \bar{x}, \bar{e})) = o_1 \in Objects(sh) \wedge o_2 \notin Objects(sh) \wedge wf(sh)$

Fig. 7. Well-formedness predicate over traces

It is easy to see that the well-formedness predicate enforces that only the main block can be selected initially, as all other local traces are excluded by the well-formedness condition, that methods can only start after they have been called, that suspension events can only occur on executing processes, etc.

3.3   Semantic Logic

In the following, we aim to state and prove properties about all possible local traces of a method or a statement in a method. To formalize this, it is convenient to allow some reflection of the trace semantics into a logical language. We call this a *semantic* logic, its models are traces. In such a logic it is natural to relate indices in traces to states and events. The construct to relate traces and states has the form $[k] \vdash \varphi$, where k is an index term, denoting the k-th element of the trace that is the current model, and φ is a first-order formula over *states*. Here "$\vdash$" is a symbol of the logic. The meaning is that in the k-th state of a model trace the predicate φ holds. Similarly, traces and events are related by $[k] \doteq t$ which says that the k-th element of the model trace is equal to the event modeled by term t.

Example 7. The following formula in semantic logic expresses that there is a future resolve event that returns Unit and in the preceding state the field fl was positive. The type **I** models trace indices, Method is the set of all method names.

$$\exists\, k \in \mathbf{I}.\ \exists\, \mathtt{m} \in \mathtt{Method}.\ \exists\, o \in \mathtt{Object}.\ \exists\, f \in \mathtt{Future}.$$
$$[k] \doteq \mathsf{futEv}(o, f, \mathtt{m}, \mathtt{Unit}) \wedge [k - 1] \vdash \mathtt{this.fl} > 0$$

The formal definition of semantic logic is straightforward, for a full treatment, we refer to [43]. Given a statement s, we assume from now on to implicitly know the method that contains it, the object it is executed on and the future is resolves. Thus we abstract the evaluation function $\mathsf{val}_{\mathsf{X},\mathsf{m},f,\sigma}(s)$ defined Sect. 3.2 and write $[\![s]\!]_\sigma$ for the set of all local traces starting in σ.

4 Behavioral Program Logic

We state the verification system as behavioral contracts in Behavioral Program Logic (BPL) [42]. This simplifies the calculus compared to [47], as well as interaction with external static analyses.

BPL is a first-order dynamic logic with a *state*-based semantics: Its models are single states inside a Kripke structure, as in standard dynamic logics such as JavaDL [14]. Nonetheless BPL allows to verify *trace* properties of statements. To enable this, the representation and semantics of trace properties are separated and encapsulated in *behavioral modalities*. A behavioral modality can either be handled by a validity calculus, ensuring that every trace of a given statement follows the specification, or it can be passed to an external analysis. Hence, a BPL *behavioral specification* consists of at least two elements: syntax and semantics. If it also has a validity calculus and an obligation schema that assigns proof obligations to methods, then it is a *behavioral type*. We first define behavioral specifications. The semantics of terms in the *behavioral language* θ maps elements of the language into formulas of the semantic logic defined Sect. 3.3. We call elements of the behavioral language *behavioral words*.

Definition 3 (Behavioral Specification). *A behavioral specification* $\mathbb{T}$ *is a pair* $(\theta_\mathbb{T}, \alpha_\mathbb{T})$, *where* $\theta_\mathbb{T}$ *is a non-empty behavioral language and* $\alpha_\mathbb{T}$ *maps elements of* $\theta_\mathbb{T}$ *into formulas of semantic logic.*

It is straightforward to define, for example, postconditions as behavioral specifications, because they are already a trace property, where only the final element of a trace is relevant, but we aim for more complex properties, for example:

Example 8 (Points-To Behavioral Specification). The behavioral specification of a *points-to (p2) analysis* specifies that the next statement reads a future resolved by a method from a set M. The constant $\mathbf{1}$ refers to the index of the first event.

$$\mathbb{T}_{p2} = (\mathcal{P}(\mathsf{M}), p2) \text{ with}$$

$$p2(M) = \exists \mathsf{X} \in \mathtt{Object}. \ \exists f \in \mathtt{Future}. \ \exists \mathtt{m} \in \mathtt{Method}. \ \exists v \in \mathtt{Val}. \ \exists i \in \mathbb{N}.$$

$$\left([\mathbf{1}] \doteq \mathsf{futREv}(\mathsf{X}, f, \mathtt{m}, v, i) \wedge \bigvee_{\mathtt{m}' \in M} \mathtt{m} \doteq \mathtt{m}'\right)$$

Intuitively, a behavioral language is a representation of a fragment of semantic logic. Such fragments are embedded into BPL with behavioral modalities of the form $[\mathsf{s} \Vdash^{\alpha_\mathsf{T}} \theta_\mathsf{T}]$. Following JavaDL, BPL uses *updates* [13] to keep track of state changes.

Definition 4 (Syntax of BPL). *Let prd range over predicate symbols, fct over function symbols, x over first-order variable names and S over sorts. As sorts we take all data types* D*, all interfaces, all class names and additionally* $\mathtt{Field}$*,* $\mathtt{Future}$*,* $\mathtt{Val}$*, and* $\mathtt{Object}$*. Formulas φ, updates U and terms t are defined by the following grammar, where $\mathtt{v}$ ranges over program variables, consisting of local variables and the special variables* $\mathtt{heap}$*,* $\mathtt{heapOld}$*,* $\mathtt{heapLast}$ *and* $\mathtt{result}$*. Let* $\mathtt{fl}$ *range over all field names and* $\mathtt{eh}$ *range over expressions without direct field access, but with the extra program variable* $\mathtt{heap}$*. Let s range over statements and* $(\theta_\mathsf{T}, \alpha_\mathsf{T})$ *over behavioral specifications.*

$$\varphi ::= prd(\bar{t}) \mid t \doteq t \mid \varphi \vee \varphi \mid \neg \varphi \mid \exists x \in S. \ \varphi \mid [\mathsf{s} \Vdash^{\alpha_\mathsf{T}} \theta_\mathsf{T}] \mid \{U\}\varphi$$

$$t ::= x \mid \mathtt{v} \mid \mathtt{fl} \mid fct(\bar{t}) \mid \mathtt{eh} \mid \mathtt{if} \ \varphi \ \mathtt{then} \ t \ \mathtt{else} \ t \mid \{U\}t$$

$$U ::= \epsilon \mid U \| U \mid \{U\}U \mid \mathtt{v} := t$$

A behavioral modality says that all traces of s starting in the current state are models of $\alpha_\mathsf{T}(\theta_\mathsf{T})$. An update describes a specific state change. Updates are *delayed substitutions*: During the proof procedure, the state changes of the statement in question (inside a behavioral modality) are accumulated in updates and simplified. The resulting substitution is then applied *once per proof path* on the modality-free verification conditions resulting from the behavioral modality.

Example 9. The following BPL formula expresses that the **get** statement reads from a future that is resolved by $\mathtt{Producer.detectNews()}$ (see Example 4).

$$\left[\mathtt{ns = fut.get} \Vdash^{p2} \{\mathtt{Producer.detectNews}\}\right]$$

Definition 5 (Semantics of BPL). *Let I be a first-order model, i.e. a mapping from function names to functions and from predicate names to predicates. Let β be a variable assignment from first-order variables to semantic values.*

- *The evaluation of terms in a state σ is a function $[\![t]\!]_{\sigma,\beta,I}$ that maps terms to domain elements.*
- *The evaluation of updates in a state σ is a function $[\![U]\!]_{\sigma,\beta,I}$ that maps updates to functions from states to states.*
- *The evaluation of formulas in a state σ is given as a satisfiability relation $\sigma, \beta, I \models \varphi$.*

Semantic evaluation is standard as in first-order logic, except for updates and behavioral modalities which are given in Fig. 8.

$$[\![\mathtt{v} := \mathtt{t}]\!]_{\sigma,\beta,I}\left(\sigma'\right) := \sigma'[\mathtt{v} \mapsto [\![\mathtt{t}]\!]_{\sigma,\beta,I}]$$

$$[\![\epsilon]\!]_{\sigma,\beta,I}(x) := x \qquad [\![U_1||U_2]\!]_{\sigma,\beta,I}(x) := [\![U_2]\!]_{\sigma,\beta,I}\left([\![U_1]\!]_{\sigma,\beta,I}(x)\right)$$

$$[\![\{U_1\}U_2]\!]_{\sigma,\beta,I} := [\![U_2]\!]_{[\![U_1]\!]_{\sigma,\beta,I}\beta,I} \qquad [\![\{U\}t]\!]_{\sigma,\beta,I} := [\![t]\!]_{[\![U]\!]_{\sigma,\beta,I},\beta,I}$$

$$\sigma, \beta, I \models \{U\}\varphi \iff [\![U]\!]_{\sigma,\beta,I}, \beta, I \models \varphi$$

$$\sigma, \beta, I \models [\mathtt{s} \overset{\alpha_{\mathsf{T}}}{\Vdash} \theta_{\mathsf{T}}] \iff \forall \theta \in [\![\mathtt{s}]\!]_{\sigma} . \, \theta, \beta, I \models \alpha_{\mathsf{T}}(\theta_{\mathsf{T}})$$

Fig. 8. Semantics of updates and behavioral modalities.

We only consider models I that map each function symbol to its natural semantics. For example, heap functions and the `heap` program variable are mapped to the theory of arrays extended for objects [58]. Central is the following connection axiom, for all heaps h, fields `fl`, and terms `t`:

$$I(\mathsf{select})\left(I(\mathsf{store})(h, \mathtt{fl}, \mathtt{t}), \mathtt{fl}\right) = \mathtt{t}$$

For the full axiomatization we refer to Beckert et al. [14]. We further assume that all first-order variables are unique (no overloading) and that the type and number of parameters for functions and predicates is well-formed. We use common abbreviations such as $\forall x \in S. \, \varphi$ for $\neg \exists x \in S. \, \neg\varphi$. We shorten comparison expressions for terms of `Bool` type by writing, e.g., `i > j` instead of $\mathtt{i} > \mathtt{j} \doteq \mathtt{True}$ and we render `select(heap, f)` as `this.f`. We use a sequent calculus to reason about validity of BPL-formulas.

Definition 6 (Sequent). *Let Γ, Δ be finite sets of BPL-formulas. A sequent $\Gamma \Rightarrow \Delta$ has the semantics $\bigwedge \Gamma \rightarrow \bigvee \Delta$. Γ is called the antecedent and Δ the succedent. A sequent $\{\gamma_1, \ldots, \gamma_n\} \Rightarrow \{\delta_1, \ldots, \delta_m\}$ is also written $\gamma_1, \ldots, \gamma_n \Rightarrow \delta_1, \ldots, \delta_m$.*

Definition 7 (Rules). *Let C, P_i be sequents. A rule has the form*

$$\textit{(name)} \; \frac{P_1 \quad \cdots \quad P_n}{C} \; cond$$

Where C *is called the conclusion and* P_i *premises, while "cond" is a decidable side condition. Rules with zero premises are admissible and called* axiom.

Definition 8 (Validity, Soundness, Calculus). *A BPL formula is* valid *if it is satisfied for all states* σ, *all variable assignments* β *and all models* I *(fixed as above). A rule is* sound *if validity of all premises implies validity of the conclusion. A* calculus *is a set of sound sequent rules.*

A behavioral type is a behavioral specification extended with (i) a proof obligation schema mapping every method in a given program to a behavioral word (its specification) and (ii) a set of sound validity rules for behavioral modalities containing the extended behavioral specification.

Definition 9 (Behavioral Type). *Let* $\mathbb{T} = (\theta_\mathbb{T}, \alpha_\mathbb{T})$ *be a behavioral specification. A behavioral type extending* $\mathbb{T}$ *is a quadruple* $(\theta_\mathbb{T}, \alpha_\mathbb{T}, \iota_\mathbb{T}, \kappa_\mathbb{T})$. *The calculus* $\kappa_\mathbb{T}$ *consists of rules over* $\theta_\mathbb{T}$ *(i.e. the conclusion must contain a behavioral modality with a behavioral word from* $\theta_\mathbb{T}$). *The obligation schema* $\iota_\mathbb{T}$ *is a map from method names* m *to pairs* $(\varphi, \theta_\mathbb{T}^m)$, *where* φ *is a first-order formula that may only contain field and local variables accessible by* m.

Not every behavioral specification needs to be extended to a behavioral type, for example, $\mathbb{T}_{p2}$ serves as an interface to an external analysis. To evaluate the formula in Example 9, the modalities can be compared against the result of a pointer analysis for futures [30]. For examples of other BPL behavioral types and a discussion on the notion of "Behavioral Type" we refer to [42].

5   Cooperative Contracts in BPL

We formulate cooperative contracts as a behavioral type in BPL, called *behavioral contract*[4]. We also define the extraction of annotated specifications to behavioral contracts and formulate the propagation of specifications described in Sect. 2.3 in terms of behavioral contracts.

Context sets are not part of behavioral contracts, but can be expressed analogously as (global) trace properties.

Compared to our previous account [47], the use of BPL vastly simplifies the verification system: First, the propagation does not require an additional intermediate representation. Second, the validity calculus operates directly on behavioral contracts and not on an *encoding* of contracts in postconditions and dedicated rules. In contrast to postcondition-based approaches [23], the calculus also does not have implicit parameters, such as call conditions.

In addition to the specification elements introduced in previous sections, we use class preconditions, which are essentially preconditions on the fields passed to the constructor.

---

[4] Due to their nature as contracts and behavioral types, not due to a relation to behavioral contracts as a subset of behavioral types as in [38].

Example 10. The following specifies that class C is initialized with a positive value for param.

```
/*@ requires this.param > 0; @*/
class C(Int param) { ... }
```

5.1   Cooperative Contracts as Behavioral Specifications

We first define suspension and resolve specifications. A suspension specification follows the structure of a suspension contract (without context sets) and consists of the frame, suspension assumption and suspension guarantee. Similarly, a resolve specification is a pair of the expected guarantee and the set of responsible methods.

Definition 10 (Suspension, Resolve Specification). *A suspension specification* Susp *is a triple* (W, ens, req), *where* $W \subseteq$ Field *is a set of fields and* $ens, req \in$ FOL *are FOL formulas. A resolve specification* Res $\in \mathcal{P}(M) \times$ FOL *is a pair* $(mtds, cond)$ *of a set of method names and a FOL formula.*

Example 11. The suspension specification for notifyClients in Example 5 is shown below, with the prettified syntax for heap access.

$$
\begin{aligned}
&\big(W = \emptyset, \\
&ens = \text{ns} \neq \text{null} \land \text{len}(\text{this.myClients}) \leq \text{this.limit} \\
&req = \text{this.service} \doteq \text{null}\big)
\end{aligned}
$$

A behavioral contract itself mirrors the structure of the cooperative contract for a method. To identify specific statements inside a method, we use program point identifiers (PPI), a generalization of the annotated names. The PPI for **await** and **get** statements is their name annotation, recorded as i in Sect. 3.2, the PPI for **return** statements is implicit and not exposed.

Definition 11 (Syntax for Behavioral Contracts). *The behavioral language* met *for contracts is a tuple* $(W, post)_{S,C}$ *with the following components:*

$S : $ PPI $\mapsto$ (Susp $\cup$ Res $\cup$ FOL)	*Program Point Specifications*
$C : $ Classes $\cup$ Methods $\mapsto$ FOL	*Call Conditions*
$W \subseteq$ Field	*Assignable fields*
$post \in$ FOL	*Postcondition*

A program-point specification S maps (i) every PPI of a suspension to a suspension specification, (ii) every PPI of a reading statement to a resolve contract, (iii) every PPI of a terminating statement to a method postcondition. Call conditions C map method names to the call precondition of the called method and class names to the class precondition.

The pair (S, C) does not change during symbolic execution: with top-down contract generation it can be seen as a lookup table for global properties. The set

W is the currently active dynamic frame. Finally, *post* is the current statement postcondition. It is *not* necessarily the postcondition of the method, but used to establish postconditions of arbitrary statements *not ending in suspension or termination*. This is needed to express loop invariants.

We say $(W, post)$ is the *active* part of the contract and $(\mathbb{S}, \mathbb{C})$ the *passive* part: The active part must be adhered to by the *currently active* statement, while the passive part serves as a specification repository for program points encountered during symbolic execution.

Example 12. Consider the following behavioral modality

$$\left[\mathsf{this.f \; = \; this.g+1; \; [atom: \; "a"] \; await \; this.f \; > \; 0; \; s; } \; \Vdash^{\mathsf{met}} \left(\{\mathsf{f}\}, \mathsf{this.g} \doteq 1\right)_{\mathbb{S},\mathbb{C}}\right]$$

The behavioral contract expresses that before the next suspension (or termination), only writes to f are allowed. The formula $\mathsf{this.g} \doteq 1$ is the statement postcondition. It does *not* need to hold at the suspension point.

5.2   Extraction and Propagation

Given a specified program P, the verification workflow consists of the following steps:

1. For each method a specification triple is extracted. Such a triple contains heap and parameter preconditions, as well as behavioral contracts. Context sets are recorded globally.
2. The behavioral contracts are propagated according to the context sets and the context sets are passed to external analyses to check whether the program adheres to them.
3. Each methods of the program is verified against its propagated behavioral contract.

Specification Extraction. All abbreviations (such as **await** $\mathsf{o!m()}$) are expanded before extraction. Syntactically, the formulas in the specification are an extension of the first-order fragment of BPL that only uses **heap** and the local variables as program variables. These may contain functions $old(\cdot)$, $last(\cdot)$ that allow its argument (either a term or a formula) to be evaluated in the heap at the prestate of the current method call and at the most recent suspension, respectively. These constructs are removed by substitutions

$$\varphi[\mathsf{heap} \setminus \mathsf{heapOld}] \text{ and } \varphi[\mathsf{heap} \setminus \mathsf{heapLast}]$$

that replace occurrences of **heap** in the argument of $old(\cdot)$, $last(\cdot)$ with ghost variables.

Given a program P, we define the extracted *passive* specification $\mathbb{S}^P, \mathbb{C}^P$:

$$\mathbb{C}^P(\text{I.m}) = \textit{requires clause of m in interface I}$$

$$\mathbb{C}^P(\text{c}) = \textit{requires clause of class c}$$

$$\mathbb{S}^P(\text{p}) = \begin{cases} \text{res(p)} & \text{if p is the PPI of a } \textbf{get} \text{ statement} \\ \text{susp(p)} & \text{if p is the PPI of a } \textbf{await} \text{ statement} \\ \text{term(p)} & \text{if p is the PPI of a } \textbf{return} \text{ statement} \end{cases}$$

For brevity, write $\mathbb{S}^W(\text{p})$ for the W component of $\mathbb{S}(\text{p})$ (if defined) and similar for the other possible components and $\mathbb{C}$. The postcondition of a return statement with PPI p is accessed simply with $\mathbb{S}(\text{p})$. The functions res, susp and term are generated as follows. For a resolve contract (the read statement possibly prefixed by an assignment) of the form

```
/*@ resolvedBy M; @*/
[atom: "name"] e.get;
```

we extract the resolve specification $\text{res(name)} = (M, \text{true})$. If no resolve contract is given, M defaults to set of all method names.

Given a suspense contract, where A_1, A_2 are sets of method and atomic segment names,

```
/*@ ensures  ens;
    requires req;
    succeeds A₁;
    overlaps A₂;
    assignable W; @*/
[sync: "name"] await g;
```

we extract the suspension specification. $\text{susp(name)} = (W, \textit{ens}, \textit{req})$. The default for state clauses is true, the default for context sets is the set of all method names and atomic block names in the class containing the specified statement, the default for the frame is the set of all fields of the class containing the statement.

Given a **return** statement with PPI p, we set its specification term(p) to the conjunction of the *ensures* clauses of (i) the contract annotated to the containing method implementation in the class and (ii) the contract annotated to the method signature declared in an interface (if such a declaration exists and true otherwise). The following is the specification of a method C.m with contracts in its class and interface I:

```
interface I {                       class C implements I {
  /*@ requires preparam;              /*@ requires preheap;
      ensures postparam;                  ensures postheap;
      succeeds A₁;                        assignable W; @*/
      overlaps A₂; @*/                  T m(...) {...}
    T m(...);                       }
}
```

The overall behavioral contract is the following triple, where the default of formulas is true and the default for sets is the set of all names (fields):

$$\left(\textit{pre}^{\text{heap}}, \textit{pre}^{\text{param}}, (W, \text{true})_{\mathbb{S}^P, \mathbb{C}^P} \right)$$

In addition to the behavioral contract we also extract a global specification:

Definition 12 (Extraction of Global Specification). *From a program* P *we extract the* global specification G *that maps each atomic segment name and each method name to a pair of sets of atomic segment and method names. Each method name is mapped to the context set pair of its method contract and each atomic segment name is mapped to the context set pair of its suspension contract. For a name a we denote the first element of such a pair with* $G^{\mathsf{Succ}}(a)$ *and the second with* $G^{\mathsf{Over}}(a)$.

Specification Propagation. Propagation uses the global specification to propagate heap preconditions. It is, however, *frame-aware*: if the propagated formula cannot possibly change its evaluation during executing an atomic segment, because it does not share any fields with the assignable clause, then the atomic segment needs not prove that it preserves the formula. It is ignored in the *overlaps* specification for propagation. It must, however, be taken into account when it is part of the *succeeds* set.

Definition 13 (Propagated Specification). *Let* P *be a program,* C, S *the passive specification of the extracted behavioral contracts,* G *the extracted global specification. The* propagated passive specification C, S_{prop} *is generated as follows. Let a be any atomic segment name.*

– *For each* $m \in G^{\mathsf{Succ}}(m')$, *let* p *be the PPI of the* **return** *statement of* m *and* ψ *the heap precondition of* m'. *Then set* $S_{\mathsf{prop}}(p) = S(p) \wedge \psi$.
– *For each* $m \in G^{\mathsf{Succ}}(a)$, *let* p *be the PPI of the* **return** *statement of* m *and* ψ *the* requires *clause of* $S(a)$. *Then set* $S_{\mathsf{prop}}(p) = S(p) \wedge \psi$.
– *For each* $m \in G^{\mathsf{Over}}(m')$, *let* p *be the PPI of the* **return** *statement of* m, W *its* assignable *set and* ψ *the postcondition of* m', *if* $\mathsf{fields}(\psi) \cap W \neq \emptyset$, *we set*

$$S_{\mathsf{prop}}(p) = S(p) \wedge ((\{\mathtt{heap} := \mathtt{oldHeap}\}\psi) \to \psi)$$

– *For each* $m \in G^{\mathsf{Over}}(a)$, *let* p *be the PPI of the* **return** *statement of* m, W *its* assignable *set and* ψ *the postcondition of* $S(a)$, *if* $\mathsf{fields}(\psi) \cap W \neq \emptyset$, *we set*

$$S_{\mathsf{prop}}(p) = S(p) \wedge ((\{\mathtt{heap} := \mathtt{oldHeap}\}\psi) \to \psi)$$

– *Analogously for atomic segment names* $a' \in G^{\mathsf{Over}}(a)$ *and* $a' \in G^{\mathsf{Over}}(m')$, *where the* ensures *clause instead of the postcondition is manipulated.*

This construction is applied recursively for all atomic segment and method names. Afterwards, the postconditions of the interface contract are made available in the resolve contracts. Let $\mathtt{r_{C.m}}$ be the PPI of the **return** statement of C.m and $S_{\mathsf{prop}}^{\mathsf{param}}(\mathtt{r_{C.m}})$ its conjunct from the interface contract. Then set

$$S_{\mathsf{prop}}^{cond}(p) = \bigvee_{\substack{\mathtt{r_{C.m}} \\ \text{C.m } implements \text{ } m \in S^{mtds}(p)}} S_{\mathsf{prop}}^{\mathsf{param}}(\mathtt{r_{C.m}}) \ .$$

5.3   Semantics of Behavioral Contracts

We require a few auxiliary definitions to locate events in traces. For each event type ev, for example, futEv, there is a predicate $\mathsf{isEv}(i)$ that holds iff the i-th element of the current trace is an event of type ev. Also predicate $\mathsf{isInvEv}(i, \mathsf{m})$ holds iff the i-th element of the current trace is an invEv on method m, and analogously for isNewEv. Similar definitions include predicate $\mathsf{isSuspEv}(i)$ that holds iff the i-th element of the current trace is an SuspBoolEv or SuspFutEv; predicate $\mathsf{isSuspEv}(i, \mathsf{p})$ holds iff the i-th element of the current trace is an SuspBoolEv or SuspFutEv at PPI p; predicate $\mathsf{isInvEvW}(i, \mathsf{m}, \mathsf{e})$ holds iff the i-th element of the current trace is an invEv on method m with value e, and analogously for isNewEvW, isFutEvW and isFutREvW.

Given a specification φ with parameters (for example, method parameters), write $\varphi(\bar{\mathsf{e}})$ for the substitution of the parameters with the corresponding terms from $\bar{\mathsf{e}}$. Given a field f, we denote the declared type of its values with T_{f}. Predicate $\mathsf{isLast}(i, j)$ holds iff j is either the final state of the current trace after i or the state before the first suspension event after i:

$$\mathsf{isLast}(i, j) \equiv j > i \wedge$$
$$\left(\left(\mathsf{isSuspEv}(j+1) \wedge \forall k \in \mathbf{I}. \; (i < k < j \rightarrow \neg\mathsf{isSuspEv}(k)) \right) \vee \right.$$
$$\left. \left(\forall k \in \mathbf{I}. \; k \leq j \wedge (i < k < j \rightarrow \neg\mathsf{isSuspEv}(k)) \right) \right)$$

Definition 14 (Semantics of Behavioral Contracts). *The semantics α of a frame W starting at trace position $i \in \mathbf{I}$ is that the trace has the same value in all fields not in W at the subsequent suspension event (or final state, if the trace has no suspension):*

$$\alpha(\mathsf{W}, i) =$$
$$\exists j \in \mathbf{I}. \; \mathsf{isLast}(i, j) \wedge \bigwedge_{\mathsf{f} \notin \mathsf{W}} \exists t_{\mathsf{f}} \in T_{\mathsf{f}}. \; \left(([i] \vdash \mathsf{this.f} \doteq t_{\mathsf{f}}) \wedge ([j] \vdash \mathsf{this.f} \doteq t_{\mathsf{f}}) \right)$$

The semantics α of a postcondition φ is that the final state is a model for φ, unless the last event is a resolve event:

$$\alpha(\varphi) = \exists max \in \mathbf{I}. \; \left(\forall i \in \mathbf{I}.i \leq max \right) \wedge \neg\mathsf{isFutEv}(max - 1) \rightarrow [max] \vdash \varphi$$

The semantics α of the call conditions $\mathbb{C}$ is that each call and each object creation has parameter values that are a model for the call (creation) precondition. The instantiation of the precondition contains no variable or field of the callee, but is evaluated in a state:

$$\alpha(\mathbb{C}) = \bigwedge_{\mathsf{m} \in \mathrm{dom}(\mathbb{C})} \forall i \in \mathbf{I}. \; \mathsf{isInvEv}(i, \mathsf{m}) \rightarrow$$
$$\left(\exists \bar{\mathsf{e}} \in \mathtt{List\text{<}Any\text{>}}. \; \mathsf{isInvEvW}(i, \mathsf{m}, \bar{\mathsf{e}}) \wedge [i+1] \vdash \mathbb{C}(\mathsf{m})(\bar{\mathsf{e}}) \right)$$
$$\bigwedge_{\mathsf{C} \in \mathrm{dom}(\mathbb{C})} \forall i \in \mathbf{I}. \; \mathsf{isNewEv}(i, \mathsf{m}) \rightarrow$$
$$\left(\exists \bar{\mathsf{e}} \in \mathtt{List\text{<}Any\text{>}}. \; \mathsf{isNewEvW}(i, \mathsf{m}, \bar{\mathsf{e}}) \wedge [i+1] \vdash \mathbb{C}(\mathsf{c})(\bar{\mathsf{e}}) \right)$$

The semantics α of the suspension specification is that at every suspension (i) the frame semantics holds until the subsequent suspension point, (ii) the ensures clause is established, and (iii) the requires clause holds. Additionally, at every return statement the corresponding postcondition holds and at every future read the correct method has been read and the conditions on the read value hold:

$$\alpha(\mathbb{S}) = \bigwedge_{p \in dom(\mathbb{S})} \forall i \in \mathbf{I}. \ \mathsf{isSuspEv}(i, p) \rightarrow [i+1] \vdash \mathbb{S}^{ens}(p) \wedge [i+3] \vdash \mathbb{S}^{req}(p)$$
$$\wedge \ \alpha(\mathbb{S}^{W}(p, i+4))$$

$$\wedge \bigwedge_{\substack{p \in dom(\mathbb{S}) \\ p \ is \ at \ \mathbf{return}}} \forall i \in \mathbf{I}. \ \forall e \in \mathsf{Any}. \ \mathsf{isFutEvW}(i, p, e) \rightarrow [i-1] \models \mathbb{S}(p)(e)$$

$$\wedge \bigwedge_{\substack{p \in dom(\mathbb{S}) \\ p \ is \ at \ \mathbf{get}}} \forall i \in \mathbf{I}. \ \forall e \in \mathsf{Any}. \ \mathsf{isFutREvW}(i, p, e) \rightarrow [i-1] \models \mathbb{S}^{cond}(p)(e)$$

The complete semantics is

$$\mathsf{met}\big((\mathbb{W}, \varphi)_{\mathbb{S}, \mathbb{C}}\big) = \exists mi \in \mathbf{I}. \ \big(\forall i \in \mathbf{I}. \ i \geq mi\big) \wedge \alpha(\mathbb{W}, mi) \wedge \alpha(\varphi) \wedge \alpha(\mathbb{S}) \wedge \alpha(\mathbb{C}) \ .$$

The formula is finite, as for any specification the domains of $\mathbb{C}$, $\mathbb{S}$ are finite.

5.4 Method Contracts as Behavioral Types

We proceed to proof obligation generation and proof calculus. The proof obligation schema is straightforward. In particular, it requires neither an encoding of frames in the postcondition like JavaDL [58] nor statements involving the event history like ABDSL [26].

Definition 15 (Proof Obligation Schema). Let P be a specified program and Mtd_P the set of its methods. Let $\big(\mathsf{pre}_\mathsf{m}^{param}, \mathsf{pre}_\mathsf{m}^{heap}, \theta_\mathsf{m}\big)_{\mathsf{m} \in \mathsf{Mtd}_\mathsf{P}}$ be the extracted and propagated set of behavioral contract triples from P. Further, given a method m, let s_m be the method body of m. The proof obligation schema is

$$\iota(\mathsf{m}) = \big(\mathsf{pre}_\mathsf{m}^{param} \wedge \mathsf{pre}_\mathsf{m}^{heap}, \theta_\mathsf{m}\big)$$

which characterizes the following proof obligations:

$$\{\mathtt{lastHeap} := \mathtt{heap}\}\{\mathtt{oldHeap} := \mathtt{heap}\}\big((\mathsf{pre}_\mathsf{m}^{param} \wedge \mathsf{pre}_\mathsf{m}^{heap}) \rightarrow [\mathsf{s}_\mathsf{m} \overset{\mathsf{met}}{\Vdash} \theta_\mathsf{m}]\big) \ .$$

The two updates save the prior state for the specifications connecting two different heaps: $\mathtt{oldHeap}$ is the heap at the beginning of method execution, $\mathtt{lastHeap}$ is the heap from the last (re-)activation. In the beginning, all heaps ($\mathtt{heap}$, $\mathtt{lastHeap}$, $\mathtt{oldHeap}$) coincide.

To formulate the proof system we need the auxiliary definitions stated in Fig. 9:

- Applying the update $U_{\mathcal{A}}$ removes ("anonymizes") all state information from the **heap** variable and saves the old state in **lastHeap**.
- Similarly, $U_{\mathcal{F}}^{\mathsf{W}}$ removes all information from all program variables in W and all heaps except **oldHeap**.
- $\mathsf{W}_\mathbf{s}'$ is the intersection of the currently active frame W and all frame specifications in $\mathbf{s}$. This is needed for loops, because the loop body $\mathbf{s}$ has to be in the frame from before the loop, as well as in the frame at the end of every iteration. These sets may differ when the loop body contains an **await**.
- fields extracts all field accesses from a set of expressions.

$$U_{\mathcal{A}} = \{\mathtt{lastHeap} := \mathtt{heap}\}\{\mathtt{heap} := \mathtt{anon}(\mathtt{heap})\}$$

$$U_{\mathcal{F}}^{\mathsf{W}} = \{\mathtt{lastHeap} := \mathtt{anon}(\mathtt{lastHeap})\}\{\mathtt{heap} := \mathtt{anon}(\mathtt{heap})\}\{\mathtt{v}_1 := v_1\}\dots\{\mathtt{v}_n := v_n\}$$

for each non-heap program variable $\mathtt{v}_i \in \mathsf{W}$ and fresh symbols v_i.

$$\mathsf{W}_\mathbf{s}' = \begin{cases} \mathsf{W} & \text{if } \mathbf{s} \text{ contains no } \textbf{await} \\ \mathsf{W} \cap \bigcap_{\mathrm{PPI}\ \mathtt{i}\ \text{in}\ \mathbf{s}} S^{\mathsf{W}}(\mathtt{i}) & \text{otherwise} \end{cases}$$

$$\mathsf{fields}(\mathsf{e}_1, \dots, \mathsf{e}_n) = \text{ fields within expressions } \mathsf{e}_1, \dots, \mathsf{e}_n$$

Fig. 9. Auxiliary definitions.

Definition 16 (Proof Calculus). *The proof system for contracts is in Fig. 10. The rules for writes to variables are similar to those for field writes to* **f**: *the generated update* $x := t$ *changes to* **heap** $:=$ **store**(heap, f, t). *Additionally* $\mathtt{f} \in \mathsf{W}$ *is added, see* **(assignF)**. *In the remaining rules we only give the version for variables.*

The rules for all statements except **return** and **skip** are given with an active statement and a continuation $\mathbf{s}$. The rules for **skip** ensure that if the statement has no continuation, a **skip** can be added.

- Rule **(assign)** turns an assignment to a variable into an update and **(assignF)** does the same for a field.
- The rule **(skI)** introduces **skip** as discussed above, **(skF)** removes a **skip** as the active statement, **(sk)** terminates symbolic execution evaluates the statement postcondition when **skip** is the sole remaining statement.
- Rule **(return)** proves the *method* postcondition at (the implicit) PPI $\mathtt{i}$ of the **return** statement. The statement postcondition needs *not* to hold here.
- Rule **(get)** has two premises: the first checks with a global points-to analysis that the correct method is synchronized. There are no rules for this modality—the branch is closed by an external analysis. The second premise generates a fresh symbol v and adds the propagated knowledge about it when symbolic execution is continued.
- Rule **(await)** checks first that the correct predicate holds before termination, and continues symbolic execution according to the specification of the suspension point. The statement postcondition needs *not* to hold here.

$$\text{(assign)} \quad \frac{\Gamma \Longrightarrow \{U\}\{x := e\}\big[s \overset{met}{\Vdash} (\mathbb{W}, \varphi)_{s,c}\big], \Delta}{\Gamma \Longrightarrow \{U\}\big[x = e;\ s \overset{met}{\Vdash} (\mathbb{W}, \varphi)_{s,c}\big], \Delta}$$

$$\text{(assignF)} \quad \frac{\Gamma \Longrightarrow \{U\}\{heap := store(heap, f, e)\}\big[s \overset{met}{\Vdash} (\mathbb{W}, \varphi)_{s,c}\big], \Delta}{\Gamma \Longrightarrow \{U\}\big[f = e;\ s \overset{met}{\Vdash} (\mathbb{W}, \varphi)_{s,c}\big], \Delta} \quad f \in \mathbb{W}$$

$$\text{(skl)} \quad \frac{\Gamma \Longrightarrow \{U\}\big[s;\ skip \overset{met}{\Vdash} (\mathbb{W}, \varphi)_{s,c}\big], \Delta}{\Gamma \Longrightarrow \{U\}\big[s \overset{met}{\Vdash} (\mathbb{W}, \varphi)_{s,c}\big], \Delta} \quad \text{s is neither } \mathbf{skip} \text{ nor composed}$$

$$\text{(skF)} \quad \frac{\Gamma \Longrightarrow \{U\}\big[s \overset{met}{\Vdash} (\mathbb{W}, \varphi)_{s,c}\big], \Delta}{\Gamma \Longrightarrow \{U\}\big[skip;\ s \overset{met}{\Vdash} (\mathbb{W}, \varphi)_{s,c}\big], \Delta} \qquad \text{(sk)} \quad \frac{\Gamma \Longrightarrow \{U\}\varphi, \Delta}{\Gamma \Longrightarrow \{U\}\big[skip \overset{met}{\Vdash} (\mathbb{W}, \varphi)_{s,c}\big], \Delta}$$

$$\text{(return)} \quad \frac{\Gamma \Longrightarrow \{U\}\{result := e\}S(i), \Delta}{\Gamma \Longrightarrow \{U\}\big[return\ e;\ \overset{met}{\Vdash} (\mathbb{W}, \varphi)_{s,c}\big], \Delta} \quad \text{i is the PPI of this } \mathbf{return}$$

$$\Longrightarrow [[sync:\ "i"]\ x = e.get;\ s \overset{p2}{\Vdash} S^{mtds}(i)]$$

$$\text{(get)} \quad \frac{\Gamma, \{U\}\{result := v\}S^{cond}(i) \Longrightarrow \{U\}\{x := v\}\big[s \overset{met}{\Vdash} (\mathbb{W}, \varphi)_{s,c}\big], \Delta}{\Gamma \Longrightarrow \{U\}\big[[sync:\ "i"]\ x = e.get;\ s \overset{met}{\Vdash} (\mathbb{W}, \varphi)_{s,c}\big], \Delta} \quad v \text{ fresh}$$

$$\Gamma \Longrightarrow \{U\}S^{ens}(i), \Delta$$

$$\text{(await)} \quad \frac{\Gamma, \{U\}U_{\mathcal{A}}(S^{req}(i) \wedge g) \Longrightarrow \Gamma, \{U\}U_{\mathcal{A}}\big[s \overset{met}{\Vdash} (S^R(i), S^{\mathbb{W}}(i), \varphi)_{s,c}\big], \Delta}{\Gamma \Longrightarrow \{U\}\big[[atom:\ "i"]\ await\ g;\ s \overset{met}{\Vdash} (\mathbb{W}, \varphi)_{s,c}\big], \Delta}$$

$$\text{(create)} \quad \frac{\Gamma \Longrightarrow \{U\}\mathbb{C}(C)(\bar{e}), \Delta \qquad \Gamma \Longrightarrow \{U\}\{x := o\}\big[s \overset{met}{\Vdash} (\mathbb{W}, \varphi)_{s,c}\big], \Delta}{\Gamma \Longrightarrow \{U\}\big[x = e.new\ C(\bar{e});\ s \overset{met}{\Vdash} (\mathbb{W}, \varphi)_{s,c}\big], \Delta} \quad o \text{ fresh}$$

$$\text{(call)} \quad \frac{\Gamma \Longrightarrow \{U\}(e \neq null \wedge \mathbb{C}(m)(\bar{e})), \Delta \qquad \Gamma \Longrightarrow \{U\}\{x := f\}\big[s \overset{met}{\Vdash} (\mathbb{W}, \varphi)_{s,c}\big], \Delta}{\Gamma \Longrightarrow \{U\}\big[x = e!m(\bar{e});\ s \overset{met}{\Vdash} (\mathbb{W}, \varphi)_{s,c}\big], \Delta} \quad f \text{ fresh}$$

$$\Gamma \Longrightarrow \{U\}I, \Delta \qquad \Gamma, \{U\}U_F^{\mathbb{W}s}(I \wedge e) \Longrightarrow \{U\}U_F^{\mathbb{W}s}\big[s \overset{met}{\Vdash} (\mathbb{W}'_s, I)_{s,c}\big], \Delta$$

$$\text{(loop)} \quad \frac{\Gamma, \{U\}U_F^{\mathbb{W}s}(I \wedge \neg e) \Longrightarrow \{U\}U_F^{\mathbb{W}s}\big[s' \overset{met}{\Vdash} (\mathbb{W}'_s, \varphi)_{s,c}\big], \Delta}{\Gamma \Longrightarrow \{U\}\big[while\ (e)\ \{s\}\ s' \overset{met}{\Vdash} (\mathbb{W}, \varphi)_{s,c}\big], \Delta}$$

$$\Gamma, \{U\}e \Longrightarrow \{U\}\big[s;s'' \overset{met}{\Vdash} (\mathbb{W}, \varphi)_{s,c}\big], \Delta$$

$$\text{(branch)} \quad \frac{\Gamma, \{U\}\neg e \Longrightarrow \{U\}\big[s';s'' \overset{met}{\Vdash} (\mathbb{W}, \varphi)_{s,c}\big], \Delta}{\Gamma \Longrightarrow \{U\}\big[if\ (e)\ then\ \{s\}\ else\ \{s'\}\ s'' \overset{met}{\Vdash} (\mathbb{W}, \varphi)_{s,c}\big], \Delta}$$

Fig. 10. Calculus for behavioral contracts

- Rules (create) and (call) handle object creation and method calls: the precondition has to be proven in one premise and a fresh symbol is used subsequently during symbolic execution. Rule (call) additionally checks that the target is not null.
- Rule (loop) is a standard loop invariant rule: The invariant formula I has to be proven when the loop is entered. This is done in the first premise. The second premise checks that I is preserved by the method body. The update mechanism removes all information from the accessed variables and heap, except that I and the guard holds. This is the only place where the statement postcondition is modified: it must be shown that the method body has the postcondition I. The mechanism for the frames is described above.
- Rule (branch) splits the proof into two branches, following the two branches of the if statement.

The rules assume a standard technique to translate expressions into terms and formulas, however, a guard e? is translated into true.

Frames are checked syntactically by computing the accessed fields in an assignment, yet our system is more precise than a purely syntactic approach: By embedding frames into symbolic execution, the check is flow- and value-sensitive. For example, it avoids to execute dead code. In addition, it is *contract-sensitive*: given multiple contracts we can check whether the frames hold for a given specification, while purely syntactic approaches cannot distinguish these cases.

We also do not require an explicit history variable keeping track of events, as the trace properties dealing with events are hidden in the behavioral modalities.

5.5   Context Sets as Global Trace Properties and Soundness

The main theorem states that in every global trace of a verified program, the projections to local traces are models for the semantics of the corresponding method contract. This requires a characterization of context sets as properties of global traces. In addition, we assume standard soundness proofs for most rules in the proof calculus. However, rules (await) and (get) *depend on non-local information*. For example, (get) is only sound if the methods that provide the read value indeed have verified soundness conditions. These rules, therefore, are part of the composition step of the main theorem.

Lemma 1. *Rules (assign), (assignF), (skI), (skF), (sk), (return), (create), (call), (loop), (branch) are sound, i.e. validity of the premises implies validity of the conclusion.*

Definition 17 (Semantics of Global Specification). *Let m be a method and p an atomic segment name. A trace sh adheres to global specification $\mathbb{G}$ if:*

- *For every invocation reaction event on m at index i, there is a future event from a method $m' \in \mathbb{G}^{\mathsf{Succ}}(m)$ or a suspension event from some $p' \in \mathbb{G}^{\mathsf{Succ}}(m)$ at index $j < i$. If these sets are empty, then i must be the first invocation reaction event on the object. Moreover, every future or suspension event with index k, such that $j < k < i$, is from some $m'' \in \mathbb{G}^{\mathsf{Over}}(m)$ or $p'' \in \mathbb{G}^{\mathsf{Over}}(m)$.*

– *For every suspension reaction event on* p *at index* i, *there is a future event from a method* $m' \in \mathbb{C}^{\mathsf{Succ}}(p)$ *or a suspension event from some* $p' \in \mathbb{C}^{\mathsf{Succ}}(p)$ *at index* $j < i$. *Moreover, every future or suspension event with index* k, *such that* $j < k < i$, *is from some* $m'' \in \mathbb{C}^{\mathsf{Over}}(p)$ *or* $p'' \in \mathbb{C}^{\mathsf{Over}}(p)$.

Given a future f in a global trace sh, let m_f be the method resolving f and θ_m its behavioral contract.

Theorem 1. *Let* P *be a program. If all method contracts can be proven, i.e. there is a proof in the calculus for the sequents in* $\iota(m)$, *and all traces* sh *generated by* P *adhere to the global specification, then for each global trace generated by* P *and each future* f *within* sh, *the projection of* sh *on* f *is a model for* θ_{m_f}:

$$sh|_f \models \mathsf{met}(\theta_{m_f})$$

Proof Sketch. The proof is by induction over the number n of reactivations and future reads in the generated trace sh.

n = 0. In the first base case there are no suspensions and future reads, hence, rules (get) and (await) are irrelevant. So all sequents in $\iota(m)$ are valid. It remains to show that the proof obligations do not discard any traces, i.e. preconditions pre^{heap}, pre^{param} hold in the first state of every projected trace $sh|_f$.
Let i be the invocation reaction of a process and m_i its method. If the semantics of the global specification holds, then before i there was a position $k < i$ with a future event that terminates a process of a method m_k in the *succeeds* set of m_i. By propagation, pre^{heap} is established here, as $\iota(m_k)$ is valid. Between k and i only methods m'_k from the *overlaps* method run on the same object, so pre^{heap} is preserved until i because $\iota(m'_k)$ is valid. Methods running on other objects are irrelevant, because they cannot access the heap of the object running m_i and pre^{heap} contains only fields of one object. Regarding pre^{param}, there is a $l < i$ with the invocation event corresponding to i. This l is issued by some other method m_l. Since $\iota(m_l)$ is valid, that call has been verified to adhere to the call conditions of $\mathbb{C}$.

n = 1. In the second base case there is exactly one future read or reactivation. Let i be the position of that event in sh. Let m_i be the method issuing the event. We distinguish the two cases:

Future Read. Let p be the PPI of the reading **get** statement. By assumption, the proof for $\iota(m_i)$ has been provided, but this does not imply that $\iota(m_i)$ is valid: Rule (get) is not sound, i.e., validity of its premises does not imply validity of its conclusion. But it is sound for the state σ before i: if its premises hold in σ, then its conclusion holds in σ. To establish this, we must show that $\{\texttt{result} := v\}\mathbb{S}^{cond}(p)$ holds in the state before i. It is sufficient to show that the read value is described by $\mathbb{S}^{cond}(p)$.
By the first rule premise, m_i is in $\mathbb{S}^{mtds}(p)$. By the second premise, the code following the **get** statement is a model for the rest of the behavioral contract, if the read value is described by $\mathbb{S}^{cond}(p)$. By propagation,

$S^{cond}(\mathbf{p})$ is the disjunction of all postconditions (from the interface, so they contain only result as a program variable).

We observe that every method not containing **await** and **get** statements is a model for its type by the above argument. To read a future, a method $\mathbf{m}_i$ must have terminated with a future event at position $k < i$. So the read value v is described by $\{\mathtt{result} := v\}post^{\mathsf{param}}$ and

$$\{\mathtt{result} := v\}post^{\mathsf{param}} \rightarrow \{\mathtt{result} := v\}S^{cond}(\mathbf{p}) \ .$$

Thus, the proof of $\iota(\mathbf{m}_i)$ describes all relevant states to conclude that the theorem statement holds.

Reactivation. Let $\mathbf{p}$ be the PPI of the reading **await** statement. This case is similar to the previous one, except one has to show that (await) is sound at i. It is sufficient to show that $S^{\mathsf{req}}(\mathbf{p}) \wedge \mathbf{g}$ can be assumed. The guard condition $\mathbf{g}$ obviously holds, as it is directly part of the semantics. The argument for $S^{\mathsf{req}}(\mathbf{p})$ is the same as in the proof in the case for $n = 0$, i.e. that pre^{heap} can be assumed at method start. The only difficulty arises when the **await** statement has to establish $S^{\mathsf{req}}(\mathbf{p})$ itself. However, if the proof of $\iota(\mathbf{m}_i)$ has been closed, then the first premise has been shown and does *not* rely on the soundness of (await): we may extract a partial proof by pruning the branch corresponding to the second premise to establish that at suspension $S^{\mathsf{req}}(\mathbf{p})$ holds.

$\mathbf{n > 1}$. Let i be the index of the last reactivation or future read event. For $sh[0 \ldots i-1]$ we can apply the induction hypothesis, i.e. every complete local trace so far was a model for its contract. Let $\mathbf{m}_i$ be the method issuing the event. We distinguish the same cases as above:

Future Read. The case for future reads is analogous to the one in base case $n = 1$. The only difference is that the read future may have been resolved by a method that contains a **get** statement itself. The soundness of (get) for those states, however, is established by the induction hypothesis.

Reactivation. This case is again analogous. The only difference is that other **await** statements may need to establish the suspension assumption (instead of the **await** statement in question), and the process of the other **await** statement has not terminated yet at i. This is covered by the same argument as in the base case $n = 1$ by extracting partial proofs for any relevant method. Otherwise, the induction hypothesis suffices. □

We integrate the pointer analysis as a behavioral specification that is obviously not complete. The appropriate notion of completeness for logics referring to external analyses remains an open question.

6   Related Work

Wait conditions were introduced as program statements for critical regions and monitors in the pioneering work of Brinch-Hansen [34,35] and Hoare [36]. Reasoning approaches for monitors are discussed by Dahl [20]. SCOOP [9] explores preconditions as wait/when conditions.

The paper [22] provided a reasoning system for distributed communications between active objects where interleaved concurrency inside each object is based on explicit release points. This paper assumes pre-conditions to hold when methods are activated, but uses a set of invariants, i.e., one monitor invariant capturing interleaving at each release point. The proof system is used to prove that a class maintains a set of monitor invariants which describe its release points. Compare with our paper, the major difference is in how release points are handled. We have more expressive language to specify other methods at the interleaving points. Thus, the proof system of [22] is more expressive than reasoning over just a single class invariant but less expressive than ours.

Previous approaches to AO verification [22, 24, 26] consider only object invariants that must be preserved by every atomic segment of every method. As discussed, this is a special case of our system. Compared to our work, this may make the specifications of methods weaker. Our work is an extension of KeY-ABS [23, 26] with the ability to specify and verify behavioral contracts for the ABS programs. KeY-ABS is based on a four-event semantics for asynchronous method calls, which introduces disjoint alphabets for the local histories of different objects. It is an extension of [5]. Invocation event in [5] is split into invocation event and invocation reaction event in KeY-ABS; completion event in [5] is split into completion event and completion reaction event in KeY-ABS. This disjoint alphabets allows to reduce the complexity of reasoning about such concurrent programs by significantly simplifying the formulas in terms of the number of needed quantifiers.

Actor services [57] are compositional event patterns for modular reasoning about asynchronous message passing for actors. They are formulated for pure actors and do not address futures or cooperative scheduling. Method preconditions are restricted to input values, the heap is specified by an object invariant. A rely-guarantee proof system [1, 41] implemented on top of Frama-C by Gavran et al. [31] demonstrated modular proofs of partial correctness for asynchronous C programs restricted to using the Libevent library.

A verification system for message passing programs written in Java and the MPJ library can be found in [56]. Compared to our work, future in [56] has different meaning. The authors modelled the communication protocol in the mCRL2 process algebra. These algebraic terms were defined as *futures* to predict how components will interact during program execution. Permission-based separation logic and model checking were applied in [56] to reason about local and global correctness of a network, respectively. Specification and verification supports message sending, receiving and broadcasting but not method contracts.

Contracts for channel-based communication are partly supported by session types [16, 37]. These have been adapted to the active object concurrency model [46], including assertions on heap memory [45], but require composition to be explicit in the specification. Stateful session types for active objects [45] contain a propagation step (cf. Sect. 2.3): Postconditions are propagated to preconditions of methods that are specified to run subsequently. In contrast, the propagation in the current paper goes in the opposite direction, where a contract specifies what a method relies on and then propagates to the method that is obliged to prove it. Session types, with their global system view, specify an obligation for a method and propagate to the methods which can rely on it.

Compositional specification of concurrency models outside rely-guarantee was mainly proposed based on separation logic [17,55], which separates shared memory regions [28] and assigns responsibilities for regions to processes. Shared regions relate predicates over the heap that must be stable, i.e. invariant, when accessed. Huisman et al. [15,61] have used permission-based separation logic to verify class invariants in multi-threaded programs, using barrier contracts. Even though approaches to specify regions precisely have been developed [19,28], their combination with interaction modes beyond heap access (such as asynchronous calls and futures) is not well explored. It is worth noting that AO do not require the concept of regions in the logic, because strong encapsulation and cooperative scheduling ensure that two threads never run in parallel on the same heap. The central goal of separation *logic*— separation of heaps—is a design feature of the AO *concurrency model*.

7   Conclusion

Preemption interferes with specification contracts in concurrent programs, because the unit of computation here differs from the unit of specification. Cooperative scheduling introduces syntactically declared program points for preemption, occupying a middle ground between no preemption (as in actors and sequential programs) and full preemption, as in multi-threaded programs.

This paper has addressed the problem of specification contracts for cooperative scheduling in active object languages. Because message passing does not correspond to transfer of control in the asynchronous setting, it is necessary to distinguish the responsibilities of the caller from the responsibilities of the callee in fulfilling the precondition of a task. We address this problem by means of pre- and postconditions at the level of interfaces, reflecting that the caller must fulfill the *parameter precondition*, and at the level of implementations, reflecting that only the callee has enough knowledge of the implementation to fulfill the *heap precondition*. We further show that by exploiting the syntactic declaration of such preemption points, it is possible to specify locally how tasks depend on each other and when different tasks may safely overlap.

Technically, the paper develops a specification language for cooperatively scheduled active objects by specifying program behavior at the possible interleaving points between tasks in terms of a concurrency context with *succeeds* and *overlaps* sets. These sets enable fine-grained interleaving behavior to be specified when required, and otherwise default into standard invariants, which weaken the specification to allow any interleaving. We formalized reasoning about such specifications in a behavioral program logic over behavioral types. It relates the trace semantics generated by execution of programs with method contracts expressed as behavioral types.

Acknowledgment. This work is supported by the SIRIUS Centre for Scalable Data Access and the FormbaR project, part of AG Signalling/DB RailLab in the Innovation Alliance of Deutsche Bahn AG and TU Darmstadt. The authors thank Wolfgang Ahrendt, Frank de Boer, and Henk Mulder for their careful reading and valuable feedback.

References

1. Abadi, M., Lamport, L.: Conjoining specifications. ACM Trans. Program. Lang. Syst. **17**(3), 507–534 (1995)
2. ABS development team: The ABS language specification, January 2018. http://docs.abs-models.org/
3. Agha, G., Hewitt, C.: Actors: a conceptual foundation for concurrent object-oriented programming. In: Shriver, B. (ed.) Research Directions in Object-Oriented Programming, pp. 49–74. MIT Press, Cambridge (1987)
4. Ahrendt, W., Beckert, B., Bubel, R., Hähnle, R., Schmitt, P.H., Ulbrich, M. (eds.): LNCS. From Theory to Practice, vol. 10001. Springer, Cham (2016). https://doi.org/10.1007/978-3-319-49812-6
5. Ahrendt, W., Dylla, M.: A system for compositional verification of asynchronous objects. Sci. Comput. Program. **77**(12), 1289–1309 (2012)
6. de Boer, F.S., Hähnle, R., Johnsen, E.B., Schlatte, R., Wong, P.Y.H.: Formal modeling of resource management for cloud architectures: an industrial case study. In: De Paoli, F., Pimentel, E., Zavattaro, G. (eds.) ESOCC 2012. LNCS, vol. 7592, pp. 91–106. Springer, Heidelberg (2012). https://doi.org/10.1007/978-3-642-33427-6_7
7. Albert, E., Flores-Montoya, A., Genaim, S., Martin-Martin, E.: May-happen-in-parallel analysis for actor-based concurrency. ACM Trans. Comput. Log. **17**(2), 11:1–11:39 (2016)
8. Armstrong, J.: Programming Erlang: Software for a Concurrent World. Pragmatic Bookshelf Series, Pragmatic Bookshelf (2007)
9. Arslan, V., Eugster, P., Nienaltowski, P., Vaucouleur, S.: SCOOP – concurrency made easy. In: Kohlas, J., Meyer, B., Schiper, A. (eds.) Dependable Systems: Software, Computing, Networks. LNCS, vol. 4028, pp. 82–102. Springer, Heidelberg (2006). https://doi.org/10.1007/11808107_4
10. Baker, H.G., Hewitt, C.E.: The incremental garbage collection of processes. In: Proceeding of the Symposium on Artificial Intelligence Programming Languages, number 12 in SIGPLAN Notices, p. 11, August 1977
11. Baudin, P., et al.: ACSL: ANSI/ISO C Specification Language. CEA LIST and INRIA, 1.4 edition (2010)
12. Baumann, C., Beckert, B., Blasum, H., Bormer, T.: Lessons learned from micro-kernel verification - specification is the new bottleneck. In: Cassez, F., Huuck, R., Klein, G., Schlich, B., (eds.) Proceedings 7th Conference on Systems Software Verification, EPTCS, vol. 102, pp. 18–32 (2012)
13. Beckert, B.: A dynamic logic for the formal verification of java card programs. In: Attali, I., Jensen, T. (eds.) JavaCard 2000. LNCS, vol. 2041, pp. 6–24. Springer, Heidelberg (2001). https://doi.org/10.1007/3-540-45165-X_2
14. Beckert, B., Klebanov, V., Weiß, B.: Dynamic logic for java. Deductive Software Verification – The KeY Book. LNCS, vol. 10001, pp. 49–106. Springer, Cham (2016). https://doi.org/10.1007/978-3-319-49812-6_3

15. Blom, S., Huisman, M., Mihelcic, M.: Specification and verification of GPGPU programs. Sci. Comput. Program. **95**, 376–388 (2014)
16. Bocchi, L., Lange, J., Tuosto, E.: Three algorithms and a methodology for amending contracts for choreographies. Sci. Ann. Comp. Sci. **22**(1), 61–104 (2012)
17. Brookes, S., O'Hearn, P.W.: Concurrent separation logic. ACM SIGLOG News **3**(3), 47–65 (2016)
18. Caromel, D., Henrio, L., Serpette, B.P.: Asynchronous and deterministic objects. In: Proceedings of the 31st ACM Symposium on Principles of Programming Languages (POPL 2004), pp. 123–134. ACM Press (2004)
19. da Rocha Pinto, P., Dinsdale-Young, T., Gardner, P.: TaDA: a logic for time and data abstraction. In: Jones, R. (ed.) ECOOP 2014. LNCS, vol. 8586, pp. 207–231. Springer, Heidelberg (2014). https://doi.org/10.1007/978-3-662-44202-9_9
20. Dahl, O.-J.: Monitors revisited. In: Roscoe, A.W., (ed.) A classical Mind: Essays in Honour of C.A.R. Hoare, pp. 93–103. Prentice Hall, Upper Saddle River (1994)
21. de Boer, F., et al.: A survey of active object languages. ACM Comput. Surv. **50**(5), 76:1–76:39 (2017)
22. de Boer, F.S., Clarke, D., Johnsen, E.B.: A complete guide to the future. In: De Nicola, R. (ed.) ESOP 2007. LNCS, vol. 4421, pp. 316–330. Springer, Heidelberg (2007). https://doi.org/10.1007/978-3-540-71316-6_22
23. Din, C.C., Bubel, R., Hähnle, R.: KeY-ABS: a deductive verification tool for the concurrent modelling language ABS. In: Felty, A.P., Middeldorp, A. (eds.) CADE 2015. LNCS (LNAI), vol. 9195, pp. 517–526. Springer, Cham (2015). https://doi.org/10.1007/978-3-319-21401-6_35
24. Din, C.C., Dovland, J., Johnsen, E.B., Owe, O.: Observable behavior of distributed systems: component reasoning for concurrent objects. J. Logic Algebraic Program. **81**(3), 227–256 (2012)
25. Din, C.C., Hähnle, R., Johnsen, E.B., Pun, K.I., Tapia Tarifa, S.L.: Locally abstract, globally concrete semantics of concurrent programming languages. In: Schmidt, R.A., Nalon, C. (eds.) TABLEAUX 2017. LNCS (LNAI), vol. 10501, pp. 22–43. Springer, Cham (2017). https://doi.org/10.1007/978-3-319-66902-1_2
26. Din, C.C., Owe, O.: Compositional reasoning about active objects with shared futures. Formal Aspects Comput. **27**(3), 551–572 (2015). https://doi.org/10.1007/s00165-014-0322-y
27. Din, C.C., Tapia Tarifa, S.L., Hähnle, R., Johnsen, E.B.: History-based specification and verification of scalable concurrent and distributed systems. In: Butler, M., Conchon, S., Zaïdi, F. (eds.) ICFEM 2015. LNCS, vol. 9407, pp. 217–233. Springer, Cham (2015). https://doi.org/10.1007/978-3-319-25423-4_14
28. Dinsdale-Young, T., da Rocha Pinto, P., Gardner, P.: A perspective on specifying and verifying concurrent modules. J. Logic. Algebraic Methods Program. **98**, 1–25 (2018)
29. Flanagan, C., Felleisen, M.: The semantics of future and an application. J. Funct. Program. **9**(1), 1–31 (1999)
30. Flores-Montoya, A.E., Albert, E., Genaim, S.: May-happen-in-parallel based deadlock analysis for concurrent objects. In: Beyer, D., Boreale, M. (eds.) FMOODS/-FORTE -2013. LNCS, vol. 7892, pp. 273–288. Springer, Heidelberg (2013). https://doi.org/10.1007/978-3-642-38592-6_19
31. Gavran, I., Niksic, F., Kanade, A., Majumdar, R., Vafeiadis, V.: Rely/guarantee reasoning for asynchronous programs. In: Aceto, L., de Frutos Escrig, D., (eds.) 26th International Conference on Concurrency Theory (CONCUR 2015), volume 42 of Leibniz International Proceedings in Informatics (LIPIcs), pp. 483–496. Schloss Dagstuhl-Leibniz-Zentrum fuer Informatik (2015)

32. Hähnle, R., Huisman, M.: Deductive software verification: from pen-and-paper proofs to industrial tools. In: Steffen, B., Woeginger, G. (eds.) Computing and Software Science. LNCS, vol. 10000, pp. 345–373. Springer, Cham (2019). https://doi.org/10.1007/978-3-319-91908-9_18

33. Halstead Jr., R.H.: Multilisp: a language for concurrent symbolic computation. ACM Trans. Program. Lang. Syst. **7**(4), 501–538 (1985)

34. Hansen, P.B.: Structured multiprogramming. Commun. ACM **15**(7), 574–578 (1972)

35. Hansen, P.B.: Operating System Principles. Prentice-Hall Inc, Upper Saddle River (1973)

36. Hoare, C.A.R.: Towards a theory of parallel programming. In: Hansen, P.B. (ed.) Operating System Techniques, pp. 61–71. Springer, New York (1972). https://doi.org/10.1007/978-1-4757-3472-0_6

37. Honda, K., Yoshida, N., Carbone, M.: Multiparty asynchronous session types. In: Proceedings of the 35th ACM SIGPLAN-SIGACT Symposium on Principles of Programming Languages, POPL 2008, pp. 273–284 (2008)

38. Hüttel, H., et al.: Foundations of session types and behavioural contracts. ACM Comput. Surv. **49**(1), 3:1–3:36 (2016)

39. Jacobs, B., Piessens, F.: The VeriFast program verifier. Technical Report CW-520, Department of Computer Science, Katholieke Universiteit Leuven, August 2008

40. Johnsen, E.B., Hähnle, R., Schäfer, J., Schlatte, R., Steffen, M.: ABS: a core language for abstract behavioral specification. In: Aichernig, B.K., de Boer, F.S., Bonsangue, M.M. (eds.) FMCO 2010. LNCS, vol. 6957, pp. 142–164. Springer, Heidelberg (2011). https://doi.org/10.1007/978-3-642-25271-6_8

41. Jones, C.B.: Tentative steps toward a development method for interfering programs. ACM Trans. Program. Lang. Syst. **5**(4), 596–619 (1983)

42. Kamburjan, E.: Behavioral program logic. In: Cerrito, S., Popescu, A. (eds.) TABLEAUX 2019. LNCS (LNAI), vol. 11714, pp. 391–408. Springer, Cham (2019). https://doi.org/10.1007/978-3-030-29026-9_22

43. Kamburjan, E.: Behavioral program logic and LAGC semantics without continuations (technical report). CoRR, abs/1904.13338 (2019)

44. Kamburjan, E.: Modular verification of a modular specification: behavioral types as program logics. Ph.D. thesis, Technische Universität Darmstadt (2020)

45. Kamburjan, E., Chen, T.-C.: Stateful behavioral types for active objects. In: Furia, C.A., Winter, K. (eds.) IFM 2018. LNCS, vol. 11023, pp. 214–235. Springer, Cham (2018). https://doi.org/10.1007/978-3-319-98938-9_13

46. Kamburjan, E., Din, C.C., Chen, T.-C.: Session-based compositional analysis for actor-based languages using futures. In: Ogata, K., Lawford, M., Liu, S. (eds.) ICFEM 2016. LNCS, vol. 10009, pp. 296–312. Springer, Cham (2016). https://doi.org/10.1007/978-3-319-47846-3_19

47. Kamburjan, E., Din, C.C., Hähnle, R., Johnsen, E.B.: Asynchronous cooperative contracts for cooperative scheduling. In: Ölveczky, P.C., Salaün, G. (eds.) SEFM 2019. LNCS, vol. 11724, pp. 48–66. Springer, Cham (2019). https://doi.org/10.1007/978-3-030-30446-1_3

48. Kamburjan, E., Din, C.C., Hähnle, R., Johnsen, E.B.: Asynchronous cooperative contracts for cooperative scheduling. Technical report, TU Darmstadt (2019). http://formbar.raillab.de/en/techreportcontract/

49. Kirchner, F., Kosmatov, N., Prevosto, V., Signoles, J., Yakobowski, B.: Frama-C: a software analysis perspective. Formal Aspects Comput. **27**(3), 573–609 (2015). https://doi.org/10.1007/s00165-014-0326-7

50. Leavens, G.T., et al.: JML reference manual. Draft revision 2344, May 2013
51. Leino, K.R.M., Wüstholz, V.: The Dafny integrated development environment. In: Dubois, C., Giannakopoulou, D., Méry, D. (eds.) Proceedings 1st Workshop on Formal Integrated Development Environment, F-IDE, EPTCS, Grenoble, France, vol. 149, pp. 3–15 (2014)
52. Lin, J.-C., Yu, I.C., Johnsen, E.B., Lee, M.-C.: ABS-YARN: a formal framework for modeling Hadoop YARN clusters. In: Stevens, P., Wąsowski, A. (eds.) FASE 2016. LNCS, vol. 9633, pp. 49–65. Springer, Heidelberg (2016). https://doi.org/10.1007/978-3-662-49665-7_4
53. Liskov, B.H., Shrira, L.: Promises: linguistic support for efficient asynchronous procedure calls in distributed systems. In: Wise, D.S. (ed.) Proceedings of the SIGPLAN Conference on Programming Language Design and Implementation (PLDI 1988), pp. 260–267. ACM Press, June 1988
54. Nakata, K., Uustalu, T.: A Hoare logic for the coinductive trace-based big-step semantics of while. Logical Methods Comput. Sci. 11(1), 1–32 (2015)
55. O'Hearn, P., Reynolds, J., Yang, H.: Local reasoning about programs that alter data structures. In: Fribourg, L. (ed.) CSL 2001. LNCS, vol. 2142, pp. 1–19. Springer, Heidelberg (2001). https://doi.org/10.1007/3-540-44802-0_1
56. Oortwijn, W., Blom, S., Huisman, M.: Future-based static analysis of message passing programs. In: Orchard, D.A., Yoshida, N., (eds.) Proceedings of the Ninth workshop on Programming Language Approaches to Concurrency- and Communication-cEntric Software, PLACES 2016, EPTCS, Eindhoven, The Netherlands, 8th April 2016, vol. 211, pp. 65–72 (2016)
57. Summers, A.J., Müller, P.: Actor services - modular verification of message passing programs. In: Thiemann, P. (ed.) ESOP 2016), vol. 9632, pp. 699–726. Springer, Heidelberg (2016). https://doi.org/10.1007/978-3-662-49498-1_27
58. Weiß, B.: Deductive verification of object-oriented software: dynamic frames, dynamic logic and predicate abstraction. Ph.D. thesis, Karlsruhe Institute of Technology (2011)
59. Wong, P.Y.H., Diakov, N., Schaefer, I.: Modelling adaptable distributed object oriented systems using the HATS approach: a fredhopper case study. In: Beckert, B., Damiani, F., Gurov, D. (eds.) FoVeOOS 2011. LNCS, vol. 7421, pp. 49–66. Springer, Heidelberg (2012). https://doi.org/10.1007/978-3-642-31762-0_5
60. Yonezawa, A., Briot, J.P., Shibayama, E.: Object-oriented concurrent programming in ABCL/1. In: Conference on Object-Oriented Programming Systems, Languages and Applications (OOPSLA 1986), vol. 21, no. 11, pp. 258–268, November 1986. SIGPLAN Notices
61. Zaharieva-Stojanovski, M., Huisman, M.: Verifying class invariants in concurrent programs. In: Gnesi, S., Rensink, A. (eds.) FASE 2014. LNCS, vol. 8411, pp. 230–245. Springer, Heidelberg (2014). https://doi.org/10.1007/978-3-642-54804-8_16

Using Abstract Contracts for Verifying Evolving Features and Their Interactions

Alexander Knüppel[1](✉), Stefan Krüger[2], Thomas Thüm[3], Richard Bubel[4],
Sebastian Krieter[5], Eric Bodden[2], and Ina Schaefer[1]

[1] TU Braunschweig, Braunschweig, Germany
{a.knueppel,i.schaefer}@tu-braunschweig.de
[2] University of Paderborn, Paderborn, Germany
{stefan.krueger,eric.bodden}@uni-paderborn.de
[3] University of Ulm, Ulm, Germany
thomas.thuem@uni-ulm.de
[4] TU Darmstadt, Darmstadt, Germany
bubel@cs.tu-darmstadt.de
[5] University of Magdeburg, Magdeburg, Germany
Sebastian.Krieter@ovgu.de

Abstract. Today, software systems are rarely developed monolithically,
but may be composed of numerous individually developed features.
Their modularization facilitates independent development and verification. While feature-based strategies to verify features in isolation have
existed for years, they cannot address interactions between features. The
problem with feature interactions is that they are typically unknown and
may involve any subset of the features. Contrary, a family-based verification strategy captures feature interactions, but does not scale well when
features evolve frequently. To the best of our knowledge, there currently
exists no approach with focus on evolving features that combines both
strategies and aims at eliminating their respective drawbacks. To fill this
gap, we introduce FEFALUTION, a feature-family-based verification approach based on *abstract contracts* to verify evolving features *and* their
interactions. FEFALUTION builds partial proofs for each evolving feature
and then reuses the resulting partial proofs in verifying feature interactions, yielding a full verification of the complete software system. Moreover, to investigate whether a combination of both strategies is fruitful,
we present the first empirical study for the verification of evolving features implemented by means of feature-oriented programming and by
comparing FEFALUTION with another five family-based approaches varying in a set of optimizations. Our results indicate that partial proofs
based on abstract contracts exhibit huge reuse potential, but also come
with a substantial overhead for smaller evolution scenarios.

1 Introduction

Today's software systems are often developed in terms of features, such as the
operating system Linux, the integrated development environment Eclipse, or

© Springer Nature Switzerland AG 2020
W. Ahrendt et al. (Eds.): Deductive Software Verification, LNCS 12345, pp. 122–148, 2020.
https://doi.org/10.1007/978-3-030-64354-6_5

the web browser Firefox. End-users can choose a subset of these features for a customized product. In such software product lines [7], the number of possible feature combinations typically grows exponentially in the number of features. This kind of variability makes their verification a non-trivial task [39], as individual features change over time due to software evolution, and it is typically impossible to foresee which product variants need to be generated. Moreover, it is infeasible to generate and verify all feature combinations for even small feature-oriented software projects.

Implementation artifacts of a feature can be modularized into plug-ins, feature modules, or aspects [7]. A major goal of modularity is to reduce complexity and to support large development teams [34]. As a side-effect, modularity allows to verify features to a certain extent in isolation. A major advantage of such *feature-based verification* is that also under evolution one only needs to verify those features that changed [39] and not the complete code base. Hoewever, verifying each feature in isolation – known as *feature-based verification* – is generally insufficient, as features interact with each other. For instance, a feature may call methods defined in other features (i.e., syntactical interaction) or it may even rely on the behavior of other features (i.e., semantic interaction) [13]. Any combination of an arbitrary subset of features may lead to a feature interaction. Hence, there is a potentially exponential number of interactions, which are typically unknown a priori.

To resolve the interaction problem, another verification strategy called *family-based verification* applies a single verification to the complete code base (i.e., the whole family of products at once) [10,15,21,23,37]. Typically, a *metaproduct* is generated by encoding the complete code base including all features into one executable product. While the family-based strategy avoids the verification of every possible feature combination separately, the verification problem is more complex and needs to be solved again whenever one of the features evolves.

Our hypothesis for this work is that a combined approach (i.e., a *feature-family-based strategy*) may be simultaneously robust against evolution of features to reduce re-verification effort and also able to deal with feature interactions. However, testing this hypothesis is a non-trivial task, as there are also numerous *optimizations* (e.g., whether method calls are inlined or abstracted) that may affect the performance and reuse potential of verification strategies in general. To this end, we focus on two open questions in this work, namely (1) *can a feature-family-based strategy reduce the verification effort for evolving features compared to a sole family-based stragey?* and (2) *how do different optimizations affect the verification of evolving features?*

To the best of our knowledge, no adequate feature-family-based approach explicitly addressing the evolution of features currently exists. Therefore, we propose FEFALUTION, a feature-family-based deductive verification approach particularly designed for evolution and for overcoming some limitations by prior work. In a feature-based phase, FEFALUTION builds partial proofs for each evolving feature by generating a *feature stub* containing all artifacts (e.g., classes, methods, and fields) that are referenced from other features. When referring to methods of other features, we use the notion of abstract contracts [11] to avoid that changes in contracts of other features influence the verification result and, thus, require a re-verification. The verification of the feature stubs results in partial proofs.

In a subsequent family-based phase based on *variability encoding* [37], FEFA-LUTION then reuses the resulting partial proofs in verifying feature interactions. Variability encoding is the process of transforming compile-time into run-time variability to reuse existing verification tools as-is [42]. We extend prior work on variability encoding for feature-oriented contracts [41] with support for abstract contracts and for partial proofs.

We focus on contract specification with the Java Modeling Language (JML) [31] and verification with KEY [1], whereas our ideas may also be applied to other specification languages and verification tools. As modularization technique, we rely on feature modules specified with feature-oriented contracts due to the available tool support for modularization and composition of contracts [41]. In detail, we make the following contributions.

- A presentation of a feature-family-based deductive verification approach called FEFALUTION, which combines the generation of feature stubs [30] and abstract contracts [11] with variability encoding [37].
- Tool support for FEFALUTION based on three existing tools, namely (1) a version of KEY that facilitates the use of abstract contracts, (2) Feature-House [4] for composing feature modules and feature-oriented contracts with support for variability encoding, and (3) FeatureIDE [40] for the generation of feature stubs.
- An empirical comparison of a total of six family-based approaches varying in specific characteristics applied to five evolution scenarios of the bank account product line.

2   Background and Running Example

In this section, we introduce the core concepts our work is based on. We briefly discuss JML specifications in general and abstract contracts in particular. As we focus on software product lines, we give a brief introduction to feature modeling, feature composition, and product-line specification.

2.1   Design by Contract

To specify a program's behavior, we follow the *design-by-contract* paradigm [33]. In design-by-contract, the program behavior is typically specified by code annotations that have to be obeyed by method implementations. Method contracts specify *preconditions* that need to be satisfied by callers and *postconditions* that callers can then rely on. Furthermore, class invariants define class-wide properties. A class invariant is established by the class' constructor and serves as an additional precondition and postcondition for each method of the class.

As specification language, we use the Java Modeling Language (JML), which implements design-by-contract for Java programs [32]. In the first listing of Fig. 1,

```
 1   class Account {                                              BankAccount
 2     static final int OVERDRAFT_LIMIT = 0;
 3     int balance = 0;
 4
 5   /*@ requires x != 0;
 6     @ ensures \result <==> (balance == \old(balance) + x);
 7     @ assignable balance; @*/
 8     boolean update(int x) {
 9       if (balance + x < OVERDRAFT_LIMIT) return false;
10       balance += x;
11       return true;
12     }
13   }
```

```
14   class Account {                                                DailyLimit
15     static final int DAILY_LIMIT = -1000;
16     int withdraw = 0;
17
18   /*@ requires \original;
19     @ ensures \original;
20     @ assignable withdraw; @*/
21     boolean update(int x) {
22       if ((x < 0 && withdraw + x < DAILY_LIMIT) ||
23         !original(x))
24         return false;
25       withdraw += x;
26       return true;
27     }
28   }
```

```
29   class Account {                              BankAccount • DailyLimit
30     static final int OVERDRAFT_LIMIT = 0;
31     int balance = 0;
32     static final int DAILY_LIMIT = -1000;
33     int withdraw = 0;
34
35   /*@ requires x != 0;
36     @ ensures \result <==> (balance == \old(balance) + x);
37     @ assignable balance; @*/
38     boolean update_wrappee_BankAccount (int x)
39     {//Lines 9 - 11}
40
41   /*@ requires x != 0;
42     @ ensures \result <==> (balance == \old(balance) + x);
43     @ assignable balance, withdraw; @*/
44     boolean update(int x) {
45       if ((x < 0 && withdraw + x < DAILY_LIMIT) ||
46         !update_wrappee_BankAccount(x))
47         return false;
48       withdraw += x;
49       return true;
50     }
51   }
```

Fig. 1. Composition of two feature modules of a bank account product line [41]

we show the contracts of method update. The listings in the figure also show the
mechanism of composition in feature-oriented programming, which we discuss
further below. The keywords **requires** (Line 5) and **ensures** (Line 6) indicate
the pre- and postcondition, respectively. The last line of the contract (Line 7)
represents the assignable clause. An assignable clause represents a set of program
locations that the method is permitted to change on return. For method update,
only field balance may change.

Contracts can be used by a theorem prover during the deductive verification process when a method invocation is encountered. Alternatively, method invocations can be treated by inlining the body of the called methods. This has several disadvantages [29], as (a) in presence of dynamic dispatch the verifier has to split the proof produced by the theorem prover into different cases, one for each overwritten method to which the method invocation might be dispatched at runtime, (b) the verification (program analysis) is no longer modular as changes to the implementation of the called method invalidate proofs for all callers, and (c) the verification becomes a closed-world analysis, as the implementation of called methods needs to be accessible in order to guarantee correctness. Furthermore, available implementations for native methods calls, however, are rarely accessible.

These disadvantages can be mitigated by using the contract of an invoked method and following the paradigm of behavioral subtyping. This way, we can avoid to enumerate all possible method implementations and only apply the most general common method contract. Additionally, contracts are usually more stable than implementations as they are only concerned with *what* is computed and not *how* the algorithm is implemented. Hence, we become independent of changes to the implementation of called methods. As inlining may produce an indefinite large call stack, contracts should reduce the proof complexity. However, it is an open question under which circumstances contracts indeed lead to less verification effort [29].

2.2   Abstract Contracts

Hähnle et al. [25] and Bubel et al. [11] propose abstract contracts for the deductive verification of evolving source code. Using abstract contracts in verification, the theorem prover creates partial proofs without relying on the concrete definitions of contracts. These partial proofs are saved and reused to save verification effort during a re-verification. Abstract contracts may reduce the overall verification effort of a program under development [11].

We illustrate the structure of abstract contracts by making the concrete contract of method update abstract. We show the method's concrete contract in Lines 5–7 in Fig. 1 and the resulting abstract contract in Fig. 2. Lines 1–3 of Fig. 2 represent the abstract section, in which placeholders for precondition, postcondition, and assignable clause are declared. Lines 4–7 consist of the placeholders' definitions and are called the concrete section. In our example, Line 1 shows the declaration of precondition placeholder updateR, which is then defined in Line 4 as x != 0. When a verification is performed based on abstract contracts, the theorem prover uses the placeholders instead of the concrete definition in the proving process.

2.3   Feature Modeling and Valid Feature Combinations

To assemble a product, feature modules are composed together. However, not all feature combinations are meaningful. For example, it is undesirable to have

```
1   /*@ requires_abs updateR;
2     @ ensures_abs updateE;
3     @ assignable_abs updateA;
4     @ def updateR = x != 0;
5     @ def updateE = \result <==>
6     @    (balance == \old(balance) + x);
7     @ def updateA = balance; @*/
8   boolean update(int x) {}
```

Fig. 2. Method *update* in role *Account* in feature *BankAccount*

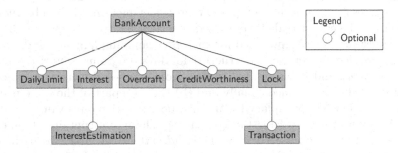

Fig. 3. Feature model of a variant of the bank account product line

features in the same product that contain code for specific operating systems. Feature models [14,28] describe valid combinations of features. The most common way to represent feature models are feature diagrams [28]. In Fig. 3, we show the feature diagram that represents our running example, being a software product line implementing a rudimentary BankAccount management system. The root feature *BankAccount* provides a base implementation. All its child features are optional and provide additional functionalities such as maximum daily withdrawal and performing updates of multiple accounts in one atomic transaction. Moreover, some dependencies are imposed on the features. In our running example, feature *InterestEstimation* requires the presence of feature *Interest* and feature *Transaction* requires the presence of feature *Lock*.

2.4 Feature Composition and Specification

In feature-oriented programming, there is a bijective mapping of *features* to so-called *feature modules*. Feature modules encapsulate all the feature's artifacts, such as part of the source code, test cases, or documentation [7]. Importantly, the granularity is not on file level, but different methods and fields of the same class may be *decomposed* into different feature modules with respect to their corresponding feature. Additionally, refined methods in a feature module can be annotated with a specification (cf. Fig. 1). For convenience, we use the terms *feature* and *feature module* interchangeably.

To generate a particular software product p, a set of selectable features $F = \{f_1, \ldots, f_n\}$ is incrementally composed together by a composition operator

$\bullet : F \times F \rightarrow F$ [2]:

$$p = f_n \bullet (f_{n-1} \bullet (\cdots \bullet (f_2 \bullet f_1))) \qquad (1)$$

For feature modules, the composition is achieved by means of superimposition [3] and for specifications, the composition is achieved by feature-oriented contract composition [41]. Both compositions are not commutative in general [5, 27, 41], such that a developer has to decide in which order features are merged together. In the following, we briefly describe both concepts.

Superimposition [3] is a simple process, where two feature modules represented as trees are recursively composed together by merging their substructures if and only if the parent node is composed and their name and type match. Such a tree structure has to be provided for each programming language individually. For instance, elements of the tree structure for Java programs comprise *packages*, *classes*, *methods*, and *fields* and two classes from composed feature modules are merged if (a) they are named equally and (b) they are part of the same package. In Fig. 1, we show an exemplary feature composition with our example product line as it is performed by FEATUREHOUSE [8]. The figure contains the method update of features *BankAccount* and *DailyLimit* in the first two listings. In the product line, feature *BankAccount* represents the base feature, with which all other features are composed, meaning that the method implementation of feature *DailyLimit* refines the method implementation of feature *BankAccount*. In the third listing, we show the result of the composition of both methods. The listing contains two methods. In method update in feature *DailyLimit* the keyword original is used (see Line 23) to call its direct predecessor in feature *BankAccount*. During composition, the keyword is replaced by a call to method update_wrappee_BankAccount (see Line 46) defined in feature *BankAccount*.

When a product is generated, its specification needs to be composed as well. While there are several approaches to realize such a contract composition [38, 41], we focus on a particular composition mechanism similar to feature-oriented method refinement on the implementational level, namely *explicit contract refinement* [41]. With explicit contract refinement, refining contracts may refer the original precondition or postcondition in their respective precondition and postcondition by keyword original [41]. Let m, m' be two methods specified with preconditions P, P' and postconditions Q, Q', respectively. Then the composition operator for explicit contract refinement is defined as:

$$\{P\}m\{Q\} \bullet \{P'\}m'\{Q'\} = \{P'[\backslash \texttt{original} \backslash P]\}m \bullet m'\{Q'[\backslash \texttt{original} \backslash Q]\} \quad (2)$$

where $P'[\backslash \texttt{original} \backslash P]$ yields the replacement of all placeholders original with precondition P in precondition P' ($Q'[\backslash \texttt{original} \backslash Q]$ is defined analogously).

2.5   Family-Based Verification

The family-based verification that we consider in this work is based on the construction of a *metaproduct*. A metaproduct combines all features of a product line into a single software product by means of *variability encoding* [43]. Essentially,

```
1    public  class Account {
2
3        boolean update(int x) {
4            if (!FM.FeatureModel.Logging) {
5                update_wrappee_DailyLimit(x);
6            } else {
7                //Body of method update from Feature Logging
8            }
9        }
10
11       boolean update_wrappee_DailyLimit(int x) {
12           if (!FM.FeatureModel.DailyLimit) {
13               update_wrappee_BankAccount(x);
14           } else {
15               //Body of method update from Feature DailyLimit
16           }
17       }
18
19       boolean update_wrappee_BankAccount(int x) {
20           //Body of method update from Feature BankAccount
21       }
22   }
```

Fig. 4. Variability encoding for method *update*

compile-time variability (i.e., the selection of composing features) is transformed into run-time variability (i.e., branching conditions). A boolean class variable is created for each feature that indicates whether a feature is selected (**true**) or not (**false**). These feature variables are then used in implementations and specifications to simulate different feature selections at run-time. Verification tools are configured to treat feature variables as uninitialized to consider all possible combinations.

However, relying only on a family-based strategy when also considering the evolution of product lines has some drawbacks, as all proofs of the former metaproduct may become invalid. For instance, when the feature model has changed, new combinations emerge that were not considered during the last verification. Moreover, a newly added feature might interact with other features. Figure 4 shows how such an interaction is established through method refinements for method update in the bank account product line when adding a new feature *Logging*. Method update is defined in feature *BankAccount* and refined in features *Logging* and *DailyLimit*. In the metaproduct, all refinements are connected using variability encoding. That is, an if-condition checking whether the respective feature is selected is added to each of the refinements. Since feature *Logging* introduced a new refinement, all update methods and all methods that call method update need to be re-verified. Therefore, one would need to regenerate the metaproduct, so that new feature *Logging* is included, and verify the new metaproduct again.

Although there is a feature-family-based approach by Hähnle and Schaefer [24] that facilitates proof reuse, it requires a refinement to have more specialized contracts than the method it refines. Feature *Logging*, however, introduces new fields and its methods use them in their contracts. Thus, their approach cannot be applied to the bank account product line under the given evolution scenario.

3   Applying Feature-Family-Based Verification Under Evolution

In this section, we introduce our reference approach following a feature-family-based verification strategy called FEFALUTION.

3.1   Overview

Our main research goal is to evaluate whether a feature-family-based verification approach may outperform existing family-based approaches for the verification of product lines under evolution. As to the best of our knowledge no such approach currently exists, we propose a novel two-phased approach following the feature-family-based strategy. Figure 5 presents an overview of FEFALUTION, which is divided into a *feature-based verification* phase and a subsequent *family-based* verification phase.

The feature-based verification phase mainly consists of two steps. First, a set of feature modules is transformed into a set of *feature stubs* (1). The reason is that feature modules do not typically constitute valid Java programs. Therefore, compiling or verifying them produces type errors. To lift a feature module to a valid Java program, we adopt and extend the concept of *feature stubs* as proposed by Kolesnikov et al. [30] to enable feature-based type checking. Feature stubs extend feature modules with additional (dummy) source code, such that all type and compilation errors are resolved. After the feature-stub generation, the feature stub contains two kinds of methods. For an easier distinction, we refer to methods that originally belonged to the feature module as *domain methods* and we refer to methods created to match calls to methods outside the feature as *method prototypes*. In addition, our realization of feature stubs also resolves dependencies on the level of contracts and adds *pure abstract contracts* to method prototypes to enable a contract-based formal verification.

Second, each method in a feature stub is verified and a corresponding proof is produced (2). For many methods, only partial (or *incomplete*) proofs exist, as they may invoke methods that are only visible in other features and whose concrete definition is therefore unknown at this stage. An additional optimization applies the feature-based verification only if a proof does not already exist in the previous version (e.g., as prevalent for any method of the initial version). Otherwise, the partial proofs of the former version are considered and a proof replay mechanism is applied to also minimize verification effort in the presence of implementation changes.

In the family-based verification phase, FEFALUTION tries to complete all partial proofs. First, the feature modules together with the feature model are used as input to generate the metaproduct (i.e., a single software product that representes the complete product line) (3). Second, FEFALUTION finalizes all partial proofs by replacing the incomplete method invocations (i.e., method prototypes) with the concrete instances and replaying these proof artifacts on the corresponding domain method of the metaproduct (4).

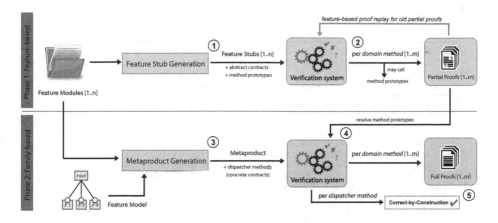

Fig. 5. Overview of FEFALUTION

An additional optimization is the generation of *dispatcher methods* to further increase the reuse potential. As illustrated in Fig. 4 and proposed by Thüm et al. [37], an if-statement is added for each *domain method* to check whether the corresponding feature is deselected. In this case, the previous method along the feature composition order is called, and introducing additional methods for the variability encoding is avoided. Yet, using only one method is impractical for our approach, as it would be more difficult to reuse partial proofs from the feature-based phase. Therefore, we also introduce *dispatcher methods* in the metaproduct, adopting parts of the variability encoding from Apel et al. [9]. Figure 7 shows an example of a dispatcher method in Line 35. Dispatcher methods serve as a connecting link between two domain methods, and we consider them to be correct-by-construction (5), as their contract only represents the case distinction between both dispatched methods. This way, the corresponding proof obligations become trivially true. In Algorithm 1, we draft our main algorithm, where we denote by DM a set of domain methods and P_{part} a set of partial proofs. We use the prime symbol (e.g., DM') to refer to the respective representation in the previous version.

Algorithm 1 FEFALUTION($\mathbb{F}$, $\mathbb{F}'$, $\mathcal{FM}$, ∂_{old}), where $\mathbb{F}$ is the set of feature modules, $\mathbb{F}'$ is the set of feature modules from the previous version, $\mathcal{FM}$ is the feature model, and $\partial_{old} : DM' \rightarrow P'_{part}$ is a function mapping domain methods $m' \in DM'$ from the previous version to their respective partial proof $p' \in P'_{part}$.

1: Create for each feature module $fm \in \mathbb{F}$ a corresponding feature stub by applying

$$s_{fm} = \text{GENERATEFEATURESTUB}(fm, \mathbb{F}, \mathcal{FM}) \qquad (3)$$

and define by $\mathbb{S}_{\mathbb{F}}$ the set of all feature stubs for feature modules $\mathbb{F}$.

2: Compute set $\mathbb{S}_{\mathbb{F}'}$ of all feature stubs for the past feature modules $\mathbb{F}'$. Define $\Delta(\mathbb{S}_{\mathbb{F}}, \mathbb{S}_{\mathbb{F}'}) \subseteq DM$ as the set of *domain methods* that changed.

3: Define $\partial : DM \rightarrow P_{part}$ as a function that maps domain methods $m \in DM$ from the current version to their respective partial proof $p \in P_{part}$ by the following case distinction:

   a. for each new domain method $m \in DM \setminus DM'$:

$$\partial(m) := \text{FEATUREBASEDVERIFICATION}(m) \qquad (4)$$

   b. for each domain method $m \in \Delta(\mathbb{S}_{\mathbb{F}}, \mathbb{S}_{\mathbb{F}'})$:

$$\partial(m) := \text{FEATUREBASEDPROOFREPLAY}(m, \partial_{old}(m)) \qquad (5)$$

   c. for each domain method $m \in DM \cap DM' \wedge m \notin \Delta(\mathbb{S}_{\mathbb{F}}, \mathbb{S}_{\mathbb{F}'})$:

$$\partial(m) := \partial_{old}(m). \qquad (6)$$

4: Compute the metaproduct mp based on the current set of future modules $\mathbb{F}$ and feature model $\mathcal{FM}$:

$$mp = \text{COMPUTEMETAPRODUCT}(\mathbb{F}, \mathcal{FM}). \qquad (7)$$

5: Define P_{part}^{ad} as the set of adapted partial proofs with respect to metaproduct mp and $\partial^{ad} : DM \rightarrow P_{part}^{ad}$ as the mapping function.

6: For all domain methods $m \in DM$, apply

$$p_{full} = \text{FAMILYBASEDVERIFICATION}(m, \partial^{ad}) \qquad (8)$$

to obtain the full proof for domain method m by completing the abstract segments in $\partial^{ad}(m)$.

3.2   From Feature Stubs to Partial Proofs

For each feature-module dependency, FEFALUTION generates a stub for the missing element. For example, consider Fig. 6. Method `transfer` of class *Transaction* contains a call to method `update`, which is part of class *Account*. Feature *Transaction*, however, neither contains the class nor the method. Thus, we generate the class and a method prototype as part of the feature stub for feature *Transaction* as shown in Fig. 6, which resolves an otherwise emerging type error. Other examples are references that access either a field or type of outside the feature as a feature-module dependency as well.

A special case of a feature-module dependency is keyword `original`. Methods may be refined multiple times by different features, which results in a *refinement chain*. The previous refinement of a method in a refinement chain can

```
1   class Transaction {
2       public boolean transfer(Account source,
3           Account destination, int amount) {
4           [...]
5           if (!source.update(-amount))
6               return false;
7           if (!destination.update(amount)) {
8               source.undoUpdate(-amount);
9               return false;
10          }
11          [...]
12      }
13  }
```

```
14  class Account {
15      /* method prototype */
16      /*@ requires_abs updateR;
17      @ ensures_abs updateE;
18      @ assignable_abs updateA; @*/
19      boolean update(int x) { return true;}
20
21      /* method prototype */
22      /*@ requires_abs updateR;
23      @ ensures_abs updateE;
24      @ assignable_abs updateA; @*/
25      boolean undoUpdate(int x) { return true;}
26  }
```

Fig. 6. Classes *Transaction* and *Account* in feature stub *Transaction*

be accessed via keyword `original`, which is replaced by a concrete instance of the respective method at compile time. Method `update`, which we show in the feature *DailyLimit* of Fig. 1, uses `original` to refer to the previous refinement. In the feature stub generation process, the keyword is replaced with a call to the newly added method prototype in the feature stub. Consider again Fig. 1 method `update` in feature *DailyLimit* of Fig. 1. FEFALUTION creates a method prototype to match the call and replaces keyword `original` with the method prototype's name.

An addition to the original feature stub generation [30] is the introduction of abstract contracts for method prototypes. Otherwise, a theorem prover would assume the absence of a specification. As no definition for a method prototype exists (i.e., for method inlining), a (partial) proof cannot be established in this case. Therefore, FEFALUTION enriches method prototypes with *pure abstract contracts* (i.e., abstract contracts without concrete definitions), which we refer to as *contract prototypes*. Figure 6 shows the contract prototypes in Lines 16–18. Using contract prototypes, a theorem prover can now incorporate `update` in its analysis. Whenever a domain method calls a method prototype, the respective obligations can not be closed by the theorem prover and remain open. Consequently, a partial (incomplete) proof is generated that, however, already may contain numerous reusable proof steps. These *abstract sections* in partial proofs are replaced in the next phase by concrete definitions to generate full proofs.

3.3 Generation and Theorem Proving of the Metaproduct

Similar to the feature stub generation, the metaproduct generation translates both the implementation and the specification. Following the variability encoding as described by Thüm et al. [37], FEFALUTION adds a new class `FeatureModel`, in which each feature of the product line is represented by a static boolean field. During verification, the theorem prover can use these feature variables to simulate all valid feature combinations. To prevent the theorem prover from simulating invalid feature combinations, FEFALUTION adds an invariant to each class representing the feature model as a propositional formula.

Afterwards, FEFALUTION adapts the *domain methods* of all features in two ways. First, as briefly described in Sect. 3.1, *dispatcher methods* are introduced to increase robustness of the domain methods. In particular, FEFALUTION uses dispatcher methods to connect domain methods of all features along the feature composition order by creating a call hierarchy. Second, as FEFALUTION has access to the information of all features and the order of composition at this stage, keyword `original` is replaced by the concrete method call. In particular, a reference to `original` is only a special case of a feature-module dependency caused by a method call across different features. As an example, consider again method `update` in feature *DailyLimit* of Fig. 1, which also contains keyword `original`. During the metaproduct generation, FEFALUTION replaces `original` with a call to the introductory method `update_BankAccount`, as can be seen in Line 22 of Fig. 7.

To encode the whole product line's variability, FEFALUTION additionally adapts the specification. Again, we partly adopt the work of Thüm et al. [37]. They enrich the method contracts in their metaproduct with an implication before each clause defining under which feature combination it must hold. As stated above, their metaproduct methods are structurally similar to our *dispatcher methods*, so we adopt the same mechanism for our *dispatcher methods*. For *domain methods*, we mostly use the contracts from the feature-based phase as-is, including the additional **requires** clause stating that the corresponding feature must be selected. The only exception is keyword `original`. FEFALUTION is able to include all information from the product line. Therefore, FEFALUTION can replace keyword `original` with the precondition or postcondition of the respective method in the call hierarchy. This way, FEFALUTION is able to resolve all syntactic and semantic feature interactions. Finally, for the metaproduct, FEFALUTION transforms all method contracts into abstract contracts – which does not change the semantics of the contracts – to ensure reusability of the partial proofs.

In the metaproduct class in Fig. 7, we also show some of the resulting contracts. For the *domain method* `update_DailyLimit`, the contract mostly stays as it was in the feature module. Only keyword `original` in the precondition and postcondition is replaced by the precondition and postcondition of the former refinement `update_BankAccount` (see Line 13 and Line 15). The contract of `dispatcher_update_DailyLimit` represents a composition of the contracts of *domain methods* `update_BankAccount` and `update_DailyLimit`. In front

```
1    public class Account {
2        static final int OVERDRAFT_LIMIT = 0;
3        int balance = 0;
4        static final int DAILY_LIMIT = -1000;
5        int withdraw = 0;
6
7        /*@ ... @*/
8        boolean update_BankAccount(int x) {
9            [...]
10       }
11
12   /*@ requires_abs update_DailyLimitR;
13    @ def update_DailyLimitR = FM.FeatureModel.DailyLimit && x != 0;
14    @ ensures_abs update_DailyLimitE;
15    @ def update_DailyLimitE =\result <==> (balance == \old(balance) + x) &&
16    @   ((FM.FeatureModel.DailyLimit ==> (!\result ==> withdraw == \old(withdraw))
17    @     && (\result <==> withdraw <= \old(withdraw))));
18    @ assignable_abs update_DailyLimitA;
19    @ def update_DailyLimitA = withdraw, balance; @*/
20       boolean update_DailyLimit(int x) {
21           [...]
22           if (!update_BankAccount(x))
23               return false;
24           [...]
25       }
26
27   /*@ requires_abs dispatch_update_DailyLimitR;
28    @ def dispatch_update_DailyLimitR = (FM.FeatureModel.BankAccount ||
29    @   FM.FeatureModel.DailyLimit) && x != 0;
30    @ ensures_abs dispatch_update_DailyLimitE;
31    @ def dispatch_update_DailyLimitE = \result
32    @   <==> (balance == \old(balance) + x);
33    @ assignable_abs dispatch_update_DailyLimitA;
34    @ def updateA = withdraw, balance; @*/
35       boolean dispatch_update_DailyLimit (int x) {
36           if (FM.FeatureModel.DailyLimit)
37               return update_DailyLimit(x);
38           return update_BankAccount(x);
39       }
40
41       /*@ ... @*/
42       boolean update(int x) {
43           if (FM.FeatureModel.Logging)
44               return update_Logging(x);
45           return dispatch_update_DailyLimit(x);
46       }
47
48       /*@ ... @*/
49       boolean update_Logging(int x) {
50           [...]
51       }
52   }
```

Fig. 7. Class *Account* after metaproduct generation

of each precondition and postcondition introduced by feature *DailyLimit*, there is an implication stating that the clause must only hold if the feature is selected (see Line 16). We do not need such an implication for feature *BankAccount*, because this feature is part of any program variant. Finally, we add a precondition stating that at least *BankAccount* and *DailyLimit* must be selected (see Lines 28–29).

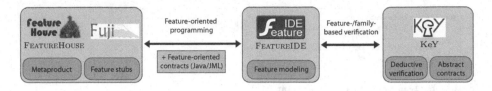

Fig. 8. Integration of FEFALUTION into the FEATUREIDE ecosystem

After the metaproduct generation, the partial poofs can be replayed on the adapted domain methods. If a proof goal remains open, this may be due to several reasons. First, a method may not fulfill its specification. In this case, either the behavior of the method or its specification needs to be changed. Second, if the contract correctly describes a method's behavior, but the theorem prover can still not close all proof goals, it might not be able to perform the necessary steps to complete the verification automatically. Still, interacting with the theorem prover may be possible. If all proof goals for the metaproduct are closed during verification, the product line is successfully verified.

4   Open-Source Tool Support

We implemented FEFALUTION as extensions to the tools FEATUREIDE and FEA-TUREHOUSE. FEATUREHOUSE [8] is a composer of software artifacts that supports feature-oriented composition for several languages. It is integrated into FEATUREIDE, an Eclipse-based IDE for feature-oriented product lines. Both tools have been extended to support (1) JML contracts and (2) variability encoding by means of the metaproduct generation technique proposed by Thüm et al. [37]. As we adopt some mechanisms of Thüm et al. [37] and rely on JML-based specification, we provide our tool support only as *extensions* to these tools. Moreover, one goal was to generate our verification objects (i.e., feature stubs and metaproduct) in such a way that they can be verified by any off-the-shelf theorem prover supporting JML contracts. However, for our approach we rely on abstract contracts and, to the best of our knowledge, only KEY provides them. Our last extension therefore integrates KEY into FEATUREIDE. In Fig. 8, we illustrate how all three tools are connected.

When a product line is to be verified, the feature-stub generation can be started for any FEATUREHOUSE project in FEATUREIDE. The family-based type check is performed automatically before the actual generation is performed by means of the tool Fuji. Fuji [6] is a compiler for feature-oriented programming but also supports family-based type checking based on a family-wide access model. After the feature-stub creation, if KEY is installed as a plugin, it is started automatically with the first feature stub loaded. A user can employ KEY's taclet *Finish abstract proof part* to reason about abstract contracts, which results in partial proofs based on the placeholders declared in the contract prototypes. Besides performing the actual verification, KEY can also save the created partial proofs in proof files on hard disk. When KEY is closed, FEATUREIDE starts a new KEY instance with the next feature stub to bypass loading each feature stub manually. To start the second phase, one needs to re-build the product line to yield the current metaproduct. After the generation, the metaproduct can be verified with KEY. For *domain methods*, the partial proofs can be reused by employing KEY's proof replay feature and closing all remaining proof goals with KEY. For *dispatcher methods*, no partial proofs are generated. After verifying all methods of the metaproduct, the product line is considered to be completely verified. Both the base tools and our extensions are open-source and available at their respective repositories.[1] [2]

5   Empirical Evaluation of Fefalution

With FEFALUTION and our given tool support, we introduced a feature-family-based verification approach, which is intended to outperform existing product-line verification approaches considering the evolution of software product lines. The above sections raise the following two important research questions that we aim to answer by means of an empirical study.

RQ–1: Does FEFALUTION reduce the overall verification effort considering product-line evolution compared to existing approaches?

RQ–2: Which impact do different optimizations of family-based verification approaches have on the verification effort?

Answering **RQ–1** is important to understand whether our instance of a feature-family-based approach (i.e., FEFALUTION) is indeed a promising alternative to sole family-based approaches. Answering **RQ–2** will help users and researchers to get insights on concrete optimizations (e.g., employing either concrete or abstract contracts, or applying proof replay) that influence the verification effort.

5.1   Case Study

Our experiment is based on the bank account product line (cf. Fig. 3) that has already been used for product-line specification and verification [41]. As FEFALUTION focuses on evolution, we developed a total of six different versions of the product line that each represent a common type of evolution scenario. All methods in each scenario are specified and can be verified automatically. We show all versions and how they are created in Fig. 9.

Scenario S_1 represents our *base line* for each evolution scenario. Scenarios S_2 and S_3 represent evolution on the implementation level by either making changes (i.e., refactorings) to the contracts or the implementation. Scenarios S_4 and S_5 represent the evolution of the feature model. In particular, we remove feature *CreditWorthiness* for scenario S_4 and add feature *Logging* to the product

---

[1] Adapted FEATUREHOUSE: https://github.com/kruegers/featurehouse.
[2] Adapted FEATUREIDE: https://github.com/kruegers/featureide.

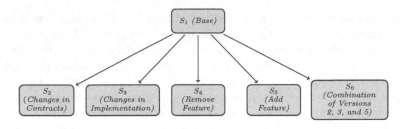

Fig. 9. Illustration of the five performed evolution scenarios

line for scenario S_5. Finally, scenario S_6 combines the changes of scenarios S_2, S_3, and S_5.

The product line for scenario S_5 has already been presented in Fig. 3. Overall, the product line for scenario S_5 consists of five classes distributed over nine features, twelve class refinements, a total of 17 unique methods specified with a contract, and six method refinements.

5.2   Experimental Design

We evaluate a total of six approaches by means of our existing tool support (cf. Sect. 4). As product-based approaches are typically inferior to family-based approaches [39], we only consider approaches that follow a family-based strategy. In particular, there exist numerous optimizations between the family-based verification approach developed in earlier work by some of the authors [37] and the feature-family-based verification approach developed in this work (i.e., FEFALUTION). Hence, to get more insights on the influence of these optimizations, we contribute four additional strategies to our comparison, where we alter some of the optimizations. We illustrate the six approaches in Table 1. Optimizations include whether (1) a feature-based phase exists, (2) abstract contracts are used to allow the creation of partial proofs, (3) method calls are treated either with inlining or contracting, (4) dispatcher methods are generated for the metaproduct to increase robustness to implementation changes, (5) proof replay is applied on features, and (6) proof replay is applied on the metaproduct.

We compare all six approaches according to our two research questions. To answer **RQ–1**, we examine the overall verification effort of all approaches. Verification effort is measured in terms of necessary proof steps, which we consider to be an adequate measurement in terms of proof complexity, and proof time in milliseconds. To answer **RQ–2**, we present the results from the perspective of product line evolution and discuss which optimizations of a verification approach have the most impact. Afterwards, we discuss the potential reuse of verification results. For the evaluation, we used a notebook with Intel Core i7-3610QM CPU @ 2.30 GHz with 12 GB RAM on Windows 10 and Java 1.8.

Table 1. Evaluated approaches and their optimizations

Approach	Feature-based phase	Abstract contract	Method call treatment with contracting	Method call treatment with inlining	Meta-product generation with dispatcher	Meta-product generation without dispatcher	Feature-based proof replay	Family-based proof replay
FEFALUTION	●	●	●	○	●	○	●	○
VA$_2$ (Metaproduct)	○	●	●	○	●	○	○	●
VA$_3$ (Concrete)	○	○	●	○	●	○	○	●
VA$_4$ (Inlining 1)	○	○	○	●	●	○	○	●
VA$_5$ (Inlining 2)	○	○	○	●	○	●	○	●
VA$_6$ (Family-based [37])	○	○	○	●	○	●	○	○

●: applied; ○ not applied

5.3 Results

We present the results in the following tables. In Table 2, we show the overall verification effort for each approach to verify all six versions (i.e., necessary proof steps, branches, and proof times) without depicting the reuse potential. In the following, we mainly discuss proof steps, as proof times and number of branches largely mirror the results and lead to similar interpretations.

Table 2. Overall verification effort for all approaches

Approach	Proof steps	Proof time (in ms)	Branches
FEFALUTION	714,762	3,372,449	7,522
VA$_2$	665,994	2,762,019	5,041
VA$_3$	363,713	598,756	6,376
VA$_4$	157,072	258,145	2,919
VA$_5$	140,492	173,387	2,995
VA$_6$	153,931	187,156	3,499

As Table 2 shows, FEFALUTION needs the most steps of all approaches for a full verification of all versions. Overall, FEFALUTION needs approximately 7% more steps than VA$_2$, 49% more than approach VA$_3$, and more than four times as much for the remaining versions VA$_4$, VA$_5$, and VA$_6$). Although the overhead itself is not a surprise to us, we did not expect the gap between using abstract contracts and concrete contracts to become this large. While approach

VA$_2$, which only consists of the family-based phase, also leads to an overhead compared to the other approaches, it nevertheless needs less effort compared to FEFALUTION.

Table 3. Overall verification effort considering proof reuse

Approach	Saved proof steps	Percentage of reused proof steps	Percentage of reused branches
FEFALUTION	128,258	17.94%	44.65%
VA$_2$	129,396	19.43%	54.48%
VA$_3$	22,920	6.30%	10.24%
VA$_4$	13,212	8.41%	14.38%
VA$_5$	13,707	9.75%	16.69%

Regarding the overall proof reuse potential, Table 3 shows that about 128,258 steps (17.94%) of the total proof steps needed by FEFALUTION could be reused. Compared to FEFALUTION and VA$_2$, the reuse potential for all other approaches is considerably smaller. To get more insights about which approach performs better on which evolution scenario, we decided to conduct a more fine-grained analysis for the reuse potential. As described before, evolution scenarios S_2 and S_3 represent additions and changes to the *implementation and specification*, whereas S_4 and S_5 represent more coarse-grained changes to the *product line* (e.g., removing a complete feature module or other changes to the feature model). In the following, we investigate both kinds of evolution individually for all six approaches.

Table 4. Reuse for versions with changes in implementation and specification

Approach	Saved proof steps	Percentage of reused proof steps	Percentage of reused branches
FEFALUTION	29,161	21.70%	60.97%
VA$_2$	29,506	23.91%	65.12%
VA$_3$	19,941	44.43%	33.01%
VA$_4$	10,630	50.47%	69.16%
VA$_5$	10,716	57.50%	79.06%

Table 4 shows that for changes that do not affect the feature model but only the implementation and specification, VA$_4$ and VA$_5$ are the most successful approaches with a reuse potential of over 50% each. The reuse potential for FEFALUTION and VA$_2$ is considerably smaller. However, when the feature model changes, as indicated by Table 5, the reuse potential for approaches VA$_3$,

VA_4, and VA_5 drop significantly, whereas FEFALUTION and VA_2 perform significantly better compared to all other approaches. Moreover, the reuse potential for FEFALUTION and VA_2 is similar in magnitude.

Table 5. Reuse for versions with changes to the feature model

Approach	Saved proof steps	Percentage of reused proof steps	Percentage of reused branches
FEFALUTION	49,439	21.47%	63.06%
VA_2	50,568	22.63%	67.82%
VA_3	1,959	1.45%	3.11%
VA_4	1,703	2.58%	5.32%
VA_5	1,870	3.18%	6.87%

5.4 Discussion

For RQ1, we conclude that FEFALUTION reveals a large overhead compared to most approaches when considering the total verification effort. When the feature model evolves, FEFALUTION achieves a higher proof reuse than approaches VA_3, VA_4, and VA_5. However, VA_2 trumps FEFALUTION both in overall verification effort and proof reuse.

The proof strategies for abstract contracts are the same as for standard reasoning. This leads to some inefficient behavior when constructing partial proofs. For instance, once the program has been symbolically executed on a branch, there are several formulas of the form `if (locset \in method_A(...)) \then phi1 \else phi2`. As `method_A` is the abstract placeholder for the assignable clause, the conditional formula cannot be simplified further and leads to a proof split. Hence, we get 2^n branches for n such formulas.

When constructing the full proofs based on these partial proofs, this means we have to show the same proof obligations for several of these branches. This is avoided in case of concrete contracts as in most cases when inserting the concrete assignable clause, the condition of the conditional formulas simplifies to true or false and hence no unnecessary proof splits occur. By improving the strategies for the partial proofs, by stopping once a program has been symbolically executed and the remaining proof goal is first-order only, the proof size reduces drastically. A simple manual emulation of such a proof strategy leads to significant improvements. For instance, for method `transfer` of feature *Transaction* in S_6, the proof size is reduced from 111,075 nodes to 34,259 nodes. Further improvements by a more intelligent expansion of the placeholders may thus lead to further improvements.

Additionally, most features that had to be re-verified in the feature-based phase in S_2 to S_6 resulted in partial proofs containing less than 50 proof steps. The potential for feature-based proof replay was therefore limited in our case study.

RQ-1: Evaluation of Fefalution

For the bank account product line, FEFALUTION revealed a slight overhead for each evolution scenario compared to the sole family-based approach (i.e., VA_2). However, our manual analysis shows also room for improvement in two directions. First, the internal expansion of abstract contracts can be improved to drastically reduce the overhead. Second, feature-based proof replay was only applicable to a limited degree, as many established partial proofs during our evaluation consisted of less than 50 proof steps. More complex evolution scenarios may lead to more significant reductions of verification effort.

To answer RQ2, we compare FEFALUTION with five other approaches that each alter a specific *optimization* (cf. Table 1). For proof composition, our results indicate that a feature-family-based approach with partial proofs based on abstract contracts does not increase the reuse potential but, in fact, reduces it slightly when compared to a sole family-based approach with the same optimizations otherwise. To determine the impact of abstract contracts in contrast to concrete contracts, we can compare the results of approaches VA_2 and VA_3. Here, the results indicate that abstract contracts represent a trade-off between an overhead for a single verification on the one hand and an increased proof reuse on the other hand. Consequently, FEFALUTION and VA_2 need more effort for a full verification, but manage to achieve a much higher reuse than VA_3. This is not surprising, as abstract contracts were designed to facilitate more proof reuse, even if that leads to a small overhead [11]. Finally, we compare the results of approaches VA_3 and VA_4 to evaluate method call handling during verification. As illustrated, treating method calls with inlining instead of contracting leads to much lower overall verification effort, which may imply that our designed case study is insufficient to showcase the benefits of contracting compared to method inlining under evolution.

RQ-2: Comparison of all Approaches

For the bank account product line, abstract contracts lead to significant overhead regarding the overall verification effort, whereas approaches using method inlining require the least amount of verification effort. Considering only the feature model evolution, potential proof reuse is 8–10 times higher with abstract contacts. Contrary, considering only the evolution of implementation and specification, potential proof reuse is only half as high.

Additionally to these results, we made an observation during the evaluation, we want to discuss in the following. The smaller a full proof of a method is the bigger partial proofs tend to become relatively. For methods that need less than 100 proof steps for full verification, partial proofs often provide already more than 70% of the needed proof steps. For methods whose proofs are larger (> 1000 proof steps), however, the partial proofs are often less than 10% of the steps needed for a full proof. Although the general notion is not surprising, the huge drop is unfortunate because it reduces the usefulness of abstract contracts and partial proofs for software systems with methods for inherently complexer correctness proofs.

5.5   Further Insights and Future Directions

Our discussion in Sect. 5.4 implies that part of the results are indeed artifacts of the used *proof strategy*. Current program verification systems including KEY are mostly optimized for finding proofs. The feature-based phase together with the generated partial proofs, however, add an additional complexity to the proof search, which amounts to the overhead we measured for the bank account product line. This could very well be a design issue in current verification systems, which need to be adapted for a feature-based framework.

There is also another possibly fruitful direction to continue this line of work that has not been explored before. In recent work, Steinhöfel and Hähnle [35] suggest *abstract execution*, which has the potential to replace or at least enhance our usage of abstract contracts. With abstract execution (1) any statement or expression can be abstract, such that more fine-grained reuse than at the method level is possible, (2) abstract contracts can specify additional properties, such as necessity for termination or return values, which makes them more flexible, and (3) abstract contracts may contain dynamic frames and can express abstract heap separation conditions. Together, this has the potential to shift the trade-off in favor of our feature-family-based approach, as abstract contracts become richer. For example, the abstract contract of the logging feature would contain a dynamic frame that forces the assignable heap logger code to be disjoint with other methods. This means one can prove at the feature level that logging does not interfere with other features. Upon composition, the dynamic frame must be instantiated and proven, but this is usually trivial.

6   Related Work

In a survey, Thüm et al. [39] classify approaches in the literature for analysis of software product lines. They differentiate the approaches into product-based, family-based, feature-based approaches, and combinations thereof. Following their classification, we categorize our approach as a feature-family-based verification approach. FEFALUTION is first such approach without restrictions on specification. We provide the first comparative evaluation of a feature-family-based approach.

Product-based approaches usually require the generation of all products. Harhurin and Hartmann [26] among others propose optimizations such as verifying only a base product and reusing the proofs for the other products. However, even for optimized approaches, for product lines with many products, too many products need to be generated, which is why we chose not to include a product-based phase in our approach.

To facilitate feature-based approaches, combinations with product-based approaches have been proposed. Thüm et al. [36], Damiani et al. [17], Delaware et al. [19,20] and Gondal et al. [22] propose approaches that first create partial proofs for all features/implementation units and then compose these to full proofs for all products. Although our approach also consists of a feature-based phase to produce partial proofs and we compose the partial proofs in a second phase, our approach performs the composition in a family-based phase instead of a product-based phase.

Thüm et al. [37] present a family-based approach, which creates one metaproduct by means of variability encoding. FEFALUTION is similar as its second phase is also family-based, and we adopt some parts of the metaproduct generation. FEFALUTION differs in that it uses a different form of variability encoding and consists of two phases to facilitate proof reuse and to incorporate the notion of evolution. We also evaluate FEFALUTION in comparison to other family-based approaches instead of comparing it to product-based approaches.

Hähnle and Schaefer [24] propose to apply the Liskov Principle to contracts in order to achieve a feature-family-based verification. Their approach requires that when a method's pre- and postconditions are modified in a delta, they must become more specific than in the original implementation unit. Similarly, assignable clauses in deltas are only allowed to be subsets of the original assignable clause. Consequently, their approach allows for a modular verification and thus a reuse of old still valid proofs but the restrictions it imposes on contract refinement limit its practicability. With FEFALUTION, we aim to achieve a similarly modular verification without restrictions on contracts.

On top of the discussed differences, none of the approaches consider product-line evolution and therefore often require a complete re-verification. In order to facilitate proof reuse, Hähnle et al. [25] propose abstract contracts. In their approach, abstract contracts are used to provide placeholders independent of the actual definition of the contracts. A theorem prover can create a partial proof with respect to the placeholders that can be used for a full verification when the concrete definitions are known. Bubel et al. [11] further explore and extend the concept and provide tool support. Bubel et al. [12] also propose the concept of *proof repositories* to explicitly address the problem of software evolution and inefficient re-verification by employing abstract contracts. Contrary to their results, applying abstract contracts to the evolution of features seems to produce a higher overhead in its current stage.

Feature-family-based approaches have also been applied to other verification techniques than theorem proving. Delaware et al. [18] define a type system based on a feature-aware subset of Java. Type safety of individual features is specified through constraints, which can then be used to guarantee the whole family's type safety by relating them to the feature model. Damiani and Schaefer [16] propose a feature-family-based type checking approach for delta-oriented product lines. They manage to partially type-check each delta in isolation before using these results for a full family-based type check. However, type checking is not sufficient to detect semantic feature interactions. Hence, we designed our approach as a deductive verification approach.

7   Conclusions

Software product-line engineering facilitates a paradigm for systematically developing a set of program variants with a common code base. To verify program variants, numerous product-based and family-based strategies were proposed over the last decade. The lack of addressing feature interactions make sole feature-based strategies less effective, but they also exhibit the potential to scale better than sole family-based approaches. The goal of this work was to systematically investigate how to reduce the verification effort of specified product lines under evolution, whilst the focus of our discussion lies on method contracts and feature-oriented programming.

To this end, we conducted an empirical study in which we compared six approaches with varying characteristics. Our evaluation was based on an existing benchmark, namely the bank account product line, comprising a base version and five common evolution scenarios. Besides measuring and discussing the overall verification effort for each scenario, we confirmed that abstract contracts are mostly valuable when the product lines evolves (e.g., adding new features). However, as method inlining performed better than contracting, we also conclude that our employed case study lacked complexity in order to draw many significant conclusions. Our proposed feature-family-based verification FEFALUTION also performed slightly worse than the sole family-based verification, which we attribute to the limited applicability of the feature-based proof replay.

Nonetheless, we argue that our initial study and tooling constitutes a first stepping stone for a more thorough investigation of the verification of evolving product lines. While the lack of adequate case studies and benchmarks is certainly adverse to our initial goal, our automatic tooling can be employed as-is to continue this line of research. Questions such as *Can* FEFALUTION *outperform the family-based strategy for any evolution scenario?* or *Will a combination of feature-based proof replay and family-based proof replay reduce the overall verification effort?* are particularly interesting to investigate in future work.

Acknowledgements. We are grateful to Stefanie Bolle for her help with the implementation and evaluation, and also to Dominic Steinhöffel for his support with KeY and abstract contracts. This work was supported by the DFG (German Research Foundation) under the Researcher Unit FOR1800: Controlling Concurrent Change (CCC).

References

1. Ahrendt, W., Beckert, B., Bubel, R., Hähnle, R., Schmitt, P.H., Ulbrich, M.: Deductive Software Verification-The Key Book. LNCS, vol. 10001. Springer, Cham (2016). https://doi.org/10.1007/978-3-319-49812-6
2. Apel, S., Hutchins, D.: A calculus for uniform feature composition. ACM Trans. Program. Lang. Syst. (TOPLAS) **32**(5), 19:1–19:33 (2010)
3. Apel, S., Lengauer, C.: Superimposition: a language-independent approach to software composition. In: Pautasso, C., Tanter, É. (eds.) SC 2008. LNCS, vol. 4954, pp. 20–35. Springer, Heidelberg (2008). https://doi.org/10.1007/978-3-540-78789-1_2

4. Apel, S., Kästner, C., Lengauer, C.: Featurehouse: language-independent, automated software composition. In: Proceedings International Conference Software Engineering (ICSE), Washington, DC, USA, pp. 221–231. IEEE (2009). ISBN 978-1-4244-3453-4

5. Apel, S., Lengauer, C., Möller, B., Kästner, C.: An algebraic foundation for automatic feature-based program synthesis. Sci. Comput. Program. (SCP) **75**(11), 1022–1047 (2010)

6. Apel, S., Kolesnikov, S., Liebig, J., Kästner, C., Kuhlemann, M., Leich, T.: Access control in feature-oriented programming. Sci. Comput. Program. (SCP) **77**(3), 174–187 (2012)

7. Apel, S., Batory, D., Kästner, C., Saake, G.: Feature-Oriented Software Product Lines. Concepts and Implementation. Springer, Heidelberg (2013). https://doi.org/10.1007/978-3-642-37521-7

8. Apel, S., Kästner, C., Lengauer, C.: Language-independent and automated software composition: the featurehouse experience. IEEE Trans. Softw. Eng. (TSE) **39**(1), 63–79 (2013)

9. Apel, S., von Rhein, A., Wendler, P., Größlinger, A., Beyer, D.: Strategies for product-line verification: case studies and experiments. In: Proceedings International Conference Software Engineering (ICSE), Piscataway, pp. 482–491. IEEE (2013). ISBN 978-1-4673-3076-3

10. Aversano, L., Di Penta, M., Baxter, I.D.: Handling preprocessor-conditioned declarations. In: Proceedings International Working Conference Source Code Analysis and Manipulation (SCAM), Washington, DC, USA, pp. 83–92. IEEE, October 2002. ISBN 0-7695-1793-5

11. Bubel, R., Hähnle, R., Pelevina, M.: Fully abstract operation contracts. In: Margaria, T., Steffen, B. (eds.) ISoLA 2014. LNCS, vol. 8803, pp. 120–134. Springer, Heidelberg (2014). https://doi.org/10.1007/978-3-662-45231-8_9

12. Bubel, R., et al.: Proof repositories for compositional verification of evolving software systems. In: Steffen, B. (ed.) Transactions on Foundations for Mastering Change I. LNCS, vol. 9960, pp. 130–156. Springer, Cham (2016). https://doi.org/10.1007/978-3-319-46508-1_8

13. Calder, M., Kolberg, M., Magill, E.H., Reiff-Marganiec, S.: Feature interaction: a critical review and considered forecast. Comput. Netw. **41**(1), 115–141 (2003)

14. Czarnecki, K., Eisenecker, U.: Generative Programming: Methods, Tools, and Applications. ACM/Addison-Wesley, New York (2000)

15. Czarnecki, K., Pietroszek, K.: Verifying feature-based model templates against well-formedness OCL constraints. In: Proceedings International Conference Generative Programming and Component Engineering (GPCE), New York, NY, USA, pp. 211–220. ACM (2006)

16. Damiani, F., Schaefer, I.: Family-based analysis of type safety for delta-oriented software product lines. In: Margaria, T., Steffen, B. (eds.) ISoLA 2012. LNCS, vol. 7609, pp. 193–207. Springer, Heidelberg (2012). https://doi.org/10.1007/978-3-642-34026-0_15

17. Damiani, F., Dovland, J., Johnsen, E.B., Owe, O., Schäfer, I., Yu, I.C.: A transformational proof system for delta-oriented programming. In: de Almeida, E.S. (ed.) Proceedings International Software Product Line Conference (SPLC), New York, NY, USA, vol. 2, pp. 53–60. ACM (2012). ISBN 978-1-4503-1095-6

18. Delaware, B., Cook, W.R., Batory, D.: Fitting the pieces together: a machine-checked model of safe composition. In: Proceedings European Software Engineering Conference/Foundations of Software Engineering (ESEC/FSE), pp. 243–252. ACM (2009)

19. Delaware, B., Cook, W., Batory, D.: Product lines of theorems. In: Proceedings Conference Object-Oriented Programming, Systems, Languages and Applications (OOPSLA), New York, NY, USA, pp. 595–608. ACM (2011). ISBN 978-1-4503-0940-0
20. Delaware, B.D.S., Oliveira, B.C., Schrijvers, T.: Meta-theory à la carte. In: Proceedings Symposium Principles of Programming Languages (POPL), New York, NY, USA, pp. 207–218. ACM (2013). ISBN 978-1-4503-1832-7
21. Fischbein, D., Uchitel, S., Braberman, V.: A foundation for behavioural conformance in software product line architectures. In: Proceedings International Workshop Role of Software Architecture for Testing and Analysis (ROSATEA), New York, NY, USA, pp. 39–48. ACM (2006)
22. Gondal, A., Poppleton, M., Butler, M.: Composing event-b specifications - case-study experience. In: Apel, S., Jackson, E. (eds.) SC 2011. LNCS, vol. 6708, pp. 100–115. Springer, Heidelberg (2011). https://doi.org/10.1007/978-3-642-22045-6_7
23. Gruler, A., Leucker, M., Scheidemann, K.: Modeling and model checking software product lines. In: Barthe, G., de Boer, F.S. (eds.) FMOODS 2008. LNCS, vol. 5051, pp. 113–131. Springer, Heidelberg (2008). https://doi.org/10.1007/978-3-540-68863-1_8
24. Hähnle, R., Schaefer, I.: A Liskov principle for delta-oriented programming. In: Margaria, T., Steffen, B. (eds.) ISoLA 2012. LNCS, vol. 7609, pp. 32–46. Springer, Heidelberg (2012). https://doi.org/10.1007/978-3-642-34026-0_4
25. Hähnle, R., Schaefer, I., Bubel, R.: Reuse in software verification by abstract method calls. In: Bonacina, M.P. (ed.) CADE 2013. LNCS (LNAI), vol. 7898, pp. 300–314. Springer, Heidelberg (2013). https://doi.org/10.1007/978-3-642-38574-2_21
26. Harhurin, A., Hartmann, J.: Towards consistent specifications of product families. In: Cuellar, J., Maibaum, T., Sere, K. (eds.) FM 2008. LNCS, vol. 5014, pp. 390–405. Springer, Heidelberg (2008). https://doi.org/10.1007/978-3-540-68237-0_27
27. Höfner, P., Möller, B., Zelend, A.: Foundations of coloring algebra with consequences for feature-oriented programming. In: Kahl, W., Griffin, T.G. (eds.) RAMiCS 2012. LNCS, vol. 7560, pp. 33–49. Springer, Heidelberg (2012). https://doi.org/10.1007/978-3-642-33314-9_3
28. Kang, K.C, Cohen, S.G, Hess, J.A, Novak, W.E., Peterson, A.S.: Feature-oriented domain analysis (FODA) feasibility study. Technical report CMU/SEI-90-TR-21, Software Engineering Institute (1990)
29. Knüppel, A., Thüm, T., Padylla, C., Schaefer, I.: Scalability of deductive verification depends on method call treatment. In: Margaria, T., Steffen, B. (eds.) ISoLA 2018. LNCS, vol. 11247, pp. 159–175. Springer, Cham (2018). https://doi.org/10.1007/978-3-030-03427-6_15
30. Kolesnikov, S., von Rhein, A., Hunsen, C., Apel, S.: A comparison of product-based, feature-based, and family-based type checking. In: Proceedings International Conference Generative Programming and Component Engineering (GPCE), New York, NY, USA, pp. 115–124. ACM (2013). ISBN 978-1-4503-2373-4
31. Leavens, G.T., Cheon, Y.: Design by contract with JML, September 2006. http://www.jmlspecs.org/jmldbc.pdf
32. Leavens, G.T., Baker, A.L., Ruby, C.: Preliminary design of JML: a behavioral interface specification language for Java. SIGSOFT Softw. Eng. Notes **31**(3), 1–38 (2006)
33. Meyer, B.: Applying design by contract. IEEE Comput. **25**(10), 40–51 (1992)
34. Parnas, D.L.: On the criteria to be used in decomposing systems into modules. Commun. ACM **15**(12), 1053–1058 (1972)

35. Steinhöfel, D., Hähnle, R.: Abstract execution. In: ter Beek, M.H., McIver, A., Oliveira, J.N. (eds.) FM 2019. LNCS, vol. 11800, pp. 319–336. Springer, Cham (2019). https://doi.org/10.1007/978-3-030-30942-8_20
36. Thüm, T., Schaefer, I., Kuhlemann, M., Apel, S.: Proof composition for deductive verification of software product lines. In: Proceedings International Workshop Variability-intensive Systems Testing, Validation and Verification (VAST), Washington, pp. 270–277. IEEE Computer (2011)
37. Thüm, T., Schaefer, I., Apel, S., Hentschel, M.: Family-based deductive verification of software product lines. In: Proceedings International Conference Generative Programming and Component Engineering (GPCE), New York, NY, USA, pp. 11–20. ACM, September 2012. ISBN 978-1-4503-1129-8
38. Thüm, T., Schaefer, I., Kuhlemann, M., Apel, S., Saake, G.: Applying design by contract to feature-oriented programming. In: de Lara, J., Zisman, A. (eds.) FASE 2012. LNCS, vol. 7212, pp. 255–269. Springer, Heidelberg (2012). https://doi.org/10.1007/978-3-642-28872-2_18
39. Thüm, T., Apel, S., Kästner, C., Schaefer, I., Saake, G.: A classification and survey of analysis strategies for software product lines. ACM Comput. Surv. **47**(1), 6:1–6:45 (2014)
40. Thüm, T., Kästner, C., Benduhn, F., Meinicke, J., Saake, G., Leich, T.: FeatureIDE: an extensible framework for feature-oriented software development. Sci. Comput. Program. (SCP) **79**, 70–85 (2014)
41. Thüm, T., Knüppel, A., Krüger, S., Bolle, S., Schaefer, I.: Feature-oriented contract composition. J. Syst. Softw. **152**, 83–107 (2019)
42. von Rhein, A., Thüm, T., Schaefer, I., Liebig, J., Apel, S.: Variability encoding: from compile-time to load-time variability. J. Logic a Algebraic Methods Program. (JLAMP) **85**(1, Part 2), 125–145 (2016)
43. von Rhein, A., Thüm, T., Schaefer, I., Liebig, J., Apel, S.: Variability encoding: from compile-time to load-time variability. J. Logic a Algebraic Methods Program. **85**(1), 125–145 (2016)

Constraint-Based Contract Inference for Deductive Verification

Anoud Alshnakat[1], Dilian Gurov[1], Christian Lidström[1],
and Philipp Rümmer[2(✉)] (iD)

[1] KTH Royal Institute of Technology, Stockholm, Sweden
{anoud,dilian,clid}@kth.se
[2] Uppsala University, Uppsala, Sweden
philipp.ruemmer@it.uu.se

Abstract. Assertion-based software model checking refers to techniques that take a program annotated with logical assertions and statically verify that the assertions hold whenever program execution is at the corresponding control point. While the associated annotation overhead is relatively low, these techniques are typically monolithic in that they explore the state space of the whole program at once, and may therefore scale poorly to large programs. Deductive software verification, on the other hand, refers to techniques that prove the correctness of a piece of software against a detailed specification of what it is supposed to accomplish or compute. The associated verification techniques are modular and scale well to large code bases, but incur an annotation overhead that is often very high, which is a real obstacle for deductive verification to be adopted in industry on a wider scale. In this paper we explore synergies between the two mentioned paradigms, and in particular, investigate how interpolation-based Horn solvers used for software model checking can be instrumented to infer missing procedure contracts for use in deductive verification, thus aiding the programmer in the code annotation process. We summarise the main developments in the area of automated contract inference, and present our own experiments with contract inference for C programs, based on solving Horn clauses. To drive the inference process, we put program assertions in the main function, and adapt our TriCera tool, a model checker based on the Horn solver Eldarica, to infer candidate contracts for all other functions. The contracts are output in the ANSI C Specification Language (ACSL) format, and are then validated with the Frama-C deductive verification tool for C programs.

1 Introduction

Static approaches in program verification, including deductive verification [1,9] and model checking [8], offer an unparalleled level of confidence that software is indeed correct, and are receiving increasing attention in industrial applications. Static verification of a program can proceed in different ways: *monolithic* approaches receive the program and some form of specification as input, and attempt to construct a mathematical argument that the program, as a whole,

© Springer Nature Switzerland AG 2020
W. Ahrendt et al. (Eds.): Deductive Software Verification, LNCS 12345, pp. 149–176, 2020.
https://doi.org/10.1007/978-3-030-64354-6_6

satisfies the specification; *modular* approaches successively subdivide the verification problem into smaller and smaller parts, and thus construct a hierarchical correctness argument. In the verification literature, many examples in this spectrum from monolithic to modular methods can be identified; for instance, the state space of a concurrent program can be explored systematically by enumerating possible interleavings, a monolithic approach applied in classical model checking [21], but it is also possible to analyse the threads of a program one by one with the help of invariants, relies, or guarantees [22,31]. Monolithic and modular methods have complementary properties; monolithic methods tend to be easier to automate, while modular methods tend to scale to larger programs or systems.

In this paper, we explore synergies between monolithic and modular methods for the verification of programs with procedures. As monolithic methods, we consider model checkers built using the concept of *constrained Horn clauses* [6, 16,20]: such tools are able to verify, among others, programs with procedures and recursion fully automatically, and can in case of success output program artefacts including loop invariants and contracts [26]. On the modular side, we target deductive Hoare logic-based verification tools, which besides the program also needs detailed intermediate program annotations as input. Such specifications are written in a richer logical language, and are in principle to be supplied by the designer of the software, since they should express his or her intention. For procedural programming languages, they are given by means of procedure contracts that capture what each procedure is obliged to achieve when called, and under what assumptions on the caller.

We argue that these two families of tools complement each other extremely well: on the one hand, model checkers can automatically compute the program annotations required by deductive verification tools, and thus be used as invariant and contract inference tools; on the other hand, deductive verification tools can act as proof checkers that independently validate the computation of a model checker. Several hybrid combination approaches are possible as well: given a program partially annotated with invariants and contracts, a model checker could add the missing annotations, or show that the existing annotations are inconsistent and need corrections. For a program that is too large to be handled by a software model checker, manually provided contracts can be used to split the program into multiple parts of manageable size. For procedures that are invoked from multiple programs, contracts inferred in the context of one program can be reused for deductive verification of another program. The long-term vision of the presented line of research is the development of a *program annotation assistant* that applies fully automatic methods, including model checking, to infer, augment, or repair the annotations needed in deductive verification.

The main contributions of the paper are (i) a brief survey of the main directions in automatic contract inference (Sect. 3); (ii) the definition of the required program encoding and annotation translation to combine the Horn clause-based software model checker TriCera with the deductive verification system Frama-C [9] (Sects. 4 and 2); and (iii) an experimental evaluation of the performance of this tool combination on benchmarks taken from the SV-COMP [5] (Sect. 6).

```
int nondet();
/*@ contract @*/
int mc91(int n) {
  if (n > 100) {
    return n - 10;
  } else {
    return mc91(mc91(n + 11));
  }
}

int main() {
  int x = nondet();
  int res = mc91(x);
  assert (x!=8 || res==91);
  assert ((x<=102) || res==x-10);
}
```

```
/*@
//Function: mc91
  requires \true;
  assigns \nothing;
  ensures (n <= 100 ==>
          \result == 91)
  ensures (n > 100 ==>
          \result == n - 10);
*/
int mc91(int n) {
  if (n > 100) {
    return n - 10;
  } else {
    return mc91(mc91(n + 11));
  }
}
```

Listing 1.1. TriCera input for the McCarthy 91 function

Listing 1.2. An example of ACSL contracts for Frama-C

Motivating Example. We first illustrate the relationship between software model checking and deductive verification, using a C-version of the well-known McCarthy 91 function as a motivating example:

$$mc91(n) = \begin{cases} n - 10 & \text{if } n > 100 \\ mc91(mc91(n + 11)) & \text{if } n \leq 100. \end{cases}$$

Today's *software model checkers* focus mainly on the verification of safety (or reachability) properties embedded in program code in the form of assertions. Model checkers aim at fully automatic verification of programs, and therefore try to prove the absence of assertion violations without requiring any further code annotations. In the implementation of the McCarthy 91 function shown in Listing 1.1, two assertions in the main function capture the post-conditions to be verified: for the input 8, the result of the McCarthy 91 is conjectured to be 91, and for any input greater than 102 the result will be the input minus 10. The main function serves as a *harness* for the verification of the function of interest. The input in Listing 1.1 can be verified automatically by state-of-the-art model checkers, for instance by the TriCera model checker considered in this paper. TriCera can handle functions either by inlining them, or by inferring function contracts consisting of pre- and post-conditions. In our example, a contract is needed, since the McCarthy 91 function is recursive; the use of a contract is enabled by the comment /*@ contract @*/. The translation of the computed contract to the specification language ACSL is discussed in Sect. 5, and the contract is shown in Listing 5.2.

Deductive verification systems such as Frama-C [9] and KeY [1], in contrast, rely to a larger degree on user-provided annotations. In the case of the McCarthy 91 function, verification cannot proceed before a suitable function contract is supplied. Annotations and specifications in Frama-C are written in the behavioural specification language ACSL, which contains constructs written in special C comments. The function contract annotation begins with /*@ and ends with */, as shown in Listing 1.2. The keyword **ensures** is used to specify post-conditions. More details on Frama-C and ACSL will be given in Sect. 4.3. The contract given in Listing 1.2 is manually written, and gives a complete specification of the function. While most deductive verification tools are not able to compute contracts, they can usually check the correctness of contracts fully automatically.

ACSL annotations required by Frama-C, or similar tools, are detailed, and thus laborious to write. As the study [24] argues, an effective combination of contracting and function inlining is indispensable for the scalability of deductive verification. Going beyond this, automating the process of inferring function contracts is clearly advantageous for the software development process: earlier studies have shown that automation is a key enabler for the wider use of formal methods in industrial settings, and that automated annotation is of particular importance [28]. In this paper, we propose to leverage the ability of software model checkers to automatically compute contracts, and this way support the deductive verification process. That is, given an input specification and C code as in Listing 1.1, we want to generate a contract similar to Listing 1.2 for use in Frama-C. This paper provides the theoretic background for such a combination, and presents first practical steps.

2   The Notion of a Contract

In this section we recall the notion of a (software) contract, and define the operators of contract refinement and composition that provide the theoretical foundation for working with contracts.

2.1   Contract Basics

For reasons of presentation, all considerations are done in the context of a simple while-language with functions, with integers as the only data-type. We further assume that function parameters are passed by value and are read-only, and that programs do not contain global variables (or other kinds of global data, like heap). All results generalise to more realistic settings, like to the specification language ACSL used by Frama-C.

Definition 1 (Contract [26]). *Suppose f is a function with formal parameters $\langle a_1, \ldots, a_n \rangle$ and a formal result variable r. A contract for f is a pair $(Pre_f, Post_f)$ consisting of a pre-condition Pre_f over the arguments $a_1, \ldots, a_n$, and a post-condition $Post_f$ over the arguments $a_1, \ldots, a_n$ and the result r.*

Pre- and post-conditions are commonly represented as formulas in first-order logic, modulo a suitable set of background theories (e.g., integers or bit-vectors). The pre-condition, denoted by the *requires* clause in ACSL, characterises the legal inputs of a function, while the post-condition, denoted by the *ensures* clause, states properties of the function result, in relationship to the arguments. In addition to pre- and post-conditions, contracts in ACSL also commonly specify modified variables in an *assigns* clause, but this is only meaningful in the presence of global variables. An example of such a contract is shown in Listing 1.2.

A contract for a function f makes it possible to carry out the task of verifying a program (that uses f) in two steps:

(i) It has to be checked that the function f *satisfies* its contract. An implementation of a function f is said to satisfy a contract $(Pre_f, Post_f)$ if every terminating run that starts in a state satisfying Pre_f ends in a state satisfying $Post_f$. In Sect. 4, contract satisfaction will be formalised through the Hoare triple $\{Pre_f\}\ S_f\ \{Post_f\}$, in which S_f is the function body of f.

(ii) The rest of the program, sometimes called the *client code*, can be verified on the basis of the contract for f, disregarding the concrete implementation of f. A contract $(Pre_f, Post_f)$ is applicable in client code if every invocation of f satisfies the pre-conditions Pre_f, and if the client code executes correctly for every potential result of f satisfying $Post_f$. In Sect. 4, the verification of client code will be formalised through a dedicated Hoare proof rule CALL.

In the case of a program with multiple functions, step (i) will be carried out for each implementation of a function in the program, so that the overall verification effort can be split into many small parts that can be handled separately or in parallel. As a result, verification of large programs can be organised in such a way that the verification effort scales roughly linearly in the size of the program, which is the key idea underlying procedure-modular (or function-modular) verification. All large-scale verification projects proceed in this modular manner.

2.2   Contract Refinement and Composition

A function implementation will generally satisfy many contracts, some of which will be sufficient to verify a given piece of client code, while others might be too weak. Different contracts might cover different aspects of function behaviour, and for instance describe the results produced for different input ranges. This motivates the study of algebraic properties of the space of contracts, an exercise that has received much attention for the case of system-level contracts [4], and to a lesser degree for contracts of functions or procedures [30]. We define notions of contract refinement, conjunction, and disjunction that exhibit several convenient properties, and that correspond to the way contracts are used in KeY [1].

We say that a contract $C = (Pre, Post)$ *refines* a contract $C' = (Pre', Post')$ (for the same function f), denoted $C \sqsubseteq C'$, if $Pre' \Rightarrow Pre$ and $Post \wedge Pre' \Rightarrow Post'$; in other words, refinement weakens the pre-condition of a contract, and strengthens the post-condition for arguments admitted by the pre-condition. Refinement has the property that if a function f satisfies the finer (and thus *stronger*, or *more precise*) contract C, then f also fulfills the more abstract one C'. Vice versa, it also means that if a client verifies by means of modular verification against the more abstract contract C' of a function, it will again do so against the finer contract C, and thus does not need to be re-verified upon refining the contract. Finally, note that the conjunction $Post \wedge Pre'$ only makes sense under the assumption that function arguments (or global variables) cannot be updated in function bodies, as stated in the beginning of Sect. 2.1. In the more general case, Pre' has to be modified to refer to the function pre-state, for instance using the \old operator in ACSL.

The relation $\sqsubseteq$ is a preorder on the set of possible contracts of a function f, i.e., it is reflexive, transitive, but clearly not anti-symmetric. As usual, this means that the preorder induces an equivalence relation $\equiv$ defined by

$$C \equiv C' \Leftrightarrow (C \sqsubseteq C') \wedge (C' \sqsubseteq C)$$

and that the quotient $\sqsubseteq / \equiv$ is a partial order. In the following, we denote the class of contracts that are equivalent to C by $[C]$, but leave out the brackets $[\cdot]$ in most formulas for sake of presentation.

Example 2. Consider a function abs that computes the absolute value of an integer x. Possible contracts for abs are:

$$C_1 : \quad (x = 5, r = 5) \qquad\qquad C_2 : \quad (x = 5, r = 6)$$
$$C_3 : \quad (x = 5, r = x) \qquad\qquad C_4 : \quad (x \geq 0, r = x)$$
$$C_5 : \quad (x \leq 0, r = -x) \qquad\qquad C_6 : \quad (true, r = |x|)$$

A standard implementation of abs will satisfy the contracts C_1, C_3, C_4, C_5, C_6, but not C_2. Contracts C_1 and C_3 are equivalent, $C_1 \equiv C_3$. Contract C_4 refines contract C_1 ($C_4 \sqsubseteq C_1$), since C_4 is more restrictive than C_1, and similarly $C_6 \sqsubseteq C_4$ and $C_6 \sqsubseteq C_5$.

The example indicates that the space of possible contracts of a function has the structure of a lattice, which is indeed the case:

Lemma 3. *Let $\mathcal{C}$ be the set of all contracts of a function f (including both satisfied and unsatisfied contracts). The partially ordered set $(\mathcal{C}/\equiv, \sqsubseteq/\equiv)$ is a bounded lattice with the bottom element $\perp = [(true, false)]$, the top element $\top = [(false, true)]$, and the binary operations:*

$$[(Pre, Post)] \sqcup [(Pre', Post')] \Leftrightarrow [(Pre \wedge Pre', Post \vee Post')] \qquad \text{(Join)}$$
$$[(Pre, Post)] \sqcap [(Pre', Post')] \Leftrightarrow \qquad\qquad\qquad\qquad \text{(Meet)}$$
$$[(Pre \vee Pre', (Pre \rightarrow Post) \wedge (Pre' \rightarrow Post'))]$$

Proof. It mainly has to be verified that the defined operations indeed describe least upper and greatest lower bounds. This can be done automatically by first-order theorem provers. □

The bottom element $\bot$ of the contract lattice is the strongest (most refined) contract, and is only satisfied by an implementation of a function that diverges for every input; the top element $\top$ is the weakest contract, and satisfied by every implementation. Joining two contracts models the case of a function f having several implementations: if two implementations of f satisfy the contracts C_1 and C_2, respectively, then both implementations will satisfy $C_1 \sqcup C_2$, and client code can be verified on the basis of this more abstract contract. The meet of two contracts merges properties of a function expressed in multiple contracts into a single, stronger contract: if an implementation satisfies both C_1 and C_2, then it will also satisfy $C_1 \sqcap C_2$ (and vice versa). The meet operation is useful, in particular, for merging multiple automatically inferred contracts, as will be discussed later in this paper.

Example 4. We consider again the contracts from Example 2. Contracts C_4 and C_5 capture different parts of the behaviour of **abs**, and the meet of the two contracts is C_6, i.e., $C_4 \sqcap C_5 \equiv C_6$.

The problem of combining contracts has also been studied in the context of Hoare inference rules. Consider a library function that is called by several client functions. The library function may then have a different contract inferred from each client context, and we want to combine these into a single contract. Owe et. al. found that two inference rules, namely a rule for generalised normalisation and the CONSEQ rule of Hoare logic (see Table 1), are sufficient to infer any Hoare triple $\{P\} \ S \ \{R\}$ from a given set of Hoare triples over the same program S that logically entail $\{P\} \ S \ \{R\}$ [30]. Combining contracts in this way, however, does not preclude the need for re-verifying clients against their contracts in the context of the new, combined contract of a library function.

3 Existing Approaches in Contract Inference

While contracts are extremely useful for verifying programs modularly, finding correct and sufficient contracts is a time-consuming and error-prone process. This section surveys the existing work on *automatic* contract synthesis, extracting contracts either from the program under verification, or from the program together with the overall properties to be verified.

3.1 Strongest Post-conditions

One line of research on inferring contracts is based on the fundamental semantic notion of *strongest post-condition* due to Dijkstra [13], sometimes also called a *function summary*. Given a program (or rather a part of a program, typically a procedure) and a *pre-condition*, i.e., a state assertion that is assumed to hold at the beginning of the execution of the program, the strongest post-condition is an assertion that captures precisely the final states of the execution. So, if the pre-condition is *true*, the strongest post-condition characterises the final states of all executions starting in any initial state. For the purposes of contract inference this is meaningful, since one obtains useful contracts even when no pre-condition has been supplied from elsewhere. The strongest post-condition provides the strongest possible contract (for the given pre-condition) and is thus ideal for procedure-modular deductive verification. However, this precision often comes at the cost of overly verbose assertions being generated. This is because the strongest post-condition, when generated automatically, will often closely reflect the program from which it is extracted, and not necessarily capture the program *intention* concisely.

Strongest post-conditions can be computed with the help of *symbolic execution* [15], at least for programs that do not contain unbounded loops. This method is a source of explosion of the size of the generated formulas, since it is path-based.

Singleton and others [36] developed an algorithm that converts the exponentially large post-conditions, resulting from a strongest post-condition computation, into a more concise and usable form. The algorithm consists of several steps. Initially, the program is converted into a passive single assignment form (essentially eliminating all assignments, which are the main source of assertion explosion). Then, from a given pre-condition (or *true*, if no better pre-condition is available), the strongest post-condition is computed by means of symbolic execution. The resulting formula is first converted into a normal form that groups subformulas into a hierarchy of cases, and is then flattened. The flattened formula is analysed for overlapping states, which are recombined into a form, in which the strongest post-condition is finally presented.

3.2   Weakest Pre-conditions

A related approach is the inference of *pre-conditions* that are sufficient to establish given post-conditions, or more generally pre-conditions that ensure that program assertions do not fail. The information captured by pre-conditions is complementary to that of post-conditions: while pre-conditions do not compare pre- and post-states, and therefore cannot specify the effect of a function, they state obligations required for correct execution of a function that need to be taken care of by the caller.

Pre-conditions can be computed in various different ways. The traditional weakest pre-condition calculus due to Dijkstra [12] transforms post-conditions to pre-conditions, and forms the basis of several deductive verification systems. Similarly to post-conditions, pre-conditions can also be computed through symbolic execution, by extracting the path constraints of all paths leading to violated post-conditions or failing assertions. An alternative approach based on a combination of abstract interpretation and quantifier elimination is presented by Moy [27]; the method is able to compute pre-conditions also in the presence of loops, but it does not always output weakest pre-conditions. Seghir and Kroening derived pre-conditions using an algorithm based on *Counterexample-Guided Abstraction Refinement* (CEGAR) [34]. Starting from an over-approximation of the weakest pre-conditions of a function, the algorithm iteratively eliminates sets of pre-states for which function execution can lead to errors, until eventually sufficient (but still necessary, i.e., weakest) pre-conditions remain. The use of CEGAR implies that also functions with loops can be handled, although in general the algorithm might not terminate; this is unavoidable since neither strongest post-conditions nor weakest pre-conditions are computable in general. An eager variant of the algorithm, which does no longer require a refinement loop is demonstrated by Seghir and Schrammel [35].

The concept of *Maximal Specification Inference* [2] generalises the inference of weakest pre-conditions and considers the specifications of multiple functions simultaneously. Given a piece of program code that uses functions $f_1, \ldots, f_n$ (e.g., taken from a library), maximal specification inference attempts to construct the weakest specifications of $f_1, \ldots, f_n$ that are sufficient to verify the overall program. Albarghouthi et al. computed weakest specifications in a counterexample-guided manner, employing multi-abduction to find new specifications [2]. The approach can be applied even when no implementations of $f_1, \ldots, f_n$ are available.

3.3   Dynamic Inference of Assertions and Contracts

Given a set of test cases that exercise a system through its state space, a tool for *dynamic contract inference* will determine conditions that hold at various program points. These conditions are candidate assertions that may hold for all program runs. The most well-known tool for dynamic contract inference is Daikon [14], which automatically detects likely invariants for multiple languages; C, C++, Java and Perl. For each language, Daikon dedicates an instrumenter to trace certain variables. The traced variables are read by the inference engine to generate likely invariants. The generated invariants are tested against their trace samples and are reported only if they pass these tests. Daikon is optimised to handle large code sizes and large numbers of invariants, e.g., by suppressing the weaker invariants.

The Daikon tool has been used for dynamic contract inference in Eiffel. Polikarpova et al. compare, on 25 Eiffel classes, the programmer-provided contracts with automatically generated ones [32]. The results from this study show that a high portion of the inferred assertions were correct and relevant, that there were around 5 times more inferred assertion clauses than programmer-provided ones, and that only about 60% of the programmer-provided assertions were covered by the automatically inferred ones. The main conclusion from this work is that the inferred contracts can be used to correct and improve the human-written ones, but that contract inference can not completely replace the manual work. As the authors comment, this should not be surprising, since automatically inferred contracts are bound to document the behaviour of the program *as it is*, rather than document its *intent*.

A related approach is used by QuickSpec [7], a tool to automatically discover laws satisfied by functional programs. QuickSpec systematically enumerates possible terms and equations about functional programs, uses random testing to eliminate laws that do not hold, and applies a congruence graph data-structure to eliminate more complicated laws that follow from known simpler equations. Like the other dynamic approaches, QuickSpec can sometimes erroneously propose laws that could not be ruled out based on the generated test cases, but experiments show that the approach performs well in practice, and is able to discover intricate facts about programs.

3.4   Property-Guided Contract Inference

The methods discussed so far are driven primarily by the considered program, and can be applied even if no specifications or properties are otherwise given. Property-guided contract inference methods, in contrast, do not attempt to find the most general contract satisfied by a function, but instead aim at discovering contracts that are just sufficient to verify some overall property of a program. The approach proposed in Sects. 4 and 5 of this paper, which is based on an encoding of programs and functions as *Constrained Horn Clauses*, falls into this category. Also weakest pre-condition methods, and in particular maximal specification synthesis [2], can start from existing specifications.

Since they do not aim for generality, property-guided methods can often find partial contracts that are more succinct than the complete contracts. For instance, by choosing stronger pre-conditions, it might be possible to find contracts that ignore complicated corner-cases, provided that they are never triggered by a program.

As a related approach, Denney and Fischer propose the use of syntactic patterns to infer annotations for automatically generated code [11]. This is feasible since generated code is very idiomatic, so that all code constructs that can possibly occur can be covered by patterns. The chosen code generator systems were AutoBayes and AutoFilter. The results show that the algorithm could successfully certify various safety properties of the generated code.

4   Deductive Verification and Horn Clauses

This part discusses the property-guided inference of contracts with the help of Horn solvers. Horn clauses, in this context often narrowed down to *Constrained Horn Clauses*, CHC, have been proposed as a uniform framework to automate the application of proof rules in deductive verification [6,16,20], lifting deductive approaches to a similar level of automation as achieved by software model checkers. Thanks to their generality, Horn solvers can be applied quite naturally to infer not only program invariants, but also contracts, from the program and properties to be verified. We start by considering different calculi for deductive verification, and their automation, before more formally defining the framework of Horn clauses.

4.1   From Hoare Logic to Horn Clauses, and Back Again

Program logics characterise the correctness of programs in terms of proof rules that can be used to derive program correctness judgements. The proof rules often require the right annotations to be provided by the user, or by some oracle; for instance, loop rules need (inductive) loop invariants to be provided, and rules for modular handling of function or method calls rely on a contract. We consider proof rules in Hoare logic [18], which express the correctness of programs in terms of Hoare triples $\{P\}\ S\ \{R\}$ with a pre-condition P, program S, and post-condition R. The triple $\{P\}\ S\ \{R\}$ expresses that every terminating run of program S that starts in a state satisfying P ends in a state satisfying R. Hoare triples can be derived using proof rules such as the ones in Table 1 and 2.

Table 1. Selection of standard hoare rules for sequential programs

$$\frac{}{\{P[x/t]\}\ x = t\ \{P\}}\ \text{ASSIGN} \qquad \frac{\{P\}\ S\ \{Q\} \qquad \{Q\}\ T\ \{R\}}{\{P\}\ S;T\ \{R\}}\ \text{COMP}$$

$$\frac{\{P \wedge B\}\ S\ \{R\} \qquad \{P \wedge \neg B\}\ T\ \{R\}}{\{P\}\ if\ B\ then\ S\ else\ T\ \{R\}}\ \text{COND} \qquad \frac{\{I \wedge B\}\ S\ \{I\}}{\{I\}\ while\ B\ do\ S\ \{I \wedge \neg B\}}\ \text{LOOP}$$

$$\frac{P \Rightarrow P' \qquad \{P'\}\ S\ \{R'\} \qquad R' \Rightarrow R}{\{P\}\ S\ \{R\}}\ \text{CONSEQ}$$

Sequential Hoare Proofs. The first selection of Hoare rules, shown in Table 1, can be used to derive properties of sequential programs without function calls. For simplicity, we assume that no distinction is made between program expressions and terms of the specification language in rule ASSIGN, and between Boolean program expressions and formulas of the specification language in the rules COND and LOOP. One rule exists for each of the program constructs, which are assignments to variables, sequential composition, conditional statements, and while loops; one further rule, the CONSEQuence rule, describes how pre-conditions can be strengthened and post-conditions be weakened. Each rule specifies that the conclusion, the Hoare triple underneath the bar, follows from the premises above the bar. In ASSIGN, the notation $P[x/t]$ denotes (capture-avoiding) substitution of all free occurrences of x in P by the term t.

During proof search, the rules are applied backwards, in a goal-directed manner. Two of the rules have formulas in their premises that do not appear in the respective conclusion; when these rules are applied backwards, these formulas need to be provided by the user: in COMP, an *intermediate assertion Q* is needed to decompose a Hoare triple into two triples, and in LOOP, a *loop invariant I* has to be specified. The framework of Horn clauses provides a general strategy to compute such verification artefacts automatically, by initially keeping the required annotations *symbolic* (i.e., by using uninterpreted predicate symbols), collecting constraints from the leaves of a proof tree, and then using a Horn solver to determine which annotations are adequate.

To implement this strategy, it is advantageous to work with slightly generalised versions of some of the rules, shown in Table 2. Compared to the rules

Table 2. Hoare rules with generalised conclusions

$$\frac{P \Rightarrow R[x/t]}{\{P\}\ x = t\ \{R\}} \ \text{Assign}' \qquad \frac{P \Rightarrow I \qquad \{I \wedge B\}\ S\ \{I\} \qquad I \wedge \neg B \Rightarrow R}{\{P\}\ while\ B\ do\ S\ \{R\}} \ \text{Loop}'$$

in Table 1, the generalised rules do not syntactically restrict the pre- and post-conditions in the conclusion; logically, the rules in Table 2 can be derived from their respective original version in Table 1 and the CONSEQ rule.

$$\frac{\dfrac{I(n, x) \wedge x < n \Rightarrow I(n, x + 1)}{\{I(n, x) \wedge x < n\}\ x = x + 1\ \{I(n, x)\}}}{\mathcal{P}}$$

$$\frac{\dfrac{n \geq 0 \Rightarrow P(n, 0)}{\{n \geq 0\}\ x = 0\ \{P(n, x)\}} \qquad \dfrac{P(n, x) \Rightarrow I(n, x) \qquad \mathcal{P} \qquad I(n, x) \wedge x \not< n \Rightarrow x = n}{\{P(n, x)\}\ while\ x < n\ do\ x = x + 1\ \{x = n\}}}{\{n \geq 0\}\ x = 0;\ while\ x < n\ do\ x = x + 1\ \{x = n\}}$$

Fig. 1. Proof for Example 5

Example 5. We show how to prove a simple Hoare triple using this approach:

$$\{n \geq 0\}\ x = 0;\ while\ x < n\ do\ x = x + 1\ \{x = n\}$$

A completely expanded proof tree for this Hoare triple is shown in Fig. 1. The proof contains applications of the rules COMP and LOOP′, both of which demand program annotations; to be able to construct a complete proof, *symbolic formulas* $P(n, x)$ and $I(n, x)$ have been inserted, involving the uninterpreted binary predicate symbols P and I applied over the program variables, allowing us to postpone the actual choice of concrete formulas at this point.

The proof's leaves, marked in grey, represent the conditions that the formulas $P(n, x)$, $I(n, x)$ have to satisfy in order to close the proof:

$$n \geq 0 \Rightarrow P(n, 0)$$
$$P(n, x) \Rightarrow I(n, x)$$
$$I(n, x) \wedge x < n \Rightarrow I(n, x + 1)$$
$$I(n, x) \wedge x \not< n \Rightarrow x = n$$

The variables n, x are implicitly universally quantified in each formula. The four conditions can be turned into *Horn clauses*, i.e., written as disjunctions with at most one positive literal each (Example 7 elaborates on this, continuing the current example), and their satisfiability can therefore be checked automatically using Horn solvers. In case of our four conditions, a Horn solver would quickly determine that the clauses are indeed satisfiable, and that one possible solution are the formulas:

$$P(n, x) \equiv n \geq 0 \wedge x = 0$$
$$I(n, x) \equiv n \geq x \wedge x \geq 0$$

To obtain a self-contained Hoare proof, we could substitute the placeholders P, I in Fig. 1 with those formulas, and observe that indeed all rule applications become valid, and the proof is well-formed.

Verification by Contract. One reason for the popularity of Horn clauses in verification is that other language features, for instance procedure calls or concurrency, can be handled in much the same way as sequential programs. We consider the case of a program containing (possibly mutually recursive) functions $f_1, \ldots, f_n$, and make the same simplifying assumptions as in Sect. 2: function parameters are passed by value and are read-only, and there are no global variables. For simplicity of presentation, it is assumed here that each function f is associated with a distinct set $\bar{a}_f = \langle a_f^1, \ldots, a_f^k \rangle$ of variables representing the formal arguments of the function, as well as a further distinct variable r_f to store the function result. Each function f is implemented through a function body S_f, which by itself is a piece of program code, and possibly contains function calls.

Table 3. Hoare rule for function calls

$$\frac{P \Rightarrow Pre_f[\bar{a}_f/\bar{t}] \qquad P \wedge Post_f[\bar{a}_f/\bar{t}] \Rightarrow R[x/r_f]}{\{P\}\ x = f(\bar{t})\ \{R\}} \text{ CALL}$$

Following the style of *design-by-contract* [26], each function f is specified with a contract $(Pre_f, Post_f)$, containing a pre-condition Pre_f over the arguments $\bar{a}_f$, and a post-condition $Post_f$ over the arguments $\bar{a}_f$ and the result r_f. To verify programs involving function calls, we need a further Hoare rule, which is shown in Table 3. The rule enables the modular verification of programs referring entirely to the function contracts, and is a simplified version of the rules that can be found in the literature (e.g., in the work by von Oheimb [29]). The two premises of the rule state that function calls have to establish the pre-conditions, and that the post-conditions can be assumed to hold for the result of the function call. To verify an end-to-end property $\{P\}\ S\ \{R\}$ of a program S, with functions $f_1, \ldots, f_n$, in a procedure-modular way, it has to be shown that (i) each function f_i satisfies its contract, which means that the Hoare triple $\{Pre_{f_i}\}\ S_{f_i}\ \{Post_{f_i}\}$ holds; and (ii) S satisfies the end-to-end property $\{P\}\ S\ \{R\}$, making use of the contracts for the functions $f_1, \ldots, f_n$.

To verify programs with function calls automatically, we can apply a similar strategy as before: we keep function pre- and post-conditions initially symbolic as formulas $Pre_f(\bar{a}_f)$ and $Post_f(\bar{a}_f, r_f)$, respectively; we collect the constraints that pre- and post-conditions have to satisfy, together with constraints on loop invariants and intermediate assertions; and finally we use a Horn solver to search for a solution of the constraints in combination. Note that we overload here the meta-symbols Pre_f and $Post_f$ used in rule CALL, with the uninterpreted predicate symbols of the symbolic formulas. Note also that while the formulas are symbolic, the terms to which the predicate symbols are applied are explicit, and thus the substitutions are carried out immediately (and not left symbolic).

Example 6. We show how to verify a program with a recursive unary function f using this strategy:

$$\{x \geq 0\} \; y = f(x) \; \{y = x\} \tag{1}$$

where the function f has the body

$$\textit{if } a_f^1 > 0 \textit{ then } \; z = f(a_f^1 - 1); r_f = z + 1 \; \textit{ else } \; r_f = 0$$

Note that the notation $r_f = t$ corresponds to a *return* statement.

$$\frac{x \geq 0 \Rightarrow Pre(x) \qquad x \geq 0 \land Po(x, r_f) \Rightarrow r_f = x}{\{x \geq 0\} \; y = f(x) \; \{y = x\}}$$

$$\frac{\dfrac{Pre(a_f^1) \land a_f^1 > 0 \Rightarrow Pre(a_f^1 - 1)}{Pre(a_f^1) \land a_f^1 > 0 \land Po(a_f^1 - 1, r_f) \Rightarrow Q(a_f^1, r_f, r_f)}}{\dfrac{\{Pre(a_f^1) \land a_f^1 > 0\} \; z = f(a_f^1 - 1) \; \{Q(a_f^1, z, r_f)\} \qquad \dfrac{Q(a_f^1, z, r_f) \Rightarrow Po(a_f^1, z + 1)}{\{Q(a_f^1, z, r_f)\} \; r_f = z + 1 \; \{Po(a_f^1, r_f)\}}}{\dfrac{\{Pre(a_f^1) \land a_f^1 > 0\} \; z = f(a_f^1 - 1); r_f = z + 1 \; \{Po(a_f^1, r_f)\}}{\mathcal{P}_1}}}$$

$$\frac{\dfrac{Pre(a_f^1) \land a_f^1 \not> 0 \Rightarrow Po(a_f^1, 0)}{\{Pre(a_f^1) \land a_f^1 \not> 0\} \; r_f = 0 \; \{Po(a_f^1, r_f)\}}}{\mathcal{P}_2}$$

$$\frac{\mathcal{P}_1 \qquad \mathcal{P}_2}{\{Pre(a_f^1)\} \; \textit{if } a_f^1 > 0 \textit{ then } z = f(a_f^1 - 1); r_f = z + 1 \textit{ else } r_f = 0 \; \{Po(a_f^1, r_f)\}}$$

Fig. 2. Hoare proofs for Example 6

The two proof trees needed to verify the program, for the overall property and the correctness of the function contract, are shown in Fig. 2, using the symbolic formulas $Pre(a_f^1)$ and $Po(a_f^1, r_f)$ for the contract and $Q(a_f^1, z, r_f)$ as intermediate assertion between $z = f(a_f^1 - 1)$ and $r_f = z + 1$. The proofs give rise to the following conditions (in the proofs in grey) about the annotations:

$$x \geq 0 \Rightarrow Pre(x)$$
$$Pre(a_f^1) \wedge a_f^1 > 0 \Rightarrow Pre(a_f^1 - 1)$$
$$Pre(a_f^1) \wedge a_f^1 > 0 \wedge Po(a_f^1 - 1, r_f) \Rightarrow Q(a_f^1, r_f, r_f)$$
$$Q(a_f^1, z, r_f) \Rightarrow Po(a_f^1, z + 1)$$
$$Pre(a_f^1) \wedge a_f^1 \not> 0 \Rightarrow Po(a_f^1, 0)$$
$$x \geq 0 \wedge Po(x, r_f) \Rightarrow r_f = x$$

A solution of the constraints is:

$$Pre(a_f^1) \equiv true$$
$$Po(a_f^1, r_f) \equiv (a_f^1 \geq 0 \wedge r_f = a_f^1) \vee (a_f^1 \leq 0 \wedge r_f = 0)$$
$$Q(a_f^1, z, r_f) \equiv z = r_f \wedge a_f^1 = z + 1 \wedge a_f^1 > 0$$

In other words, it has been shown that the function f satisfies the contract $C = (true, (a_f^1 \geq 0 \wedge r_f = a_f^1) \vee (a_f^1 \leq 0 \wedge r_f = 0))$, and that C is sufficient to verify the client program (1). It can be noted that C, for reasons of readability, can be decomposed into $C \equiv C_1 \sqcap C_2$, with simpler contracts $C_1 = (a_f^1 \geq 0, r_f = a_f^1)$ and $C_2 = (a_f^1 \leq 0, r_f = 0)$.

4.2 Constrained Horn Clauses

We now introduce the framework of constrained Horn clauses more formally. Throughout the section, we assume that some background theory has been fixed, for instance the theory of Presburger arithmetic, of fixed-length bit-vectors, or of arrays. Given a set X of first-order variables, a *constraint language* is then a set *Constr* of first-order formulas over the background theory and X; in practice, often the constraint language is restricted to quantifier-free formulas.

We then consider a set R of uninterpreted fixed-arity relation symbols, which represent set-theoretic relations over the domain described by the background theory. Relation symbols are used as symbolic formulas (e.g., I, Pre, etc.) in the previous section.

A *(constrained) Horn clause* is a formula $B_1 \wedge \cdots \wedge B_n \wedge C \rightarrow H$ where

- $C \in Constr$ is a constraint over the chosen background theory and X;
- each B_i is an application $p(t_1, \ldots, t_k)$ of a relation symbol $p \in R$ to first-order terms over X;
- H is similarly either an application $p(t_1, \ldots, t_k)$ of $p \in R$ to first-order terms, or *false*.

The first-order variables in a clause are implicitly universally quantified. H is called the *head* of the clause, and $B_1 \wedge \cdots \wedge B_n \wedge C$ the *body*. In case $C = true$, we often leave out C and just write $B_1 \wedge \cdots \wedge B_n \rightarrow H$.

Horn solvers are tools for computing (symbolic or syntactic) solutions of Horn clauses. A syntactic solution of a set HC of Horn clauses maps every relation symbol $p(x_1, \ldots, x_n)$ (with $p \in R$) to a constraint over the arguments $x_1, \ldots, x_n$ in the chosen constraint language, in such a way that substituting the formulas for the relation symbols makes all clauses valid. Tools like Spacer [25] or Eldarica [19] can compute solutions of Horn clauses over a number of background theories fully automatically, with the help of model checking algorithms including CEGAR and IC3.

Example 7. The four conditions extracted in Example 5 can be turned into Horn clauses with just a minor change of notation. The clauses are formulated over the set $R = \{P, I\}$ of binary relation symbols, and the first-order variables n, x are implicitly universally quantified:

$$n \geq 0 \rightarrow P(n, 0)$$
$$P(n, x) \rightarrow I(n, x)$$
$$I(n, x) \wedge x < n \rightarrow I(n, x + 1)$$
$$I(n, x) \wedge x \not< n \wedge x \neq n \rightarrow \textit{false}$$

It can be noted that the formulas given in Example 5 are indeed a syntactic solution of the clauses.

4.3 Tool Support

We conclude the section by discussing the model checkers and deductive verification tools used in the rest of the paper.

TriCera. There are several verification tools implementing the verification strategy outlined in Sect. 4.1, including the tool SeaHorn [17] for C programs, and JayHorn [23] for Java. TriCera,[1] the tool used in our experiments, is a software model checker for C programs following the same methodology. TriCera was originally a spin-off of the C front-end that was used in the Horn solver Eldarica, and later extended to also support computation of function contracts, and to handle heap-allocated data-structures. TriCera primarily targets the Horn solver Eldarica as back-end, but can also output Horn clauses to interface other solvers.

Eldarica. Eldarica [19][2] is a solver for Horn clauses with constraints over a number of possible theories. Eldarica combines Predicate Abstraction with the Counterexample-Guided Abstraction Refinement (CEGAR) algorithm to automatically check whether a given set of Horn clauses is satisfiable. Eldarica first appeared as a solver for Horn clauses over Presburger arithmetic in 2013. Over the last years, various further features have been added to the tool, and it

---

[1] https://github.com/uuverifiers/tricera.
[2] https://github.com/uuverifiers/eldarica.

can now solve problems over the theories of integers, algebraic data-types, bit-vectors, and arrays. Eldarica can process Horn clauses and programs in a variety of formats, implements sophisticated heuristics to solve tricky systems of clauses without diverging, and offers an elegant API for programmatic use.

Frama-C. Frama-C is a tool for static analysis of C code [9]. There are several plugins available that perform different analyses. On such plugin is WP, which uses deductive verification to verify functional properties of programs [9]. To perform verification Frama-C uses function contracts to specify behaviours of functions, and to this end it has its own specification language called ACSL (ANSI C Specification Language). Function contracts are annotated in the source code as a special type of C comments, and a contract generally consists of pre-conditions and post-conditions, expressed using the keywords **requires** and **ensures**, respectively. An example can be seen in Listing 1.2.

The deductive verification performed by the WP plugin is based on Weakest Pre-condition calculus [12], which defines for a statement S a function from any post-condition Q to a pre-condition P', such that P' is the weakest pre-condition where the Hoare triple $\{P'\}\ S\ \{R\}$ holds. This mapping can be seen as a modification of the Hoare logic rules presented in Sect. 4.1, and verification of a Hoare triple $\{P\}\ S\ \{R\}$ can then be performed by computing the weakest pre-condition P' and proving that $P \Rightarrow P'$. The WP plugin verifies, and reports, for each annotation (e.g., assertions and invariants) whether it is valid. The overall program is said to be valid if all annotations are valid. The verification process is function-modular, i.e., when a function call is reached the tool checks that the caller fulfills the pre-condition of the called function, and, if so, assumes that the post-condition hold after the function. Verification that the callee fulfills the contract is then performed separately, similarly to the proof in Fig. 2.

5 Synthesising Contracts for Frama-C

This section describes how the model checker TriCera is used to synthesise contracts that can be verified in Frama-C, and the reason for doing so.

The way TriCera is used to synthesise contracts is by verifying that all assertions in the program hold. As a side effect of this, contracts for all individual functions are generated, as part of the Horn clause solution. Through an extension to TriCera, these contracts are then syntactically transformed into ACSL, and verified in Frama-C. Using a deductive verifier to verify the program again, with the newly generated contracts, increases confidence in the verification result. Frama-C is a well established tool that is generally considered trustworthy, and using several verification techniques naturally increases confidence.

Extracting contracts from model checking can also help in other respects. Contracts can be used when a program is modified to speed up the re-verification process: all contracts that are still satisfied by a modified function can be kept and reused. Contracts can also be applied to gradually modularise verification efforts, and in this way improve scalability. Since model checking is automatic but

---

mc914/2: $((({\_1} + -1 * {\_0}) = 0) \;\&\; ((100 + -1 * {\_0}) >= 0))$

mc913/2: $((({\_1} + -1 * {\_0}) = 0) \;\&\; ((-101 + {\_0}) >= 0))$

...

mc91_pre/1: true

...

mc91_post/2: $((((!((10 + ({\_1} + -1 * {\_0})) = 0) \;|\; ((-101 + {\_0}) >= 0)) \;\&\; (!((-91 + {\_1}) = 0) \;|\; ((101 + -1 * {\_0}) >= 0))) \;\&\; (((10 + ({\_1} + -1 * {\_0})) = 0) \;|\; ((-91 + {\_1}) = 0)))$

Listing 5.1. A portion of TriCera's solution output for Listing 1.1.

not function modular, it is by itself limited in scalability. By relying mainly on the result of Frama-C, contract synthesis is complementary to writing contracts manually. Modules that are too large to be model-checked can still be verified and the result combined with verification of other modules, where all contracts have been synthesised automatically. Finally, having explicit contracts is useful for verification of code external to the code base used to synthesise the contracts, for example when the latter is a library.

In the present paper, we assume a context where there are properties to be verified at the C module level. Even though the contracts do not give a complete specification of function, they are still of interest in this context, since they will always be sufficient to prove the desired properties at the module level.

TriCera does currently not support the full C language, and only has limited support for heap, arrays, pointers, and structs. As such, properties related to memory safety cannot be verified, and contracts not be generated. We therefore limited our experiment to programs over arithmetic data-types.

5.1   Syntactical Transformation

Our starting point for producing ACSL contracts is the Horn clause solution output in Prolog format by TriCera. A part of the Horn clause solution for the example in Listing 1.1 is shown in Listing 5.1. Each line of the output contains a formula that defines one of the predicates from the Horn clauses.

In TriCera's solution, the pre-state prior to entering the function, and the post-state after exiting the function are identified with the names `func_pre` and `func_post`. Those were split from other statements such as the main invariant and the conditions of functions at different states. The pre-state and post-state formulas correspond to the pre-condition and post-condition, i.e, the function contract. After extracting the contracts, they were properly rearranged twice. The first rearrangement was with respect to the function name. The second rearrangement was required to ensure that the pre-condition precedes the post-condition of each function. Thus, the order is compliant with ACSL annotations.

```
/*@
//Function: mc91
   requires \true;
   ensures (\result − \old(n) != −10 || \old(n) >= 101) &&
           (\result != 91 || 101 >= \old(n)) &&
           (\result − \old(n) == −10 || \result == 91);
*/
```

Listing 5.2. The final result of pretty-printing an ACSL contract, when using the harness from Listing 1.1

TriCera uses the symbols $\_0, \_1, \ldots \_n-1$ to represent to index function arguments and program variables. For outputting contracts, those symbols were again replaced with the original program variables. A few more syntactical modifications were necessary in order to adhere to the ACSL format, as follows:

(i) Logical symbols (&, |, =) were replaced with the C equivalents (&&, ||, ==).
(ii) Boolean literals (`true`, `false`) were replaced with the corresponding ACSL primitives (\true, \false).
(iii) Variable values before execution (`value_old`) were replaced with the equivalent ACSL construct (\old(value)).
(iv) The keywords for pre- and post-states (`func_pre`, `func_post`) were replaced with ACSL keywords for pre- and post-conditions (`requires`, `ensures`).

To form more readable contracts, we used (and extended) the existing pretty-printer from Princess [33], the theorem prover included in TriCera and Eldarica. Pretty-printing eliminated most of the parentheses in the output, and applies further simplifications to the formulas, leading to more legible ACSL. The final result is shown in Listing 5.2. With some manipulations of the formula it is easy to see that this is equivalent to the contract in Listing 1.2. Furthermore, we can see that the contract is a complete specification of the function, despite the input specification not asserting properties for all executions.

5.2 Contracts for Different Assertions

In the generation of ACSL contracts, the result highly depends on the choice of the logical formula in the assertions. For example, in Listing 1.1, if the harness is altered to only have the assertion `assert(res>0);`, then the generated post-condition is `ensures \result >= 91;`, and if altering the harness to have only the assertion `assert(res==91 || res==x-10);`, the generated post-condition is `ensures \result == 91 || (\result-\old(n)==-10 && \old(n)>=101);` (in both cases the pre-condition is simply `true`). Both post-conditions are verified in Frama-C as `valid`, and proven to be correct with respect to the test harness.

There is no guarantee of completeness of the generated contract, it will simply be sufficient to verify what was asserted about the function, as well as be sound with regard to recursive calls. However, in many cases, such as in the example just shown in Listing 5.2, the contract will be stronger than what was asserted in the harness function.

5.3 Contracts for Client Code and Libraries

As explained above, the function contracts that are inferred are sufficient for the calling function to be verified, but are not necessarily the *strongest* (or *most precise*) contracts that the respective functions fulfill. As such, if a function is used in more than one client program (say it is a library function), the contract extracted in the context of one client might not be sufficient in the context of another client. If we have several clients using the same library function, the contracts inferred individually in each client can be combined to a single contract that allows all client code to be verified.

Depending on the context in which a function is called, the pre-condition generated by TriCera will vary. For example, if, as in Listing 1.1, the function inputs are unconstrained, the pre-condition generated tends to be \true. This is because the function is in fact model-checked for all possible states w.r.t. the affected variables. In this case, the generated contracts can be combined by simply creating a new post-condition that is the conjunction of all generated post-conditions. In Frama-C this can be achieved by including all the generated **ensures** clauses, since this is semantically equivalent to having one **ensures** clause that is the conjunction of all the expressions. The new contract C will then refine all the generated contracts $C_1, \ldots, C_n$, as defined in Sect. 2.2.

A more interesting case is when a function is called in a context where the variables are assigned a specific value, or their possible values are a subset of the total range. In this case TriCera will generate a pre-condition allowing only the values that can possibly occur in the calling context. For example, consider the **cmp** function seen in Listing 5.3, which is used as an example in the paper by Singleton et al. [36] discussed in Sect. 3.1. For some harness, TriCera will generate the clause **requires b == 5 && a == 5;** as pre-condition, with the post-condition **ensures \result == 0 && \old(b) == 5 && \old(a) == 5;**, and for some other harness the two clauses **requires b == 7 && a == 5;** and **ensures \result == -1 && \old(b) == 7 && \old(a) == 5;** will be generated. Note that the post-conditions contain redundant equalities over the variables in the pre-state, an artefact of the use of constant propagation in the Horn solver. In this case we cannot use conjunctions of the contracts to create a new contract. Ignoring the fact that the post-conditions would be incompatible, the specification resulting from contract conjunction would not give enough information to the caller about which input would create the respective output. Instead one can use each pair of pre- and post-conditions (P_i, Q_i) to form an implication $P_i \Rightarrow Q_i$, to create a new post-condition that is the conjunction of all these implications. This follows the meet operation defined in Sect. 2.2, and

```
int cmp(int a, int b) {
    int c = a;
    if (c < b) {
        return −1;
    } else {
        if (c > b) {
            return 1;
        }
        return 0;
    }
}
```

Listing 5.3. C implementation of an integer comparison function.

thus we have that the new contract $C = C_1 \sqcap \cdots \sqcap C_n$, where $C_1, \ldots, C_n$ are the generated contracts.

An equivalent result can also be achieved by using the ACSL construct behavior. Behaviours are used specifically to specify several pre- and post-condition pairs, which is also evaluated similarly to the meet operation on contracts. The two approaches are semantically equivalent, and as long as we also keep the disjunction of pre-conditions will have no effect on verification completeness. Without the pre-condition, the contract might not be possible to prove. An obvious example is when the pre-condition contains auxiliary assertions, for example about memory validity, since then the resulting specification might not be possible to prove because of run-time exceptions not related to executions considered in the particular contexts from which the contracts were generated.

Listing 5.4 shows an example of three automatically inferred contracts that have been manually conjoined using the Frama-C behavior construct as outlined above, into a single contract that can be verified in Frama-C, and which allows the clients from which the original, now conjoined, contracts where generated to be verified. By using this approach, it also possible to instruct Frama-C to prove that the behaviours are disjoint, and that they form a complete specification, if desired, by using the ACSL keywords disjoint and complete. Completeness means that the assumptions of the behaviours covers all possible states as specified by the pre-condition, i.e. that the pre-condition implies that at least one of the assumptions of the behaviours hold. Disjointness refers to the assumptions of the behaviours not overlapping, i.e. that the pre-condition implies that no two assumptions of the behaviours hold at the same time.

6   A Case Study Using SV-COMP Benchmarks

This section describes how the TriCera contract generation was evaluated using SV-COMP verification tasks, and the results thereof. The case study is a

```
/*@
    requires  a == b || a < b || a > b;
    assigns \nothing;
    behavior eq:
        assumes b == a;
        ensures \result == 0 && \old(b) == \old(a);
    behavior lt :
        assumes b − a >= 1;
        ensures \result == −1;
    behavior gt:
        assumes a − b >= 1;
        ensures \result == 1;
    complete behaviors;
    disjoint  behaviors;
*/
```

Listing 5.4. Frama-C contract resulting from the conjoining of different inferred contracts for the function in Listing 5.3.

continuation of previous work on using model checking based on Constrained Horn Clauses to verify and infer contracts for industrial software [3].

The authors of the present paper are not aware of any existing techniques for C code contract inference, and cannot therefore make a comparative evaluation. Instead, a subset of a collection of verification tasks commonly used to evaluate verification techniques was used to carry out initial experiments with the contract inference performed by TriCera.

6.1 SV-COMP Verification Tasks

The International Competition on Software Verification (SV-COMP) is an annual competition to assess the state-of-the-art software verification tools [5]. The collection of verification tasks used in this competition is maintained in an open-source repository, and has been contributed by multiple research and development groups [37].

The SV-COMP repository was chosen as the main method to test the automatically generated contracts. The benchmark suite was limited to 12 folders of C implementation files. The selected verification tasks focused on checking loops and recursions. The tested properties varied in nature, and included, for example, overflow and (un)reachability checks.

It was necessary to edit the source files to prepare them for contract generation, and also to process them correctly with TriCera. The main changes included:

- Some source files included loops directly inside a main function, but no function calls. In such files the loops were moved to separate functions, and contracts generated for those auxiliary functions. New variables were introduced to store the returned values, and used in the properties to be verified in the outer function.

- Tasks with the expected verification result FALSE, i.e., a counterexample to safety, were modified to produce the answer TRUE.
- Some source files used the function VERIFER_error() to express assertions. Such function calls were changed to the statement assert(0).
- The reserved keyword _Bool is not supported by TriCera. Source files using this data-type were fixed by adding a typedef enum {false, true} _Bool;

The experiments were performed in a virtual machine running Ubuntu 17.10, on a host machine with an Intel Core i5-7500 CPU @ 3.40 GHz. Three of the four CPU cores, and 3.8 GiB memory, were allocated to the virtual machine. The verification time limit was set to 60 min. Where we report average contract generation times, the test cases that timed out were excluded.

6.2   Results

The following verification results focus on whether functions meet their generated contracts, so the result is considered to be positive (i.e., verified) when the postcondition is verified as Valid using Frama-C. Some results also specify whether the pre-condition was verified as Valid, which means that it holds at all call sites (including both the harness function and recursive calls). A result of Unknown means that Frama-C terminated but was unable to prove the assertion, and Timeout means that the verification attempt did not terminate within the time limit.

Overall Results. In total there were 129 verification tasks tested using TriCera. For 110 of these, a contract could be generated within the set time limit, whereas 19 tasks timed out. Out of the 110 generated contracts, 78 could be immediately verified by Frama-C. An additional 20 tasks could be verified after manually adding loop annotations (i.e., variant, invariant and assigns). The rest of the verification tasks could not be verified. The average contract generation time was 19 s, with the minimum and maximum being 1.3 s and 17 min, respectively. The detailed results are divided into two parts based on whether the files contained functions with loops or recursion.

Programs with Loops. This part of the experiment was conducted over 66 source files, which were selected from 10 different folders of the SV-COMP benchmark repository. The test suite contained both For and While loops, and also some cases of nested loops. Programs had between 10 and 50 lines of code (measured using the tool CLOC [10]).

Of the 66 programs with loops, 13 did not have a contract generated within the time limit, and were ignored for the rest of the analysis. Of the 53 for which a contract was generated, 22 could immediately be verified with Frama-C, in addition to 20 more verified after manually adding loop annotations. The primary

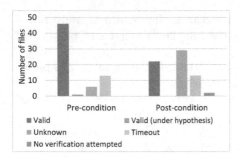

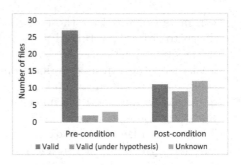

Fig. 3. Results of verifying generated contracts for files containing loops in Frama-C.

Fig. 4. Results of verifying generated contracts for files with loops in Frama-C, after adding loop annotations.

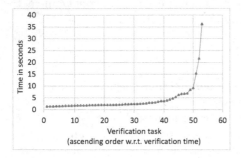

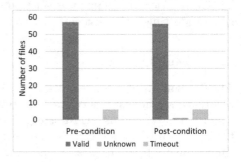

Fig. 5. Time spent in running both verification and contract generation in TriCera of functions that contain loops.

Fig. 6. Results of verifying generated contracts for files with recursive functions in Frama-C.

verification result is shown in Fig. 3 in terms of pre-condition and post-condition verification status in Frama-C. In Fig. 4, the verification result after manually adding loop annotations can be seen, for the files which were not already successfully verified. In several of these cases, Frama-C verified the assertions as valid under some hypothesis, which means that the result depended on other assertions that could not be verified. In almost all cases, this dependence were the manually added loop annotations that could not be verified.

The average contract generation time was 4.2 s, the minimum 1.4 s, and the maximum 36 s (Fig. 5). The horizontal axis views a series of verification tasks, while the vertical axis shows the ascending order of the required time.

Programs with Recursion. This part of the experiment was conducted over 63 source files that contained recursive functions, selected from 2 folders of the SV-COMP benchmark repository. These files all contained a main function, which could be used as a harness, calling recursive functions. Thus, the source code did not require to be rewritten in the same manner as the files containing loops. The source code included both single and nested recursive (up to 4) functions. Programs had between 18 and 66 lines of code.

Of the 63 programs with recursion, 6 failed the contract generation time limit. Of the 57 programs with generated contracts, 56 could be verified with Frama-C. Figure 6 shows the final result of the contracts tested using Frama-C. No further additions were required to verify those files.

The average contract generation time was 33 s, with the minimum 1.3 s and maximum 17 min (Fig. 7).

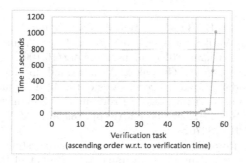

Fig. 7. Time spent in running both verification and contract generation in TriCera of functions that contain recursion.

Summary. The case study used the SV-COMP repository as the source to test the inferred contracts. There were no further assertions added to the source files, and only 5 files required assumption statements in order to generate the contracts (e.g. to ensure that a random value assigned to a loop guard variable is always positive). Around 77.3% of files with loops (excluding the time outs) and 98.2% of files with recursion were verified with Frama-C. The overall time varied from a few seconds to 17 min.

The tasks with loops demanded extensive manual work because of the missing `invariant`, `variant` and `assigns` loop annotations. However, the recursive tasks were straightforward, and minimal code alterations were made.

7   Conclusions

This paper surveys existing work on automatic inference of program contracts, proposes a property-guided method to compute contracts with the help of Horn solvers, and provides experimental evidence that such an approach indeed works on a selection of SV-COMP benchmarks. Our implementation, at this point, is a proof of concept, and more work is needed to handle real-world C programs: in particular, inference not only of contracts but also of loop invariants, and inference of contracts also in the presence of arrays, heap-allocated data-structures, and pointers. Within those restrictions, we believe that the experimental results are encouraging, and that the proposed combination of deductive verification technology with model checking algorithms can significantly extend the reach of both paradigms.

Acknowledgements. This work has been partially funded by the Swedish Governmental Agency for Innovation Systems (VINNOVA) under the AVerT project 2018-02727, by the Swedish Research Council (VR) under grant 2018-04727, and by the Swedish Foundation for Strategic Research (SSF) under the project WebSec (Ref. RIT17-0011).

References

1. Ahrendt, W., Beckert, B., Bubel, R., Hähnle, R., Schmitt, P.H., Ulbrich, M. (eds.): Deductive Software Verification - The KeY Book - From Theory to Practice. LNCS, vol. 10001. Springer, Cham (2016). https://doi.org/10.1007/978-3-319-49812-6
2. Albarghouthi, A., Dillig, I., Gurfinkel, A.: Maximal specification synthesis. In: Bodík, R., Majumdar, R. (eds.) Proceedings of the 43rd Annual ACM SIGPLAN-SIGACT Symposium on Principles of Programming Languages, POPL 2016, St. Petersburg, FL, USA, 20–22 January 2016, pp. 789–801. ACM (2016). https://doi.org/10.1145/2837614.2837628
3. Alshnakat, A.: Automatic verification of embedded systems using horn clause solvers. Master's thesis, Uppsala University, Department of Information Technology (2019)
4. Benveniste, A., et al.: Contracts for system design. Found. Trends Electron. Des. Autom. **12**(2–3), 124–400 (2018)
5. Beyer, D.: Software verification and verifiable witnesses. In: Baier, C., Tinelli, C. (eds.) TACAS 2015. LNCS, vol. 9035, pp. 401–416. Springer, Heidelberg (2015). https://doi.org/10.1007/978-3-662-46681-0_31
6. Bjørner, N., Gurfinkel, A., McMillan, K., Rybalchenko, A.: Horn clause solvers for program verification. In: Beklemishev, L.D., Blass, A., Dershowitz, N., Finkbeiner, B., Schulte, W. (eds.) Fields of Logic and Computation II. LNCS, vol. 9300, pp. 24–51. Springer, Cham (2015). https://doi.org/10.1007/978-3-319-23534-9_2
7. Claessen, K., Smallbone, N., Hughes, J.: QUICKSPEC: guessing formal specifications using testing. In: Fraser, G., Gargantini, A. (eds.) TAP 2010. LNCS, vol. 6143, pp. 6–21. Springer, Heidelberg (2010). https://doi.org/10.1007/978-3-642-13977-2_3
8. Clarke, E.M., Henzinger, T.A., Veith, H., Bloem, R.: Handbook of Model Checking. Springer, Cham (2018). https://doi.org/10.1007/978-3-319-10575-8
9. Cuoq, P., Kirchner, F., Kosmatov, N., Prevosto, V., Signoles, J., Yakobowski, B.: Frama-C: a software analysis perspective. In: Eleftherakis, G., Hinchey, M., Holcombe, M. (eds.) SEFM 2012. LNCS, vol. 7504, pp. 233–247. Springer, Heidelberg (2012). https://doi.org/10.1007/978-3-642-33826-7_16
10. Danial, A.: Cloc - count lines of code. http://cloc.sourceforge.net/
11. Denney, E., Fischer, B.: A generic annotation inference algorithm for the safety certification of automatically generated code. In: Jarzabek, S., Schmidt, D.C., Veldhuizen, T.L. (eds.) Generative Programming and Component Engineering, 5th International Conference, GPCE 2006, Portland, Oregon, USA, 22–26 October 2006, Proceedings, pp. 121–130. ACM (2006), https://doi.org/10.1145/1173706.1173725
12. Dijkstra, E.W.: Guarded commands, non determinacy and formal derivation of programs. Commun. ACM **18**(8), 453–457 (1975). http://doi.acm.org/10.1145/360933.360975
13. Dijkstra, E.W.: A Discipline of Programming. Prentice-Hall, Englewood Cliffs (1976). http://www.worldcat.org/oclc/01958445

14. Ernst, M.D., et al.: The daikon system for dynamic detection of likely invariants. Sci. Comput. Program. **69**(1–3), 35–45 (2007). https://doi.org/10.1016/j.scico.2007.01.015

15. Gordon, M., Collavizza, H.: Forward with Hoare. In: Roscoe, A.W., Jones, C.B., Wood, K.R. (eds.) Reflections on the Work of C.A.R. Hoare. LNCS, pp. 101–121. Springer, London (2010). https://doi.org/10.1007/978-1-84882-912-1_5

16. Grebenshchikov, S., Lopes, N.P., Popeea, C., Rybalchenko, A.: Synthesizing software verifiers from proof rules. In: PLDI, pp. 405–416 (2012). http://doi.acm.org/10.1145/2254064.2254112

17. Gurfinkel, A., Kahsai, T., Komuravelli, A., Navas, J.A.: The SeaHorn verification framework. In: Kroening, D., Păsăreanu, C.S. (eds.) CAV 2015. LNCS, vol. 9206, pp. 343–361. Springer, Cham (2015). https://doi.org/10.1007/978-3-319-21690-4_20

18. Hoare, C.A.R.: An axiomatic basis for computer programming. Commun. ACM **12**(10), 576–580 (1969). http://doi.acm.org/10.1145/363235.363259

19. Hojjat, H., Rümmer, P.: The ELDARICA horn solver. In: 2018 Formal Methods in Computer Aided Design, FMCAD 2018, Austin, TX, USA, 30 October–2 November 2018. IEEE (2018). https://doi.org/10.23919/FMCAD.2018.8603013

20. Hojjat, H., Rümmer, P., Subotic, P., Yi, W.: Horn clauses for communicating timed systems. In: Bjørner, N., Fioravanti, F., Rybalchenko, A., Senni, V. (eds.) Proceedings First Workshop on Horn Clauses for Verification and Synthesis, HCVS 2014, Vienna, Austria, 17 July 2014. EPTCS, vol. 169, pp. 39–52 (2014). https://doi.org/10.4204/EPTCS.169.6

21. Holzmann, G.J.: The model checker SPIN. IEEE Trans. Softw. Eng. **23**(5), 279–295 (1997)

22. Jones, C.B.: Developing methods for computer programs including a notion of interference. Ph.D. thesis, University of Oxford, UK (1981). http://ethos.bl.uk/OrderDetails.do?uin=uk.bl.ethos.259064

23. Kahsai, T., Rümmer, P., Sanchez, H., Schäf, M.: JayHorn: a framework for verifying java programs. In: Chaudhuri, S., Farzan, A. (eds.) CAV 2016. LNCS, vol. 9779, pp. 352–358. Springer, Cham (2016). https://doi.org/10.1007/978-3-319-41528-4_19

24. Knüppel, A., Thüm, T., Padylla, C., Schaefer, I.: Scalability of deductive verification depends on method call treatment. In: Margaria, T., Steffen, B. (eds.) ISoLA 2018. LNCS, vol. 11247, pp. 159–175. Springer, Cham (2018). https://doi.org/10.1007/978-3-030-03427-6_15

25. Komuravelli, A., Gurfinkel, A., Chaki, S.: SMT-based model checking for recursive programs. In: Biere, A., Bloem, R. (eds.) CAV 2014. LNCS, vol. 8559, pp. 17–34. Springer, Cham (2014). https://doi.org/10.1007/978-3-319-08867-9_2

26. Meyer, B.: Applying "design by contract". IEEE Comput. **25**(10), 40–51 (1992). https://doi.org/10.1109/2.161279

27. Moy, Y.: Sufficient preconditions for modular assertion checking. In: Logozzo, F., Peled, D.A., Zuck, L.D. (eds.) VMCAI 2008. LNCS, vol. 4905, pp. 188–202. Springer, Heidelberg (2008). https://doi.org/10.1007/978-3-540-78163-9_18

28. Nyberg, M., Gurov, D., Lidström, C., Rasmusson, A., Westman, J.: Formal verification in automotive industry: enablers and obstacles. In: Margaria, T., Steffen, B. (eds.) ISoLA 2018. LNCS, vol. 11247, pp. 139–158. Springer, Cham (2018). https://doi.org/10.1007/978-3-030-03427-6_14

29. Oheimb, D.: Hoare logic for mutual recursion and local variables. In: Rangan, C.P., Raman, V., Ramanujam, R. (eds.) FSTTCS 1999. LNCS, vol. 1738, pp. 168–180. Springer, Heidelberg (1999). https://doi.org/10.1007/3-540-46691-6_13

30. Owe, O., Ramezanifarkhani, T., Fazeldehkordi, E.: Hoare-style reasoning from multiple contracts. In: Polikarpova, N., Schneider, S. (eds.) IFM 2017. LNCS, vol. 10510, pp. 263–278. Springer, Cham (2017). https://doi.org/10.1007/978-3-319-66845-1_17

31. Owicki, S.S., Gries, D.: An axiomatic proof technique for parallel programs I. Acta Inf. **6**, 319–340 (1976). https://doi.org/10.1007/BF00268134

32. Polikarpova, N., Ciupa, I., Meyer, B.: A comparative study of programmer-written and automatically inferred contracts. In: Rothermel, G., Dillon, L.K. (eds.) Proceedings of the Eighteenth International Symposium on Software Testing and Analysis, ISSTA 2009, Chicago, IL, USA, 19–23 July 2009, pp. 93–104. ACM (2009). https://doi.org/10.1145/1572272.1572284

33. Rümmer, P.: A constraint sequent calculus for first-order logic with linear integer arithmetic. In: Cervesato, I., Veith, H., Voronkov, A. (eds.) LPAR 2008. LNCS (LNAI), vol. 5330, pp. 274–289. Springer, Heidelberg (2008). https://doi.org/10.1007/978-3-540-89439-1_20

34. Seghir, M.N., Kroening, D.: Counterexample-guided precondition inference. In: Felleisen, M., Gardner, P. (eds.) ESOP 2013. LNCS, vol. 7792, pp. 451–471. Springer, Heidelberg (2013). https://doi.org/10.1007/978-3-642-37036-6_25

35. Seghir, M.N., Schrammel, P.: Necessary and sufficient preconditions via eager abstraction. In: Garrigue, J. (ed.) APLAS 2014. LNCS, vol. 8858, pp. 236–254. Springer, Cham (2014). https://doi.org/10.1007/978-3-319-12736-1_13

36. Singleton, J.L., Leavens, G.T., Rajan, H., Cok, D.R.: Inferring concise specifications of APIs. CoRR abs/1905.06847 (2019). http://arxiv.org/abs/1905.06847

37. SV-Comp: Collection of verification tasks. https://github.com/sosy-lab/sv-benchmarks

From Explicit to Implicit Dynamic Frames in Concurrent Reasoning for Java

Wojciech Mostowski[✉]

Computing and Electronics for Real-time and Embedded Systems (CERES),
Halmstad University, Halmstad, Sweden
wojciech.mostowski@hh.se

Abstract. In our earlier work we presented a method for formal verification of concurrent Java programs based on Dynamic Logic and symbolic permissions. Embedded within the *explicit* dynamic frames method realised through JML* specifications, permissions to heap locations and the actual heap location values are tracked separately and require two independent and often overlapping frame specifications. This is in contrast to well established Separation Logic and sibling frameworks, where program frames are inferred from permission annotations that already provide implicit framing information.

In this paper we show how to avoid redundant frame specifications and move towards the *implicit* framing approach in our method. We strive to keep as much as possible of the existing reasoning framework to preserve the general verification philosophy and implementation of our verification tool, the KeY verifier. We achieve our goal by only a small alteration of the existing proof obligation generation without changing any core part of the underlying logic, in particular, we maintain its closed character. However, even though specifications become more natural and less redundant, the *indirect* character of the specifications introduces a clear performance penalty for the verification engine.

We then proceed to a brief discussion why, under our minimal approach assumptions, this extension is still not sufficient to translate Separation Logic specifications into our framework.

1 Introduction

In our previous work [28] we have devised a permission-based verification method for concurrent Java programs and implemented it in the KeY verifier [1]. The program logic of KeY is Dynamic Logic for Java. On the specification layer KeY uses the Java Modelling Language (JML) [21] and the dynamic frames specification method as originally proposed by Kassios [19] and later adapted to KeY and JML by Weiß [34]. The building blocks of our extension to verify concurrent Java programs with KeY are symbolic permissions [17] and reasoning with multiple program heaps [27]. The result is a fully functional and modular verification system for concurrent Java programs; however, due to the use of *explicit* framing, our method is conceptually different from the other existing permission-based methods.

© Springer Nature Switzerland AG 2020
W. Ahrendt et al. (Eds.): Deductive Software Verification, LNCS 12345, pp. 177–203, 2020.
https://doi.org/10.1007/978-3-030-64354-6_7

Permission-based reasoning is an established method for verifying concurrent programs with design-by-contract [26] style specifications, classically enriched with *fractional* permissions [11]. In the context of concurrent execution, permission annotations protect access to heap locations for each thread. Adherence to these annotations is verified locally for each thread and primarily establishes non-interference of threads; programs are guaranteed to be free of data races. The program logic most commonly used for this is Separation Logic [4,33] or an equivalent reasoning framework [32]. Separation Logic builds on top of Hoare Logic [16] and provides a fundamental treatment of the program heap that resolves memory aliasing issues. In particular, Separation Logic specifications (with or without permissions) provide implicit information about the memory or heap frame of the verified program.

Our verification method is not built on Separation Logic, but on the mentioned dynamic frames method realised through JML specifications and implemented in Java Dynamic Logic. While this provides very similar functionality, frames have to be given explicitly in our specifications. Moreover, we use two heaps in our specifications, one that stores actual heap memory contents and one that stores permissions, so we have to explicitly state two separate frame specifications. While we argued for this explicit approach to be advantageous for two reasons (modularity of specifications w.r.t. the use of permissions and overall specification precision) it is a matter of fact that our specifications contain redundant information that could be inferred instead. This is exactly the method employed in the *implicit* dynamic frames (IDF in short) approach [32,35], and we already noted [28] that *"It is also possible to achieve full IDF-style framing in our framework, however, we have chosen not to do so (yet)."* In this paper, we follow up on this statement and show which changes to our reasoning framework are necessary to support the IDF specification methodology in KeY. We concentrate on framing alone, and keep the explanations about the other aspects of concurrent verification (like locking and permission transfers) to a bare minimum. In particular, many of our examples can remain in the sequential setting without the loss of generality. Nevertheless, this work is considered in the concurrent context as the permissions that provide the framing information are used to show thread non-interference.

Our goal is to adapt the existing logic and keep its all (implemented) features, rather than to build a new reasoning system with a fully reworked proof system. However, despite only minor changes actually necessary to achieve our goal, introducing implicit framing incurs performance penalties. Namely, additional quantified formulas are introduced which in turn may require suitable instantiations (possibly manual/interactive). Moreover, even with this implicit framing it is actually not possible to provide a direct translation of Separation Logic specifications to our framework, because of the still existing conceptual differences between the KeY method and Separation Logic frameworks. As we explain it later, the culprit is that Separation Logic specifications would have to be treated as *executable* statements in KeY, and this has consequences for the design of the verification process.

Paper Outline. In Sect. 2 we summarise our earlier results [28]; we recap the main ideas behind verifying concurrent programs with permissions and show how this is realised in our framework with explicit dynamic frames. Section 3 explains implicit dynamic frames (IDF) and discusses the changes necessary to enable IDF-style specifications in our setting [28], this is followed by an example of a new specification in Sect. 4. Then, in Sect. 5 we explain the core problems behind the translation of Separation Logic annotated programs to be verified by KeY. Finally, Sect. 6 summarises the paper and discusses future work.

2   Permission-Based Reasoning with Explicit Frames

The context of our work is formal specification of functional, design-by-contract properties for Java programs (in general, imperative object-oriented programs) and source code-based verification of these properties using a suitable program logic and theorem proving. Our concrete setting is the Java Dynamic Logic (Java DL from now on) implemented in the KeY verification system [1] that employs symbolic execution and provides a user-friendly automated and inter-active verification facilities for a very large subset of Java. Specifications are written in a flavour of the Java Modelling Language [21] called JML* which essentially extends the classic JML to handle dynamic frames specifications. Dynamic frames are a powerful solution to handle one of the core problems of verifying imperative programs that operate on a heap (more generally, accessing memory through pointers), namely that of program framing. Frame specifications allow us to keep the changed memory context of the verified program constrained and in turn enable efficient modular verification. In the following, we explain the explicit dynamic frames as implemented in KeY using a simple example.

2.1   Basic Dynamic Frames in JML*

The essence of specifying and reasoning about programs using explicit dynamic frames is the introduction of memory location sets into the specification language as first class citizens and allowing them to be embedded within abstract predicates [19]. Location set expressions are primarily used in the specification of procedures' write-frames, so called assignable clauses, and in the specification of read-frames, so called accessible clauses, the latter for *pure* program procedures that do not change the state of the program and can be used in specifications.

Dynamic Frames Example. A classic, albeit minimalistic example of a Java program annotated with JML* is shown in Fig. 1. The frames are expressed using abstraction through the JML model field fp (Line 3) representing the footprint of an ArrayList object. Later on, when translated to Java DL, this model field becomes an *observer symbol* – a heap and object reference dependent function symbol. This is important, as we will use such functions for our implicit frame representation, too. A read-frame is specified with the **accessible** keyword (Line 6), and a write-frame is specified with the **assignable** keyword

(Line 11). Both frame clauses are effectively lemmas. Consequently, one is obliged to show that the lemma holds by showing that the corresponding method adheres to the limits of the frame, and then the lemma can be used to support proofs that involve the use of the method. For mutator methods, the **assignable** clause is used to anonymise[1] the corresponding locations of the program when the method contract is modularly applied in the proof to discharge a method call. The **accessible** clause is used in the context of read-only methods to establish the equivalence of two expressions under two states when the expressions are specified not to depend on locations changed between the two states, i.e., locations other than the ones specified in the **accessible** clause. In our example, size() is guaranteed to always evaluate to the same value in all states in which the object field s is not changed. The key feature is the *dynamic* character of the frames. Being specified with a model field that can be constrained using an arbitrary specification, the frame definition can change over time during program execution. Hence, the mentioned heap and object dependent function representation in the logic is used for model fields, and more generally also for model methods [29]. Classically, linked data structures would have such changing object footprint specified recursively. Our array list example here is fully static in this respect, the model field fp is a constant location set with an explicit, non-recursive definition (Line 3).

```
   public class ArrayList {
2      Object[] cnt; int s;
       //@ model \locset fp = s, cnt, cnt[*];
4
       //@ ensures \result == s;
6      //@ accessible fp;
       /*@ pure @*/ int size() { return s; }
8
       //@ requires size() < cnt.length;
10     //@ ensures size() == \old(size()) + 1;
       //@ assignable fp;
12     void add(Object o) { cnt[s++] = o; }
   }
```

Fig. 1. A simple array list specified (incompletely) with explicit frames.

Dynamic Frames in Java Dynamic Logic. In Java DL suitable mechanisms are devised to both show the framing lemmas to hold and to use them in the proofs [34]. Java DL is an extension of first order typed logic with modalities that embed Java programs to be verified. For a piece of Java program p and a property formula ϕ, the box modality $[p]\phi$ expresses partial correctness – if program p

---

[1] In other formalisms this is called *havocing* [22], but the principle is the same.

terminates, then its final state should satisfy ϕ. The diamond modality $\langle p \rangle \phi$ expresses total correctness – program p is required to terminate and the resulting final state should satisfy ϕ. For each Java method specified with "**requires** pre" and "**ensures** post" clauses a proof obligation of the following form is generated to show method() correct:

$$\widehat{pre} \rightarrow \langle \mathrm{method}(); \rangle \widehat{post}$$

where $\widehat{pre}$ and $\widehat{post}$ are translations of the corresponding JML* assertions into first order logic expressions of Java DL. The verification process then proceeds by symbolically executing the program statements in method() into a symbolic state characterised by parallel logic variable assignments $\{a_1 := v_1 \| \ldots \| a_n := v_n\}$ and applying the result to $\widehat{post}$, and then checking the first order validity of the resulting formula. Applying the symbolic state to the formula is essentially equivalent to the Weakest Precondition calculus [12]. Updates to the heap triggered by the assignments in the verified program are reflected in a dedicated variable $heap$ and handled using the theory of arrays [25].

For framing, an **assignable** clause is shown to be correct for a given method by proving the following formula:

$$\forall_{o:Object,f:Field}(o, f) \in \widehat{frame} \lor select(heap, o, f) = select(heapAtPre, o, f) \quad (1)$$

where $\widehat{frame}$ is the translation of the assignable clause from JML* and depends on $heapAtPre$. Variable $heapAtPre$ is the snapshot of the $heap$ variable taken before the method call, and $select$ is the theory of arrays selection function to read values from the given heap variable. For readability, from this point on we use @ as a shortcut notation for the heap selection function, as follows:

$$select(heap, o, f) \equiv o.f@heap$$

For our example in Fig. 1 the following proof obligation for the method add(Object o) is generated:

$$
\begin{aligned}
&self \neq null \land o \neq null \land ArrayList :: size(heap, self) < length(self.cnt@heap) \rightarrow \\
&\quad \{heapAtPre := heap\}\langle \\
&\qquad \mathtt{self.add(o);} \\
&\quad \rangle \, ArrayList :: size(heap, self) = ArrayList :: size(heapAtPre, self) + 1 \land \\
&\qquad \forall_{o:Object,f:Field} \\
&\qquad\quad (o, f) \in ArrayList :: fp(heapAtPre, self) \lor o.f@heap = o.f@heapAtPre
\end{aligned}
$$
$$(2)$$

In this formula, $ArrayList :: size$ and $ArrayList :: fp$ are observer function symbols. They represent the pure method size() and the model field fp, respectively, both of which depend on the current heap and object reference in question. After checking certain conditions related to inheritance [29], these functions can be expanded according to their definitions. Variable $self$ is a representative of objects of type ArrayList, while the expression $\{heapAtPre := heap\}$ is the initial symbolic state that records the pre-state of the method call. This symbolic state is then extended and completed by symbolically executing statements from method add() using Java DL calculus rules.

Any contract proven correct this way can then be used as a lemma in a modular proof to discharge a call to the corresponding method in any client code. The current symbolic state of the client program under verification is modified as follows. Heap locations listed in the method frame are anonymised, while other locations are guaranteed not to be affected by the method call. This anonymised state is freshly described by adding the method's postcondition to the sequent. More concretely, for discharging a call to add(), state anonymisation is performed by modifying the current heap in the following way:

$$heapAfterAdd := anon(heap, ArrayList::fp(heap, list), anonHeapAdd) \qquad (3)$$

The new heap *heapAfterAdd* replaces the old heap and the postcondition of add() is added to describe this new heap. The *anon* function creates a new heap as follows. If the location is *not* listed in the second parameter (here the footprint fp of some array list object *list*) then the value is taken from the heap in the first parameter (here *heap*). Otherwise, the value of the location is taken from the third parameter, here a fresh heap variable *anonHeapAdd*. Effectively, this makes the heap locations within the method frame undefined.

Similar proof obligations and mechanisms are used to show the **accessible** clauses correct. The main difference is that a location set disjointness condition is used instead to show the independent evaluation of the corresponding observer functions under non-overlapping read-frames. However, we do not quote them here, as they are not essential to our presentation, more details can be found elsewhere [29]. For clarity, we also skip the Java exception handling or object creation issues.

2.2 Permission Annotations to Handle Concurrency

The sequential setting presented so far assumes that programs run in isolation as the only process or thread with no external interactions or data sharing. A common extension to design-by-contract specification style to enable verification of concurrent programs is to add permission annotations to specifications. In the context of the currently running thread, such annotations guard every heap location access with either a partial permission that gives the running thread a read access to the underlying heap location, or with a full permission that gives the thread a write access. Permissions are typically modified at call sites, i.e., method invocations or thread dispatching. Permissions are *accounted* for in each thread separately and guarantee non-interference of threads, i.e., that the program is free of data races, as no two threads are allowed to have conflicting access to the same heap location.

Classically, rational fractions are used for permissions [11], 1 represents a full write permission, and any fraction smaller than 1 is a partial read permission. However, other permissions systems like tree-permissions [13] are also possible, and we developed symbolic permissions [17] for our approach. Furthermore, typically permissions are embedded within Separation Logic like formalism [32,33],

```
public class Counter {
  private int c; //@ monitor Perm(this.c, 1);

  public void increase() { synchronized(this) { this.c++; } }
}
```

Fig. 2. An example resource invariant with a permission annotation.

as they are a generalisation of the points-to predicate expressing an access right to the underlying heap location. During program analysis, permissions can be transferred between threads. Permission transfers typically occur when synchronisation primitives are used, like locks or semaphores, and when threads are spawned or joined. To achieve permission transfers, fractional permissions can be split and recombined, while our symbolic permissions [17] can be explicitly transferred between objects or threads.

Figure 2 shows a minimalistic example of a permission annotated program using an *artificial* Separation Logic JML notation and fractional permissions. This example makes use of a resource invariant [31], specified with the **monitor** keyword, to track the access that the Java locking mechanism gives to the shared counter field **this.c**. The lock is simply the object itself, and it is engaged by enclosing the critical section of the program in the **synchronized** block. Within the scope of this block, permissions declared in the resource invariant are temporarily transferred from the resource invariant to the currently running thread granting this thread the right to change **this.c**. Apart from the **synchronized** primitive, the Java API provides a complete concurrency framework [20] with an assortment of synchronisation classes. For this Java concurrency API simple resource invariants are not sufficient and more involved specifications are needed [3]. However, the underlying idea remains the same – API contracts declare how permissions are transferred between the synchroniser and the currently running thread to grant sufficient access rights to perform operations on the shared data.

Finally, note that permission-based specifications extend the classic design-by-contract specifications and can still be used to establish functional properties of verified programs. However, the scope of the functional properties is limited; heap locations potentially modified by other threads, i.e., ones that the current thread does not hold any permissions to, can never be relied on in the context of the local thread. For example, no functional specification can be given for **this.c** outside of the **synchronized** block, in particular in the contract of increase(), due to the lack of a suitable permission. It is possible to employ mechanisms based on histories to state properties about heap locations without permissions [10], however, it goes beyond the scope of this paper.

2.3   Permission Annotations for Dynamic Frames in JML*

In our previous work [28] we also equipped KeY with permissions to handle concurrency. However, we did not follow precisely the ideas of permission-based reasoning just described, most of which have their roots in Separation Logic. Our goal was to employ a minimal extension of the existing mechanisms in KeY, so we concentrated on adapting to the explicit dynamic frames methodology to enable permission-based reasoning, rather than changing it completely to move towards a Separation Logic like framework and loosing many of the existing features and extensions of Java DL implemented in KeY.

Additionally, we developed the mentioned symbolic permission system [17] tailored to KeY. In short, permission values can be abstracted by stating the read or write access that the permission grants, and permissions have the usual properties, e.g., that a write permission implies a read one. Moreover, we can specify explicit permission transfers between named objects. We refer the reader to [17] for a full account, including formal definitions and mechanically proved consistency properties, here we just use simple examples and explain them briefly in the process.

Supporting permissions in Java DL is achieved by operating on two heaps simultaneously [27] – the regular memory heap as before, and an additional permission heap that tracks permissions to the corresponding heap locations. These two heaps are integrated into the logic, but they are also made explicit in JML* specifications to allow the separation of functional properties (actual values on the heap) and non-interference properties (permissions to heap locations). Not surprisingly, the two heaps are named heap and permissions, and they are given *separate* framing specifications. In many cases, the **assignable** permission frames are actually empty, but not for methods and programming constructs that transfer permissions, e.g., mutual exclusion or sharing locks used to access data of another thread. Java DL extends naturally to deal with the extra permission heap, e.g., formulas (1) and (3) from Sect. 2.1 simply include two heaps. Finally, through the use of abstract predicates [29], flexible means are provided to enable fully modular and abstract specifications, which include generic treatment of Java synchronisation classes [3, 28].

2.4   ArrayList Example with Permissions

In Fig. 3 a specification of ArrayList extended to include permissions is shown. For illustration, it also adds very simple locking routines to show how permissions can be transferred. However, the specification shown here is not generic, locking and synchronisation is normally treated more comprehensively with parametric specifications of the API as mentioned above. As before, a footprint for objects of this class is declared as a model field and it includes all the fields and data stored within these fields (Line 3). The specification of size() now requires a read permission to **this**.s to be present (Line 5), so that the method body can indeed read s. The permission is specified with \readPerm(\perm(s)), where \perm is an access operator to read values of the permissions heap, instead of the regular heap, and \readPerm is simply a predicate that establishes the underlying permission to be at least a read one for the *current thread*. Furthermore, the method now has two **accessible** clauses (Line 7–Line 8). On the regular heap, it reads object fields declared in the footprint, and the same locations are accessed

```java
   public class ArrayList {
2     Object[] cnt; int s;
      //@ model \locset fp = s, cnt, cnt[*];
4
      //@ requires \readPerm(\perm(s));
6     //@ ensures \result == s;
      //@ accessible<heap> fp;
8     //@ accessible<permissions> fp;
      /*@ pure @*/ int size() { return s; }
10
      //@ requires \readPerm(\perm(cnt));
12    //@ requires \writePerm(\perm(s));
      //@ requires \writePerm(\perm(cnt[s]));
14    //@ requires size() < cnt.length;
      //@ ensures size() == \old(size()) + 1;
16    //@ assignable<heap> fp;
      //@ assignable<permissions> \nothing;
18    void add(Object o) { cnt[s++] = o; }

20    //@ ghost Object lock;

22    //@ requires \writePermObject(lock, \perm(s));
      //@ requires \writePermObject(lock, \perm(cnt[*]));
24    //@ ensures \perm(s) == \transferPermAll(lock, \ct,
          ↪ \old(\perm(s)));
      //@ ensures \perm(cnt[*]) == \transferPermAll(lock, \ct,
          ↪ \old(\perm(cnt[*])));
26    //@ assignable<heap> \nothing;
      //@ assignable<permissions> s, cnt[*];
28    native void lock();

30    //@ requires \writePerm(\perm(s));
      //@ requires \writePerm(\perm(cnt[*]));
32    //@ ensures \perm(s) == \returnPerm(\ct, lock, \old(\perm(s)));
      //@ ensures \perm(cnt[*]) == \returnPerm(\ct, lock,
          ↪ \old(\perm(cnt[*])));
34    //@ assignable<heap> s, cnt[*];
      //@ assignable<permissions> s, cnt[*];
36    native void unlock();
   }
```

Fig. 3. Explicit frames specification with permissions.

on the permissions heap. This symmetry is natural for a read-only method – to access any field of the object a corresponding permission has to be checked and hence the location is also accessed on the permissions heap. Note that putting the complete footprint fp as declared in this class in either **accessible** clause of size() is a large over-approximation, as it only reads s. This is exactly what the permission in the precondition specifies and the precondition alone *should* be sufficient to define the read-frame of this method.

Compared to the size() method, the state changing method add() does not have the same frame symmetry for its **assignable** clauses. It modifies the contents of the array cnt at the s position (cnt[s]), and then it modifies field s (Line 18). The array reference cnt is only read, not modified. Hence, the corresponding permissions are added to the precondition of add() (Line 11–Line 13). The **assignable** clause for the base heap (Line 16) is again an over-approximation, and it includes all locations in the footprint fp, while the **assignable** clause for the permissions heap is empty (Line 17). This is because no permissions are modified by the add() method, they are only read to check the corresponding access rights. As above, the locations that the method reads or writes are already determined by the permissions declared in the precondition, moreover, this information is more precise than the **assignable** clause.

Locks. Finally, two methods to provide a locking mechanism for list updating are specified for further illustration. Both lock() and unlock() are native, it is assumed that a suitable low-level implementation (e.g., using atomic variables and/or compare-and-swap operations) is provided. On the specification level, we need to model the equivalent of a resource invariant [31] to have a *placeholder* for permissions associated with the lock. For this, the ghost lock object (Line 20) is used to hold the permission rights to the corresponding locations when the lock is not engaged, and upon locking these rights are temporarily transferred to the currently running thread to be later returned back to the lock upon unlocking. This also means that we actually allow arbitrary objects to hold permissions, not only threads. A client application would typically call lock() first before calling add() to get the corresponding access rights to modify the list. For simplicity, we assume that read access to the cnt array is globally given to all threads.

Compared to the add() method, for the locking method the **assignable** clause for the regular heap is empty (Line 26), while for the permissions heap it is not (Line 27); the sole purpose of the locking method is to modify permissions to the associated heap locations, not the contents of the heap itself. The actual shape and type of permission change are given by the permission transfer and return functions. Upon locking *all* access rights are transferred from the lock object to the currently running thread \ct (Line 24–Line 25), and upon unlocking all these rights are returned to the lock again (Line 32–Line 33). The transfer and return functions take \old permissions from the permission heap, modify them accordingly, and return fresh permissions that are stored on the permissions heap again.

The permissions to s and cnt[*] specified in the preconditions of lock() (Line 22–Line 23) and unlock() (Line 30–Line 31) are used to establish the lock engagement state, i.e., lock() should be only called when the said permissions belong to the lock meaning that the lock is not engaged and it holds all the permissions. The predicate \writePermObject is a generalisation of the \writePerm predicate to any object. This allows us to specify where, besides the current thread, the permissions reside at the given state. In fact, \writePerm(p) is a syntactical shortcut for \writePermObject(\ct, p). The ability to assign permissions to objects other than the currently running thread is also the counterpart of lock-sets [15] in other formalisms to effectively solve the problem of specifying the lock engagement state.

Symmetrically, unlock() should only be used after lock() has been used first and the associated rights were granted to the currently running thread. Finally, note the **assignable** frame for the regular heap of the unlock() method (Line 34). Even though the method is only operating on permissions to return the rights from the current thread to the lock, it is necessary to anonymise the corresponding locations on the regular heap after the permissions are completely returned to the lock. This forces the current thread to forget about heap values that it lost permissions to.

In concurrent reasoning the specifications themselves have to be framed with respect to permissions. That is, pre- and postconditions are only allowed to refer to heap locations for which there is at least a read permission specified within the same condition. Since locations without access rights can be potentially modified by other threads it is not sound to refer to their values in any way. In [28] we showed how our specifications are checked to be self-framed with respect to permissions by proving a suitable proof obligation. All frames shown so far are given statically through the corresponding specification clauses. However, in the proof obligation for showing self-framing the frame of the specification expression is constructed dynamically *on-the-fly*. This on-demand frame construction gives us the base to also construct the **accessible** and **assignable** clauses on-demand and allow for implicit method framing based on permission specifications.

3   Transformation to Implicit Dynamic Frames

Our explicit frame specifications with permissions exhibit substantial redundancy – the **assignable** and **accessible** clauses are essentially obsolete. The precondition provides the complete framing information for a given method – a read permission indicates that a method might access a heap location (previously indicated in the **accessible** clause) and the write permission indicates that a method might modify a heap location (previously indicated in the **assignable** clause). More importantly, no heap access (read or write) in the code would be allowed without a corresponding permission annotation, hence the permission annotations provide complete framing specification. This is exactly the approach that the *implicit dynamic frames* (IDF) method employs [24, 35].

The fine points to address in order to extract a usable frame from permission specifications are the following. First of all, the permission annotations indicate what precise accesses are forthcoming in the corresponding method on the *regular* heap. They do not, however, give the same information as to what can happen on the permissions heap. In particular, a write permission to a location clearly indicates that this location is to be changed on the regular heap, hence the location is technically in the assignable frame for heap, but it does not mean that the same location would change on the permissions heap. Most often, permissions are just checked (read) and are not modified. Putting this location in the assignable set for permissions is an over-approximation that has to be accounted for. Secondly, in the modular proof when heap locations are anonymised following the schema in formula (3) in Sect. 2.1, we still need a reference (through a defined function symbol) to a complete set of locations modified by the method, which in the explicit approach is just given.

3.1   Implicit Frames for the Regular Heap

The permissions specified in the precondition indicate precisely what kind of access a given heap location will be subjected to during the execution of the method within the context of the currently running thread. A read permission indicates that a location needs to be read, a write permission indicates that the corresponding location is going to be either read or changed. Thus, a method that has only read permissions specified in the precondition is a pure method, one previously specified with the **accessible** clause, while a method with write permissions is a mutator method, one previously specified with the **assignable** clause. With permissions, no additional proof obligation of the form given in formula (1) in Sect. 2.1 is needed to check this implicit framing, this is achieved by permission tracking. In particular, if the method tries to write a heap location without a corresponding permission, the proof will not succeed indicating that the method tries to change locations outside of its prescribed write frame expressed with permissions. Similarly, no heap locations can be read without a corresponding read permission. Thus, with permissions one can skip the framing part of the generated proof obligation, e.g., in formula (2) the last two lines are not necessary.

3.2   Implicit Frame Extraction

Although the frame does not have to be explicitly checked for correctness, the precise information about heap locations in the frame is still needed to dispatch method calls modularly. That is, the application of the anonymisation function (3) to the current symbolic state needs the set of heap locations that constitute the write frame of the method.

The main idea to solve this issue is to apply the same principle as with abstract frame specifications given through model field definitions. Recall our ArrayList example where the heap footprint for the complete class was given through the fp model field. The anonymisation formula refers to the corresponding state observing symbol:

$$heapAfterAdd := anon(heap, ArrayList :: fp(heap, list), anonHeapAdd)$$

The footprint observer function $ArrayList :: fp$ refers to specific heap locations through the explicit definition of the model field fp given in Fig. 1, Line 3, this is called a *functional* represents clause. A corresponding Java DL axiomatic definition is generated for the proof allowing to unfold $ArrayList::fp$ into these specific heap locations. In this case, the definition is the following:

$$\forall_{h:Heap,l:ArrayList} ArrayList::fp(h,l) = \{(l,s),(l,cnt)\} \cup allElements(l.cnt@h)$$

meaning that for a particular heap h and `ArrayList` object l, an occurrence of $ArrayList::fp(h,l)$ can be replaced with the right-hand side of this definition, where $allElements$ denotes a location set of all elements of the given array.

Following this principle, it is sufficient to introduce another state observing function for the given method's frame, one that instead *fishes out* heap locations from the method's precondition by having a suitable definition. This definition is inevitably indirect. Intuitively, it states that the result of the function is a set of heap locations *such that* a write permission to each of these locations is specified in the method's precondition. Such indirect definition is resemblant of a *relational* model field definition where a specification for the model field is given through the \such_that JML clause. This allows one to specify a relation that the result should satisfy using any suitable predicates or expressions, rather than giving an explicit functional expression defining the result.

Hence our new observer function $writeFrameMethodX$ (for some method X, here add) captures the permissions from X's precondition with the following definition in Java DL:

$$\forall_{h:Heap,l:ArrayList,p_1:Object} \quad \forall_{o:Object,f:Field}$$
$$((\{\text{permissions} := permsPreAdd(h,l,p_1) \,\|\, \text{heap} := h\}\widehat{preAdd} \rightarrow$$
$$writePerm(o.f@permsPreAdd(h,l,p_1))) \rightarrow$$
$$(o,f) \in ArrayList::writeFrameAdd(h,l,p_1))$$
$$\wedge \tag{4}$$
$$((\neg\{\text{permissions} := anon(fullPerms,(o,f),permsPreAdd'(h,l,p_1)) \,\|$$
$$\text{heap} := h\}\widehat{preAdd} \rightarrow \neg readPerm(o.f@permsPreAdd'(h,l,p_1))) \rightarrow$$
$$(o,f) \notin ArrayList::writeFrameAdd(h,l,p_1))$$

Because method parameters $p_1,\ldots,p_n$ (here $n = 1$) may occur in $\widehat{preAdd}$ and consequently affect the frame, our frame observer function now also depends on these method parameters to make it specific to a particular method call. Otherwise, the h and l quantified variables make the definition specific to a given program state represented by heap h and call object l. Thus, every instantiation of this definition will receive concrete instances of h, l, and $p_{1...n}$ to make the definition specific to a particular call site.

Let us first discuss the top implication in (4). It is important to capture the permissions *only* from the precondition and not from anywhere else in the proof context. The permission heap function symbol $permsPreAdd$ (similarly the $'$ version in the lower part of the formula) is introduced, but otherwise left undefined, to bind the evaluation of permissions to one method call site and consequently one particular instance of the precondition. Expression $\widehat{preX}$ is a translation of the precondition of method X from JML*, and with the state update expression $\{\text{permissions} := permsPreX(h,l,p_{1...n}) \,\|\, \text{heap} := h\}$ in front of it we localise permission expressions and the rest of the precondition to the current program state identified by the heap variable h, call object l, and method parameters $p_{1...n}$, i.e., a particular call site. Overall, the top expression defines the location set that the result of $writeFrameMethodX$ should contain, namely, it binds them to locations with a write permission in the precondition.

The bottom implication of our definition takes care of specifying locations that are *not* in the frame. This is equally, if not more, important to enable complete reasoning. Here, the anonymisation function serves the purpose of splitting the evaluation of the precondition into two heap spaces. The $permsPreX'$ heap is concerned with locations appearing in the precondition, while the $fullPerms$ heap is where all other permissions reside, i.e., all permission queries in this space evaluate to *true*. Effectively, when the expression is instantiated with a heap location (o, f) that does not appear in the precondition, all permissions in $\widehat{preX}$ are trivially true which in turn qualifies (o, f) to be excluded from the frame. Otherwise, if a permission to (o, f) does appear in $\widehat{preX}$ we check if it is a read permission only, in which case it is also excluded from the write-frame. All other locations would indicate a write permission in the precondition, in which case the complete bottom implication is inconclusive for the location exclusion and instead the top implication already discussed applies for inclusion of these locations in the frame.

For each of the methods in the class we need a separate observer function of this kind, here we have exemplified this with a definition for method add. Conceptually, this follows the idea of model methods presented in [29], only here we provide a relational definition for a method specific, auto-generated observer symbol. It refers verbosely to a copy of the method's precondition to filter out locations with and without a write permission by intricate manipulation of the permissions heap variable. These intricacies shall become more clear when we show the example in Sect. 4. Intuitively, this manipulation is necessary for the following reasons. In our setting, missing permissions for locations do not explicitly imply that there is no write permission on that location, it only leaves the given location with a "don't know" status. If that explicit information implication held, a much simpler definition for (4) with equivalence and no bottom implication would suffice:

$$writePerm(o.f@permsPreAdd(h, l, p_1))) \leftrightarrow$$
$$(o, f) \in ArrayList::writeFrameAdd(h, l, p_1))$$

Thus, there is the need to split the permission space to make the non-specified permissions explicit. On top of that, just a read permission but not a write one should still exclude the corresponding location from the write-frame.

This covers constructing a write-frame previously given explicitly with an **assignable** clause. For pure methods, one needs to have a read-frame previously specified with an **accessible** clause. The solution is very similar. In the top implication, the only change is that we are looking for locations with a read permission, not necessarily a write permission. For the bottom implication, we modify the negated permission check so that any location that is not specified in the precondition at all is excluded from the frame, while any specified location gives an inconclusive result and the top implication applies. The corresponding definition of $ArrayList :: readFrameSize$ for the size method reads as follows:

$$\forall_{h:Heap,l:ArrayList} \quad \forall_{o:Object,f:Field}$$
$$(({\text{permissions}} := permsPreSize(h,l) \parallel {\text{heap}} := h\}\widehat{preSize} \rightarrow$$
$$readPerm(o.f@permsPreSize(h,l))) \rightarrow$$
$$(o,f) \in ArrayList :: readFrameSize(h,l)) \tag{5}$$
$$\wedge$$
$$((\neg\{\text{permissions}} := anon(fullPerms,(o,f),permsPreSize'(h,l)) \parallel$$
$$\text{heap} := h\}\widehat{preSize} \rightarrow writePerm(o.f@permsPreSize'(h,l))) \rightarrow$$
$$(o,f) \notin ArrayList :: readFrameSize(h,l))$$

Practicality. Our frame collection formula (4) is essentially a relational JML* **represents** clause with a specifically tailored definition. However, relational represents clauses are often advocated against, see for example [14, Sect. 9.2.1.5]. In particular, relations given by such clauses do not have to specify unique results of the corresponding observer functions, moreover, additional conditions have to be checked for the satisfiability of all existing relational represents clauses. Finally, just reasoning about function symbols with relational definitions is more complicated hindering the verification performance and possibly requiring manual proof interactions (after all, universal quantification over several variables is involved in our frame definition). Because of these issues and still existing problems to comprehensively treat true Separation Logic specification style in KeY (see upcoming Sect. 5) we have opted not to implement this extension in KeY to test it in practice. Nevertheless, should the need to implement this arise, we still need to treat framing for the permissions heap along the regular heap.

3.3   Implicit Framing for the Permissions Heap

Contrary to the regular heap, the presence of a write permission in the specification does not, in general, imply that the permissions heap is modified within the body of the method. In fact, the most common case is that a write permission is given to allow a corresponding write access on the regular heap, while the permission heap itself stays unchanged. In our example in Fig. 3 only the synchronisation methods lock and unlock actually change the locations on the permissions heap, even though write permissions to heap locations are also stated in the add method (Line 12–Line 13). Thus, putting a location into the write-frame of the permissions heap based on the corresponding write permission *might be* a large over-approximation. Many locations included in the frame this way will stay unchanged nevertheless and to express this lack of change, suitable statements have to be included in the postcondition.

On the other hand, *synchronisation* methods, like our lock and unlock methods, may change both read and write permissions mentioned in the specification, while not changing the regular heap locations at all. That is, a specified read permission can also mean that the permission itself might be changed, while the corresponding location on the regular heap cannot change.

Unfortunately, we have not found a way to avoid this over-approximation. All locations for which any permission is mentioned in the specification have to be assumed to be changing on the permission heap and included in the corresponding permissions frame. The additional complication is that we now need to consider permissions residing with other objects than the current thread. For synchronisation methods a permission that is modified does not necessarily have to be assigned to the current thread, but instead it is "produced" by the method by transferring it from another object, e.g., a lock. The lock() method does exactly that in our example in Fig. 1. In the following we show how the frame extraction is done in this context and also how to extend the specification mechanism for permissions to easily declare locations over-approximated by this method to be non-changing permissions nevertheless.

3.4   Frame Extraction for the Permissions Heap

The method for collecting permissions heap locations is very similar to the read-frame collection one for the regular heap in (5). As before, we are interested in any permission, not just a write one. This is because a synchronisation method may wish to also modify a permission that is not necessarily a write permission. Counting semaphore or a similar multi-read synchroniser would be an example here. A slight modification is that we now need to collect permissions for any object that may hold them, i.e., apart from the current thread also for any locks that might be holding them at the time of the call. This requires introducing an existential quantifier to account for these other objects. The complete definition for our frame observer function for method add reads:

$$
\begin{aligned}
\forall_{h:Heap,l:ArrayList,p_1:Object} \quad &\forall_{o:Object,f:Field} \\
&((\{\text{permissions} := permsPreAdd(h,l,p_1) \,\|\, \text{heap} := h\}\widehat{preAdd} \to \\
&\quad \exists_{r:Object} readPermObject(r,o.f@permsPreAdd(h,l,p_1))) \to \\
&\quad\quad (o,f) \in ArrayList :: permissionsFrameAdd(h,l,p_1)) \\
&\land \\
&((\neg\{\text{permissions} := anon(fullPerms,(o,f),permsPreAdd'(h,l,p_1)) \,\| \\
&\quad \text{heap} := h\}\widehat{preAdd} \to \\
&\quad\quad \exists_{r:Object} writePermObject(r,o.f@permsPreAdd'(h,l,p_1))) \to \\
&\quad\quad\quad (o,f) \notin ArrayList :: permissionsFrameAdd(h,l,p_1))
\end{aligned}
\tag{6}
$$

As before, the state update expressions $\{\cdot\}$ takes care of bringing the context of the precondition to the corresponding regular and permissions heaps. The presence of any read permission owned by any object qualifies the corresponding location to be in *permissionsFrameX*, while permissions not present in the precondition are excluded from the frame.

3.5 Specification Extension to "Repeat" Permissions

As explained above, such dynamically created frames resulting from (4), (5), or (6) may result in an over-approximation, i.e., the underlying locations on either of the heaps do not really change while permissions for these locations have to be stated to allow the program to operate on them. In particular, our add() method does not change the permissions heap at all, while applying (6) puts (l, s), (l, cnt), and $(l.cnt@h, l.s@h)$ in the frame. We propose to use an additional keyword \samePerm, and similarly \sameValue for the regular heap (although the use of \sameValue would be less common). The expression \samePerm(1) is a simple syntactical equivalence for \perm(1) == \old(\perm(1)). The resulting need to specify all non-changing permissions in postconditions to enable precise reasoning is not surprising, Separation Logic-like specifications are also required to do so. However, in our case such annotations are not necessary if the method is declared to be **pure** in the first place, which assumes upfront that no locations on either of the heaps are changed.

4   ArrayList Example with Implicit Frames

Figure 4 shows the specification of the program in Fig. 3 modified to suit the IDF specification approach following the ideas just described. Explicit frames are now entirely gone, permission expressions imply the frame for both the regular heap and the permissions heap. The regular heap frame is extracted using (4) and, in particular, for the method add() results in locations this.s and this.cnt[this.s]. For the permissions frame, (6) is applied and results in also this.cnt being in the frame, due to the read permission in Line 8. Because none of the permissions to these locations are modified in add(), the permissions have to be repeated with the \samePerm operator in the postcondition (Line 13–Line 15).

The precondition for lock() does not specify any permissions for the current thread, only for the lock object that holds the needed permissions (Line 20–Line 21). The resulting write-frame for the regular heap is thus empty. This is actually correct, the current thread would not have any information about the locations being acquired through locking before the call to lock() anyhow, hence these locations are out of scope. Applying (6) to the precondition of lock() results in the permissions frame with locations this.s and this.cnt[*] as these permissions are specified to belong to the lock at the time of the call. For the unlock() method, these locations have write permissions specified in the precondition for the current thread (Line 26–Line 27) and hence they form the write-frame for the regular heap, according to (4). This is again correct, upon unlocking the current thread looses all permissions to these locations and hence information about their values on the regular heap has to be erased, the write-frame with these locations ensures that. However, if the unlock() method would not be giving up all access permissions to all locations and leaving the current thread with, say, still a read permission, then we would use the \sameValue operator for these locations on the regular heap in the postcondition of unlock().

```
   public class ArrayList {
2     Object[] cnt; int s;

4     //@ requires \readPerm(\perm(s));
      //@ ensures \result == s;
6     /*@ pure @*/ int size() { return s; }

8     //@ requires \readPerm(\perm(cnt));
      //@ requires \writePerm(\perm(s));
10    //@ requires \writePerm(\perm(cnt[s]));
      //@ requires size() < cnt.length;
12    //@ ensures size() == \old(size()) + 1;
      //@ ensures \samePerm(\perm(s));
14    //@ ensures \samePerm(\perm(cnt));
      //@ ensures \samePerm(\perm(cnt[s]));
16    void add(Object o) { cnt[s++] = o; }

18    //@ ghost Object lock;

20    //@ requires \writePermObject(lock, \perm(s));
      //@ requires \writePermObject(lock, \perm(cnt[*]));
22    //@ ensures \perm(s) == \transferPermAll(lock, \ct,
          ↪ \old(\perm(s)));
      //@ ensures \perm(cnt[*]) == \transferPermAll(lock, \ct,
          ↪ \old(\perm(cnt[*])));
24    native void lock();

26    //@ requires \writePerm(\perm(s));
      //@ requires \writePerm(\perm(cnt[*]));
28    //@ ensures \perm(s) == \returnPerm(\ct, lock, \old(\perm(s)));
      //@ ensures \perm(cnt[*]) == \returnPerm(\ct, lock,
          ↪ \old(\perm(cnt[*])));
30    native void unlock();
   }
```

Fig. 4. Implicit Dynamic Frames specification in JML* for the ArrayList class.

This would indicate that the information about values stored in these locations can be retained due to at least a read permission remaining with the current thread. According to (6), the frame of the permissions heap for unlock() is the same as for lock(), only the permissions are specified for the current thread in the precondition of unlock() (Line 26–Line 27) and not the lock object.

Frame Collection for add(). For further illustration, we show the concrete instance of the write-frame extraction function (4) for method add(). We assume that the first quantifier is already instantiated to a particular program state represented by heap h_0, list object l_0, and call parameter p_{1_0}. We also assume that the list size requirement in the precondition is know to be true from the proof context and we only show permissions. Finally, we substitute the heaps as specified in the update expressions $\{\cdot\}$ in (4):

$$\forall_{o:Object,f:Field}$$
$$((\, readPerm(l_0.cnt@permsPreAdd(h_0, l_0, p_{1_0})) \wedge$$
$$writePerm(l_0.s@permsPreAdd(h_0, l_0, p_{1_0})) \wedge$$
$$writePerm(l_0.cnt@h_0[l_0.s@h_0]@permsPreAdd(h_0, l_0, p_{1_0})) \rightarrow$$
$$writePerm(o.f@permsPreAdd(h_0, l_0, p_{1_0}))) \rightarrow$$
$$(o, f) \in writeFrame(h_0, l_0, p_{1_0}))$$
$$\wedge$$
$$((\neg(readPerm(l_0.cnt@anon(fullPerms, (o, f), permsPreAdd'(h_0, l_0, p_{1_0}))) \wedge$$
$$writePerm(l_0.s@anon(fullPerms, (o, f), permsPreAdd'(h_0, l_0, p_{1_0}))) \wedge$$
$$writePerm(l_0.cnt@h_0[l_0.s@h_0]@anon(fullPerms, (o, f),$$
$$permsPreAdd'(h_0, l_0, p_{1_0}))))$$
$$\rightarrow \neg readPerm(o.f@permsPreAdd'(h_0, l_0, p_{1_0}))) \rightarrow$$
$$(o, f) \notin writeFrame(h_0, l_0, p_{1_0}))$$

The top level quantifier can now be instantiated with an arbitrary heap location (o, f) to establish its inclusion or exclusion in $writeFrame$. The interesting cases are (l_0, cnt), (l_0, s), and any (o_0, f_0) not mentioned in the precondition. Instantiating with (l_0, cnt) and reducing $anon$ functions results in:

$$((readPerm(l_0.cnt@permsPreAdd(h_0, l_0, p_{1_0})) \wedge$$
$$writePerm(l_0.s@permsPreAdd(h_0, l_0, p_{1_0})) \wedge$$
$$writePerm(l_0.cnt@h_0[l_0.s@h_0]@permsPreAdd(h_0, l_0, p_{1_0})) \rightarrow$$
$$writePerm(l_0.cnt@permsPreAdd(h_0, l_0, p_{1_0}))) \rightarrow$$
$$(l_0, cnt) \in writeFrame(h_0, l_0, p_{1_0}))$$
$$\wedge$$
$$((\neg(readPerm(l_0.cnt@permsPreAdd'(h_0, l_0, p_{1_0})) \wedge$$
$$writePerm(l_0.s@fullPerms) \wedge$$
$$writePerm(l_0.cnt@h_0[l_0.s@h_0]@fullPerms)) \rightarrow$$
$$\neg readPerm(l_0.cnt@permsPreAdd'(h_0, l_0, p_{1_0}))) \rightarrow$$
$$(l_0, cnt) \notin writeFrame(h_0, l_0, p_{1_0}))$$

In the top implication, since the read permission on (l_0, cnt) does not imply a write permission, this location cannot be included in the frame. In the bottom implication, the first two write permission predicates on the $fullPerms$ heap are trivially true leaving:

$$\neg readPerm(l_0.cnt@permsPreAdd'(h_0, l_0, p_{1_0})) \rightarrow$$
$$\neg readPerm(l_0.cnt@permsPreAdd'(h_0, l_0, p_{1_0}))$$

as a condition to exclude (l_0, cnt) from the frame, which obviously holds.

Instantiating with (l_0, s) results in:

$$((readPerm(l_0.cnt@permsPreAdd(h_0, l_0, p_{1_0})) \wedge$$
$$writePerm(l_0.s@permsPreAdd(h_0, l_0, p_{1_0})) \wedge$$
$$writePerm(l_0.cnt@h_0[l_0.s@h_0]@permsPreAdd(h_0, l_0, p_{1_0})) \rightarrow$$
$$writePerm(l_0.s@permsPreAdd(h_0, l_0, p_{1_0}))) \rightarrow$$
$$(l_0, s) \in writeFrame(h_0, l_0, p_{1_0}))$$
$$\wedge$$
$$((\neg(readPerm(l_0.cnt@fullPerms) \wedge$$
$$writePerm(l_0.s@permsPreAdd'(h_0, l_0, p_{1_0})) \wedge$$
$$writePerm(l_0.cnt@h_0[l_0.s@h_0]@fullPerms)) \rightarrow$$
$$\neg readPerm(l_0.s@permsPreAdd'(h_0, l_0, p_{1_0}))) \rightarrow$$
$$(l_0, s) \notin writeFrame(h_0, l_0, p_{1_0}))$$

The write permission on (l_0, s) in the top implication can be established to hold, hence the location is included in *writeFrame*. In the bottom implication, the premiss reduces to:

$$\neg writePerm(l_0.s@permsPreAdd'(h_0, l_0, p_{1_0})) \rightarrow$$
$$\neg readPerm(l_0.s@permsPreAdd'(h_0, l_0, p_{1_0}))$$

which in general does not hold, hence (l_0, s) cannot be excluded from the frame.

Finally, instantiating with an arbitrary (o_0, f_0) that is not referenced in the precondition we get:

$$((readPerm(l_0.cnt@permsPreAdd(h_0, l_0, p_{1_0})) \wedge$$
$$writePerm(l_0.s@permsPreAdd(h_0, l_0, p_{1_0})) \wedge$$
$$writePerm(l_0.cnt@h_0[l_0.s@h_0]@permsPreAdd(h_0, l_0, p_{1_0})) \rightarrow$$
$$writePerm(o_0.f_0@permsPreAdd(h_0, l_0, p_{1_0}))) \rightarrow$$
$$(o_0, f_0) \in writeFrame(h_0, l_0, p_{1_0}))$$
$$\wedge$$
$$((\neg(readPerm(l_0.cnt@fullPerms) \wedge$$
$$writePerm(l_0.s@fullPerms) \wedge$$
$$writePerm(l_0.cnt@h_0[l_0.s@h_0]@fullPerms)) \rightarrow$$
$$\neg readPerm(o_0.f_0@permsPreAdd'(h_0, l_0, p_{1_0}))) \rightarrow$$
$$(o_0, f_0) \notin writeFrame(h_0, l_0, p_{1_0}))$$

In the top implication, no permission to (o_0, f_0) is found, hence it cannot be included in the frame. In the bottom implication, all permissions in the precondition refer to the *fullPerms* heap, which makes all permission predicates true. Consequently, the innermost premiss is false and the outer premiss is true leading to the exclusion of (o_0, f_0) from the frame.

In the end, the frame contains the two locations with a write permission in the precondition, (l_0, s) and $(l_0.cnt@h_0, l_0.s@h_0)$, while all other locations are explicitly excluded from the frame.

5 Separation Logic vs. the KeY Framework

One of the goals of shifting towards the IDF specification style is to reduce the redundancy that we have in our explicit approach. The other goal would be to also enable translation and verification of Separation Logic specifications within the KeY framework. In fact, this work was originally started in the context of the VerCors project [2] with the intention of verifying Separation Logic annotated concurrent data structures implementations with KeY. In [32] it has been shown that IDF and Separation Logic are essentially equivalent with respect to expressiveness of specifications, and the VerCors toolset [9] is implemented based on this observation. Namely, permission-based Separation Logic specifications are translated into the IDF-based Chalice [24] language and then verified automatically using the Chalice tool. Hence now, having the method for implicit framing in KeY, a similar translation should be possible to bridge Separation Logic with KeY. However, with the current method this is still not possible in a simple way, i.e., with relatively minor changes to the logic and maintaining the overall philosophy and implementation of KeY. The problem lies in the conceptual difference of how specifications are treated in Java DL and in Separation Logic. In essence, Separation Logic specifications would have to be treated as *executable* statements with consequences on the design of the calculus and basic proof obligation construction in KeY. In Java DL specifications are pure first order logic expressions and are kept separate from the verified programs. This does not mean that such translation is not at all possible (it most certainly is), but not when assuming a simple adaptation of the existing verification infrastructure of KeY. We elaborate on this in the following.

5.1 Multiplicative Character of Separation Logic

In literature [32,33] the separating conjunction operator of Separation Logic is described as *multiplicative*. In practice, this means that it is a "sequential" operator, in the sense that the evaluation of one expression depends on the evaluation of the previous one. This is a characteristic of program statements, rather than pure logical expressions. In particular, two fractional permission expressed in Separation Logic with $Perm(x, \frac{1}{2}) * Perm(x, \frac{1}{2})$ evaluate to $Perm(x, 1)$, while $Perm(x, 1) * Perm(x, 1)$ evaluates to falsity. With regular first order conjunction the expressions would evaluate to $Perm(x, \frac{1}{2})$ and $Perm(x, 1)$, respectively.

5.2 Separation Logic Assertions as Program Statements

This suggests that Separation Logic is, in a way, *state-full*. It is easier to see this when one analyses how IDF specifications of Chalice are translated to first order logic formulas [32] through the Boogie language [22] with the inhaling and exhaling operations on the heap and permission mask structures.

For reasoning about programs, Chalice uses the Weakest Precondition calculus [12]. However, unlike in the classic WP method, the pre- and postconditions, or generally program annotations, are part of the verified program stated with dedicated **assume** and **assert** statements, rather than formulas that the WP calculus is applied to. More precisely, consider verification of a simple Java method with the following specification:

```
//@ requires x >= 0;
//@ ensures x > 0;
  void increase() { x = x + 1; }
```

Putting aside the fact that variable x resides on the heap in Java, classically one would construct and evaluate the following WP formula:

$$x \geq 0 \rightarrow wp(\text{x = x + 1}; \,|\, x > 0)$$

The "classic" evaluation of this proceeds by substituting $x + 1$ for x in the postcondition $x > 0$ and then checking the validity of the resulting formula $x \geq 0 \rightarrow x + 1 > 0$ which obviously holds. When the **assume** and **assert** statements are used instead, the WP formula takes a slightly different shape:

$$wp(\textbf{assume } x >= 0; x = x + 1; \textbf{ assert } x > 0; \,|\, true)$$

The WP evaluation rule for **assert** simply conjuncts the corresponding formula with the postcondition, while the **assume** statement checks if the assumption formula implies the current postcondition. In effect, the same first order formula is created as in the classic case. Thus, for basic sequential reasoning without heap structures these two methods are equivalent.

However, for Separation Logic expressions with permissions, this is not the case. In the scope of the WP correctness formula in Chalice/Boogie there is also a logic variable H that represents the heap, and the permission mask P, essentially equivalents of our heap and permissions heaps in Java DL. The **assert** and **assume** statements not only add formulas to the WP postcondition expression, but they also manipulate, by means of WP substitution, the H and P variables to store and update heap locations and permission values of the verified program. The operations on H and P to discharge the permission in the specifications are called exhaling and inhaling, respectively, and their names already indicate a state changing operation. In particular, on exhaling permissions are taken away from the permission mask P, literally by subtracting permission values stated in the formula from the current values of permissions stored in the mask P. The corresponding WP rule in [32] states:

$$wp(\textbf{exhale}(Perm(o.f, \pi)) \,|\, \varphi) = wp(\textbf{assert } P[o, f] \geq \pi; P[o, f] := P[o, f] - \pi, \varphi)$$

where π is some fractional permission to location $o.f$. Exhaling is in fact an operator to include a specification expression as a program statement. The effective result is modifying the program state represented by permission mask P (and heap H in some other WP rules) to evaluate Separation Logic formulas, witnessed with the explicit state assignment in the above rule.

5.3   Consequences for the Java DL Calculus

There are many similarities between Chalice and KeY here. Two heap variables are used in each approach, heaps use what is referred to as *total semantics*, meaning that there is one heap variable that stores the complete image of the program heap. This is opposed to approaches where the heap is divided into several small *partial* heaps, one for each *separate* location – a more natural notion for Separation Logic, and in fact called *classical* Separation Logic. Also the last step of evaluating the correctness formula on the symbolic state in Java DL is essentially the same as the Weakest Precondition calculus.

The differentiating point in the two verification methods is where the expressions translated from the corresponding specifications end up in proof obligations or correctness formulas. In Java DL these expression are strict first order logic constructs and exist exclusively outside of the program code and never affect the program state (but are themselves affected by program statements). In Chalice, the expressions are part of the verified program code and *do* affect the representation of the program state. This conceptual difference makes it problematic to translate Separation Logic specifications within the KeY framework in a straightforward way. One sensible solution would be to *execute* Separation Logic specifications as program statements in the scope of Java DL modalities to evaluate Separation Logic atomic formulas *sequentially* as explained above.

Another alternative would be to move from the total heap semantics towards partial heaps in Java DL to bring it closer to Separation Logic, like it is done in VeriFast [18]. While having very good support for multiple heaps and multiple heap variables in the logic itself, the whole specification translation and symbolic execution mechanism of KeY would have to be adapted. Moreover, according to [32], partial heap semantics is more suitable for programming languages with manual memory allocation and deallocation, like C, while Java has garbage collection and works better with total heaps.

Finally, one could try to implement a mechanism to translate Separation Logic assertions to pure first order expression by means of a directly applicable footprint operator that can be applied to extract footprints of specification expressions in an explicit fashion (as opposed to the very implicit way we presented in this paper) and apply set operations to the resulting footprints to impose Separation Logic semantics, e.g., set disjointness operator to ensure heap separation condition of the separating conjunction. Such a footprint operator and a corresponding method of translating Separation Logic to Dafny [23] through Region Logic [5] is presented in [6]. However, the original approach has some shortcomings, e.g., the footprint operator presented in [6] applied to an existential quantifier gives a very over-approximated location set of *all* existing heap locations. This work has been later improved in [7], however, the entire revised approach presented in [7] is to combine two logics together (Separation Logic and Region Logic) rather than to provide the translation between them, as they are argued not to be compatible for this purpose (e.g., Separation Logic does not allow cyclic heap structures, while Region Logic does).

All our proposed methods of verifying Separation Logic are either imprecise, or require a redesign of Java DL and proof obligation generation mechanism of KeY. These are not simple adaptations, while the only added value would be a different specification paradigm rather than actually improved expressiveness.

Furthermore, one would also have to consider the preservation of other existing KeY extensions, in particular the complete non-interference calculus and implementation for proving data security properties [8]. Consequently, providing a proper support for Separation Logic in KeY would require a major reconstruction of the logic and its implementation along with all side developments.

Thus, we have decided not to implement this extension in KeY, essentially because of little added value as just explained. Our explicit frames framework enhanced with symbolic permissions provides the same practical expressiveness and functionality as permission-based Separation Logic, however, it involves a different specification paradigm of separately specifying properties and frames over two explicit heaps. In essence, very similar mechanisms appear in the process of translating and proving Chalice programs correct, our approach simply exhibits more of this process directly to the user. We could argue that this actually gives the user more control over the specification and verification process.

6   Conclusion

Starting with briefly explaining the explicit dynamic frames verification method as implemented in KeY, and basic concepts of permission-based reasoning, we summarised the extension to KeY and its logic to support permission-based reasoning, and showed how to shift this explicit approach towards the implicit dynamic frames paradigm. Purposely, we discussed only the framing issues, while there are several other aspects of modular verification that we did not address here, like abstract predicates [29], loop specifications, exception handling, object creation, (non-)termination, etc. [1]. All these, even though affected by what we proposed here, extend naturally to the modified handling of frames.

Despite not concluding the presented work with a working implementation in KeY, we find the lessons learned very valuable to take a different path towards supporting Separation Logic in KeY, which is likely to result in an entirely different verification framework.

Related Work. We related our efforts to the relevant work of others in the course of the paper, yet, we sum it up here for better overview.

The initial IDF idea was described in [35] and represent the first ideas to bridge Separation Logic with dynamic frames style of reasoning, but without support for permission-based reasoning yet. A complete reasoning framework is presented in [35], including methods of constructing explicit frames out of implicit specifications. Interestingly, in [35] a keyword **untouched** is also used, which is similar to our **\samePerm**, but can be applied more generally to a complete predicate instead of a single location, but with essentially the same meaning, namely that heap locations are preserved. The work presented in [35] eventually shifted towards pure Separation Logic approach [18].

The Chalice specification language and verification tool [24] is also IDF-based, it supports the verification of a basic imperative concurrent language based on permission annotations. In [32] it is shown that the Chalice approach is equivalent to intuitionistic Separation Logic, and this fact is utilised in the

VerCors toolset [2,9] which translates permission-based Separation Logic specifications and Java programs to Chalice.

The Chalice framework eventually shifted towards a more generic framework for concurrent verification, which is now implemented in the Viper tool and uses the intermediate specification language Silver [30], yet, most of the principles developed earlier for Chalice are maintained. New versions of Chalice and the VerCors toolset are now interfaced to Viper.

Finally, in [6] a translation method from Separation Logic to Dafny [23], which is also based on *explicit* dynamic frames, through the use of Region Logic [5] is presented. The work has some deficiencies which were addressed in [7] where a combination of the two logics is proposed instead of a translation. Interestingly, in [7] in their related work section the authors say:

> *Recently, Mostowski and Ulbrich [MU15] (our earlier version of [29]) replace ghost fields with model methods that allow method contracts to dynamically dispatch through abstract predicates. However, neither KeY nor JML addresses the problem of connecting SL to RL and mixing specification styles.*

This is precisely what we attempt with this paper. The ideas from [7] have not been yet implemented in a tool either, although a plan for a prototype implementation using Z3 is mentioned.

Future Work. Despite the conscious decision the skip the implementation in KeY for now, we still consider the implementation and experimentation with case studies a possible continuation of this work. Otherwise, rather than proposing an IDF translation path to support Separation Logic in KeY, a different approach could be developed, one that is more *native* in its nature.

Acknowledgments. This work was partly supported by the Swedish Knowledge Foundation grant for the AUTO-CAAS project.

References

1. Ahrendt, W., et al.: The KeY platform for verification and analysis of Java programs. In: Giannakopoulou, D., Kroening, D. (eds.) VSTTE 2014. LNCS, vol. 8471, pp. 55–71. Springer, Cham (2014). https://doi.org/10.1007/978-3-319-12154-3_4
2. Amighi, A., Blom, S., Darabi, S., Huisman, M., Mostowski, W., Zaharieva-Stojanovski, M.: Verification of concurrent systems with VerCors. In: Bernardo, M., Damiani, F., Hähnle, R., Johnsen, E.B., Schaefer, I. (eds.) SFM 2014. LNCS, vol. 8483, pp. 172–216. Springer, Cham (2014). https://doi.org/10.1007/978-3-319-07317-0_5
3. Amighi, A., Blom, S., Huisman, M., Mostowski, W., Zaharieva-Stojanovski, M.: Formal specifications for Java's synchronisation classes. In: Lafuente, A.L., Tuosto, E., (eds.) 22nd Euromicro International Conference on Parallel, Distributed, and Network-Based Processing, pp. 725–733. IEEE Computer Society (2014)
4. Amighi, A., Haack, C., Huisman, M., Hurlin, C.: Permission-based separation logic for multithreaded Java programs. Log. Meth. Comput. Sci. **11**, 2–65 (2015)

5. Banerjee, A., Naumann, D.A., Rosenberg, S.: Regional logic for local reasoning about global invariants. In: Vitek, J. (ed.) ECOOP 2008. LNCS, vol. 5142, pp. 387–411. Springer, Heidelberg (2008). https://doi.org/10.1007/978-3-540-70592-5_17

6. Bao, Y., Leavens, G.T., Ernst, G.: Translating separation logic into dynamic frames using fine-grained region logic. Technical report CS-TR-13-02a, Computer Science, University of Central Florida, March 2014

7. Bao, Y., Leavens, G.T., Ernst, G.: Unifying separation logic and region logic to allow interoperability. Formal Aspects Comput. **30**(3), 381–441 (2018)

8. Beckert, B., Bruns, D., Klebanov, V., Scheben, C., Schmitt, P.H., Ulbrich, M.: Information flow in object-oriented software. In: Gupta, G., Peña, R. (eds.) LOP-STR 2013. LNCS, vol. 8901, pp. 19–37. Springer, Cham (2014). https://doi.org/10.1007/978-3-319-14125-1_2

9. Blom, S., Huisman, M.: The VerCors tool for verification of concurrent programs. In: Jones, C., Pihlajasaari, P., Sun, J. (eds.) FM 2014. LNCS, vol. 8442, pp. 127–131. Springer, Cham (2014). https://doi.org/10.1007/978-3-319-06410-9_9

10. Blom, S., Huisman, M., Zaharieva-Stojanovski, M.: History-based verification of functional behaviour of concurrent programs. In: Calinescu, R., Rumpe, B. (eds.) SEFM 2015. LNCS, vol. 9276, pp. 84–98. Springer, Cham (2015). https://doi.org/10.1007/978-3-319-22969-0_6

11. Boyland, J.: Checking interference with fractional permissions. In: Cousot, R. (ed.) SAS 2003. LNCS, vol. 2694, pp. 55–72. Springer, Heidelberg (2003). https://doi.org/10.1007/3-540-44898-5_4

12. Dijkstra, E.W.: A Discipline of Programming. Prentice Hall Inc., Upper Saddle River (1976)

13. Dockins, R., Hobor, A., Appel, A.W.: A fresh look at separation algebras and share accounting. In: Hu, Z. (ed.) APLAS 2009. LNCS, vol. 5904, pp. 161–177. Springer, Heidelberg (2009). https://doi.org/10.1007/978-3-642-10672-9_13

14. Grahl, D., Bubel, R., Mostowski, W., Schmitt, P.H., Ulbrich, M., Weiß, B.: Modular specification and verification. Deductive Software Verification – The KeY Book. LNCS, vol. 10001, pp. 289–351. Springer, Cham (2016). https://doi.org/10.1007/978-3-319-49812-6_9

15. Haack, C., Huisman, M., Hurlin, C.: Reasoning about Java's reentrant locks. In: Ramalingam, G. (ed.) APLAS 2008. LNCS, vol. 5356, pp. 171–187. Springer, Heidelberg (2008). https://doi.org/10.1007/978-3-540-89330-1_13

16. Hoare, C.A.R.: An axiomatic basis for computer programming. Commun. ACM **12**, 576–580 (1969)

17. Huisman, M., Mostowski, W.: A symbolic approach to permission accounting for concurrent reasoning. In: 14th International Symposium on Parallel and Distributed Computing (ISPDC 2015), pp. 165–174. IEEE Computer Society (2015)

18. Jacobs, B., Smans, J., Philippaerts, P., Vogels, F., Penninckx, W., Piessens, F.: VeriFast: a powerful, sound, predictable, fast verifier for C and Java. In: Bobaru, M., Havelund, K., Holzmann, G.J., Joshi, R. (eds.) NFM 2011. LNCS, vol. 6617, pp. 41–55. Springer, Heidelberg (2011). https://doi.org/10.1007/978-3-642-20398-5_4

19. Kassios, I.T.: The dynamic frames theory. Formal Aspects Comput. **23**, 267–288 (2011)

20. Lea, D.: The java.util.concurrent synchronizer framework. Sci. Comput. Programm. **58**(3), 293–309 (2005)

21. Leavens, G.T., Baker, A.L., Ruby, C.: Preliminary design of JML: a behavioral interface specification language for Java. SIGSOFT **31**(3), 1–38 (2006)

22. Leino, K.R.M.: This is Boogie 2. Technical report, Microsoft Research (2008)
23. Leino, K.R.M.: Dafny: an automatic program verifier for functional correctness. In: Clarke, E.M., Voronkov, A. (eds.) LPAR 2010. LNCS (LNAI), vol. 6355, pp. 348–370. Springer, Heidelberg (2010). https://doi.org/10.1007/978-3-642-17511-4_20
24. Leino, K.R.M., Müller, P., Smans, J.: Verification of concurrent programs with chalice. In: Aldini, A., Barthe, G., Gorrieri, R. (eds.) FOSAD 2007-2009. LNCS, vol. 5705, pp. 195–222. Springer, Heidelberg (2009). https://doi.org/10.1007/978-3-642-03829-7_7
25. McCarthy, J.: Towards a mathematical science of computation. Inf. Process. **1962**, 21–28 (1963)
26. Meyer, B.: Applying "design by contract". Computer **25**(10), 40–51 (1992)
27. Mostowski, W.: A case study in formal verification using multiple explicit heaps. In: Beyer, D., Boreale, M. (eds.) FMOODS/FORTE -2013. LNCS, vol. 7892, pp. 20–34. Springer, Heidelberg (2013). https://doi.org/10.1007/978-3-642-38592-6_3
28. Mostowski, W.: Dynamic frames based verification method for concurrent Java programs. In: Gurfinkel, A., Seshia, S.A. (eds.) VSTTE 2015. LNCS, vol. 9593, pp. 124–141. Springer, Cham (2016). https://doi.org/10.1007/978-3-319-29613-5_8
29. Mostowski, W., Ulbrich, M.: Dynamic dispatch for method contracts through abstract predicates. In: Chiba, S., Südholt, M., Eugster, P., Ziarek, L., Leavens, G.T. (eds.) Transactions on Modularity and Composition I. LNCS, vol. 9800, pp. 238–267. Springer, Cham (2016). https://doi.org/10.1007/978-3-319-46969-0_7
30. Müller, P., Schwerhoff, M., Summers, A.J.: Viper: a verification infrastructure for permission-based reasoning. In: Jobstmann, B., Leino, K.R.M. (eds.) VMCAI 2016. LNCS, vol. 9583, pp. 41–62. Springer, Heidelberg (2016). https://doi.org/10.1007/978-3-662-49122-5_2
31. O'Hearn, P.W.: Resources, concurrency and local reasoning. Theor. Comput. Sci. **375**(1-3), 271–307 (2007)
32. Parkinson, M.J., Summers, A.J.: The relationship between separation logic and implicit dynamic frames. In: Barthe, G. (ed.) ESOP 2011. LNCS, vol. 6602, pp. 439–458. Springer, Heidelberg (2011). https://doi.org/10.1007/978-3-642-19718-5_23
33. Reynolds, J.C.: Separation logic: a logic for shared mutable data structures. In: 17th IEEE Symposium on Logic in Computer Science, pp. 55–74. IEEE Computer Society (2002)
34. Schmitt, P.H., Ulbrich, M., Weiß, B.: Dynamic frames in Java dynamic logic. In: Beckert, B., Marché, C. (eds.) FoVeOOS 2010. LNCS, vol. 6528, pp. 138–152. Springer, Heidelberg (2011). https://doi.org/10.1007/978-3-642-18070-5_10
35. Smans, J., Jacobs, B., Piessens, F.: Implicit dynamic frames: combining dynamic frames and separation logic. In: Drossopoulou, S. (ed.) ECOOP 2009. LNCS, vol. 5653, pp. 148–172. Springer, Heidelberg (2009). https://doi.org/10.1007/978-3-642-03013-0_8

Formal Analysis of Smart Contracts: Applying the KeY System

Jonas Schiffl[1]([envelope]), Wolfgang Ahrendt[2], Bernhard Beckert[1], and Richard Bubel[3]

[1] Karlsruher Institut für Technology, Karlsruhe, Germany
{jonas.schiffl,beckert}@kit.edu
[2] Chalmers Tekniska Högskola, Gothenburg, Sweden
ahrendt@chalmers.se
[3] Technische Universität Darmstadt, Darmstadt, Germany
bubel@cs.tu-darmstadt.de

Abstract. Smart contracts are programs running on decentralized, distributed ledger platforms. Rigorous formal analysis of these programs is highly desirable because they manage valuable assets and therefore are a prime target for security attacks. In this paper, we show that the computation model of smart contracts allows the application of formal methods designed for analysing single-threaded imperative programs. We discuss different classes of correctness properties and the formal methods that may be applied. Furthermore, we show how deductive program verification in particular can be used to prove correctness of smart contracts, and we discuss two approaches where we have applied the program verification tool KeY.

1 Introduction

Smart contracts are programs that run on a blockchain infrastructure. They are a prime target for security attacks, because they usually manage resources representing valuable assets. Moreover, their source code is visible to potential attackers. Due to their distributed nature, bugs are hard to fix. Thus, they are susceptible to attacks exploiting programming errors. This makes rigorous formal analysis of smart contracts highly desirable.

Even though the distributed applications that are implemented by smart contracts can be quite complex, individual contracts and their functions are small and simple enough to make formal analysis feasible. And – quite often – precise (informal) descriptions of their required properties are available.

Smart contract are binding "contracts" (only) in the sense that they are immutable and are deterministically and automatically executed by the platform on which they run. They are (only) "smart" in the sense that they define and implement some non-trivial business logic or protocol for handling digital assets. But in the end, smart contracts are just computer programs representing a reactive system. They are amenable to formal analysis and program verification, and they are great use cases for the application of formal methods.

W. Ahrendt et al. (Eds.): Deductive Software Verification, LNCS 12345, pp. 204–218, 2020.
https://doi.org/10.1007/978-3-030-64354-6_8

There are many different components at different levels in a smart contract platform which together produce a single, shared view of the state of a distributed system. That includes implementations of a blockchain data structure, network protocols, consensus protocols, cryptographic functionality, compilers and virtual machines supporting the smart contract programming language. In the following, we focus on formal verification of smart contracts themselves, as opposed to verifying the correctness of the underlying components.

In this paper, we show that the architecture of platforms running smart contracts offers an abstract computation model that yields itself naturally to the application of formal methods designed for analysing single-threaded imperative programs at the source or byte code level (Sect. 2).

We discuss different classes of correctness properties of smart contracts and the formal methods that may be applied to analyse or verify them (Sect. 3).

Then, in Sect. 4, we show how deductive program verification in particular can be used to prove functional correctness of smart contracts and discuss two approaches where we have applied the program verification tool KeY, namely (a) *VeriSmart* to verify smart contracts in the Hyperledger Fabric framework, which are implemented in Java and specified using the Java Modeling Language, and (b) *Javadity* to verify Ethereum smart contracts.

2   An Abstract View of a Smart Contract Network

2.1   Smart Contracts

Smart contracts are programs which offer services to participants in a distributed network. They are written in high-level programming languages and rely on some form of underlying infrastructure to ensure that function calls are executed in a deterministic, reproducible way, despite an inherently decentralised architecture.

Though there is no universally accepted definition for what constitutes a smart contract, the general consensus is that they have the following features in common: they run on a blockchain infrastructure, i.e., they work in conjunction with a distributed, immutable ledger; they can take control over assets on that ledger; and they do so in an automated and deterministic fashion, thereby enabling parties, who do not necessarily trust each other, to rely on them. Depending on the platform, smart contracts can be deployed either by every network participant or by the network administration. Interaction with a smart contract is done by calling its (public) functions. Reading from and writing to the distributed ledger is possible only through smart contracts.

This has several implications for a programming model which aims to subsume different varieties of smart contracts. One implication concerns the memory model which differs from that of other programming languages: In the context of smart contracts, there is an abstraction of the ledger representing the "world state" of the system. During program execution there are also other, volatile kinds of memory like heaps, call stacks and more with different life times.

Furthermore, distributed ledgers usually manage some kind of resource, e.g., in the form of digital currency or tokens representing real-world assets. Smart

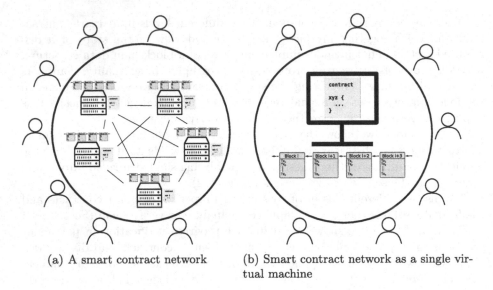

(a) A smart contract network   (b) Smart contract network as a single virtual machine

Fig. 1. Smart contract networks and their abstraction towards the user

contracts manage these resources using mechanisms for transferring ownership built into the distributed ledger infrastructure.

2.2   Smart Contract Networks

Much of the complexity of a smart contract platform is hidden from the user (i.e., someone who does not run a node, but merely uses the services provided by a smart contract). For these users, the platform behaves like a single computer. Smart contracts, in turn, behave like applications running on that computer.

Figures 1a and 1b illustrate this abstraction. In reality, a smart contract platform consists of many servers, each of them with their own version of the blockchain and, therefore, of the state of the network. Each user is connected to the network through a small subset of all nodes (Fig. 1a).

From the perspective of a user, however, the platform behaves like a single computer, on which different programs (smart contracts) are available. The user competes with other users over computation resources on that machine (Fig. 1b).

This abstract machine, which constitutes the basis for our approach to formal verification of smart contracts, can be described as follows: A smart contract platform behaves like a (non-distributed) single-core machine, on which applications take requests (in the form of function calls) from clients. The execution of a request (a transaction) is atomic and sequential. The machine's storage is a key-value database in which serialized objects are stored at unique addresses. The storage can only be modified through client requests. The overall state of the storage is determined entirely by the order in which requests are taken. No assumptions can be made about the relationship between the order of requests made by the clients and the actual order of execution. However, it can be assumed that every request is eventually executed. All requests are recorded, even if they do not modify the state or are malformed.

In summary, an application on a smart contract platform behaves very much like a standard Java program, with one important distinction: There is no persistent heap. Whenever some data needs to be preserved outside of a function, it has to be serialized and stored externally.

Our perspective on smart contract verification builds on this abstraction. While the underlying components, like cryptography and consensus, all require verification of some sort, we focus on formal verification of the programs running on the abstract machine.

In the remaining paper we look in particular at two instances of smart contract networks, Ethereum [20] and Hyperledger Fabric [4].

Ethereum. The smart contract network Ethereum comes with a cryptocurrency called Ether. Ethereum is a distributed computing platform for smart contracts, which are executed on the Ethereum Virtual Machine (EVM). There are several higher-level languages that can be compiled into EVM bytecode, a popular representative of these languages is Solidity[1]. Execution of bytecode instructions on the EVM consumes a resource called *gas*. Upon executing a smart contract one has to provide sufficient gas. If the execution costs exceed the provided amount of gas, the execution is aborted and has no effect.

Hyperledger Fabric. Hyperledger Fabric [4] is a system for deploying and managing private, permission-based blockchain networks. Smart contracts (called "chaincode") can be written in Go, Javascript, or Java. The underlying data structure is a blockchain in which assignments are recorded that assign a values (in the form of serialized records) to keys (keys are of type string). Chaincode functions provide controlled access to the storage. They operate on an abstraction of the blockchain called the world state, which holds only the current value for each key, as opposed to the entire history of assignments.

3   Properties of Smart Contracts and Their Formal Analysis

What is true for all areas of programming is also true for smart contracts: they may contain errors, in the sense that under certain circumstances, they may exhibit behavior which was not intended by the programmer, or may not be expected by most users. What makes this application area different from many others is that smart contract manage real values (like cryptocurrencies). Therefore, in most deviations from expected bahavior, someone will lose, and someone

---

[1] https://solidity.readthedocs.io.

will win. For the potential winner, it is highly attractive to provoke the deviating bahavior. Moreover, the code is open to other agents – or even to everyone, on some platforms like Ethereum. Errors are therefore likely to be discovered and exploited, to provoke a flow of resources which favours the exploiting party, at the expense of other users, in ways not intended by the programmer or the other users. In other words, most errors manifest a vulnerability, exploitable by an attacker. Note that the user of a smart contract can be another smart contract – a programmed user, so to speak. In the same way, attackers are often programmed, to scale up the damage for some, and the gain for others.

In the following, we discuss different classes of desired properties of smart contracts, which make certain errors (and their exploitation) impossible or less likely. We also discuss methods to either ensure these properties, or reveal their violation. While we give pointers to some related work on this topic, we do not aim at a complete literature review here.

3.1   Absence of Known Anti-patterns and Vulnerabilities

The developing field of smart contracts has brought with it its own set of problematic patterns, which are easily introduced by programmers who are not entirely familiar with the programming model of smart contracts in general, or of the specific platforms they are using. These patterns can then lead to unexpected behavior as well as safety and security issues.

One source of vulnerabilities, certainly in Ethereum, is the fact that each transfer of cryptocurrency is treated as a method call, leading to a passing of control to the receiver of the transfer. In the given sequential, synchronous execution model, the transferring contract can only continue once the receiving contract returns control. But in between, the receiving contract may call back into the sending contract (reentrance). This scenario may not have been foreseen by the programmer, and can therefore easily lead to unintended behavior.

More concretely, a typical source of reentrance bugs in Ethereum/Solidity is the execution of code after transferring money using the `call.value` operation, with the intention that the internal data reflects the transfer that just happened. In case of reentrance, however, such 'cleaning up' code may not be executed before another transfer happens, based on outdated data.

Consider the following simple example

```
function noMoreDebts() {
  receiver.payback{value:ownedMoney}();
  this.ownedMoney = 0;
}
```

At first, control is passed to the other contract as the receiver's payable `payback` method is invoked passing the money owned in Ether. The called contract's programmer may have overridden the invoked `payback` method such that it calls (directly or indirectly) the method `noMoreDebt` of the sender's contract again, such that the receiver gets her/his money several times as the value of field `ownedMoney` has not yet been updated to reflect that there are no more debts.

A simple way to check against these kind of bugs is to define an anti-pattern that matches operations where the control flow continues after the execution of a call that passes value in form of Ether.

Other anti-patterns and vulnerabilities specific to the Ethereum platform include (1) locked funds, where currency cannot ever be retrieved from a contract account, (2) contracts which can be killed by an arbitrary account instead of only their owner or other trusted parties, and (3) contracts which depend on a block's time-stamp or the ordering of transactions (cf. [13,16]).

In some cases, lightweight static analysis tools like Solcheck[2] and Solium[3] can be used to detect these kinds of anti-patterns. These tools are fast and efficient to use, but they can only find errors that are detectable by purely syntactic static analysis. Even then, they do not claim absence of false positives or false negatives.

In order to detect safety issues more reliably, a more in-depth semantic analysis is required. There exist several tools in this area of smart contract security, each with a slightly different focus. All of them attempt to show the presence of certain vulnerability patterns, as opposed to showing that the program fulfills a given specification.

OYENTE [13] is a tool which employs symbolic execution to detect the following vulnerabilities: dependence on transaction ordering, dependence on time stamps, mishandled exceptions, and reentrance.

Maian [16] is similar to OYENTE in that it aims to detect the presence of a set of vulnerabilities, namely "suicidal" contracts (i.e., contracts which can be killed by accounts other than their creator), "prodigal" contracts which give away funds to arbitrary addresses, and "greedy" contracts which can lock funds indefinitely.

Mythril[4], Manticore [15], and Slither [9] are more recent, but use the same underlying approach of symbolic execution and checking whether reachable states violate a given property, although the variety of built-in vulnerability specifications and the feasibility of user-defined specifications is increased. Slither also extracts the control flow graph of smart contracts and provides a single static assignment form on which other analyses have been implemented, e.g., data dependency analyses.

All tools in this section are bounded by the depth of symbolic execution, which means they will not detect errors which require a larger depth to occur, and they will report false positives. Nevertheless, the use of this kind of tool has been reported to be very useful in practice [11] as a support for manual professional code auditings.

The importance of the approach described here, i. e., detecting the presence of certain vulnerabilities, is also evidenced by the fact that there exists a registry where such vulnerabilities are collected and described[5].

---

[2] https://git.io/fxXeu.
[3] https://git.io/fxXec.
[4] https://github.com/ConsenSys/mythril.
[5] https://swcregistry.io/.

In Hyperledger Fabric, smart contracts can be written in one of several general-purpose programming languages, like Go or Java. Some features of these languages, e.g., non-determinism within a function call, or global variables, do not make sense in smart contracts and should therefore be regarded as anti-patterns. The Chaincode Scanner tool[6] is a simple static checker for detecting this kind of errors. Apart from that, to our knowledge, there are no tools for formal verification of Hyperledger Fabric smart contracts.

3.2 Termination

Smart contracts on the most common platforms are written in Turing-complete programming languages (although there is research arguing that Turing-completeness is not necessary for smart contracts and should be discarded in order to simplify formal verification; cf. [19]). Therefore, a platform cannot know in advance whether a given smart contract function will terminate. How to deal with this problem depends on the specifics of the platform.

In Hyperledger Fabric smart contracts, there is no general mechanism to ensure termination. If a node detects that a function execution exceeds a time limit, it can abort the execution and return an error. Therefore, an honest caller has no benefits from making the call. However, denial-of-service attacks are plausible. Therefore, formal analysis of termination is in the interest of all honest nodes prior to installing a smart contract. In Fabric's private, permission-based model, nodes which dishonestly introduce non-terminating functions could be excluded from the network, reducing the incentive for such behavior, and possibly making termination less of a problem.

In Ethereum, termination is guaranteed by the concept of gas. This means there is an associated cost for the execution of each instruction, paid by the calling account, and earned by the miner who executes the contract. When a caller initiates a transaction, they have to provide an amount of gas (which has a price in cryptocurrency). If the execution of the transaction exceeds the provided amount of gas, then the execution is aborted, and all effects of the computation are undone, with the exception of the gas, which is transferred to the executing miner anyway. This means that rather than deciding whether a program terminates or not, the more interesting question for Ethereum is how much gas needs to be provided for a specific call depending on the provided input and the state of the involved contracts. This kind of analysis can be performed by resource analysis tools like COSTA [3].

3.3 Functional Correctness of Individual Transactions

Correctness of smart contract applications cannot be captured by generic properties or the absence of anti-patterns alone. There has to be some formal specification describing the expected behavior of a program. Smart contract functions, which are atomic and deterministic, are the basic modules of smart contracts

---

[6] https://chaincode.chainsecurity.com/.

(much like methods are basic components of object-oriented programs), and therefore also the basic targets for correctness verification. Traditionally, functional specifications of computational units (methods/functions) are expressed with precondition-postcondition pairs, where the precondition states conditions the caller has to satisfy, and the postcondition states what the unit has to guarantee in its poststate (provided the precondition was satisfied in the prestate). However, the smart contract ecosystem is by design a trust-less environment, such that an application should not assume anything about the calls it receives. We therefore do not see that preconditions have a major role to play in the functional specification of smart contracts. Postconditions, contract invariants, and code assertions remain as key elements of smart contract specification.

Examples of specific properties of a single transaction include functional correctness statements (e.g., "the specified amount is deducted from the account if sufficient funds are available, otherwise the account remains unchanged") and statements about what locations on the ledger a transaction is allowed to modify.

An approach to verification of single transaction correctness using the Why3 verification platform has been proposed [7]. Its approach consists of a translation from EVM Bytecode to the F* language, from which verification conditions can be generated (if provided with a specification). However, no actual implementation has been published.

The solc-verify tool targets Solidity source code instead of bytecode. `require` and `assert` statements are translated to method pre- and postconditions, respectively. Additional specification in the form of function pre- and postconditions as well as invariants over the contract state can be provided. The annotations are in propositional logic with equality and cannot refer to local variables. The annotated contract is then translated to the Boogie intermediate verification language [12]. From there, verification conditions for the Z3 SMT solver can be generated.

The approaches using the KeY tool also target the correctness of individual function calls. They are discussed in Sect. 4.

3.4 Trace Properties

While correctness of single transactions is a necessary prerequisite for the correctness of a smart contract, there are properties which inherently are properties of transaction traces, in so far as they cannot be expressed as properties of individual transactions. Formalisms to express such properties include automata (of some sort) and temporal logics. Note that the degree of non-determinism in transaction traces is very high (even if the individual transactions are deterministic). The code base does not contain any 'main' routine. Instead, users can file transaction requests, freely choosing among the available functions and according call parameters. In addition, the order in which transaction request appear is typically chosen non-deterministically as part of forming a consensus in the smart contract network (typically chosen by the miners). With this degree of non-determinism and dependence on the environment, certain classes of properties may only hold in trivial cases, like (linear) liveness properties (something will happen eventually). Other classes of temporal properties may be more relevant, and desirable, like for instance reachability (e.g., "if you put money in, there is always a way to get it back again"), expressible in branching time logic. One may also want to prove that the number of transactions needed to reach a certain outcome (e.g., "get money back") cannot be increased by adversarial transaction invocations.

The VerX tool [17] allows for custom specification of temporal safety properties for Ethereum smart contracts. Properties are expressed in Past LTL [14]. Functions are symbolically executed. The implicit loop over all possible function calls is dealt with through predicate abstraction.

3.5 Hyperproperties

Even if the execution of each individual transaction is strictly regulated, and checked by the network, the miners can freely choose the scheduling of the various transaction requests. It is therefore a relevant question whether the code of smart contracts is vulnerable to scheduling attacks. Here, a smart contract is 'scheduling robust' with respect to some application-specific metric if that metric cannot be optimised for any of the smart contract users via reordering of the user requests (function calls). The issue of scheduling attacks is very specific for the smart contract domain; other areas of computation where scheduling is relevant usually do not allow untrusted parties to perform the scheduling.

It is crucial to note that scheduling robustness (with respect to whatever metric) is not a property, but a *hyperproperty*. Normal properties are satisfied, or violated, by individual system traces. Hyperproperties instead are *properties of sets of traces*, meaning that every set of traces satisfies or violates the property. The most prominent examples of hyperproperties appear in the context of security, like *noninterference*. Hyperproperties were introduced in [8], including the special case of *hypersafety* (refutable by a set of finite trace prefixes), and *k-hypersafety* (where the prefixes of at most k traces are needed for refutation). We note here that scheduling robustness is an instance of *2-hypersafety*, because it can be refuted by observing *two* schedulings (of the same set of requests) which differ in the given metric of benefit for some user.

Concerning the verification of hyperproperties, it was shown in [8] that k-hypersafety can be reduced to plain safety of a different system. The does, however, not automatically imply a feasible verification procedure. If a hyperproperty is simple enough that a sound approximation of the real system is sufficient, verification can be done with model checking [10]. This will however be the exception in the smart contract domain, where computation on values play a dominant role. Here, deductive verification is more appropriate. An overview of deductive verification of certain classes of hyperproperties is given in [6].

In our setting, the different traces do not differ in their inputs (as in many other cases of hyperproperties), but originate in the *non-deterministic processing of the same input* (here the set of function calls appearing in the network). Scheduling robustness means that the given metric cannot distinguish the variation in resolving the non-determinism. This is related to the security notion of *observational determinism*, studied in [18].

4 Using the KeY Verification System

The KeY tool [1] is a program analyses and verification system for sequential Java and JavaCard programs. It is used for deductive verification of functional properties as well as for automated test generation, symbolic state debugging and even for the verification of relational properties like information flow security.

So far, there are two approaches for applying formal methods to smart contracts using the KeY tool. Both approaches focus on the verification of functional properties for Hyperledger Fabric and Ethereum smart contracts.

4.1 Verification of Hyperledger Fabric Chaincode

In the VeriSmart project, KeY was applied as a tool for formal verification of Hyperledger Fabric smart contracts.

The difference between a normal Java program and the computational model described in Sect. 2 is in the storage: while Java programs operate on a heap, a Fabric smart contract operates on an (abstracted) key-value database storing serialized objects. In a case study demonstrating how to use KeY to prove the correctness of Hyperledger Fabric chaincode functions [5], this difference was addressed by an extension of the KeY tool,[7] including a model of the ledger on a logical level, an axiomatisation of the read/write interface of the Fabric ledger, and the introduction of abstract data types for each type of object that is managed by the smart contract.

While our approach views the storage as a key-value datbase, at the time we decided to stay closer to the actual ledger data structure, instead of directly modelling the storage as a map (KeY has preliminary support for maps).

The Fabric ledger was modelled as a *sequence* of *entries* within the KeY tool, with *sequence* being the existing KeY sequence type and *entry* a newly defined KeY abstract data type that represents a key-value pair. The sequence was added as a JML ghost field `ledger` to the concrete Fabric Java API. Like its counterpart, the Fabric ledger, the `ledger` is append-only. Conceptually, the value of an entry with key k in the abstract database can be determined by looking for the last *entry* with key k in the sequence and retrieving its value.

The Fabric Java API provides three basic methods for accessing the ledger: `getState()`, `putState()`, and `delSate()`. These API methods were axiomatically specified in order to allow reasoning about reading from and writing to the ledger in KeY. For example, the semantics of the `putState(int key, byte[] value)` method is that an entry consisting of `key` and `value` is appended to the `ledger` sequence.

---

[7] Available at https://key-project.org/chaincode.

Before being written to the ledger, objects are serialized:

```
Object o1 = someObject;
putState(key, serialize(o1));
Object o2 = deserialize(getState(key));
```

This has to be reflected in KeY; we need to be able to derive that o1 is equal to o2. To achieve this, we introduce a supertype of all types which get stored on the ledger. Subtypes must implement the `serialize()` and `deserialize()` methods, which are, again, axiomatically specified so that the above equality can be inferred.

Additional abstract data types are introduced in KeY for each of the types which are stored on the ledger. They are an intermediate representation between the Java object and its serialized form, such that the specification of the serialization and deserialization operations can refer to an instance of the abstract type. The sequent calculus rules which are required to reason about the new types are created automatically upon loading an annotated file in KeY.

As an example for the above, consider a smart contract which implements an auction. One might want to specify the `closeAuction()` method as follows:

```
/*@ ensures read(ID) != null ==> read(ID).closed;
 @ ensures (\forall Item i \in read(ID).items;
 @          i.owner_id == read(ID).highestBidderID);
 @*/
void closeAuction(int ID) { ... }
```

This JML specification is somewhat simplified for readability; the `read` function is an abstraction for accessing the ledger, i.e., reading and deserializing the object at the given location. The specification states that, if the auction object at ID is not null, then after execution of the `closeAuction()` method the `closed` flag must be correctly set; furthermore all items in the auction must belong to the highest bidder (as indicated by the `owner_id` attribute). For the correctness proof in KeY, the logical rules necessary for handling the data types stored on the ledger (in this case, auctions, items, and participants) are created automatically. The proof requires some user interaction, since the new rules have not yet been included in the automation mechanism of the prover.

4.2 Verification of Solidity Contracts

In Javadity [2] we explored how to make use of existing program verification tools for other programming languages (here: Java) in order to verify smart contracts. The intention was to be able to use mature tools out-of-the-box for specification and deductive verification. In this section we sketch our approach briefly and discuss the challenges. For more details see [2].

Javadity focused on the verification of functional properties of smart contracts written in the most popular language, named Solidity. We did *not* consider gas mechanics, except for assuming that any call may fail due to running out of gas reasons, exceptions etc. Our main idea was to translate Solidity contracts into

Java (or more precise, JavaCard) classes. This required addressing the following challenges (among others): (i) support for Solidity types (e.g. uint) and concepts (e.g., modifiers), (ii) interaction with the blockchain, and (iii) transaction abort due to an exception.

We explain our solution referring to the small example in Fig. 2, which shows the Solidity version of a casino contract on the left side, and its translated version on the right side. In brief, each contract is translated into a JavaCard class of the same name which inherits from a pre-defined class Address. The Address class provides the built-in functionality for sending, receiving and transferring Ether. In addition to Address, further pre-defined classes exist for providing an API to the underlying ledger as well as for modelling Solidity-specific types like uint. For the latter see line 4 in Fig. 2b, where the storage variable balance of type uint has been translated into a Java field of the same name with interface type Uint256. Arithmetic operations on uint are translated into semantic-preserving method invocations declared by the interface.

```
1   contract Auction {
2     address payable auctionOwner;
3     uint balance;
4     bool closed = false;
5     ...
6
7     function closeAuction() public {
8       require(acutionOwner==msg.sender)
9       uint tmp = balance;
10      balance = 0;
11      closed = true;
12      msg.sender.transfer(tmp);
13    }
14  }
```

```
1   class Auction extends Address {
2     Address auctionOwner;
3     //@ invariant closed ==> (balance == 0);
4     Uint256 balance;
5     boolean closed = false;
6     ...
7
8     public void require(boolean b) {...}
9
10    /*@ public normal_behavior
11      @ requires auctionOwner == msg.sender;
12      @ ensures closed;
13      @*/
14    public void closeAuction() {
15      require(auctionOwner == msg.sender)
16      Uint256 tmp = balance;
17      balance = Uint256.ZERO;
18      closed = true;
19      msg.sender.transfer(tmp);
20    }
21  }
```

(a) Auction contract in Solidity

(b) Auction contract translated into Java (with JML specifications)

Fig. 2. Translation from Solidity to Java

The translation also supports a restricted version of modifiers, where the statement _; (placeholder for the function's body to which the modifier is attached) must occur only once as last statement. This allows us to translate modifiers into methods, and to invoke these as first statements in the bodies of the Java methods resulting from the translation of a Solidity function annotated with the corresponding modifiers.

To be able to capture state-rollback in case a function execution fails (e.g., not enough gas or an exception), we lifted the transaction concept of JavaCard. In short, for each method m there is an external call wrapper call_m which wraps the invocation of m inside a JavaCard transaction.

The verification of the contracts was then achieved by specifying the translated contracts with the Java Modeling Language and to load the annotated methods into the KeY verifier, which also supports JavaCard's transaction mechanism. In the example, the JML specification consists of an invariant stating that the value of field `balance` is zero if the auction ended. The method specification of `closeAuction` states that if the caller is the auction owner then the auction is closed afterwards.

Although our approach works in principle and avoids the need for a specific Solidity verifier, there were some drawbacks with the above solution. One problem which severely compromised automation was the need to translate the primitive datatype `uint` into a reference type in Java. This caused a considerable overhead for the verifier as all mathematical operations and comparisons became method invocations on objects. Another problem are slightly converging semantics and resulting restrictions, e.g. there can be no nested transactions due to using JavaCard's transaction mechanism.

5   Conclusion and Future Work

We hope we could convince the reader of the contribution that contemporary deductive verification techniques can make to ensuring smart contract safety. We identified typical properties that are of general interest in this domain, and addressed specification and verification of functional properties for two particular instances of smart contract platforms, namely Hyperledger Fabric and Ethereum.

For future work we want to address the limitations that we encountered in Sect. 4.2 concerning an exact mapping of Solidity and Java semantics and that the proof methodology in presence of a hostile environment is not the best possible match. For these reasons, we decided to adapt KeY to support Solidity natively and to provide a tailored specification and proof methodology. The latter is necessary as despite Solidity being a sequential language there is loss of control similar to distributed languages when calling into another contract.

More generally, KeY will be extended to enable verification of trace properties of smart contracts. A concrete approach to this challenge is the implementation of history constraints which can be added to the specification of a contract, stating that every transition between two states of a trace has to fulfill a given property. Furthermore, it would be interesting to investigate how reasonable assumptions about transaction liveness on a given smart contract platform can be used to reduce the verification of concrete liveness properties to more feasible verification tasks.

References

1. Ahrendt, W., Beckert, B., Bubel, R., Hähnle, R., Schmitt, P.H., Ulbrich, M. (eds.): Deductive Software Verification - The KeY Book: From Theory to Practice. LNCS, vol. 10001. Springer, Cham (2016). https://doi.org/10.1007/978-3-319-49812-6

2. Ahrendt, W., et al.: Verification of smart contract business logic: exploiting a Java source code verifier. In: Hojjat, H., Massink, M. (eds.) FSEN 2019. LNCS, vol. 11761, pp. 228–243. Springer, Cham (2019). https://doi.org/10.1007/978-3-030-31517-7_16

3. Albert, E., Correas, J., Gordillo, P., Román-Díez, G., Rubio, A.: GASOL: gas analysis and optimization for ethereum smart contracts. In: Biere, A., Parker, D. (eds.) TACAS 2020. LNCS, vol. 12079, pp. 118–125. Springer, Cham (2020). https://doi.org/10.1007/978-3-030-45237-7_7

4. Androulaki, E., et al.: Hyperledger fabric: a distributed operating system for permissioned blockchains. In: Proceedings of the Thirteenth EuroSys Conference, EuroSys 2018, pp. 30:1–30:15. ACM (2018). https://doi.org/10.1145/3190508.3190538

5. Beckert, B., Herda, M., Kirsten, M., Schiffl, J.: Formal specification and verification of hyperledger fabric chaincode. In: Bai, G., Biswas, K. (eds.) 3rd Symposium on Distributed Ledger Technology (SDLT-2018) Co-Located with ICFEM 2018: the 20th International Conference on Formal Engineering Methods, November 2018. https://symposium-dlt.org/

6. Beckert, B., Ulbrich, M.: Trends in relational program verification. Principled Software Development, pp. 41–58. Springer, Cham (2018). https://doi.org/10.1007/978-3-319-98047-8_3

7. Bhargavan, K., et al.: Formal verification of smart contracts: short paper. In: Proceedings of the 2016 ACM Workshop on Programming Languages and Analysis for Security - PLAS 2016, pp. 91–96. ACM Press, Vienna (2016). https://doi.org/10.1145/2993600.2993611. http://dl.acm.org/citation.cfm?doid=2993600.2993611

8. Clarkson, M.R., Schneider, F.B.: Hyperproperties. J. Comput. Secur. 18(6), 1157–1210 (2010). https://doi.org/10.3233/JCS-2009-0393

9. Feist, J., Grieco, G., Groce, A.: Slither: a static analysis framework for smart contracts. In: Proceedings of the 2nd International Workshop on Emerging Trends in Software Engineering for Blockchain, WETSEB@ICSE 2019, Montreal, QC, Canada, 27 May 2019, pp. 8–15. IEEE/ACM (2019). https://doi.org/10.1109/WETSEB.2019.00008

10. Finkbeiner, B., Rabe, M.N., Sánchez, C.: Algorithms for model checking HyperLTL and HyperCTL*. In: Kroening, D., Păsăreanu, C.S. (eds.) CAV 2015. LNCS, vol. 9206, pp. 30–48. Springer, Cham (2015). https://doi.org/10.1007/978-3-319-21690-4_3

11. Groce, A., Feist, J., Grieco, G., Colburn, M.: What are the actual flaws in important smart contracts (and how can we find them)? arXiv:1911.07567 [cs] (2020)

12. Leino, K.R.M.: This is boogie 2. Manuscript KRML 178(131), 9 (2008)

13. Luu, L., Chu, D.H., Olickel, H., Saxena, P., Hobor, A.: Making smart contracts smarter. In: Proceedings of the 2016 ACM SIGSAC Conference on Computer and Communications Security, CCS 2016, pp. 254–269. Association for Computing Machinery, New York (2016). https://doi.org/10.1145/2976749.2978309

14. Manna, Z., Pnueli, A.: Temporal Verification of Reactive Systems. Springer, New York (1995). https://doi.org/10.1007/978-1-4612-4222-2

15. Mossberg, M., et al.: Manticore: a user-friendly symbolic execution framework for binaries and smart contracts. In: 2019 34th IEEE/ACM International Conference on Automated Software Engineering (ASE), pp. 1186–1189. IEEE (2019)

16. Nikolić, I., Kolluri, A., Sergey, I., Saxena, P., Hobor, A.: Finding the greedy, prodigal, and suicidal contracts at scale. In: Proceedings of the 34th Annual Computer Security Applications Conference, ACSAC 2018, San Juan, PR, USA, pp. 653–663. ACM, New York (2018). https://doi.org/10.1145/3274694.3274743

17. Permenev, A., Dimitrov, D., Tsankov, P., Drachsler-Cohen, D., Vechev, M.: VerX: safety verification of smart contracts. In: 2020 IEEE Symposium on Security and Privacy, SP, pp. 18–20 (2020)
18. Roscoe, A.W.: CSP and determinism in security modelling. In: IEEE Symposium on Security and Privacy. IEEE Computer Society (1995)
19. Sergey, I., Kumar, A., Hobor, A.: Scilla: a smart contract intermediate-level language. arXiv preprint arXiv:1801.00687 (2018)
20. Wood, G.: Ethereum: a secure decentralised generalised transaction ledger. Ethereum Project Yellow Paper 151, 1–32 (2014)

Feasibility and Usablility

A Tutorial on Verifying LinkedList Using KeY

Hans-Dieter A. Hiep(✉)(iD), Jinting Bian, Frank S. de Boer, and Stijn de Gouw

CWI, Science Park 123, 1098 XG Amsterdam, The Netherlands
{hdh,j.bian,frb,stijn.de.gouw}@cwi.nl

Abstract. This is a tutorial paper on using KeY to demonstrate formal verification of state-of-the-art, real software. In sufficient detail for a beginning user of JML and KeY, the specification and verification of part of a corrected version of the `java.util.LinkedList` class of the Java Collection framework is explained. The paper includes video material that shows recordings of interactive sessions, and project files with solutions. As such, this material is also interesting for the expert user and the developer of KeY as a 'benchmark' for specification and (automatic) verification techniques.

Keywords: Program correctness · Linked list · Theorem proving · KeY

1 Introduction

Software libraries are the building blocks of many programs that run on the devices of many users every day. The functioning of a system may rely for a large part on its used software libraries. A small error present in a heavily-used software library could lead to serious unwanted outcomes, such as system outages and failures. Using informal root cause analysis [16], one could find from a system failure its root causes, which may include programming errors. But root cause analysis can only be applied *after* a failure has happened. To prevent certain failures from happening in the first place, program correctness is of the utmost importance. Although establishing program correctness seems to be an expensive activity, it may be worthwhile for critical software libraries, such as the standard library that all programs rely on.

This tutorial intends to show how we take an existing Java program that is part of the Java standard library, and study it closely to increase our understanding of it. If we are only interested in showing the presence of an issue with the program, e.g. that it lacks certain functionality, it suffices to show an example run which behaves unexpectedly. But to reach the conclusion that no unexpected behavior ever results from running the program, first requires a precise specification of what behavior one expects, and further requires a convincing argument that all possible executions of the program exhibit that behavior.

© Springer Nature Switzerland AG 2020
W. Ahrendt et al. (Eds.): Deductive Software Verification, LNCS 12345, pp. 221–245, 2020.
https://doi.org/10.1007/978-3-030-64354-6_9

We take a formal approach to both specification and reasoning about program executions, allowing us to increase the reliability of our reached conclusions to near certainty. In particular, the specifications we write are expressed in the Java Modeling Language (JML), and our reasoning is tool-supported and partially automated by KeY. To the best of the authors' knowledge, KeY is the only tool that supports enough features of the Java programming language for reasoning about real programs, of which its run-time behavior crucially depends on the presence of features such as: dynamic object creation, exception handling, integer arithmetic with overflow, `for` loops with early returns, nested classes (both static and non-static), inheritance, polymorphism, erased generics, etc.

As a demonstration of applying KeY to state-of-the-art, real software, we focus on Java's `LinkedList` class, for two reasons. First, a (doubly-)linked list is a well-known basic data structure for storing and maintaining unbounded data, and has many applications: for example, in Java's secure sockets implementation[1]. Second, it has turned out that there is a 20-year-old bug lurking in its program, that might lead to security-in-depth issues on large memory systems, caused by the overflow of a field that caches the length of the list [12]. Our specification and verification effort is aimed at establishing the absence of this bug from a repaired program.

This article is based on the results as described in another closely related paper [12]. That paper provides a high-level overview on the specification and verification effort of the linked list class as a whole, for a more general audience. In the present article, more technical details on how we use the KeY theorem prover are given, and we give more detail concerning the production of the proofs. In particular, this tutorial consists of the on-line repository of proof files [11], and on-line video material that shows how to (re)produce the proofs [10]: these are video recordings of the interactive sessions in KeY that demonstrates exactly what steps one could take to complete the correctness proofs of the proof obligations generated by KeY from the method contracts.

We see how to set-up a project and configure the KeY tool (Sect. 2). We then study the source code of the `LinkedList` to gain an intuitive understanding of its structure: how the instances look like, and how the methods operate (Sect. 3). We formulate, based on previous intuition, a *class invariant* in JML that expresses a property that is true of every instance (Sect. 4). An interesting property that follows from the class invariant, that is used as a separation principle, is described next (Sect. 5). To keep this presentation reasonably short, we further focus on the methods which pose the main challenges to formal verification, `add` and `remove`. We give a *method contract* for the `add` method that describes its expected behavior and we verify that its implementation is correct (Sect. 6). The difficulty level increases after we specify the `remove` method (Sect. 7), as its verification requires more work than for `add`. We study a deeper method that `remove` depends on, and finally use *loop invariants* to prove the correctness of `remove`. We conclude with some proof challenges for the reader's recreation of further specifications and (in)formal proofs (Sect. 8).

---

[1] E.g. see the JVM internal class `sun.security.ssl.HandshakeStateManager`.

2   Preliminaries

Table 1. Directory structure of project files. The `src` directory contains the Java classes we want to specify and verify. The `jre` directory contains stub files, with specifications of unrelated classes. The `LinkedList.java` file is the source file we end up with after following this tutorial. The `proof` directory contains the completed proofs.

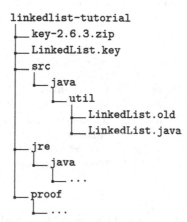

```
linkedlist-tutorial
├── key-2.6.3.zip
├── LinkedList.key
├── src
│   └── java
│       └── util
│           ├── LinkedList.old
│           └── LinkedList.java
├── jre
│   └── java
│       └── ...
└── proof
    └── ...
```

First we set-up the project files needed to use KeY. The project files are available on-line [11]: these can be downloaded and include the KeY software version that we use. After unpacking the project files, we end up with the directory structure of Table 1.

The original source file of `LinkedList.old` was obtained from OpenJDK version `jdk8-b132`. The original has been pre-processed: generic class parameters are removed, and all methods and nested classes irrelevant to this tutorial are removed. Both the removal of generics and the stub files in the `jre` folder were generated automatically, using the Eclipse extensions for KeY. Repeating those steps is not necessary here.

Over the course of the next sections, we modify the original source file and add annotations to formally specify its behavior, and helper methods for presenting intermediary lemmas. The annotations are usual Java comments, and thus ignored when the file is read by a Java compiler. The helper methods introduce slight performance overhead (of calling a method that performs no operations, and immediately returning from it); it is clear that these do not change the original behavior of the program.

2.1   KeY Settings Set-Up

To produce proofs in KeY, the first step is to set-up KeY's proof strategy and taclet options. This has to be done only once, as these taclet settings are stored per computer user. Sometimes, KeY overwrites or corrupts these settings if different versions are used. To ensure KeY starts in a fresh state, one can remove

Table 2. (a) Proof search strategy (b) Taclet options

Max. rule applications	1000	JavaCard	Off
Stop at	Default	Strings	On
Proof splitting	Delayed	Assertions	Safe
Loop treatment	Invariant	BigInt	On
Block treatment	Contract	Initialization	Disable static ...
Method treatment	Contract	Int Rules	Java semantics
Dependency contract	On	Integer Simpl. Rules	Full
Query treatment	Off	Join Generate	Off
Expand local queries	On	Model Fields	Treat as axiom
Arithmetic treatment	Basic	More Seq. Rules	On
Quantifier treatment	No splits	Permissions	Off
Class axiom rule	Off	Program Rules	Java
Auto induction	Off	Reach	On
User-defined taclets	All off	Runtime Exceptions	Ban
(a)		Sequences	On
		Well-def. Checks	Off
		Well-def. Operator	L
		(b)	

the `.key` directory from the user's home directory, and clean out preferences from the `.java/.userPrefs` directory by deleting the `de/uka/ilkd/key` hierarchy containing `prefs.xml` files[2]. Now start up KeY, and the example selection screen appears (if not, selecting File▷ Load Example opens the same screen). Load any example, to enter proof mode.

First, we set-up a proof strategy: this ensures the steps as done in the videos can be reproduced. On the left side of the window, change the settings in the Proof Search Strategy tab to match those of Table 2a. We ensure to use particular taclet rules that correctly model Java's integer overflow semantics. Select Options▷ Taclet Options, and configure the options as in Table 2b. The taclet options become effective after loading the next problem. We do that now: the main proof file `LinkedList.key` can be loaded, and a Proof Management window opens up, showing a class hierarchy and its methods. A method is not shown when no specifications are present. After giving specifications below, more methods can be selected in this window.

3   Structure and Behavior of `java.util.LinkedList`

In this section we walk through part of the source code of Java's linked list: see the `LinkedList.old` file. Over the course of this tutorial, we add annotations at the appropriate places. We finally obtain the `LinkedList.java` file.

---

[2] On Windows, the preferences are instead stored in the Windows Registry. Use the `regedit` tool and clean out under `HKEY_CURRENT_USER\Software\JavaSoft\Prefs` or `HKEY_CURRENT_USER\Software\Wow6432Node\JavaSoft\Prefs` the same hierarchy. On Mac OS, open a terminal, change directory to `~/Library/Preferences` and delete `de.uka.ilkd.plist`.

```
1    package java. util ;
2
3    public  class  LinkedList {
4
5        transient  int  size  =  0;
6        transient  Node  first ;
7        transient  Node  last;
8
9        public  LinkedList()  {}
```

Listing 1. The `LinkedList` class fields and constructor (begin of file).

Our `LinkedList` class has three attributes and a constructor (Listing 1): a `size` field, which stores a cached number of elements in the list, and two fields that store a reference to the first and last `Node`. The public constructor contains no statements: thus it initializes `size` to zero, and `first` and `last` to `null`.

The linked list fields are declared transient and package private. The transient flag is not relevant to our verification effort. The reason the fields are declared package private seems to prevent generating accessor methods by the Java compiler. However, in practice, the fields are treated as if they were private.

```
65       private  static  class  Node {
66           Object item;
67           Node next;
68           Node prev;
69
70           Node(Node prev, Object element, Node next) {
71               this .item = element;
72               this .next = next;
73               this .prev = prev;
74           }
75       }
76
77   }
```

Listing 2. The `Node` nested class fields and constructor (end of file).

The `Node` class is defined as a private static nested class to represent the containers of items stored in the list (Listing 2). A static nested private class behaves like a top-level class, except that it is not visible outside the enclosing class. The nodes are doubly-linked, that is, each node is connected to its preceding node (through field `prev`) and succeeding node (through field `next`). These fields contain `null` in case no preceding or succeeding node exists. The data itself is contained in the `item` field of a node.

```
39          // implements java.util.Collection.add
40          public boolean add(Object e) {
41              linkLast(e);
42              return true;
43          }
```

Listing 3. The method `add`.

The method `add` for adding elements to the list, takes one argument, the item to add (Listing 3). The informal Java documentation for `Collection` specifies it always returns `true`. The implementation immediately calls `linkLast`.

```
45          // implements java.util.Collection.remove
46          public boolean remove(Object o) {
47              if (o == null) {
48                  for (Node x = first; x != null; x = x.next) {
49                      if (x.item == null) {
50                          unlink(x);
51                          return true;
52                      }
53                  }
54              } else {
55                  for (Node x = first; x != null; x = x.next) {
56                      if (o.equals(x.item)) {
57                          unlink(x);
58                          return true;
59                      }
60                  }
61              }
62              return false;
63          }
```

Listing 4. The method `remove`.

The method `remove` for removing elements, also takes one argument, the item to remove (Listing 4). If that item was present in the list, then its first occurrence is removed and `true` is returned; otherwise, if the item was not present, then the list is not changed and `false` is returned.

Presence of the item depends on whether the argument of the remove method is `null` or not. If the argument is `null`, then it searches for the first occurrence of a `null` item in the list. Otherwise, it uses the `equals` method, that every `Object` in Java has, to determine the equality of the argument with respect to the contents of the list. The first occurrence of an item that is considered equal by the argument is then returned. In both cases, the execution walks over the linked list, from the first node until it has reached the end. In the case that the node was found that contains the first occurrence of the argument, an internal method is called: `unlink`, and afterwards `true` is returned.

Observe that the linked list is not modified if `unlink` is not called. Although not immediately obvious, this requires that the `equals` method of every object cannot modify our current linked list, for the duration of the call to `remove`. When the `remove` method is called with an item that is not contained in the list, either loop eventually exits, and `false` is returned.

```
11      void linkLast(Object e) {
12          final Node l = last;
13          final Node newNode = new Node(l, e, null);
14          last = newNode;
15          if (l == null) first = newNode;
16          else l.next = newNode;
17          size++;
18      }
```

Listing 5. The internal method `linkLast`.

The internal method `linkLast` changes the structure of the linked list (Listing 5). After performing this method, a new node has been created, and the `last` field of the linked list now points to it. To maintain structural integrity, also other fields change: if the linked list was empty, the `first` field now points to the new, and only, node. If the linked list was not empty, then the new last node is also reachable via the former last node's `next` field. It is always the case that all items of a linked list are reachable through the `first` field, then following the `next` fields, and also for the opposite direction.

```
20      Object unlink(Node x) {
21          final Object element = x.item;
22          final Node next = x.next;
23          final Node prev = x.prev;
24          if (prev == null) { first = next;}
25          else {
26              prev.next = next;
27              x.prev = null;
28          }
29          if (next == null) {last = prev;}
30          else {
31              next.prev = prev;
32              x.next = null;
33          }
34          x.item = null;
35          size--;
36          return element;
37      }
```

Listing 6. The internal method `unlink`.

The internal method `unlink` is among the most complex methods that alters the structure of a linked list (Listing 6). The method is used only when the linked list is not empty. Its argument is a node, necessarily one that belongs to the linked list. We first store the fields of the node in local variables: the old item, and next and previous node references.

After the method returns, the argument fields are all cleared, presumably to help the garbage collector. However, other fields also change: if the argument is the first node, the `first` field is updated; if the argument is the last node, the `last` field is updated. The predecessor or successor fields `next` and `prev` of other nodes are changed to maintain the integrity of the linked list: the successor of the unlinked node becomes the successor of its predecessor, and the predecessor of the unlinked node becomes the predecessor of its successor.

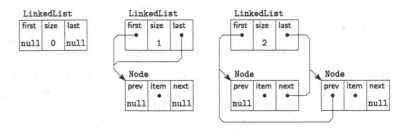

Fig. 1. Three example linked lists: empty, with a chain of one node, and with a chain of two nodes. Items themselves are not shown.

3.1   Expected and Unexpected Method Behavior

We draw pictures of linked list instances to understand better how the structure looks like over time. In Fig. 1, we see three linked list instances. The left-most linked list is an object without any items: its `size` is zero. When we perform `add` with some item (it is not important what item), a new node is created and the first and last pointers are changed to point to the new node. Now the `prev` and `next` fields of the new node are `null`, indicating that there is no other node before and there is no other node after it. Also, the `size` field is increased by one. Adding another item further creates another node, that is linked up to the previous node properly; the `last` field is then pointed to the newly created node. In the third instance, suppose we would perform `remove` with the first item. We would then have to unlink the node, see the code of `unlink` in Listing 6: the new value of `first` becomes the value of `next` which is the last node, and the value of `prev` of the succeeding node becomes the value of `prev` of the node that is unlinked, which is `null`. We thus end up in a similar situation as the second instance (except for the item that may be different). Removing the last item brings us back into the situation depicted by the first instance.

An important aspect of the implementation of our linked list is the cached `size` field: it represents the number of nodes that form a chain between `first` and `last`. It turns out an overflow may happen under certain conditions [12].

Consider two facts: Java integer primitives are stored in signed 32-bit registers, and it is possible to create a chain that is larger than the maximum positive value that can be stored in such fields, $2^{31} - 1$. Now, the cached size and the actual size no longer correspond. In the methods we have seen above, this seems to be no issue. But another method of the linked list may be used to demonstrate the key problem: toArray. The intention of toArray is to give back an array containing all the items of the list (see Listing 7). There are two problems: after the overflow has occurred and the size is negative, the toArray throws an unexpected NegativeArraySizeException. Also, after adding more items that brings the size back to a positive integer, e.g. adding $2^{32} + 1$ items in total, the array is of the wrong (positive) size and cannot contain *all* items of the list, and an IndexOutOfBoundsException is thrown.

```java
public Object[] toArray() {
    Object[] result = new Object[size];
    int i = 0;
    for (Node x = first; x != null; x = x.next)
        result[i++] = x.item;
    return result;
}
```

Listing 7. The method toArray has unexpected behavior.

3.2   Verification Goal

We thus revise the source code and add a method that implements an overflow check (see Listing 8). The intention is that the overflow is signalled before it occurs, by throwing an exception. This ensures that the integrity of the linked list is always maintained. We modify the add method, and perform a call to this checkSize() method before invoking linkLast.

```java
// new method, not in original LinkedList
private void checkSize() {
    if (size == Integer.MAX_VALUE)
        throw new IllegalStateException (...);
}
```

Listing 8. A new internal method checkSize.

Our aim in this tutorial is to keep the discussion general enough, without losing interesting particular details. We apply step-wise refinements to our arguments, where we start with a higher-level intuition and drill-down on technical details as they become relevant. The reader can always see the video material; but, a high-level intuition seems essential for following along.

Our specification and verification goals comprise two points:

1. Specification captures the 'intended' behavior of the methods with respect to its structural properties: in particular, we abstract away from all properties pertaining to the contents of the linked list.

2. Verification ensures the overflow bug no longer happens in the revised linked list: the actual number of nodes and the cached size are always the same.

The first point depends on the aim of a verification attempt. Are we using the specification to verify correctness of clients of the linked list? Then properties of the contents of a linked list are essential. But, for our purpose of showing the absence of an overflow bug, we abstract away some properties of the contents of linked lists. However, this abstraction is not yet fully complete, and the complete abstraction from contents is left as a proof challenge to the reader (see Sect. 8).

The second point deserves an introduction: how can we be sure that in every linked list the number of nodes and the value stored in the `size` field are the same? Can we keep the number of nodes bounded by what a Java integer can represent? Keeping this number in a ghost field is not sufficient, since the number of nodes depends on the success of a `remove` call: removing an item not present in the linked list should not affect its size, while removing an item that is present decreases its size by one. We refine: we could keep track of the items that are stored by the linked list. The structure to collect these items cannot be a set of items, since we could have duplicate items in the list. A multiset of items, the contents of a linked list, seems right: the size field of the linked list must be the same as the size of its contents, and the remove method is only successful if its argument was contained before the call.

However, working with multisets is quite unnatural, as the `remove` method removes the first item in the list. That can be refined by specifying the contents as a sequence of items instead. Although this could work in principle, a major difficulty when verifying the `remove` method is to give an argument as to why the method terminates. This requires knowledge of the linking structure of the nodes. We could relate the sequence of items to a traversal over nodes, saying that the first item of a linked list is found in the node by traversing `first`, and the item at index $0 < i < n$ is found in the node by traversing `first` and then `next` for $i - 1$ times. Formalizing this seems quite difficult, and as we shall see, not even possible in first-order logic.

Hence, we end up with our last refinement: we keep a sequence of nodes in a ghost field. From this sequence, one obtains the sequence of items. We relate the sequence of nodes to the linked list instance and require certain structural properties to hold of the nodes in the sequence. The length of this sequence is the actual number of nodes, that we show to be equal to the cached size.

4   Formulating a Class Invariant

We now formalize a class invariant, thereby characterizing all linked list instances. We focus on unbounded linked lists first, as these are the structures we intend to model: so most properties are expressed using KeY's unbounded integer type \ bigint. Only at the latest we restrict the size of each linked list to a maximum, as a limitation imposed by the implementation. The setting in which to do our characterization is multi-sorted first-order logic. This logic is presented in a simplified form, leaving out irrelevant details (such as the heap): the full logic used by KeY is described in Chapter 2 of [13].

Consider the following sorts, or type symbols: *LinkedList* for a linked list, *Node* for a node, *Object* for objects and *Null* for `null` values. We have a type hierarchy, where *Null* is related to *LinkedList* and *Node*, and *LinkedList* and *Node* are both related to *Object*. This means that any object of sort *Null* is also an object of sort *LinkedList* and *Node*. Moreover, every object that is a linked list is also of type *Object*, and similar for nodes. We have the following signature: *first* : *LinkedList* → *Node* and *last* : *LinkedList* → *Node* for the `first` and `last` fields of linked lists, and *prev* : *Node* → *Node*, *item* : *Node* → *Object*, and *next* : *Node* → *Node* for the `prev`, `item` and `next` fields of nodes. Further, we assume there is exactly one object of *Null* sort, which is the `null` constant, for which above functions are left undefined: `null` is a valid object of the `LinkedList` and `Node` Java types, but one may not access its fields.

We search for an axiomatization that characterizes linked list instances. One can find these axioms by trial and error. We start listing some (obvious) axioms:

1. $\forall x^{LinkedList}; (x \neq \text{null} \rightarrow (first(x) \neq \text{null} \leftrightarrow last(x) \neq \text{null}))$
   Every linked list instance either has both first and last set to `null`, or both point to some (possibly different) node.
2. $\forall x^{LinkedList}; (x \neq \text{null} \rightarrow (first(x) \neq \text{null} \rightarrow prev(first(x)) = \text{null}))$
   The predecessor of the first node of a linked list is set to `null`.
3. $\forall x^{LinkedList}; (x \neq \text{null} \rightarrow (last(x) \neq \text{null} \rightarrow next(last(x)) = \text{null}))$
   The successor of the last node of a linked list is set to `null`.
4. $\forall x^{Node}; (x \neq \text{null} \rightarrow (prev(x) \neq \text{null} \rightarrow next(prev(x)) = x))$
   Every node that has a predecessor, must be the successor of that predecessor.
5. $\forall x^{Node}; (x \neq \text{null} \rightarrow (next(x) \neq \text{null} \rightarrow prev(next(x)) = x))$
   Every node that has a successor, must be the predecessor of that successor.

These axioms are not yet sufficient: consider a linked list, in which its first and last nodes are different and both have neither a predecessor nor a successor. This linked list should not occur: intuitively, we know that the nodes between first and last are all connected and should form a doubly-linked 'chain'. Moreover, for every linked list, this chain is necessarily finite: one can traverse from first to last by following the next reference a finite number of times. This leads to a logical difficulty.

Proposition 1. *It is not possible to define the reachability of nodes of a linked list in first-order logic.*

Proof. Let x be a linked list and y a node: there is no formula $\phi(x, y)$ that is true if and only if $next^i(first(x)) = y$ for some integer $i \geq 0$.[3] Suppose towards contradiction that there is such a formula $\phi(x, y)$. Now consider the infinite

---

[3] $next^i$ is not a function symbol in first-order logic but an abbreviation of a finite term built by iteration of i times *next*, where $next^0(x) = x$ and $next^i(x) = next(next^{i-1}(x))$ for all $i > 0$.

set Δ of first-order formulas $\{\phi(x,y)\} \cup \{\neg(\textit{next}^i(\textit{first}(x)) = y) \mid 0 \le i\}$. Let Γ be an arbitrary finite subset of Δ. Consider that there must exists some j such that $\Gamma \subseteq \{\phi(x,y)\} \cup \{\neg(\textit{next}^i(\textit{first}(x)) = y) \mid 0 \le i < j\}$, so we can construct a linked list with j nodes, and we interpret x as that linked list and y as the last node. Clearly $\phi(x,y)$ is true as the last node is reachable, and all $\neg(\textit{next}^i(\textit{first}(x)) = y)$ is true for all $0 \le i < j$ because j is not reachable within i steps from the first node. Since Γ is arbitrary, we have established that all finite subsets of Δ have a model. By compactness, Δ must have a model too. However, that is contradictory: no such model for Δ can exists, as neither $\phi(x,y)$ and $\textit{next}^i(\textit{first}(x)) \ne y$ for all integers $0 \le i$ can all be true. $\qquad\square$

We extend our signature to include other sorts: sequences and integers. These sorts are interpreted in the standard model. A schematic rule to capture integer induction is included in KeY (see [13, Section 2.4.2]). Sequences (see [13, Chapter 5.2]) have a non-negative integer length n, and consist of an element at each position $0 \le i < n$. We write $\sigma[i]$ to mean the ith element of sequence σ, and $\ell(\sigma)$ to mean its length n.

Intuitively, each linked list consists of a sequence of nodes between its first and last node. Let instanceof$_{Node}$: Object be a built-in predicate that states that the object is not null and of sort $Node$. A *chain* is a sequence σ such that:

(a) $\forall i^{\text{int}}; (0 \le i < \ell(\sigma) \rightarrow \text{instanceof}_{Node}(\sigma[i]))$
   All its elements are nodes and not null
(b) $\forall i^{\text{int}}; (0 < i < \ell(\sigma) \rightarrow prev(\sigma[i]) = \sigma[i-1])$
   The predecessor of node at position i is the node at position $i - 1$
(c) $\forall i^{\text{int}} : (0 \le i < \ell(\sigma) - 1 \rightarrow next(\sigma[i]) = \sigma[i+1])$
   The successor of node at position i is the node at position $i + 1$

Let $\phi(\sigma)$ denote the above property that σ is a chain. If $\ell(\sigma) = 0$ then $\phi(\sigma)$ is vacuously true: the empty sequence is thus a chain. We now describe properties $\psi_1(\sigma,x)$ and $\psi_2(\sigma,x)$ that relate a chain σ to a linked list x. These denote the following intuitive properties: there is no first and last node and the chain is empty, or the chain is not empty and the first and last node are the first and last elements of the chain.

$$\psi_1(\sigma,x) \equiv (\ell(\sigma) = 0 \wedge \textit{first}(x) = \textit{last}(x) = \text{null})$$
$$\psi_2(\sigma,x) \equiv (\ell(\sigma) > 0 \wedge \textit{first}(x) = \sigma[0] \wedge \textit{last}(x) = \sigma[\ell(x) - 1])$$

6. $\forall x^{LinkedList}; (x \ne \text{null} \rightarrow \exists \sigma^{\text{sig}}; (\phi(\sigma) \wedge (\psi_1(\sigma,x) \vee \psi_2(\sigma,x))))$
   Every linked list necessitates the existence of a chain of either property

Further, we require that the size field of the linked list and the length of the chain are the same: this property is essential to our verification goal. The size field is modeled by the function $size$: $LinkedList \rightarrow int$, and we require its value (1) to equal the length of the chain, and (2) to be bounded by the maximum value stored in a 32-bit integer. In formulating above properties in JML, we skolemize the existential quantifier using a ghost field: see Listing 9. This has the additional benefit that we can easily refer to the chain ghost field in specifications.

```
/*@ nullable @*/ transient Node first;
/*@ nullable @*/ transient Node last;
//@ private ghost \seq nodeList;
/*@ invariant
  @   nodeList.length == size &&
  @   nodeList.length <= Integer.MAX_VALUE &&
  @   (\forall \bigint i; 0 <= i < nodeList.length;
  @       nodeList[i] instanceof Node) &&
  @   ((nodeList == \seq_empty && first == null && last == null)
  @   || (nodeList != \seq_empty && first != null &&
  @         first.prev == null && last != null &&
  @         last.next == null && first == (Node)nodeList[0] &&
  @         last == (Node)nodeList[nodeList.length-1])) &&
  @   (\forall \bigint i; 0 < i < nodeList.length;
  @       ((Node)nodeList[i]).prev == (Node)nodeList[i-1]) &&
  @   (\forall \bigint i; 0 <= i < nodeList.length-1;
  @       ((Node)nodeList[i]).next == (Node)nodeList[i+1]);
  @*/
```

Listing 9. The class invariant of LinkedList expressed in JML.

The class invariant is implicitly required to hold for the **this** object when invoking methods on a linked list instance. In particular, for the constructor of the linked list, the class invariant needs to be established after it returns. In Listing 10, we state that the constructor always constructs a linked list instance for which its chain is empty. The proof of the correctness follows easily: at construct time, the fields (including the ghost field) of the linked list instance are initialized with their default values. This means the size is zero, and the first and last references are **null**, and the ghost field is the empty sequence.

```
/*@
  @ public normal_behavior
  @   ensures nodeList == \seq_empty;
  @*/
public LinkedList() {}
```

Listing 10. The method contract of the constructor of LinkedList in JML.

For verifying the constructor above, see the video [1, 0:23–0:53], where the relevant video material is between timestamps 0:23 and 0:53.

5   The Acyclicity Property

An interesting consequence of the class invariant is the property that traversal of only **next** fields is acyclic. In other words, following only **next** references of any node that is present in a chain never reaches itself. The acyclicity property implies there is a number of times to follow the **next** reference until the last node is reached. For the last node, this number is zero (the last node is already reached). A symmetric property holds for **prev** too.

We logically specify the acyclicity property as follows. Let σ be the chain of a non-empty linked list x for which the class invariant holds. The following holds:

$$\forall i^{\text{int}}; (0 \le i < \ell(\sigma) - 1 \rightarrow \forall j^{\text{int}}; (i < j < \ell(\sigma) \rightarrow \sigma[i] \ne \sigma[j]))$$

Let n abbreviate $\ell(\sigma)$. By contradiction: assume there are two indices, $0 \le i < j < n$, such that the nodes $\sigma[i]$ and $\sigma[j]$ are equal. Then it must hold that for all k such that $j \le k < n$, the node $\sigma[k]$ is equal to the node $\sigma[k - (j - i)]$: by induction on k. Base case: if $k = j$, then node $\sigma[j]$ and node $\sigma[j - (j - i)]$ are equal by assumption, since $\sigma[j - (j - i)] = \sigma[i]$. Induction step: suppose node at $\sigma[k]$ is equal to node at $\sigma[k-(j-i)]$. We must show if $k+1 < n$ then node $\sigma[k+1]$ equals node $\sigma[k+1-(j-i)]$. This follows from the fact that $\sigma[k+1] = next(\sigma[k])$ and $\sigma[k + 1 - (j - i)] = next(\sigma[k - (j - i)])$ for $k < n - 1$, since σ is a chain and the chain property (c) of last section. Now we have established, for all $j \le k < n$, node $\sigma[k]$ equals node $\sigma[k - (j - i)]$. In particular, this holds when k is $n - 1$, the index of the last node: so we have $\sigma[n - 1] = \sigma[n - 1 - (j - i)]$. Since the difference $(j - i)$ is positive, we know $\sigma[n - 1 - (j - i)]$ is not the last node. By the linked list property 3 we have $next(last(x)) = $ **null** and by $\psi_2(\sigma, x)$ we have $last(x) = \sigma[n - 1]$: so we have $next(\sigma[n - 1]) = $ **null**. By the chain properties (c) and (a) we have $next(\sigma[n-1-(j-i)]) = \sigma[n-(j-i)]$ and instanceof$_{Node}(\sigma[n-(j-i)])$, respectively. From the latter we know $\sigma[n-(j-i)] \ne$ **null**. So we have $next(\sigma[n-1-(j-1)]) \ne$ **null**. But this is a contradiction: if nodes $\sigma[n-1]$ and $\sigma[n-1-(j-i)]$ are equal then their **next** fields must also have equal values, but $next(\sigma[n-1]) = $ **null** and $next(\sigma[n-1-(j-i)]) \ne$ **null**!

```
/*@ private normal_behavior
  @ requires true;
  @ ensures (\forall \bigint i;
  @    0 <= i < (\bigint)nodeList.length − (\bigint)1;
  @   (\forall \bigint j; i < j < nodeList.length;
  @    nodeList[i] != nodeList[j ]));
  @*/
private /*@ strictly_pure @*/ void lemma_acyclic() {}
```

Listing 11. The method of a lemma added to `LinkedList` expressed in JML.

For verifying the lemma as formalized in Listing 11, see the video [2].

6   The add Method

Due to the revision of the source code, the add method now calls `checkSize` first (see Listing 8) to ensure that the size field does not overflow when we add another item. This means that the add method has two expected behaviors: the normal behavior when the length of the linked list is not yet at its maximum, and the exceptional behavior when the length of the linked list is at its maximum.

In the normal case, we expect the `add` method to add the given argument as an item to the linked list. Thus the sequence of nodes must become larger. We further specify the position where the item is added: at the end of the list. If add return normally, it returns true. In the exceptional case, we expect that an exception is thrown. We formalize the contract for `add` in Listing 12.

```
/*@
  @ public normal_behavior
  @   requires nodeList.length + (\bigint)1 <= Integer.MAX_VALUE;
  @   ensures
  @     nodeList == \seq_concat(\old(nodeList),
  @       \seq_singleton(nodeList[nodeList.length-1])) &&
  @     ((Node)nodeList[nodeList.length-1]).item == e &&
  @     \result;
  @ public exceptional_behavior
  @   requires nodeList.length == Integer.MAX_VALUE;
  @   signals_only IllegalStateException;
  @   signals (IllegalStateException e) true;
  @*/
public boolean add(/*@ nullable @*/ Object e) {
    checkSize(); // new
    linkLast(e);
    return true;
}
```

Listing 12. The `add` method with its method contract expressed in JML.

Since the `add` method calls the deeper methods `checkSize` and `linkLast`, we may employ their method contracts when verifying this method. So, before we verify `add`, we specify and verify these methods first.

We expect `checkSize` to throw an exception if the length of the linked list is too large to add another element, and it returns normally otherwise: see Listing 13 for its specification. Verification of `checkSize` in both normal and exceptional cases is done automatically by KeY, as can be seen in [1, 0:54–1:24].

```
/*@
  @ private exceptional_behavior
  @   requires nodeList.length == Integer.MAX_VALUE;
  @   signals_only IllegalStateException;
  @   signals (IllegalStateException e) true;
  @ private normal_behavior
  @   requires nodeList.length != Integer.MAX_VALUE;
  @   ensures true;
  @*/
```

Listing 13. The method contract in JML of the `checkSize` method.

For the `linkLast` method, we assume that the length of the linked list is smaller than its maximum length, so we can safely add another node without causing an overflow of the size field. When adding a new node, the resulting chain now is an extension of the previous chain, and additionally the class invariant holds afterwards—this is an implicit post-condition. Since we modify the chain, we need a `set` annotation that changes the ghost field.

```
/*@
  @ normal_behavior
  @   requires
  @     nodeList.length + (\bigint)1 <= Integer.MAX_VALUE;
  @   ensures
  @     nodeList == \seq_concat(\old(nodeList),
  @       \seq_singleton(nodeList[nodeList.length−1])) &&
  @     ((Node)nodeList[nodeList.length−1]).item == e;
  @*/
void linkLast(/*@ nullable @*/ Object e) {
    final Node l = last;
    final Node newNode = new Node(l, e, null);
    last = newNode;
    if (l == null) first = newNode;
    else l.next = newNode;
    size++;
    //@ set nodeList = \seq_concat(nodeList,\seq_singleton(last));
}
```

Listing 14. The `linkLast` method with its method contract expressed in JML.

The verification of this method is no longer fully automatic, see [1, 1:25–6:52].

Observe that there are two different situations we have to deal with: either the linked list was empty, or it was not. If the linked list was empty, then `last` is `null`, and we not only set the `last` field but also the `first`. Otherwise, if the linked list was not empty, we update the former last node to set its `next` field. The challenge is to prove that the class invariant holds after these heap updates, knowing that the class invariant holds in the before heap. The main insight is that the creation of a new node does not alias with any of the existing nodes, and that the modification of the `next` field only affects the old last node. Intuitively, we have a proof situation with two heaps as depicted in Fig. 2.

The properties (b) on page 12, that fixes `prev` fields to point to the previous node in the sequence, and (c), that fixes `next` fields to point to the next node in the sequence, of the chain are the remaning goals in [1, 3:58]. Proving (b) is straightforward if one makes a distinction between old nodes and the new node. Proving (c) in the 'heap after' involves two cases: either the index is between 0 and less than $\ell(\sigma) - 2$, or it used to be the last node and now has index $\ell(\sigma) - 2$. In the former case, the heap update has no effect, as we can show that these nodes are separate from the old last node because they differ in the old value of the next field. In the latter case, the heap update can be used to prove the property directly.

Finally, we can verify the `add` method: see [1, 6:58] for the normal behavior case, and [1, 8:09] for the exceptional behavior case.

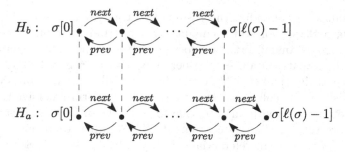

Fig. 2. The heap before (H_b) consists of an arbitrary chain of nodes. In the heap after (H_a) the dashed lines show which objects are identical to the heap before. The old last node at $\sigma[\ell(\sigma) - 1]$ has a different value for its *next* field in the heap after: this must be the result of a heap update. The new last node is not created in the heap before: indeed, it is the result of creating a new node.

7   The remove Method

The **remove** method takes as argument an object; it searches the linked list for the first node which contains the argument as an item. If found, it unlinks the node from the linked list. Using this intuition, we specify the **remove** method contract. Like with the **add** method, there is a deeper method that is called, **unlink**, which we have to specify and verify first.

An immediate difficulty in specifying the **remove** method contract is that its intended behavior depends on the behavior of the **Object.equals** method. Namely, the informal Java documentation states that the first element occurrence in the list that is 'equal to' the argument must be removed. Equality can be user-defined by overriding the **equals** method! We solve this difficulty by assuming a method contract for the equality method, see Listing 15.

```
/*@ public normal_behavior
  @   requires true;
  @   ensures \result == self.equals(param0);
  @*/
public /*@ helper strictly_pure @*/
boolean equals(/*@ nullable @*/ Object param0);
```

Listing 15. The **equals** stub method with its method contract expressed in JML.

We declare the equality method to be strictly pure, which implies that it must be a side-effect free and terminating method (see [13, Section 7.3.5]). Each strictly pure method is also directly accessible as an observer symbol (a function symbol) that can be used in specifications (see [13, Section 8.1.2]). However, no obvious relation between the possibly overridden equality method and its observer symbol is present. The intention of the contract given in Listing 15 is to relate the outcome of the method call of **equals** to the observer symbol *equals*, and this furthermore requires that the implementation is deterministic.

The ramifications of adding this assumed contract are not clear. We note that there are Java classes for which equality is not terminating under certain circumstances. Even `LinkedList` itself does not have a terminating equality, where two linked lists that contain each other may lead to a `StackOverflowError` when testing their equality. This example is described in the Javadoc [14] of the linked list: "Some collection operations which perform recursive traversal of the collection may fail with an exception for self-referential instances where the collection directly or indirectly contains itself." Another approach is to specify the outcome of equality as referential equality only, e.g. see [15, Section 4.4].

Now we can specify the behavior of `remove`. It can be seen as consisting of two cases: either its result is `true` and it has removed the first item equal to its argument from the list, or its result is `false` and the argument was not found and thus not removed. In the first case, the number of elements decreases by one. In the second case, the number of elements in the linked list remains unchanged. See Listing 16.

```
/*@
 @ public normal_behavior
 @   requires true;
 @   ensures \result == false ==>
 @     (\forall \bigint i; 0 <= i < \old(nodeList.length);
 @     (o==null ==> \old(((Node)nodeList[i]).item) != null) &&
 @     (o!=null ==> !\old(o.equals(((Node)nodeList[i]).item)))) &&
 @     nodeList == \old(nodeList);
 @   ensures \result == true ==>
 @     (\exists \bigint j; 0 <= j < \old(nodeList.length);
 @       (\forall \bigint i; 0 <= i < j;
 @       (o==null ==> \old(((Node)nodeList[i]).item) != null) &&
 @       (o!=null ==> !\old(o.equals(((Node)nodeList[i]).item)))) &&
 @     nodeList == \seq_concat(\old(nodeList)[0..j],
 @       \old(nodeList)[j+1..\old(nodeList.length)]) &&
 @     (o==null ==> \old(((Node)nodeList[j]).item) == null) &&
 @     (o!=null ==> \old(o.equals(((Node)nodeList[j]).item))));
 @*/
```

Listing 16. The `remove` method contract expressed in JML.

It is important to note that we make use of JML's `\old` operator to refer to the equality observer symbol in the old heap. Using equality in the new heap is a different observation; and it should not be possible to verify the remove method in this case. To see why, consider two linked list instances x and y: we add x to itself, and to y we add x and then y. Now we perform the `remove` operation on y with y as argument. Clearly x and y are not equal, because they have a different length. But the second item is y itself, and y equals y, so it is removed: see Fig. 3. In the resulting heap, both x and y contain x as only item: thus, x and y are equal. If we would observe equality in the new heap, then the implementation is incorrect: the item to remove should not be the second but the first!

Before we can verify the `remove` method, we must specify and verify its deeper method: `unlink`. Within the method of unlink we have to update the chain ghost

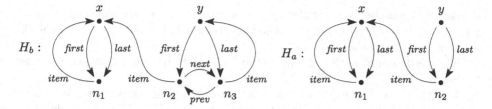

Fig. 3. The situation (H_b) before **remove** is invoked on y with argument y, and after (H_a). The result of this operation is that y's second node n_3 is unlinked, hence the first node n_2 becomes the last node and its next pointer is cleared: now x and y are equal because they have the same length, and they have the same item, namely x.

field as well, to remove a node from the sequence, so we add a set annotation to the method body. Additionally, we make use of the lemma **lemma_acyclic** by calling it as a first statement of the method. See Listing 17. This method call is also not present in the original definition for **unlink**, but we already argued that it does not affect behavior.

```
/*@ normal_behavior
  @   requires nodeList != \seq_empty &&
  @     0 <= nodeIndex < nodeList.length &&
  @     (Node)nodeList[nodeIndex] == x;
  @   ensures \result == \old(x.item) &&
  @     nodeList == \seq_concat(\old(nodeList)[0..nodeIndex],
  @       \old(nodeList)[nodeIndex+1..\old(nodeList).length]) &&
  @     nodeIndex == \old(nodeIndex);
  @*/
/*@ nullable @*/ Object unlink(Node x) {
    lemma_acyclic(); // new
    //@ set nodeList = \seq_concat(\dl_seqSub(nodeList,0,nodeIndex),
\dl_seqSub(nodeList,nodeIndex+1,\dl_seqLen(nodeList)));
    // rest of method body
    ...
```

Listing 17. The first part of method **unlink** and its method contract. Note that the @set annotation must not contain a new line, but kept on a single line: otherwise KeY 2.6.3 cannot load the source file. Here, /*@ @*/ does not work.

An interesting aspect of the specification of **unlink** is its use of a *ghost parameter*. Although KeY does not directly support ghost parameters, we are able to work around that by adding the parameter as a ghost field to our class:

//@ private ghost \bigint nodeIndex;

Its value is left undefined for the most part of the lifetime of the linked list, until we are about to invoke **unlink**. In particular, the ghost parameter contains the index of the node argument, thereby requiring that the node object passed in is part of the chain. In the following discussion, let I be the node index ghost parameter and σ the chain of the linked list: then $\sigma[I]$ is assumed to be the node argument of the method `unlink`.

The verification of the unlink method is not fully automatic, see the five videos [3–7].

Verifying unlink consists of four main cases: these correspond to the possible branches of the two if-statements (see Listing 6). The challenge again is to reestablish the class invariant in the heap after the method completes. The main insight is that, by the acyclicity property, all the nodes are separate: this allows us to distinguish the heap updates to apply only to the node that is actually affected, while leaving the other nodes equal to the situation in the heap before. The three important cases are depicted in Figs. 4, 5, 6 (compare with Fig. 2).

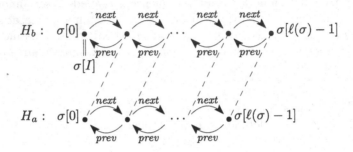

Fig. 4. The heap before (H_b) consists of a chain σ with $\ell(\sigma) \geq 2$. The dashed lines show which objects are identical in the heaps. Interpreting $\sigma[I]$ in the new heap gives $\sigma[I+1]$ in the old heap, as I does not change. The **first** field of the linked list has changed (not shown), and the second node in the old heap now has **null** as **prev**. Moreover, the **next** and **prev** field of the unlinked node have been set to **null** (not shown).

1. Suppose the test of both if-statements evaluate to true: for node x, it holds that $\mathrm{next}(x) = $ **null** and $\mathrm{prev}(x) = $ **null**. Then we know the list consists of exactly one node, as the node we are unlinking is the first and the last node. So I cannot be larger than 0. In the case the node index is zero, the class invariant is proven automatically [3, 7:25].

2. Suppose the test of the first if-statement evaluates to true, but the test of the second if-statement evaluates to false: for node x, it holds that $\mathrm{next}(x) \neq $ **null** and $\mathrm{prev}(x) = $ **null**. We thus know that the list consists of at least two nodes, and it is the first node we are unlinking. Thus, I cannot be larger than 0. If the node index is zero, the class invariant is not proven automatically [4, 2:40], but we have two open goals corresponding to the chain properties (b) and (c), cf. proof of `linkLast`. Our situation is different now, see Fig. 4. Here our insight applies: because of acyclicity, we know all nodes are different. Thus, an update of $\sigma[I]$'s fields do not affect the other nodes. When proving (c) this is sufficient as no next field of nodes in the new chain are changed compared

to the old heap [4, 10:14–15:28]. When proving (b), we furthermore make a case distinction between the new first node and the other nodes: the former follows from the heap update, the latter from the old invariant [4, 3:27–10:13].

3. Suppose the test of the first if-statement evaluates to false, and the test of the second to true: for node x, it holds that $next(x) = $ null and $prev(x) \neq$ null. This means that the list consists of at least two nodes, and it is the last node we are unlinking. Proof is similar to the previous case: see Fig. 5 and [5].

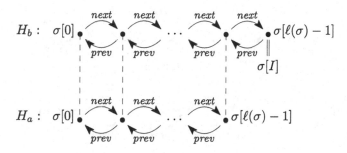

Fig. 5. The heap before (H_b) consists of a chain σ with $\ell(\sigma) \geq 2$. The dashed lines show which objects are identical in the heaps. Interpreting $\sigma[I]$ in the new heap is invalid, as $I = \ell(\sigma)$ in the new heap. The **last** field of linked list has changed (not shown), and the before last node in the old heap now has **null** as **next** field.

4. Suppose both tests of if-statements evaluate to false: for node x, it holds that $next(x) \neq$ null and $prev(x) \neq$ null. This implies that the list consists of at least three nodes: where x is some 'interior' node. This part of the proof is the largest, as it involves many case distinctions. Up to the point where the class invariant is established in the heap after goes as before, except for (b) and (c). Keep in mind the situation as depicted in Fig. 6, and see [6,7]. We distinguish the two cases:

(b) Establishing the **prev** field property of the chain involves the following observation: there are three cases. First case, for all nodes at an index $0 \leq i < I$ in the old heap, we know they are identical to the nodes at the same index in the new heap. We know the heap is updated to assign the **prev** field of $\sigma[I+1]$ in the old heap, and by acyclicity we know this node is separate from the nodes all before $\sigma[I]$ in the old heap. Second case, $\sigma[I]$ interpreted in the new heap is identical to $\sigma[I+1]$ in the old heap, and precisely for this node the **prev** field was updated to become $\sigma[I-1]$ in the old heap (which is $\sigma[I]$ in the new heap). Third and last case, for all nodes at an index $I+1 < i < \ell(\sigma)$ in the old heap, we know they are identical to the nodes at $\sigma[i-1]$ in the new heap. Again, by acyclicity we know that the node $\sigma[I+1]$ in the old heap is separate from the nodes with a higher index, so we know their **prev** field cannot be affected by the update.

(c) Establishing the next fields property of the chain is very similar, but with the index offset by one. Observe that the next field of $\sigma[I-1]$ in the old heap is updated to $\sigma[I+1]$ in the old heap. Thus the three cases are: first, for the nodes with index $0 \leq i < I-1$ in the old heap, second, for the node $\sigma[I-1]$ in the old heap, and third, for the nodes with index $I < i < \ell(\sigma)$ in the old heap.

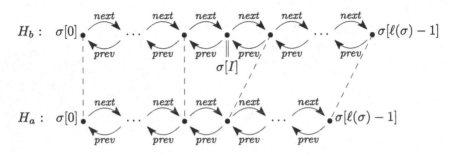

Fig. 6. The situation (H_b) consists of a chain σ with $\ell(\sigma) \geq 3$. The index I remains unchanged in the heaps, thus $\sigma[I]$ in the heap after is equal to $\sigma[I+1]$ in the heap before. The following fields are updated in the new heap: the next field of the node at $\sigma[I-1]$ in the old heap becomes the node at $\sigma[I+1]$ in the old heap, and the prev field of the node at $\sigma[I+1]$ in the old heap becomes the node at $\sigma[I-1]$ in the old heap. In the new heap these two nodes are present in succession in the chain, thus satisfying the chain properties (b) and (c).

Now that we have established that unlink removes a node from the chain while maintaining the class invariant, we can return to the verification of the remove method. The remove method iterates over the linked list until it has obtained a node to remove. However, the termination of this iteration is not obvious. Moreover, before invoking the unlink method, we need to specify the value of its ghost parameter: the index corresponding to the node. So, before we can verify the remove method, we add three kinds of annotations to its source: a ghost variable for maintaining the current index, a loop invariant that establishes termination and maintains the class invariant, and a set annotation before invoking the unlink method (see Listing 18).

```
public boolean remove(/*@ nullable @*/ Object o) {
    //@ ghost \bigint index = −1;
    if (o == null) {
        /*@ maintaining 0 <= (index + 1) &&
          @   (index + 1) <= nodeList.length;
          @ maintaining (\forall \bigint i; 0 <= i < (index + 1);
          @     ((Node)nodeList[i]).item != null);
          @ maintaining (index + 1) < nodeList.length ==>
          @   x == nodeList[index + 1];
          @ maintaining
          @   (index + 1) == nodeList.length <==> x == null;
          @ decreasing nodeList.length − (index + 1);
          @ assignable \strictly_nothing; */
        for (Node x = first; x != null; x = x.next) {
            //@ set index = index + 1;
            if (x.item == null) {
                //@ set nodeIndex = index;
                unlink(x);
                return true;
            } }
    } else {
        /*@ maintaining 0 <= (index + 1) &&
          @   (index + 1) <= nodeList.length;
          @ maintaining (\forall \bigint i; 0 <= i < (index + 1);
          @     !o.equals(((Node)nodeList[i]).item));
          @ maintaining (index + 1) < nodeList.length ==>
          @   x == nodeList[index + 1];
          @ maintaining
          @   (index + 1) == nodeList.length <==> x == null;
          @ decreasing nodeList.length − (index + 1);
          @ assignable \strictly_nothing; */
        for (Node x = first; x != null; x = x.next) {
            //@ set index = index + 1;
            if (o.equals(x.item)) {
                //@ set nodeIndex = index;
                unlink(x);
                return true;
    } } }
    return false;
}
```

Listing 18. The JML annotations of method `remove`. We use a slightly unnatural initial value for the index ghost variable, since the KeY 2.6.3 parser does not recognize the @set annotation if it appears after the if-statement.

The verification of above method is not fully automatic, see [8,9]. The proof consists of two parts, corresponding to the branches of the if-statement. In the proof, one shows (among other properties) that the loop invariant holds initially, after each iteration, and at the end of the loop. It is important to note that ($index + 1$) is equal to the length of the chain precisely when the end of the loop has been reached. This holds since we use the `next` field to traverse the chain, and only the last node has a `null` successor. Moreover, the distance to the last node decreases each iteration, and this distance is bounded from below by zero: thus the loop must terminate. Moreover, the loop is *strictly pure*, as it never modifies the heap in any of its completed iterations. The exceptional case is the last iteration in which the `remove` method returns early. Due to the early return, the loop invariant no longer needs to be shown (and so also not its heap purity). For reasons of limited space, further examination of its proof is left as a challenge to the reader.

8   Conclusion

Over the course of this paper, we have studied two essential methods of Java's `LinkedList` class: `add` and `remove`. The original implementation contains an overflow bug, and we have looked at a revised version that imposes a maximum length of the list. Furthermore, we have set out to verify that the overflow bug indeed no longer occurs. Towards this end, we have formally specified a class invariant and method contracts, with two goals: establishing the absence of the overflow bug, and capturing the 'essential' behavior of the methods with respect to the structural properties of the linked list. All methods have been formally verified [11] using the KeY theorem prover, and video material shows how [10].

A number of proof challenges were left for the reader:

Challenge 1. Describe (informally) the high-level steps of the correctness proof of `remove`.

Challenge 2. The proofs shown in the videos may not be the shortest and could contain detours: find proofs that have a fewer number of (interactive) steps.

Challenge 3. Make use of `assignable` and `accessible` clauses in JML with dynamic footprints (see [13, Section 9.3]): does this make the proofs shorter?

Challenge 4. Write a specification and verify the correctness for these linked list methods: `linkFirst`, `linkBefore`, `node`, `indexOf`, `clear`.

Challenge 5. Refine the specifications to relate the items in the 'heap before' to the items in the 'heap after', e.g. all items in the heap before `add` is called must remain at the same position in the heap after, and verify the correctness with respect to the refined contracts.

Challenge 6. Abstract the specifications from properties related to items, i.e. only show that the class invariant is maintained by the methods: can the proof still be done?

References

1. Bian, J., Hiep, H.A.: A Tutorial on Verifying LinkedList Using KeY: Part 1 (2020). https://doi.org/10.6084/m9.figshare.11662824
2. Bian, J., Hiep, H.A.: A Tutorial on Verifying LinkedList Using KeY: Part 2 (2020). https://doi.org/10.6084/m9.figshare.11673987
3. Bian, J., Hiep, H.A.: A Tutorial on Verifying LinkedList Using KeY: Part 3a (2020). https://doi.org/10.6084/m9.figshare.11688816
4. Bian, J., Hiep, H.A.: A Tutorial on Verifying LinkedList Using KeY: Part 3b (2020). https://doi.org/10.6084/m9.figshare.11688858
5. Bian, J., Hiep, H.A.: A Tutorial on Verifying LinkedList Using KeY: Part 3c (2020). https://doi.org/10.6084/m9.figshare.11688870
6. Bian, J., Hiep, H.A.: A Tutorial on Verifying LinkedList Using KeY: Part 3d (2020). https://doi.org/10.6084/m9.figshare.11688984
7. Bian, J., Hiep, H.A.: A Tutorial on Verifying LinkedList Using KeY: Part 3e (2020). https://doi.org/10.6084/m9.figshare.11688891
8. Bian, J., Hiep, H.A.: A Tutorial on Verifying LinkedList Using KeY: Part 4a (2020). https://doi.org/10.6084/m9.figshare.11699178
9. Bian, J., Hiep, H.A.: A Tutorial on Verifying LinkedList Using KeY: Part 4b (2020). https://doi.org/10.6084/m9.figshare.11699253
10. Bian, J., Hiep, H.A.: A Tutorial on Verifying LinkedList Using KeY: Video Material (2020). https://doi.org/10.6084/m9.figshare.c.4826589.v2
11. Hiep, H.A., Bian, J., de Boer, F.S., de Gouw, S.: A Tutorial on Verifying LinkedList Using KeY: Proof Files (2020). https://doi.org/10.5281/zenodo.3613711
12. Hiep, H.-D.A., Maathuis, O., Bian, J., de Boer, F.S., van Eekelen, M., de Gouw, S.: Verifying OpenJDK's LinkedList using KeY. TACAS 2020. LNCS, vol. 12079, pp. 217–234. Springer, Cham (2020). https://doi.org/10.1007/978-3-030-45237-7_13

References

13. Ahrendt, W., Beckert, B., Bubel, R., Hähnle, R., Schmitt, P.H., Ulbrich, M. (eds.): Deductive Software Verification - The KeY Book - From Theory to Practice. LNCS, vol. 10001. Springer, Cham (2016). https://doi.org/10.1007/978-3-319-49812-6
14. Bloch, J., Gafter, N.: Collection (Java Platform SE 8). https://docs.oracle.com/javase/8/docs/api/java/util/Collection.html. Accessed 23 Jan 2020
15. Huisman, M.: Verification of Java's AbstractCollection class: a case study. In: Boiten, E.A., Möller, B. (eds.) MPC 2002. LNCS, vol. 2386, pp. 175–194. Springer, Heidelberg (2002). https://doi.org/10.1007/3-540-45442-X_11
16. Rooney, J.J., Heuvel, L.N.V.: Root cause analysis for beginners. Qual. Prog. **37**(7), 45–56 (2004)

The VerifyThis Collaborative Long Term Challenge

Marieke Huisman[1], Raúl Monti[1], Mattias Ulbrich[2], and Alexander Weigl[2(✉)]

[1] University of Twente, Enschede, The Netherlands
{m.huisman,r.e.monti}@utwente.nl
[2] Karlsruhe Institute of Technology, Karlsruhe, Germany
{ulbrich,weigl}@kit.edu

Abstract. Over the last years, we have seen tremendous progress in the area of deductive program verification. To demonstrate this progress, and to bring the area of deductive program verification even further, we have proposed the VerifyThis Collaborative Long Term Challenge, which calls upon the program verification community to verify different aspects of a realistic software application over a period of several months. Goal of the challenge is to foster collaboration in order to verify a realistic and industrially-relevant software application. This paper outlines the considerations that we made when selecting the challenge, and discusses how we believe it will encourage collaboration. It presents the software application that was selected for the challenge in 2019–2020, discusses the practical set up of the challenge, and briefly reports on the received solutions and an online workshop where the different solutions were presented.

1 Introduction

Over the last 20 years, enormous progress has been made in the area of program verification [10]. This progress can be witnessed for example by the development of large, non-trivial case studies, such as the verification of the TimSort implementation in the shipped Java libraries [9], or the parallel nested depth first search [23]. Another evidence of the progress of program verification tools are the outcomes of program competitions, such as VerifyThis [12–16] and VSComp [8,18], where we see a steady increase in the complexity of challenges that have been posed (and solved). However, program verification competitions encourage competition rather than collaboration, and moreover they always impose a strict time constraint, ranging from 90 min per challenge (VerifyThis), to a time-span of 2 days for 4 challenges (VSComp). Thus, though program verification competitions are very useful, given the way that they currently are executed, they do not give a full account of what can be achieved with deductive program verification techniques in general. And in particular, they do not address the question whether deductive software verification techniques are suitable for realistic, industrial-size software.

W. Ahrendt et al. (Eds.): Deductive Software Verification, LNCS 12345, pp. 246–260, 2020.
https://doi.org/10.1007/978-3-030-64354-6_10

Moreover, we see that program verification tools are mainly developed in isolation, i.e., every tool implements its own techniques without benefitting from results obtained by other tools. We feel that this situation needs be changed: every program verification tool has its own strengths and weaknesses, and applying them on large real-world examples can be hampered by these weaknesses. Thus, these weaknesses need to be addressed, and rather than doing this for each verification tool individually, we believe that this should be done by collaboration and exchange.

Therefore, we asked ourselves what could be achieved in the area of program verification if (a) we as the program verification community collaborated and (b) the time constraints were removed? To answer this question, and in particular to encourage more collaboration within the program verification community, we have launched the *VerifyThis Collaborative Long Term Challenge*. The idea behind this challenge is to propose a single, large, industrially-relevant software application, which can benefit from formal verification, but that is too large and complex for a single verification tool. It is our hope that people contributing to this challenge all verify different aspects of the application, and that they exchange results, in order to verify together (almost) all relevant aspects of the application. We hope that the challenge will be of interest also to the larger program verification community, using techniques such as (bounded) model checking, static analysis and symbolic evaluation, and not just deductive software verification. Section 4.2 lists a variety of verification missions that show that the chosen challenge can be attractive to many communities. It is our belief that if the program verification community combines forces, we will be able to show that program verification can produce relevant results for real systems with acceptable effort.

This paper describes the set up of the VerifyThis Collaborative Long Term Challenge. In particular, we discuss the considerations that we took into account when selecting the challenge (for 2019–2020, the selected challenge is the verification of the OpenPGP Key Server), the overall set up of the challenge, and the actions and measurements that we have taken to actually foster collaboration. The main goal of this paper is to document and outline our considerations when setting up the challenge, and to help future challenge developers with their selection process.

Originally, it was planned that the long term challenge would end with a presentation session during the VerifyThis competition event. We briefly report on the five solutions that were handed in, on an online workshop that was held in April 2020 in which the different (partial) solutions to the challenges have been presented, and on lessons learnt.

The remainder of this paper is organized as follows. Section 2 discusses some earlier long term verification challenges, and compares their goals and set up with the current one. Section 3 then discusses the considerations that we took into account for selecting the challenge, and how this challenge can be used to encourage collaboration within the verification community. Section 4 discusses the particular challenge selected for 2019–2020, while Sect. 5 discusses the practical set up of the challenge, and the measures we took to foster collaboration. It reports on the submitted solutions and experiences from the online workshop.

2   Related Community Challenges

We are not the first to propose a community challenge, or grand challenge. As stated by Bicarregui, Hoare and Woodcock [5]:

> Grand challenges have a long history. From the problem of longitude in the 18th century, through Hilbert's programme for 20th-century mathematics, to the space race of the 1960s, grand challenges have led to considerable innovation and have accelerated engineering and technological advancement towards their goal.

This section discusses some earlier grand challenges in the area of program verification.

The Steam Boiler Case Study [1, 2] is the first competition of formal program specification and development methods that we are aware of. Originally, this challenge was proposed to the participants of a 1995 Dagstuhl seminar. The challenge had a competitive character: its intention was to challenge the formal specification community to apply their methods to a non-trivial non-academic case study of a steam boiler control system. The organizers gave a lot of freedom to the participants in how they wanted to address the challenge:

> We deliberately abstained from imposing any specific constraints on the expected solution. The idea was not to exclude any approach and to permit each method to be shown at its best, be it by providing a formal requirement specification, an architectural design, a sequence of stepwise refinements, an executable program or an analysis and proof of behavioural properties one wants to guarantee for the system.

Interestingly, the challenge proposers noticed that the internet helped tremendously to improve communication between the challenge participants, and to ensure that the competition is conducted on a universal scale. When preparing our challenge, we realized that enabling an efficient and lively communication between challenge participants is still critical for its success.

In 2000, the *Mondex case study* was presented [25]. This case study is a bit different: originally it was not designed as community challenge, but rather as a case study for the formal modelling, specification and verification of a smart card electronic cash system. The original case study was developed in Z, but quickly it was picked up as an interesting case study by other groups working on verification of smart card applications. The Mondex case study has solutions in Z, KeY, KIV, Alloy.

The *Verifying Compiler: A Grand Challenge for Computing Research* was proposed by Hoare [11] in 2003. This grand challenge eventually led to a repository of verified software [5]. In his original proposal, Hoare identified a set of criteria that distinguish a *grand challenge* in science or engineering from other research problems:

A grand challenge represents a commitment by a significant section of the research community to work together towards a common goal, agreed to be valuable and achievable by a team effort within a predicted timescale.

We feel that much of the spirit of Hoare's grand challenge is similar to ours. However, Hoare's grand challenge was even larger than ours, and did not focus so much on one particular application.

In 2007, Joshi and Hoare proposed a challenge to build a *verifiable filesystem* [17]. They propose this smaller challenge as a stepping stone towards the original verifying compiler grand challenge. They identified this particular challenge because:

> [it was of] sufficient importance that successful completion of the mini challenge would have an impact beyond the verification community.

Interestingly, in their paper they also describe other challenge options that they considered, such as the verification of the Linux Kernel, but which they discarded because its complexity and size seemed too large for a reasonable challenge.

3   Challenge Selection

One of the most important aspects of the VerifyThis Collaborative Long Term Challenge is the selection of the software system serving as the challenge. We identified various criteria that we believe would attract the interest of the verification community, and also carefully considered how the challenge could pave the way for potential collaboration between researchers working on different formal verification techniques.

3.1   Criteria for Challenge Selection

We composed the following list with properties that we consider that a suitable target application for the proposed kind of challenge should possess:

- The application should be a *real piece* of software; possibly part of a relevant production system. This would make it attractive for people to participate: it will give them the satisfaction of contributing to a relevant problem given that their verification efforts will concern the properties of a real software system.
- The application should be *open source*: researchers must be able to publish adaptations, modifications, and analyzes without restrictions.
- Even though the application should be written in a real-world language (and be executable), the involved challenges should be of a *language-independent nature*, such that it can be convincingly transferred to other similar programming languages, and participation in the challenge is not restricted to people that work on a program verification tool for exactly the right language.

- The application should be easily *decomposable*, i.e., it should be possible for people to focus on only a part of the complete application, without the need to fully specify and verify the complete application. We believe that decomposability is also essential to enable collaboration.
- The application should be real, but *not over-complex*, i.e., it should be possible for participants to get a good overall understanding of the application without too much effort. After that, they can concentrate on those parts of the application that they wish to verify.
- The *core functionality* of (at least part of) the application should be simple and *well-understood*.
- It should be possible to attack the verification of the application at *different levels*: a participant might start with a highly simplified version of the code and then refine this into a more realistic version. It should also be possible to first concentrate on the key characteristics, and then later extend it in different directions, for example considering error handling or performance optimizations.
- It should be possible to point out a *varied collection of relevant and interesting aspects* in the project that people could try to verify, such as:
  - algorithmic properties, e.g., finding a crucial loop invariant;
  - optimization-related properties, e.g., preservation of correctness when a cache is used, the application is optimized for speed etc.;
  - heap shape specifications and suitable framing conditions;
  - runtime safety; i.e., absence of runtime exceptions (to attract the automatic verification community)
  - concurrency-related properties;
  - exception handling;
  - bounded loops and bit arithmetic (to attract bounded checkers); and
  - behavioural protocols (to attract modelling community).

Importantly, the aspects to verify should not feel artificial, i.e., they should be related to real reliability aspects of the code.

Candidates. In our search we considered several software applications as candidate challenges. The *GNU Multiple Precision Arithmetic Library (GMP)* is a library for infinite-precision arithmetic. Together with the *GNU Scientific Library (GSL)* it provides a feature-rich set on mathematical algorithms, which makes it highly relevant and widely used. Both were not further investigated because they do not contain any concurrent algorithms. The same reasons are also valid for *Eigen* – a C++ library for linear algebra. Boost libraries, like *Graph* or *Parallel*, were declined because of their complexity and their heavy use of template programming, which renders them very C-specific. We also considered to propose a collection of algorithms as provided by a standard text book, like [24]. Such algorithms are practical and important, but we felt that they were not realistic enough. Probably such algorithms are better suited for the on-site VerifyThis program verification competition (i.e., as a 90 min challenge). Cryptographic algorithms are highly relevant in daily use. Therefore we looked at *Bouncy castle* – a library providing cryptographic implementations for the

Java Crypto API. However, cryptographic algorithms are not easy to specify, and their formal verification requires a substantial amount of mathematical reasoning. Finally, we also considered several libraries for distributed computation, such as Apache Hadoop and Thrill, but for these libraries we felt it was unclear what would actually be the desired properties to verify.

3.2 Encouraging Collaboration

As mentioned above, the VerifyThis Collaborative Long Term Challenge has been particularly designed with the goal in mind to incite collaboration between the participants. In fact, we feel that to further advance the field of formal program verification, more collaboration between different techniques and tools is essential.

Two unrelated tools can seldom make use of each other's results easily, mostly because combining fundamentally different techniques is inherently difficult. The common specification languages Java Modelling Language (JML) [19] and the ANSI/ISO-C specification Language (ACSL) [4] are designed to be applicable in different verification scenarios (e.g., deductive verification and runtime assertion checking). Even for these limited scopes, coming up with an indisputable, common language semantics is difficult (the runtime semantics of ACSL differs from that for deductive verification [21], and verification tools differ in how they verify JML specifications [6]).

This challenge has the potential for the program verification community to investigate ways of how results of one verification endeavour can be used in another. To achieve this goal, it is important that the challenge is formulated on a very general level that is not restricted to a particular sub-community. Section 4.2 reports on some relevant questions that exemplify that variety of different property types that can be specified and verified using different approaches. The more concrete situation should allow collaborating partners to identify what guarantees the results obtained in a different formal system imply in their formalism, and how these results can be encoded in their verification context.

We illustrate the potential for collaboration by a hypothetical example. An automatic static analysis may be able to infer that a module of the software only changes a number of memory locations. The analysis can produce results quickly without much specification overhead set since it answers a specialized question. This allows one to focus during the verification of heavyweight functional specifications on the already intricate interactive task to craft the relevant auxiliary specifications (contracts and loop specifications) that are usually required on such occasions. The results of the scalable framing analysis can be used as additional assumptions in the functional verification making it more precise.

4   The OpenPGP Key Server

As the target for the 2019–2020 challenge, we chose a modern public key server called HAGRID[1] This section introduces this application, and its verification missions.

When using public key encryption and signatures in e-mails, one challenge is to obtain the public key of recipients. To this end, public key servers have been installed that can be queried for public keys. The most popular[2] public key server OpenPGP was recently shown to have severe security flaws. There was no protection on who could publish a key for an e-mail address and no protection on the amount of data published. This opened the gate for a broad range of dangerous attacks such as the ones presented at CVE-2019-13050[3], or the ones described in the blog post of the HAGRID's developers. Moreover, the old key server software SKS did not conform to the General Data Protection Regulation (GDPR) and had performance issues.

As a consequence, the OpenPGP community decided to implement a new server framework that manages the access to public keys. The new official server is called HAGRID, it is open source[4], and it is already in production. HAGRID is written in the programming language Rust and comprises some 6,000 lines of code in total[5].

HAGRID represents a modern piece of code, with both an acceptable size and complexity, which makes it an excellent challenge application. Furthermore, it is currently in use by many pervasive applications such as *GPGTools, Enigmail, OpenKeychain, GPGSync, Debian* and *NixOS*, which implies that its verification will have an important impact towards security and efficiency of software that is in use daily. What is more, its architecture comprehends many interesting aspects for verification, such as database consistency, concurrency, efficiency and functional correctness, scoping a wide range of interests of the software verification community. This also makes it suitable to encourage interaction between members of the verification community, which can attack complementary verification problems over the single challenge program.

4.1   The Verifying Key Server

While HAGRID is the *reference implementation*, and the final goal is to verify it, we decided to define a more general *verifying* key server. This allows us to have a less restrictive starting point for verification by abstracting from HAGRID's particular implementation decisions. It also establishes clear bases for abstraction decisions to be made at the time of verifying with specific tailored tools.

---

[1] See https://sequoia-pgp.org/blog/2019/06/14/20190614-hagrid/.
[2] It is the default server used by the Thunderbird public-key engine *Enigmail* for instance.
[3] See https://access.redhat.com/articles/4264021.
[4] Available at https://gitlab.com/hagrid-keyserver/hagrid, (2020-04-29).
[5] Not including the underlying web framework or GPG library code.

The server is essentially a database that allows users to store their public key for their e-mail address, to query for keys for e-mail addresses and to tracelessly remove e-mail-key pairs from the database. To avoid illegal database entry and removal actions, confirmations are sent out to the e-mail addresses of issuing users upon an addition or removal request.

The server possesses a web frontend which accepts requests from users or via restful API. It additionally possesses a connection to a database from which it reads key-value pairs and writes to it, and a channel for sending e-mails. Figure 1 presents a schematic overview of the architecture. The key server can be separated into three components: the *webserver* (frontend), the *key manager* (backend), and the key *database*. At the core of the server, there are four operations that can be triggered from outside the server via HTTP-API-requests to the web frontend. The operations are:

Request adding a key. A user can issue a request for storing a key for a particular e-mail address. To avoid that anybody can store a key for someone else's e-mail address, the key is not directly stored into the database, but stored intermediately. The user retrieves a confirmation code via the given e-mail to verify the specified address. Only once the confirmation code is activated, will the address be actually added to the database.

Querying an e-mail address. Any user can issue a request for learning the key(s) stored with a concrete and verified e-mail address. Unlike on the old public server, queries for patterns are not allowed. Public keys that have been (verified) removed or have not yet been confirmed must not be returned in queries.

Request removing a key. The user can request the removal of the association between a key and an e-mail address. The process begins with the confirmation via the e-mail address: The user enters one of their previously confirmed addresses. The server sends an e-mail to this address containing a link. Behind this link, there is a website that allows the removal of the key's association.

Confirming a request. Additions and removals are indirect actions. Instead of modifying the database directly, they issue a (secret and random) confirmation code. Confirmation of the code is performed using this operation. If the provided code is one recently issued then the corresponding operation (addition/removal) is finalized.

The challenge we propose focuses on the key manager component of the server. This is a program that must provide implementations for the operations outlined above.

Nevertheless, multiple extensions to the *verifying server* can impose a bigger verification challenge for the participants. We encouraged participants to also look at this. One would maybe want to verify the database or the REST-API. One would usually want to abstract from the programming language unless the verification tool is prepared for it, but on the other hand may decide to be as faithful as possible to HAGRID's implementation, and thus as close as possible to the real code. Other verification possibilities go in the direction of improving the

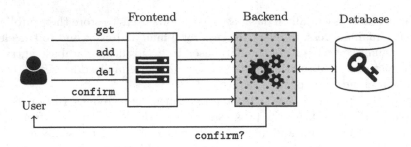

Fig. 1. Schematic of the key server architecture

reference implementation, for instance by increasing the server's performance by using more sophisticated search-friendly data structures.

4.2 Missions

The HAGRID server is a complex software system which has been chosen as the target for the long term challenge since it provides verification challenges on many different levels of *abstraction*, *complexity* and regarding many different *requirement aspects* (e.g., safety, security, performance properties). This section identifies different verification tasks (called missions) for the different abstraction levels and aspects.

One design decision of the challenge is to leave it to the participating teams on which actual artefact(s) they contribute a verification result. Depending on the addressed mission, different artefacts suggest themselves:

1. the existing production HAGRID reference implementation in Rust;
2. a new implementation (in any programming language) of the core functionality satisfying a basic set of natural language requirements available on the challenge website; or
3. a suitable abstraction from the code level to model a particular aspect (the protocol, memory, key handling, ...).

This also accommodates for the fact that contemporary verification approaches are heterogeneous in the languages and specification techniques they support. By opening the choice of language and implementation layout, the scope of the challenge has considerably broadened. Moreover, it allows also for an adjustable degree of algorithmic complexity: The data structures used in a re-implementation may range from rather simple ones (e.g., two arrays containing the email addresses and the associated keys), over more complex (e.g., a hash map with concurrent data access) up to an implementation that satisfies real-world requirements regarding, e.g., efficiency and memory consumption. This allows the contributing teams to choose their initial level and also to advance in the course of the challenge.

Moreover, an implementation may make use of underlying (provenly or assumedly correct) libraries and middleware layers (e.g., by assuming method contracts/function summaries and (object) invariants).

The first suggested mission of the VerifyThis Collaborative Long Term Challenge is the least specific task and allows many formal code analysis tools to participate. Verification tools that run fully automatically (in particular the participating tools in the SVCOMP[6] competition series) are particularly well suited to contribute solutions to this challenge and to show that results can be obtained without further user input. For this foundational verification question, no formal (full) specification is required.

Mission 1 (Safety). *Verify that the chosen implementation of the key server does not exhibit undesired runtime effects (e.g., no runtime exceptions in Java, or no undefined behaviour in C).*

Traditionally, the challenges in VerifyThis on-site competitions are more heavyweight, with concrete application-specific functional requirements on the used data structures that go beyond safety conditions and assertion checking. They strive to establish properties that require a logical formalisation against which the code needs to be verified. Unlike Mission 1, this *functional* verification requires knowledge about what the system has to compute, i.e., a specification must be provided. Depending on the complexity of the code and specification (and verification technique), the verification may then run automatically, or (in many cases) requires some form of user guidance (on top of the specification).

Mission 2 (Functionality). *Formalize the natural language functional requirements from the challenge description as formal specifications for the core operations. Verify that the implementation of the operations satisfies your formalisation.*

One example for a functional property of the key server is that if an e-mail address is queried, a key stored for this e-mail address is returned if there is one in the database.

Typically, especially for imperative (object-oriented) programming languages, functional verification is performed modularly by specifying *contracts* for each function (method) according to the design-by-contract paradigm and then proving them correct individually.

Other formal method traditions focus less on the operational effects of individual functions in form of contracts, but allow one to model the evolution of the entire system over time using a temporal or state-based formalism. This is particularly the case for model checking approaches where properties of the interaction protocol can then be analyzed on an implementation-independent level.

Mission 3 (Protocol). *Specify the temporal protocol behaviour of the key server. Identify relevant temporal properties for the key server and prove them satisfied by the protocol.*

---

[6] See https://sv-comp.sosy-lab.org.

Mission 3 deals with somewhat different properties than functional verification. It is a good candidate for a collaborative verification effort in the sense of Sect. 3.2: One team of participants may prove properties of the protocol using an approach designed for that purpose (e.g., model checking), whereas another team verifies that the implementations of the operations adhere to their abstractions. Tools have complementary strengths: Model checking cannot go into implementational details on the programming language level, and for deductive verification, encoding protocols is cumbersome, error-prone and little efficient.

There is a school of formal modelling techniques that allows one to model systems on a rather abstract level, but with mathematical rigour. These models can then be formally refined into more concrete detailed versions, and eventually into executable code. Prominent representatives are (Event-)B, Abstract State Machines or Z.

Mission 4 (Refinement). *Encode the natural language requirements from the challenge description as a mathematically rigour system model. Refine the abstract model in one or more steps into an executable program.*

Again this mission provides great potential for collaboration if abstract system verification meets program verification.

Not every system property can be formalised as functional property (Mission 2); for instance privacy properties require different verification techniques.

Mission 5 (Privacy). *Specify and prove that the key server adheres to privacy principles. In particular: (a) only exact query match results are ever returned to the user issuing a query, and (b) deleted information cannot be retrieved anymore from the server.*

One concrete example is that if an e-mail address has been deleted from the system, no information about the e-mail address is kept in the server. Classical non-interference analyses (from type-theoretical and dependency-graph-based statistical analyses to deductive analysis) allow formal methods to be applied to this mission.

There are more security-related properties for the key server since that has to produce and distribute random confirmation codes. A key server should be analysed w.r.t. cryptographic-related questions, too.

Mission 6 (Randomness). *Prove that any created confirmation code is (a) randomly chosen (i.e., that every string from the range is equally likely), (b) cannot easily be predicted, and (c) is never leaked, except as the return value of the issuing operation.*

Another field of interesting properties (that also have been addressed in VerifyThis onsite events recently) are questions around concurrency. They often are related to the actual implementation.

Mission 7 (Thread safety). *Specify and verify that your implementation is free of data races, where data races arise when concurrent processes try to access* *a common memory location simultaneously. For concurrent applications, also absence of deadlock and livelock are important requirements.*

The key server as a software system providing a critical infrastructure also has relevant properties concerning its availability, its resource consumption or its performance. They are worth being formally analysed and their analysis can likely benefit from guarantees obtained during analyses of functional aspects.

Mission 8 (Non-functional properties). *Identify, specify and verify non-functional properties of the key server concerning worst case execution times and worst case memory consumption of the operations (or other relevant non-functional properties).*

5 Realisation

Finally, we discuss some practical aspects of how we have set up the challenge and report on the experiences that we gained after the submission of the solutions.

5.1 Practical Set-Up

The VerifyThis Collaborative Long Term Challenge was launched in August 2019, and submitted solutions were due end of March 2020. Participants were invited to present their results during the on-site VerifyThis program verification competition (co-located with ETAPS in April 2020). In addition, the plan to compose a special issue with (partial) solutions to the challenge was announced.

Two crucial aspects of the long-term challenge were (1) to get people started, and (2) to ensure that people continue working on the challenge. To achieve this, we had set up several means of communication.

First of all, we have the website https://www.verifythis.github.io, which serves as the entry point to the challenge and is the main source of up-to-date information. The website has several functions. First of all, it informs the community about the challenge and its current state by showing (preliminary) results and news. It also provides information to the participants, such as an overview of the other participants and artefacts that participants have made available for reuse. We decided for a website hosted by Github, as this makes it easy for participants to contribute to the website, either via the issue tracker or a via pull request. We tried to encourage the participants to use this public repository by themselves.

In addition, we also created a mailinglist[7], such that both organisers and participants could communicate with each other directly. We had considered using a collaborative development platform such as Slack, but decided not to do this, because we felt that most of our potential participants would prefer communication by email.

---

[7] verifythis-ltc@lists.kit.edu.

5.2 Submissions

At the end of the submission period, we had received five contributions from different teams using different verification approaches and tools. Three of them focused on functional specification (mostly missions 1 and 2), two considered security-related aspects (mission 5). Short papers describing the solutions can be found in the informal proceedings [20].

Submissions for functional properties were written in different programming (and specification) languages and verified with different deductive verification tools (SPARK [22], Why3 [7], and Java+JML with KeY [3]). All specifications followed similar ideas: They specified the functional key server interface using contracts that formally capture the effects of requests on the database (represented by some form of ADT). The Why3 solution targetted a file-based database backend, whereas the other two solutions modelled it as an in-memory database.

The other two submissions provided a security testing framework for the keyserver based on history traces (in Scala), and a formulation of information flow security properties with declassification in a variant of separation logic for security properties. In particular, revocation of key entries was identified here as an interesting challenge for non-interference approaches.

5.3 Experiences

We observed that the communication channels were used less frequently than we expected. We assume that the mailing list was perhaps not the best medium for the purpose. Moreover, new collaboration ideas did not spark between different approaches or tools during the offline period. We summise that a stronger incentive for collaboration could be given by additional meetings during the runtime of the challenge. These could either be real-world meetings or could be performed online.

Since the workshop originally planned in late April 2020 had to be postponed (due to the Covid-19 pandemic), we set up an online meeting – close to the original workshop date – at which the participants and interested parties could discuss the challenge, their solutions and perhaps identify synergies and common ideas.

The half-day online event received considerable attention (over 30 participants; more than would have been expected for the online event). Similarities and differences between the approaches were identified and discussed. The contributors agreed that the LTC should not be called terminated, but that further work and collaboration would improve their work. As a concrete idea for cooperation, it was identified that explicitly modelling the history of requests can be adapted in deductive specifications from the security testing approach.

The ETAPS conference (and with that its workshop) was postponed for several months. The organisers and participants agreed to meet again when ETAPS is held for an updated report on the collaboration and solutions to the challenges.

6   Conclusion

We received many positive reactions from the community since the start of this challenge, and we hope that this will also lead to interesting and unexpected verification outcomes. Ultimately, we hope that the challenge will bring the formal verification community a step closer to its ultimate goal: the usage of formal analysis in the daily software development process, by providing better insights into the obstacles and potentials for the use of formal techniques, and therewith helping the participants to further improve their approaches and tools.

In addition to tool improvements, we also hope that the VerifyThis Collaborative Long Term Challenge will diminish the gap between different formal verification approaches, and will foster more collaboration within the verification community.

References

1. Abrial, J.-R., Börger, E., Langmaack, H.: The steam boiler case study: competition of formal program specification and development methods. In: Abrial, J.-R., Börger, E., Langmaack, H. (eds.) Formal Methods for Industrial Applications. LNCS, vol. 1165, pp. 1–12. Springer, Heidelberg (1996). https://doi.org/10.1007/BFb0027228

2. Abrial, J.-R., Börger, E., Langmaack, H. (eds.): Formal Methods for Industrial Applications. LNCS, vol. 1165. Springer, Heidelberg (1996). https://doi.org/10.1007/BFb0027227

3. Ahrendt, W., Beckert, B., Bubel, R., Hähnle, R., Schmitt, P.H., Ulbrich, M. (eds.): Deductive Software Verification - The KeY Book - From Theory to Practice, LNCS, vol. 10001. Springer, Heidelberg (2016). https://doi.org/10.1007/978-3-319-49812-6

4. Baudin, P., Filliâtre, J.C., Marché, C., Monate, B., Moy, Y., Prevosto, V.: Acsl: Ansi/iso c specification language. Reference manual. http://www.frama-c.com/download/acsl.pdf

5. Bicarregui, J., Hoare, C.A.R., Woodcock, J.C.P.: The verified software repository: a step towards the verifying compiler. Formal Asp. Comput. 18(2), 143–151 (2006). https://doi.org/10.1007/s00165-005-0079-4

6. Boerman, J., Huisman, M., Joosten, S.: Reasoning about JML: differences between KeY and OpenJML. In: Furia, C.A., Winter, K. (eds.) IFM 2018. LNCS, vol. 11023, pp. 30–46. Springer, Cham (2018). https://doi.org/10.1007/978-3-319-98938-9_3

7. Filliâtre, J.-C., Paskevich, A.: Why3 — Where programs meet provers. In: Felleisen, M., Gardner, P. (eds.) ESOP 2013. LNCS, vol. 7792, pp. 125–128. Springer, Heidelberg (2013). https://doi.org/10.1007/978-3-642-37036-6_8

8. Filliâtre, J., Paskevich, A., Stump, A.: The 2nd verified software competition: experience report. In: Klebanov, V., Beckert, B., Biere, A., Sutcliffe, G. (eds.) Proceedings of the 1st International Workshop on Comparative Empirical Evaluation of Reasoning Systems, Manchester, United Kingdom, June 30, 2012. CEUR Workshop Proceedings, vol. 873, pp. 36–49. CEUR-WS.org (2012)

9. de Gouw, S., de Boer, F.S., Bubel, R., Hähnle, R., Rot, J., Steinhöfel, D.: Verifying openjdk's sort method for generic collections. J. Autom. Reasoning 62(1), 93–126 (2019). https://doi.org/10.1007/s10817-017-9426-4

10. Hähnle, R., Huisman, M.: Deductive software verification: from pen-and-paper proofs to industrial tools. In: Steffen, B., Woeginger, G. (eds.) Computing and Software Science. LNCS, vol. 10000, pp. 345–373. Springer, Cham (2019). https://doi.org/10.1007/978-3-319-91908-9_18

11. Hoare, C.A.R.: The verifying compiler: a grand challenge for computing research. J. ACM **50**(1), 63–69 (2003). https://doi.org/10.1145/602382.602403

12. Huisman, M., Monahan, R., Mostowski, W., Müller, P., Ulbrich, M.: VerifyThis 2017: A program verification competition. Technical Report, Karlsruhe Reports in Informatics (2017)

13. Huisman, M., Monahan, R., Müller, P., Paskevich, A., Ernst, G.: VerifyThis 2018: A program verification competition. Technical Report, Inria (2019)

14. Huisman, M., Monahan, R., Müller, P., Poll, E.: VerifyThis 2016: A program verification competition. Technical Report TR-CTIT-16-07, Centre for Telematics and Information Technology, University of Twente, Enschede (2016)

15. Huisman, M., Klebanov, V., Monahan, R.: VerifyThis 2012. Int. J. Softw. Tools Technol. Transf. **17**(6), 647–657 (2015)

16. Huisman, M., Klebanov, V., Monahan, R., Tautschnig, M.: VerifyThis 2015: a program verification competition. Int. J. Softw. Tools Technol. Transf. **19**(6), 763–771 (2017)

17. Joshi, R., Holzmann, G.J.: A mini challenge: build a verifiable filesystem. Formal Asp. Comput. **19**(2), 269–272 (2007). https://doi.org/10.1007/s00165-006-0022-3

18. Klebanov, V., et al.: The 1st verified software competition: experience report. In: Butler, M., Schulte, W. (eds.) FM 2011. LNCS, vol. 6664, pp. 154–168. Springer, Heidelberg (2011). https://doi.org/10.1007/978-3-642-21437-0_14

19. Leavens, G.T., Baker, A.L., Ruby, C.: JML: a java modeling language. In: Formal Underpinnings of Java Workshop (at OOPSLA'1998), pp. 404–420. Citeseer (1998)

20. Huismann, M., Monti, R.E., Ulbrich, M., Weigl, A. (eds.): VerifyThis Long-term Challenge 2020. In: Proceedings of the Online-Event (Mai 2020). https://doi.org/10.5445/IR/1000119426

21. Maurica, F., Cok, D.R., Signoles, J.: Runtime assertion checking and static verification: collaborative partners. In: Margaria, T., Steffen, B. (eds.) ISoLA 2018. LNCS, vol. 11245, pp. 75–91. Springer, Cham (2018). https://doi.org/10.1007/978-3-030-03421-4_6

22. McCormick, J.W., Chapin, P.C.: Building High Integrity Applications with SPARK. Cambridge University Press, Cambridge (2015). https://doi.org/10.1017/CBO9781139629294

23. Oortwijn, W., Huisman, M., Joosten, S., van de Pol, J.: Automated verification of parallel nested DFS (2019), submitted

24. Sedgewick, R., Wayne, K.: Algorithms, 4th edn. Addison-Wesley, Amsterdam (2011)

25. Stepney, S., Cooper, D., Woodcock, J.: An Electronic Purse: Specification, Refinement and Proof. Technical Report PRG-126, Oxford University Computing Laboratory, July 2000. http://www.cs.kent.ac.uk/pubs/2000/1527

Usability Recommendations for User Guidance in Deductive Program Verification

Sarah Grebing and Mattias Ulbrich[✉]

Karlsruhe Institute of Technology, Karlsruhe, Germany
ulbrich@kit.edu

Abstract. Despite the increasing degree of automation, user input for guiding proof search and construction is still needed in interactive deductive program verification systems, even more so as the size of the investigated programs gets larger and the properties to be verified gain in complexity. We will present recommendations for the design of user interfaces in deductive program verification systems. The goal is to always provide the user with an easy but in depth understanding of the current proof status and guide him towards next expedient interactions. These recommendations are conclusions from a qualitative study with users of the KeY system and from our own experience in using and building different interactive verification systems. We will present the user study together with a summary of the main observations and insights.

1 Introduction

In recent years, methods for deductive program verification have made considerable progress, such that more and more proofs can be found automatically by verification systems. With the growing success of automatic verification engines, the programs and properties that can be formally verified become more and more sophisticated. They are likely to be part of a distributed system, to operate on complex data structures or to involve concurrency. First proof attempts for a verification task are likely to remain unfinished either because the code does not satisfy the specification or because the information given is not sufficient to guide the automation to a successful proof; a loop invariant may for instance be correct, but too weak. To proceed in the verification process, it is hence crucial for the user to be able to understand the reason for a failed proof attempt to either remedy the flaw or to provide the right guidance. Due to the mentioned rising complexity of programs and specifications fit for verification, users more and more face the challenge that they have to understand and interact on larger and more complex proof situations. It is evident that good presentation and interaction concepts are needed to allow the community to advance the boundary of feasible proofs. The main contributions of this article are design recommendations for user interaction in deductive verification systems. They

© Springer Nature Switzerland AG 2020
W. Ahrendt et al. (Eds.): Deductive Software Verification, LNCS 12345, pp. 261–284, 2020.
https://doi.org/10.1007/978-3-030-64354-6_11

are kept very general to be relevant (mostly) regardless of the analysed programming language, the specification and deduction method, or the verification interaction paradigm. The recommendations are derived from conclusions drawn from a qualitative user study that we have conducted with users of the deductive program verification system KeY [1] and from our experiences using and designing program verification systems.

Interaction in deductive program verification can be provided in several different ways and on different levels of abstraction. We introduce and discuss the different interaction paradigms used in deductive program verification systems today in Sect. 2.

The qualitative user study presented in Sect. 3 has been performed with experienced users (intermediate and expert level) of KeY. The KeY system has been explicitly designed for both automatic and interactive program verification. The goal of the user study was to learn about the typical interaction process with KeY, and how a new interaction feature can improve it. We designed the experiment as a semi-structured interview in which the participants were asked to solve small verification challenges while thinking aloud. The obtained data allowed us to build a model of the observed user interaction.

From this model, the interview transcript, and our experience with using and designing interactive systems, we distilled what we consider the five most important aspects for a successful user interaction concept and present them in the form of recommendations in Sect. 4. These recommendations are mostly concerned with the presentation of proofs to users and their possibilities to browse and advance it.

This article is by no means the first one investigating user interaction in deductive verification. We report in Sect. 5 on a number of research results on topics that are related to this article.

2   Interaction in Deductive Program Verification

The task of proving properties of programs is both a theoretically undecidable problem and in practice often hard to achieve. This has two implications: 1) there will always be correctly specified programs for which no proof can be found automatically, and 2) it is in general not possible to know if a begun proof belongs to a correct statement or cannot be closed.

While there are also more lightweight verification tasks (e.g., to search for null pointer accesses) that can often be addressed fully automatically without further user input, sophisticated properties about programs that operate on complex data structures usually require some form of user interaction to guide the verification system. This guidance can take place as annotations within the program code, within the specification, or within the logical representation of the proof. Three main styles have emerged as prominent interaction styles for proof construction today: direct manipulation, text-based/script-based, and annotation-based interaction. Some modern verification system implementations combine different interaction styles. They have a dominant interaction styles, but incorporate elements of other styles. This can be either one-directional delegation

(Why3 exports interactive obligations to Coq, for instance) or a bi-directional cooperation (like in KeYmaera X where interactive proof and proof script co-evolve).

Annotation-Based Interaction. The user interacts by adding annotations to the program source code in form of, e.g., contracts, loop invariants or ghost code. Annotations are translated into verification conditions that need to be proved. The details of this translation are hidden from the user. The prover acts like a black-box that only reports success or failure of a given annotation without providing insight into intermediate proof states.

The main advantage of this interaction paradigm is that the interaction takes place solely on the original representation of the problem. The annotations are thus comprehensible and directly linked to the source code. However, the required amount of guiding annotations in the source code may clutter it and thus reduce its comprehensibility. Another disadvantage is that, if a proof fails, there may be little insight that the user gains. The verification system may be able to produce a counterexample which witnesses that the assertion is indeed wrong and which can be presented in terms of program entities as a variable assignment (or a trace of assignments). But often, the verification fails without further information (e.g., if a timeout is hit). Then some systems may still provide tools to inspect statistics about the proof search (e.g., the number of quantifier instantiations) to allow reconsidering the annotations [16].

Examples for annotation-based verification systems are VCC [19], Dafny [34], Spec♯ [8], OpenJML [18], or Frama-C [30].

Script-Based/Text-Based Interaction. In the script-based interaction style, the user interacts with the prover using a proof language. In state-of-the-art systems, proof script languages vary between a declarative and a more imperative style. The program and its annotations have first to be encoded onto a logical representation of the proof obligation, and users interact on this encoded representation with the proof system.

The proof steps in scripts are formulated using proof commands. The proof commands that contribute to proof construction (proper proof commands) comprise calculus rules and tactics, and invocations of external solvers. Improper commands do not advance the proof, but are there for inspection purposes [46], e.g., what-if analyses or counterexample generation.

A simple text-based interaction can also be realized using a command-language interaction (CLI). Here, users provide proof commands which are directly evaluated by the verification system giving direct feedback.

The script-based interaction is a more sophisticated form of the textual interaction paradigm. Proof scripts may also contain control flow structures to combine the commands to more complex actions. The effect of an action is usually presented to the user in a text-based fashion, often only perceivable after the execution of a whole script. As a proof scripting language is a special type of programming language, constructs for modularization are incorporated which allow the user to decompose large proofs into more understandable portions. Compared to direct manipulation interaction, the proof steps can be more coarse-grained. Depending on the proof language, it is also possible to express the proof plan on a more abstract level than on the level of single calculus rule applications. However, state-of-the-art systems using text-based interaction allow only for a limited insight into the logical level of proofs, e.g., viewing intermediate proof states of built-in proof strategies is not always possible. As the proof representation and the actual proof problem are often shown to the user as two different views or representations, the user typically has to translate from the proof state back to the corresponding problem state.

Examples for script-based systems include Isabelle/HOL [40], Coq [14], or PVS [42].

Direct Manipulation Interaction. In the direct manipulation interaction style, the user interacts on the logical representation of the problem and on the *proof input artifacts*, i.e., the annotated program. The user provides the source code and its specification and lets the system transform the input into a proof obligation. Proof construction is done using the mouse by pointing onto formulas and applying calculus rules on mouse clicks. Additionally, the prover's proof search strategies can be configured and invoked by the user. The advantage of this interaction style is that the user has all necessary information available to make informed decisions about the next proof step. Interaction on the input artifacts includes that the user provides the auxiliary and requirement specification respectively corrects or adjusts the annotations or the source code. The user has full proof control in this interaction style. However, the interaction can be tedious as repetitive actions require the user to perform each interaction by clicking.

When the user encounters an error, either in the annotation or the source code, the large amount of available information makes error recovery a more time-consuming task: after correcting the error, the user needs to find the proof state again, that they examined when they discovered the error. A further difficulty for the user in this setting is that interaction takes places on two different representations – the input representation and the logical representation of the proof state. To be able to interact effectively, the user needs to relate these two representations.

Examples for verification systems that allow for direct manipulation interaction are the KeY system [1], KeYmaera X [43] or KIV [7].

3   User Study with Users of the KeY System

We performed an explorative formative user study with intermediate and expert users of the KeY system where we used interview sessions together with practical tasks.

Our goal of performing the user study was (a) to gain insight into the proof processes using the KeY system and (b) to test if improved exploration mechanisms can help the user in bridging the gap between the concrete proof state and the model of the proof. We also wanted to gain insights into further room for improvement of the target of evaluation.

3.1   Target of Evaluation

The KeY system [1] is an interactive theorem prover for the verification of properties of Java programs, in particular to establish their functional correctness and non-interference (absence of insecure information flow). The tool is open source and can be obtained from its webpage http://www.key-project.org. It is developed at the Karlsruhe Institute of Technology, the Technical University of Darmstadt and the Chalmers University of Technology in Gothenburg. KeY has recently been successfully applied to verify real world Java programs, of which two recent examples are implementations of Timsort [22] and Dual-Pivot Quicksort [13].

KeY uses Java source code as input language and as the language in which code fragments occur in dynamic logic formulas. Java programs can be annotated with annotations in the Java Modeling Language (JML) [32]. The annotated source code is then translated into a proof obligation in Java dynamic logic and discharged using a sequent calculus [12].

KeY has an explicit proof object, i.e., KeY's user interface shows a representation of the current proof where all intermediate proof states can be inspected by the user. The user interface (see Fig. 1) contains two different views on the proof state, the proof tree (①), and the node view (②), where the sequents are shown.

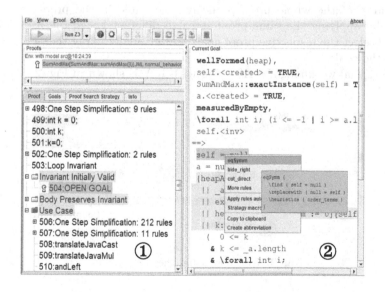

Fig. 1. User interface of the KeY system

The proof tree is a more high-level view on the proof state and contains all calculus rule-applications performed so far, as well as labels for the different proof branches in case the proof splits. Rule applications for symbolic program execution are highlighted with a different background color in the proof tree, to allow the user to distinguish these nodes from nodes where logical calculus rules have been applied. In comparison, the node view is a more detailed view and can be obtained by selecting a proof node. This view shows the (intermediate) proof obligation in the form of a textual representation of the sequent.

In its current implementation (after the user study), KeY also provides a view containing the JML-annotated Java source code (not shown in Fig. 1). After symbolic execution steps have been applied in the proof, the view highlights the code lines that have been executed symbolically in relation to a selected node in the proof tree.

Proof construction in KeY is performed only by using direct manipulation (see Fig. 1). The user points to a term of the sequent in the node view and selects it by clicking, applicable calculus rules are then shown and the user can choose the appropriate rule. If a rule application requires additional parameters, an input dialog with drag-and-drop support is presented. Additionally, KeY offers several automatic proof search strategies (also called *macro* steps).

For easy reversibility of actions, users can click onto the proof tree and undo the actions of a whole subtree easily if they encounter that the automatic strategy has performed unexpected steps that led the proof in a wrong direction. The way in which the direct manipulation interaction is implemented in KeY supports the user in focusing on one proof goal at a time, without losing the contextual information of the general proof as the information about the current state in the context of the whole proof is always accessible in the proof tree. When repeatedly applying the same proof steps to different goals, the user needs to find and select the respective proof goals and manually apply the proof steps to each of the goals.

The typical workflow of verification with KeY is shown in Fig. 2:

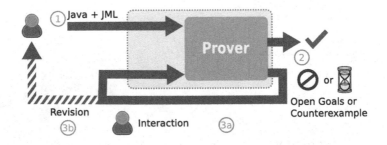

Fig. 2. Workflow using the KeY system

Initially, the user provides the proof input artifacts (step 1). After starting the automatic proof search, the result (step 2) is (a) the successful verification of the program or (b) either a counterexample or a proof with open goals that remain to be shown. In the latter case, the user may interact directly with KeY (step 3a) by interactively applying calculus rules (common examples are quantifier instantiations or logical cuts). Alternatively, the user may revise the program or specification (step 3b). Often, verifying programs in KeY involves both kinds of interactions, interspersed by automated proof search.

3.2 Methodology: Interviews with Practical Tasks

As evaluation method we used semi-structured interviews, in which mainly open-ended questions have been asked. In a structured interview, the interviewer has a script that contains the questions that will be asked *exactly* as noted. Semi-structured interviews are more flexible: the interviewer is allowed to explore topics raised by participants without having to exactly comply to the script. The participants' responses have been recorded for later analysis. Compared to questionnaire-based query methods, an advantage of semi-structured interviews is that the interviewer was able to react flexibly to the participants' responses if an answer was unclear or more detail to an issue was desired.

We enriched the interviews by adding tasks and scenarios. Users had to perform verification tasks in different variants of the investigated verification system. This allowed exploring opinions and expectations of participants towards the presented artifacts and highlighted possibilities for improvement. While performing the tasks users were repeatedly encouraged to *think-aloud*, i.e., to verbalize which actions they performed and why they were performing them.

We included tasks in the interviews where the users were only able to use a limited set of KeY's features – features that do not change the proof state. The key idea behind this limitation was to explore whether all information for estimating and assessing the current proof state is presented by the system, such that the user does not need to modify the proof state for exploration reasons.

We also included tasks where the users were able to use a mocked implementation of a new interaction mechanism that showed them information about the history of formulas during proof construction (described in [25]). The key idea here was to explore whether this new view on the proof state is helpful in the comprehension and estimation of the current proof without the need of changing the proof state.

To avoid experimenter-bias, the interview was carried out by a student assistant (master-level) possessed an understanding of the basic concepts of the KeY system and of formal verification in general, but was not involved in the design of the user study[1]. Thus, the interview was naturally focussed on more fundamental questions rather than drifting into technical details (which might have happened if a domain or tool expert had asked the questions). Moreover, since the designer of the study did not ask the questions directly, the dangers of suggestive formulations or of forcing the discussion into a direction, were actively reduced.

---

[1] A discussion of the experiences with a setup in which a non-expert interviewer mitigates the experimenter-bias can also be found in [10,11].

On the other hand, this setup also is susceptible to errors in the interview itself, e.g., in cases where the interviewer does not notice that a participant got stuck or does not recognise a fundamental problem in the course of action. To overcome this potential weakness, the test manager was part of the team, but was only allowed to interfere if a technical issue arose.

In the following we will briefly present some details on the design of the user study, the participants and the evaluation method. A more detailed description can be found in [25].

Participants. The profile of an ideal user for our study is someone who uses the KeY system in their daily work and is not part of the KeY development team. We recruited intermediate and expert users of the system, as novice users may not yet have mastered the learning curve of the KeY system and may not have the necessary domain knowledge to use the program verification system effectively. Had we included novice users in the user study, we would have moved the focus of the usability of the system towards its learnability.

However, users with the desired profile are rare. Firstly, KeY is a system being developed in academia where its purpose is also to showcase new research results in software verification. Therefore, KeY users are often also KeY developers. Secondly, KeY is a sophisticated system with many powerful functionalities which expect a high level of expertise and experience on the user's part. These two conditions already limit the user base drastically, compared to a study on general purpose software systems. With our requirement to only include intermediate and expert users, we limit the chance of finding suitable participants even more.

We therefore loosened the criteria for the selection of participants by allowing users who used the system for case studies. Additionally, we also allowed participants to take part in the study who develop at the core of the system or extensions of the system. We are aware that these participants can be biased in their opinions about specific parts of the system. However, to be able to extend the system with new methods a certain knowledge about the usage of the system and the domain is necessary and in many cases these participants used the system for the verification of programs (e.g., in case studies) before.

The loosened selection criteria for participants have been the following:

- intermediate or expert user of KeY,
- (daily) usage of KeY for program verification tasks or case studies, and
- part of the KeY development team.

We have been able to recruit nine participants. This number may seem rather small, especially if compared with user studies for general purpose software systems. However, the number was sufficient for performing an explorative study where the goal was to study the context of use, to uncover issues in using the system and to assess the effectiveness of a newly introduced feature (described below). To make statistically significant propositions about the usability of the system or perform a summative user study, a quantitative study would have been required.

Test-Design and Script-Design. We planned a session time of approximately 70 min for each interview session. We structured the usability test into different phases[2]: introduction, warm-up task, and cool-down phase. In the *introduction phase* the users were interviewed by the moderator about their experiences using the KeY system. The *warm-up phase* started with an interview about the proof process of the participants using the KeY system. Then the participants were asked to specify and verify a Java method within the time frame of 10–15 min. We did not restrict the usage of system features in the warm-up phase. Our intention for this phase was to get insight into how users of KeY use the KeY system to find a proof.

Based on the focus group discussions presented in [10,11,25], we prototypically implemented a mechanism to support the display of the origin of a formula in the KeY system: It allowed the user to select a formula in the open goal and retrieve the path from the open goal to the original proof obligation in which the formula was affected by rule applications, in the following also called *origin of a formula*. Our intention with this mechanism was to support users to bridge the gap between the user's model of the proof and the current proof presented in KeY, as the user is able to trace back the history of a selected formula and see the changes during the proof process. A more detailed description of this mechanism can be found in [25].

The main part of the interview session was a task phase, in which users should explore the mock-up version of the newly created feature that allows one to locate the origin of an expression within the open goal. We divided this phase into four tasks: The users were challenged with (a) partial first-order logic proofs (with obfuscated symbol names) and (b) partial correctness proofs for a method contract. Both tasks had to be conducted once with the help of the origin-location mechanism and once without.

The questions were for all four tasks identical: The user should describe the proof situation, they should name the history of two formulas of the open goal and name the next step to continue the proof process. At the end of the task phase the users were asked about their expectations about parent formulas of a given formula and proof.

In the *cool-down* phase participants were interviewed again about the new mechanism, the origin of a formula feature, and possible application areas in the context of proving a program correct. Furthermore, we asked about room for improvement of the verification system.

As the task of specifying and verifying a piece of software may have a large completion time, we chose

1. to leave out the specification task,
2. to present partially finished proofs to the participants (explaining them the situation in the proof process), and

---

[2] See https://formal.iti.kit.edu/~grebing/SWC/ for the full script in German and [25] for a more detailed description of the user study.

3. not to wait until the users successfully finish the proof. We rather stopped the task either when an error was found, a subtask was successfully closed or the threshold time for the task was reached.

3.3 Data Analysis Methodology

To evaluate the interview part of the study, we used qualitative content analysis, similar to the methods described by Kuckartz [31]. We used an inductive categorization: we started by associating the given answers to the questions and in the context of the posed question we categorized the answers. The inductive categories were formed alongside with the script and the comments by the participants.

To analyze the participants' interactions with the tool (during the aforementioned tasks), we chose to use sequence models to capture the sequences of actions we observed during the study. These per-user sequence models were aggregated for all participants to a single large sequence model by assigning categories to sequence of actions capturing the intents of the users. For example, assume a user selected a formula on the sequent, selected a specific rule, and then applied this selected rule. This specific sequence of actions was abstracted to the category *Interactive Proof Search*[3].

4 Recommendations for Interactive Program Verification Systems

One starting point for determining the requirements for interactive program verification systems is to identify the main activities and phases when proving programs correct – such as formalizing requirements, developing a coarse proof plan or analysing a single proof goal with the intention to establish the next proof command. Given the proof activities of the user, each of these activities can be analyzed w.r.t. which properties make the activity challenging and abstract mechanisms for user support can already be sketched. Our user studies described in Sect. 3 provide further input for this analysis.

The answers to our interview questions and the observations of the user interactions provided indications that lead to the following requirements for an interactive deductive program verification system. Along with the user study as a source for evidence also our long-term experiences in building and using program verification systems lead to the following requirements:

Recommendation 1. *Partition proof obligations into understandable subtasks.*

Observation: *Users struggle with localizing the problem in case of a failed proof attempt.*

---

[3] Examples for (consolidated) sequence models from the user study can be found in [25].

Any failing proof attempt is a frustrating event. In general, it is unclear if the specification does indeed not hold or if the verification system is too weak to close the proof. For a productive work with the verifier, it is important to recover as soon as possible. Experience shows that finding the location within the program to which a failed proof attempt corresponds is essential for being able to understand the proof state, and thus for being able to analyse the situation, act and eventually recover. Usually, this location is represented by the sequence of statements (the partial program path) executed prior to a failed assertion. In the studies, it became apparent that for many participants, a considerable amount of the available time was spent for such localisations.

The control flow structure of the program can be used to naturally divide the proof obligation into subtasks. In this context, the aspects that localize a subtask in the program are:

1. the statement where symbolic execution ended,
2. its program path,
3. the type of the unproved assertion (e.g., nullpointer check, postcondition, . . .), and
4. a counterexample with concrete values for variables (if available).

In cases where the program or the specification contain a flaw, an inspection of the concerned localized pieces of specification and code often allow identifying that flaw rather quickly without having to look into the proof. It seems that once the user's attention has been drawn to the right spot, looking for an expected (and locally fixable) problem is a lot more promising than without the localization.

In our experience, the observations can be transferred to the situation where the proof is possible in principle, but cannot be found due an incompleteness in proof automation. Understanding the location and reason of the failure is important to be able to provide guiding user input accordingly.

Many deductive verification engines rely on the weakest precondition calculus to produce verification conditions. They can either emit individual separate verification conditions for each assertion or one large condition integrating all aspects of a method contract verification. The user interaction concept of the verification system Why3, for instance, supports the latter mode (which may be faster if it works). In case of a failing method verification, the user can decide to produce numerous smaller conditions and verify them independently to start their analysis of the situation.

Recommendation 2. *Provide different views onto proof artifacts and put the views into relation.*

Observation: *Users alternate between proof state and program when inspecting the proof (state).*

For program verification proofs, the program code and its specification have to be brought together (possibly with more artifacts like mathematical theories or data type definitions). Both for proof comprehension and for proof construction, it is important to understand the relation between elements in these different domains to be able to successfully guide the verification tool. Although the proof state presentation in our user study contained all necessary information from the different domains, the study showed that users switched between the source code of the program (together with the specification) and the proof state presentation back and forth. This indicates that an integrated domain-spanning presentation is difficult to interpret and that instead the interplay of presentations from the different domains should be improved. This is important because switching between two different presentations requires a context switch which demands efforts from the user to regain orientation.

Two of the factors that make proof comprehension a challenging task are (a) the large size of proof representations (both of single proof states, and of the overall proof) and (b) the fact that program verification proofs contain information about the program and the mathematical logical proof interwoven. For example, in KeY all information is intentionally presented in a uniform syntax in the proof state in dynamic logic such that the user can advance the proof state with uniform rules. At the same time, in large proofs, it is challenging for the user to differentiate between both kinds of information.

This interweaving of information is not an issue specific to the KeY system, rather it is a peculiarity of the problem and task domain. The amount of information presented is large on the global, as well as on the local level: the proof tree contains a large amount of proof steps and each sequent can contain a large amount of formulas, sometimes filling several screens. Furthermore, the formulas on the sequent can each become large and complex in their structure, e.g., formulas that formalize the heap contents. The information structure therefore requires the user to search through a lot of information to identify the relevant information for the next promising step.

Instead of mixing the presentation of the different domain artifacts, like program code and logical representation in one sequent, as it was the case in the verification system under evaluation, it is also possible to show the domain artifacts separately. This separation of the different domain artifacts allows one to use already existing tailor-made interaction concepts and supporting functionalities for the construction and comprehension of these artifacts – integrated development environments for interacting with source code is one example for software systems that support the user with functionalities such as syntax highlighting, structuring the source code into more manageable modules and collapsing and unfolding of structured elements (loops, methods, functions, . . .).

Another important aspect of proof presentation became apparent in the user study through the observed user intents when switching between the different domain artifacts: relating the components of the currently visible proof state to the program and the specification. Besides trying to relate the symbols occurring in the proof state with elements of the program or specification, furthermore, users tried to match the proof tree against program execution paths.

The relations between the domain artifacts and dependencies between components are often implicit and users need to keep them in mind while proving or invest resources to search for these dependencies. These hidden dependencies, as they are called by Blackwell and Green [15], should be made visible to the user.

In our user study for example, we observed that the participants searched for the relation between the proof state in KeY and the annotated program in a text editor for the proof construction task as well as for the task where the proof state had to be explained to the moderator. To simplify this task, KeY provides proof search strategies that focus either on performing logical steps or on the steps that perform symbolic execution.

Based on these observations concerning the presentation of different domain artifacts in program verification systems we recommend that:

1. the different domain artifacts can be shown on the screen at the same time,
2. the different domain artifacts can be presented in their domain-specific manner (e.g., the program source code in a presentation similar to an IDE), and
3. the verification system can point out the relation between the corresponding domain artifacts in different presentations explicitly (e.g. by highlighting).

The recommendation about the presentation of artifacts also follows a guideline for general theorem prover interfaces, where it is advised that multiple views on the proof state should be given to the user to support the user in the complex task of theorem proving [20]. Similarly, this principle can also be formed for software debugging systems, where different views are used to present a potentially complex and large program state to the user. With the help of these views in software verification systems, users could focus on their preferred representation of information in the current proof situation. Going beyond that, to enable the user to flexibly switch contexts as necessary and to adhere to the usability principle of customizability, users should be able to request these views (or remove them from the screen) at any time to choose the amount and type of information suitable for the current task of the verification process.

Structuring the proof state into different views allows the user to focus on specific parts of the proof problem: either on the general structure of the proof in relation to the program or on single proof goals. We propose at least one view each onto the source code, the specification, the current proof state, and a view containing an abstract overview of the proof, e.g., a proof tree or a similar representation.

The different proposed views we consider for program verification should allow the user to maintain the relation between the program and the proof obligation by providing means to inspect the relations between the different proof artifacts shown in the views. This contributes to the principle of displaying only relevant information to the user according to Eastaughffe [20] – by separating the interwoven information, the user is able to focus on the relevant information by choosing the preferred view.

Following these recommendations results in the ability to construct proofs using different interaction styles, which follows the usability principle of flexibility. This principle was also identified by Easthaughffe to be an important feature of theorem provers. According to this principle, different views should help the user to form different models of the proof task, to be able to choose the most appropriate one for deciding the next goal-directed action.

Recommendation 3. *Provide means to hide details where necessary and allow stepwise refinement.*

Observation: *Users abstracted from details of the proof state (in particular, the proof tree) to gain an overview and stepwise refined to specific parts of the proof state (in particular branching nodes and leaves of the proof tree).*

In the user study, a central point of investigation was how participants retrieve information from the presentation in KeY. For gaining the orientation, all information is presented, as described in the last section; however, the user is overwhelmed by the amount of information. The relevant information is not clearly visible at first sight. Each participant followed their own process to identify parts of the proof state to the mental model, e.g., to the annotated program.

One reoccurring pattern was that participants zoomed into the proof from an overview to individual proof nodes or even to single formulas. The revelation of relevant information was often an unanticipated result (for the user) in this process. One example from our user study, where this became apparent, occurred while users searched for hints for the next action by scrolling through the proof tree.

One further conclusion from this observation is that we recommend that the user be supported in their efforts by adequate search functionalities in the verification tool. As an reaction to the user study, we have implemented that and a highlighting functionality that allows one or adapt the formula presentation according to a search expression.

A second observable pattern was that participants investigated specifically selected nodes (following their personal exploration strategies). We assume that they selected those nodes that gave them reference points that helped them to search for more details and to relate this to other nodes. These reference points are often nodes that have a direct relation to the proof input artifacts. The information retrieval in the user study was a time-consuming task and showed that there is still room for improvement. Different types of information that should be presented separately to support the users' mental models are presented interwoven with each other, as also described in Recommendation 2.

As presented in the last section, the large amount of information and the interweaving of the different kinds of information may result in situations where users might abandon the proof and restart it with a different proof search strategy. For example, one participant lost the overview of the proof and stated that they would start the proof process over again using a different interaction strategy (by invoking the macro "Autopilot") and proceeding with manual steps afterwards.

As a conclusion of our observations we recommend that a user should have the possibility to gain an abstract overview of the proof and the proof progress as well as the possibility to focus on specific parts of the open proof to be able to inspect these parts in isolation. One example, how such user support may be achieved is implemented in the verification prototype DIVE [23]. This system provides different views onto the proof and the proof state and allows shifting from an abstract overview to the single verification conditions and the proof script.

The first view the system presents to the user contains an overview of all verification conditions together with information about their context in terms of methods and classes. Furthermore, the user has access to information about the proof state of each verification condition (*closed*, *open*, or *needs attention*, because a change in the proof obligation has occurred and invalidated old proofs). The user can choose a verification condition and the system switches/shifts views such that the user is able to inspect the proof state and at a later stage also the proof script.

Together with the different, related views on the proof from Recommendation 2, users should be able to trace relations between the contents of the proof state and other domain artifacts and access further information to these artifacts if requested.

Recommendation 4. *Allow using a combination of different interaction styles.*

Observation: *The way users construct proofs is highly dependent on the problem at hand and the user's preferences.*

A verification system that builds on a general logical calculus usually has many ways in which a proof can be conducted. Moreover an interactive system often allows its users to reach a goal by performing different interaction steps. KeY as such a system has many degrees of freedom for gaining orientation in the proof or advancing it.

Some tasks in our user study required the users to construct a (partial) proof or to gain orientation in a partial proof. In the course of the user study we were not able to identify a single, uniform course of action that all participants would follow. The way in which our participants interacted with the proof system differed according to the type of the proof problem, the users' preferences, their experiences with KeY and their expectations about the situation at hand.

Conclusions from the user study and our experiences in using different verification systems are that software verification systems should offer alternative interaction styles to the user for proof construction and that switching between these styles should be *seamless*. This recommendation adheres to the usability principle of substitutivity of interactions which states that a user should have different ways to perform the same interactions.

One example from the user study for which users desired improvements and where a combination of different interaction styles would have been helpful was the repeated application of similar proof steps to different proof states. In particular, one possibility to improve interaction in this case would be to combine script-based interaction with direct manipulation. One way to leverage the benefits of both interaction styles would be that the initial interaction on a proof state is given by the user via direct manipulation, after which a proof script is automatically constructed from this direct manipulation interaction. This textual representation of the action can then be edited further by the user, e.g., to include repetitive application to other proof states.

This combination of interaction styles would also support users when they try to regain the orientation in a proof after changing the proof input artifacts and reloading proofs. A text-based presentation of a proof in form of a script together with debugging features like breakpoints and stepping functionalities improve orientation in the proof [24]. Furthermore, users can then also formulate proof-specific script macros which then may be reused on different proof branches, easing repetitive interactions.

Recommendation 5. *Provide support for explorative actions and easy reversion of actions.*

Observation: *Finding the right specification and to perform a closed proof is an iterative process.*

At the beginning of a proof, the user may have a rough proof plan, but does not yet know which exact proof strategy will lead to a closed proof. One option to find a proof is by *explorative actions* (i.e., learning by "trial-and-error"). In our user study, we were able to observe actions where users tried different proof strategies in KeY and reverted them after inspection of the resulting proof states. A further observation in the study was that users performed a stepwise refinement of the specification and used the tool to validate the result. We therefore argue that such explorative actions should be supported by an interactive proof system, especially since this helps the user identifying the right strategy for the proof. A similar problem occurs already when performing mathematical proofs with pen and paper. One strategy for mathematicians when dealing with unfinished proofs, is to use explorative actions to determine promising proof steps. Such actions can be side-calculations with concrete values or adding assumptions and proceeding with the proof process in order to determine whether these changes would result in a complete proof. Evidence for this trial-and-error approach can also be found in an interview with Gert Faltings presented in [36], where it was stated that in some cases proof search also contain trial-and-error phases, if the mathematician does not know directly how to proceed. Explorative actions are also often performed after considerable progress in the proof, when the user has already familiarised with a proof situation. In the local context users can then, e.g., try out different alternatives or instantiate concrete expressions for variables.

We recommend that in order to support this task, the user needs the possibility to perform sequences of trial-and-error actions. These actions have to be easily reversible, e.g., the user has to be able to recover previous proof states. Furthermore, keeping track of the user's actions should be mandatory for the system, e.g., by an interactive log containing the explorative actions. An interactive log allows users to reconsider previously applied explorative actions, also after reverting them, and furthermore allows to reapply actions after discovering that previously explored actions could be more promising.

One exemplary idea for a proof exploration mechanism is presented in [25] for the KeY system. The user has the possibility to engage a proof exploration mode. In this mode, the user can change the proof state arbitrarily (outside the laws of the logic) to perform a *"what-if" analysis* on the modified proof state. After this changing the proof state into a hypothetical proof goal, the user can continue the proof in the usual manner. If the proof branch where the changes had been applied could be closed, the user has learned that their presumption was correct and could now trace back the changes performed prior to the hypothetical proof in order to apply them to the proof input artifacts. If the changes did not lead to a successful proof, the user can access the changes in the interaction log of KeY and revert the changes to find back to the proof state from where the proof exploration mode started. KeY supports this orientation further by highlighting the proof nodes where exploration steps had been performed to.

5   Related Work

While we focused on program verification systems in this article, concerning related work we will also take into consideration the closely related domain of interactive theorem provers. Recommendations for systems of either domain may be similar and can be applied to the respective counterpart, however in some cases the recommendations may differ where the peculiarities of the domains of importance.

The first part of this section is concerned with publications giving recommendations for usability guidelines or usability principles for general interactive theorem provers, partly based on conclusions from usability evaluations.

One type of usability evaluation are questionnaire-based, e.g., using Green and Petre's Cognitive Dimensions questionnaire [15]. Two examples for work based on this questionnaire are the evaluation of different proof systems to develop a list of desirable features for educational theorem provers by Kadoda, Stone, and Diaper [29], as well as the evaluation of the KeY system in previous work [9].

Other evaluation methods include recording and inspecting user interactions, followed with user interviews, like the work of Aitken et al. [2–4] who evaluated the HOL theorem prover and the proof assistant Isabelle in collaboration with HCI experts. The goal of this work was to study the activities performed by users of interactive provers during the proof process to obtain an interaction model of the users. In their work the authors propose to use typical user errors as usability metric and they compared provers w.r.t. these errors. Based on the results, suggestions for improvements of the systems have been proposed, such as improved search mechanisms and improved access to certain proof-relevant components.

Hentschel, Hähnle, and Bubel [27] empirically evaluated two different user interfaces for the KeY system, the traditional interface and an interface similar to a software debugger with focus on the proof input artifacts. The focus of the user study was on comparing the interfaces regarding their support to understand the proof state. Similar to our observations they describe that users searched for the relation between the proof state and annotated program.

Merriam and Harrison [37,38] have evaluated interfaces of three theorem provers: CADiZ, IMPS and PVS. In this work they have identified four key activities in the interactive proof process where the user needs support from the proof system: planning, reuse, reflection and articulation. The three theorem provers have been examined with respect to these activities. Based on these results, gaps in user support of the theorem provers have been identified as well as points in the systems' interfaces where the user can make errors that cost a lot of time to recover from.

Völker [44] published a position paper on requirements and design issues of user interfaces for provers. He presented difficulties in the design of user interfaces of theorem provers developed in academia, including that focusing on the design of user interfaces is a time-consuming task and little reward is given for building elaborated user interfaces. The focus of this work was on theorem provers of the HOL family and PVS and included a requirement analysis based on scenarios using the scenario method and resulted in a high-level description of the interaction with the proof system to build requirements for theorem prover user interfaces.

Ouimet and Lundqvist [41] evaluated the system ESC/Java against identified issues that have to be addressed in order to have a widespread use of theorem provers, e.g., the large proof size and number of proof steps.

Further examples for the usability evaluation of proof assistants and proof planners using different evaluation methods include, e.g., the CLAM proof planner [28], the Alloy Analyzer [45] or NuPRL [17].

The second part of this section presents related work on usability guidelines and considerations on the usability of interactive theorem provers, partly resulting in the implementation of user interfaces.

Usability guidelines for tactic-based interactive theorem provers include providing different complementary views of the proof construction with the possibility to choose among them, offering meaningful operations on each view, the flexibility of proof commands and the focus on relevant information for the user [20].

Similarly to complementary views, Völker [44] suggested to offer complementary interaction styles, i.e., text-based as well as graphical interaction in cases there is no clear advantage for either of both interaction styles. Additionally, he identified requirements for usable theorem prover user interfaces contributing to the principle of *least effort*: Examples include auto-completion for proof commands or filtering information to ease the identification of relevant information for making decisions in the proof process.

Lowe et al. [35] present undesirable features of interactive theorem provers focusing on feedback of the system and describe their approach to building a co-operative theorem prover. In their work they have implemented an interface, called BARNACLE, for the CLAM prover. CLAM allows explanations for failing and succeeding preconditions of tactics, which should make proofs more comprehensible for the users. To allow for more human-readable explanations the authors have reconstructed the explanations of CLAM for BARNACLE.

Archer and Heitmeyer [5] have developed the TAME interface on top of the prover PVS to reduce the distance between manual proofs and proofs by automation. TAME is able to prove properties of timed automata using so called *human-style reasoning*. Proof steps in TAME are intended to be close to the large proof steps performed in manual proofs. The authors have developed strategies on top of the PVS strategies that match more closely the steps performed by humans. The goal is to provide evidence and comprehension of proofs for domain but not proof experts.

In the work of Goguen [21], three user roles that can be represented by one single user have been identified: the prover, the reader and the specifier. Each of these roles has different requirements for the interactive proof system and some of the requirements can be conflicting. The author claims that users of theorem provers need precise feedback on the failure of a proof attempt at the (sub)goal level. Goguen presented a proof approach where users should form the high-level proof plan and leave the "low-level computations" to the automatic prover is presented. Alongside, a user interface for the proof assistance tool Kumo was implemented.

There are different opinions in the related work about the benefits of offering the user a visual representation of the proof tree. While it can serve as an aid for orientation and abstraction [20], also evidence for being not helpful was assembled in [44]. Similarly, Goguen [21] argues that an unstructured proof tree is not easy to use as the users need to orient themselves in the proof tree.

In this last part of related work we will take a look at examples of verification systems and interactive theorem provers that already include parts of the recommendations for good usability or are designed according to usability principles. In the description of the systems we focus on those parts that are relevant to our suggested usability recommendations.

One example for a system combining direct manipulation as well as text-based interaction for proof construction is KeYmaera X [39]. The design of the user interface is based on existing work on general usability guidelines, HCI principles and requirements for user interfaces of theorem provers. These findings and principles are extended or specialized for the combination of direct manipulation with text-based user interaction in the domain of program verification. The user interaction and user interface of KeYmaera X follows the principles *familiarity, traceability, tutoring, flexibility* and *experimentation* [39]. Proof exploration is supported by using different functionalities: Users can retrieve suggestions for rule applications and a detailed view containing information about state changes when applying a rule. Furthermore, counterexamples and simulations can be generated. The current proof state is represented in a tabbed view, where each tab contains the sequent of an open goal. However, instead of a proof tree, deduction paths are shown in KeYmaera X, which can be retrieved by step-wise expanding details of the path in a tab, starting at the open goal.

This solution also allows focusing on the different steps on a proof branch. With progressing proof, this view may become cluttered as a deduction path may contain a large number of proof steps. Structuring of proof goals is also possible in KeYmaera X: users can change the sequent view by hiding formulas.

Concerning our recommendation to be able to inspect relations between proof artifacts, KeY supports the user in this task by depicting the relation between the proof input artifacts, the source code and the proof state, in an additional window. This feature was implemented in the KeY system in response to our user study presented in this work.

Why3 provides an overview of the proof progress and the hierarchical structure of a proof by depicting the verification conditions and their proof status. It is possible to use different means to discharge the proof verification conditions. Besides the use of SMT solvers, it is possible to perform interactive verification using the Coq system [14]. The relation between the verification conditions and the proof input artifacts is presented by highlighting relevant statements in the proof input artifacts. The relation between the formula in Coq and the proof input artifacts gets lost during transformation. Furthermore, the user needs to switch between two systems and thus two user interfaces – Why3 and Coq – which requires the user to gain orientation and to perform a context switch, which may be cognitively challenging.

Auto-active software verification systems, such as VCC [19] and Dafny [33], provide the feedback of the proof attempt on the program level. In these systems with their integration into an IDE the relation to the proof input artifacts is directly visible for the user. Users retrieve information about conditions that do not hold on specific program locations and retrieve the values of variables for a program path for inspection.

The KIV verification system [7,26] presents different views with different purposes to the user. The user has access to the proof tree, the current goal, editors for the theorems and the specification as well as managing the theorem base. Each view should support users in specific tasks, thus each view contains actions and features that are necessary for the specific task, e.g., the current goal view shows the applicable rules and has context-sensitive support for rule application using direct manipulation.

Similar to the KeY system, the representation of the proof object in KIV is the proof tree which is the central structure for proof comprehension and proof construction. KIV allows for direct manipulation with context-sensitive rule suggestions, similar to KeY. KIV contains a correctness management that takes care of the dependencies affected by changes of theorems and lemmas supporting users in the iterative proof process. KIV is integrated into the IDE Eclipse, which allows one to use the usual support for writing code.

The two general-purpose interactive theorem provers Isabelle/HOL [40] and Coq [14] natively offer text-based interaction for proof construction and are extended by elements that allow direct manipulation. In both systems the script serves as focus for proof construction and feedback to the user is given by presenting goal states and icons in the editor's gutters or by color coding. The user is able to gain insight into the way proofs are constructed by step-wise executing the proof script and being able to revert script commands. Proof navigation can be performed by clicking on the proof script statement. The approach of Coq additionally allows the user to apply tactics using point-and-click similar to KeY.

For the general purpose theorem prover Isabelle the additional user interface PGWin [6] also allows for a combination of the two interaction styles text-based and direct manipulation interaction. This interface is a combination of two existing interfaces of Isabelle. The direct manipulation interface IsaWin that follows a notepad metaphor and iconifies domain elements was combined with the proof management interface ProofGeneral. PGWin as the combination contains both representations – the proof text and the iconified representation. The user can choose which representation to use to construct proofs.

6   Conclusion

Despite recent advances, program verification of sophisticated functional properties for non-trivial programs remains a challenging and time-consuming task that requires some form of user inspection and interaction. In this article, we presented central recommendations for the design of user guidance in interactive program verifiers based on the observations of a user study that we conducted

The study revealed that one central issue for interaction in program verification is the large amount of potentially relevant information from different sources available during the proof. Moreover, it became apparent during the user study that there is no single, general proof process or interaction concept that all users follow. Instead the proof process depended on individual preferences and on the verification task at hand. The user study supported the prevalent notion that program verification can be characterized by a series of many iterations of failed proof attempts, either leading to changes in the program or specification, or to a successful proof.

Consequently, the five recommendations made in this article suggests that interactive program verifiers should

- *decompose tasks and presented information*
  by dividing proof obligations into subtasks and presenting proof states separated into multiple views,
- *support different personal interaction preferences*
  by allowing a combination of different interaction styles, providing different views on the state, and supporting information abstraction and refinement, and
- *make an effort to make proving understandable*
  by supporting proof inspections (via views, counterexamples, abstractions) and proof exploration (via hypothetical proof modification).

The user study has been conducted based on the (semi-)interactive program verifier KeY, but the obtained results and recommendations have been generalised such that they can also be applied to other solvers.

References

1. Ahrendt, W., Beckert, B., Bubel, R., Hähnle, R., Schmitt, P.H., Ulbrich, M. (eds.): Deductive Software Verification - The KeY Book: From Theory to Practice, LNCS, vol. 10001. Springer (2016). https://doi.org/10.1007/978-3-319-49812-6
2. Aitken, J.S., Gray, P., Melham, T., Thomas, M.: Interactive theorem proving: an empirical study of user activity. J. Symbolic Comp. **25**(2), 263–284 (1998)
3. Aitken, J.S., Melham, T.F.: An analysis of errors in interactive proof attempts. Interact. Comput. **12**(6), 565–586 (2000)
4. Aitken, S., Gray, P., Melham, T., Thomas, M.: A study of user activity in interactive theorem proving. In: Task Centred Approaches To Interface Design, pp. 195–218. Dept. of Computing Science (1995), gIST Technical Report G95.2
5. Archer, M., Heitmeyer, C.: Human-style theorem proving using PVS. In: Gunter, E.L., Felty, A. (eds.) TPHOLs 1997. LNCS, vol. 1275, pp. 33–48. Springer, Heidelberg (1997). https://doi.org/10.1007/BFb0028384
6. Aspinall, D., Lüth, C.: Proof general meets isawin: combining text-based and graphical user interfaces. Electr. Notes Theor. Comput. Sci. **103**, 3–26 (2004). https://doi.org/10.1016/j.entcs.2004.09.011
7. Balser, M., Reif, W., Schellhorn, G., Stenzel, K., Thums, A.: Formal system development with KIV. In: Maibaum, T. (ed.) FASE 2000. LNCS, vol. 1783, pp. 363–366. Springer, Heidelberg (2000). https://doi.org/10.1007/3-540-46428-X_25
8. Barnett, M., Leino, K.R.M., Schulte, W.: The spec# programming system: an overview. In: Barthe, G., Burdy, L., Huisman, M., Lanet, J.-L., Muntean, T. (eds.) CASSIS 2004. LNCS, vol. 3362, pp. 49–69. Springer, Heidelberg (2005). https://doi.org/10.1007/978-3-540-30569-9_3
9. Beckert, B., Grebing, S.: Evaluating the usability of interactive verification system. In: Proceedings, 1st International Workshop on Comparative Empirical Evaluation of Reasoning Systems (COMPARE), Manchester, UK, June 30, 2012. CEUR Workshop Proceedings, vol. 873, pp. 3–17. CEUR-WS.org (2012). http://ceur-ws.org/Vol-873
10. Beckert, B., Grebing, S., Böhl, F.: How to put usability into focus: Using focus groups to evaluate the usability of interactive theorem provers. In: Benzmüller, C., Paleo, B.W. (eds.) Proceedings Eleventh Workshop on User Interfaces for Theorem Provers, Vienna, Austria, 17th July 2014. Electronic Proceedings in Theoretical Computer Science, vol. 167, pp. 4–13. Open Publishing Association (2014). https://doi.org/10.4204/EPTCS.167.3
11. Beckert, B., Grebing, S., Böhl, F.: A usability evaluation of interactive theorem provers using focus groups. In: Canal, C., Idani, A. (eds.) SEFM 2014. LNCS, vol. 8938, pp. 3–19. Springer, Cham (2015). https://doi.org/10.1007/978-3-319-15201-1_1
12. Beckert, B., Klebanov, V., Schlager, S.: Dynamic logic. In: Beckert, B., Hähnle, R., Schmitt, P.H. (eds.) Verification of Object-Oriented Software. The KeY Approach. LNCS (LNAI), vol. 4334, pp. 69–177. Springer, Heidelberg (2007). https://doi.org/10.1007/978-3-540-69061-0_3
13. Beckert, B., Schiffl, J., Schmitt, P.H., Ulbrich, M.: Proving JDK's dual pivot quicksort correct. In: Paskevich, A., Wies, T. (eds.) VSTTE 2017. LNCS, vol. 10712, pp. 35–48. Springer, Cham (2017). https://doi.org/10.1007/978-3-319-72308-2_3
14. Bertot, Y., Castran, P.: Interactive Theorem Proving and Program Development: Coq'Art The Calculus of Inductive Constructions. Texts in Theoretical Computer Science An EATCS Series, 1st edn. Springer, Berlin (2004). https://doi.org/10.1007/978-3-662-07964-5

15. Blackwell, A., Green, T.R.: A cognitive dimensions questionnaire (v. 5.1.1). www.cl.cam.ac.uk/~afb21/CognitiveDimensions/CDquestionnaire.pdf, Feb 2007
16. Bormer, T.: Advancing Deductive Program-Level Verification for Real-World Application: Lessons Learned from an Industrial Case Study. Ph.D. thesis, Karlsruhe Institute of Technology (2014). https://doi.org/10.5445/IR/1000049792
17. Cheney, J.: Project report - theorem prover usability. Technical report (2001). http://homepages.inf.ed.ac.uk/jcheney/projects/tpusability.ps, report of project COMM 64
18. Cok, D.R.: OpenJML: JML for Java 7 by extending OpenJDK. In: Bobaru, M., Havelund, K., Holzmann, G.J., Joshi, R. (eds.) NFM 2011. LNCS, vol. 6617, pp. 472–479. Springer, Heidelberg (2011). https://doi.org/10.1007/978-3-642-20398-5_35
19. Dahlweid, M., Moskal, M., Santen, T., Tobies, S., Schulte, W.: VCC: Contract-based modular verification of concurrent C
20. Easthaughffe, K.A.: Support for interactive theorem proving: some design principles and their application. User Interfaces for Theorem Provers (UITP 1998) (1998)
21. Goguen, J.: Social and semiotic analyses for theorem prover user interface design. Formal Aspects Comput. **11**, 11–272 (1999)
22. de Gouw, S., Rot, J., de Boer, F.S., Bubel, R., Hähnle, R.: OpenJDK's java.utils.collection.sort() is broken: the good, the bad and the worst case. In: Computer Aided Verification - 27th International Conference, CAV 2015, San Francisco, CA, USA, July 18–24, 2015, Proceedings, Part I. pp. 273–289 (2015)
23. Grebing, S., Klamroth, J., Ulbrich, M.: Seamless interactive program verification. In: 11th Working Conference on Verified Software: Theories, Tools, and Experiments (VSTTE 2019) (July 2019, to appear)
24. Grebing, S., Luong, A.T.T., Weigl, A.: Adding text-based interaction to a direct-manipulation interface for program verification - lessons learned. In: Jamnik, M., Lüth, C. (eds.) 13th International Workshop on User Interfaces for Theorem Provers (UITP 2018) (July 2018, to appear)
25. Grebing, S.C.: User interaction in deductive interactive program verification. Ph.D. thesis, Karlsruhe Institute of Technology, October 2019. https://doi.org/10.5445/IR/1000099121
26. Haneberg, D., et al: The user interface of the KIV verification system - a system description. In: Proceedings of the User Interfaces for Theorem Provers Workshop (UITP 2005) (2005)
27. Hentschel, M., Hähnle, R., Bubel, R.: An empirical evaluation of two user interfaces of an interactive program verifier. In: Lo, D., Apel, S., Khurshid, S. (eds.) Proceedings of the 31st IEEE/ACM International Conference on Automated Software Engineering, ASE 2016, Singapore, 3–7 September, 2016, pp. 403–413. ACM (2016). https://doi.org/10.1145/2970276.2970303
28. Jackson, M., Ireland, A., Reid, G.: Interactive proof critics. Formal Aspects Comput. **11**(3), 302–325 (1999)
29. Kadoda, G., Stone, R., Diaper, D.: Desirable features of educational theorem provers: A Cognitive Dimensions viewpoint. In: Proceedings of the 11th Annual Workshop of the Psychology of Programming Interest Group (1996)
30. Kirchner, F., Kosmatov, N., Prevosto, V., Signoles, J., Yakobowski, B.: Frama-C: a software analysis perspective. Formal Aspects Comput. **27**(3), 573–609 (2015). https://doi.org/10.1007/s00165-014-0326-7
31. Kuckartz, U.: Qualitative Inhaltsanalyse. Computerunterstützung. Grundlagentexte Methoden, Beltz Juventa, Methoden, Praxis (2014)

32. Leavens, G.T., Baker, A.L., Ruby, C.: Preliminary design of JML: a behavioral interface specification language for Java. SIGSOFT/SEN **31**(3), 1–38 (2006)
33. Leino, K.R.M., Wüstholz, V.: The Dafny integrated development environment. In: Dubois, C., Giannakopoulou, D., Méry, D. (eds.) Proceedings 1st Workshop on Formal Integrated Development Environment, F-IDE 2014, Grenoble, France, 6 April 2014. EPTCS, vol. 149, pp. 3–15 (2014). https://doi.org/10.4204/EPTCS. 149.2
34. Leino, R.: Dafny: An automatic program verifier for functional correctness. Microsoft Research, April 2010. https://www.microsoft.com/en-us/research/publication/dafny-automatic-program-verifier-functional-correctness/
35. Lowe, H., Cumming, A., Smyth, M., Varey, A.: Lessons from experience: Making theorem provers more co-operative. In: Proceedings 2nd Workshop User Interfaces for Theorem Provers (1996)
36. Melis, E.: How mathematicians prove theorems. In: In Proceedings of the Annual Conference of the Cognitive Science Society, pp. 624–628. Lawrence Erlbaum Associates, Publisher (1994)
37. Merriam, N.A., Harrison, M.D.: Making design decisions to support diversity in interactive theorem proving. User Interfaces **98**, 112 (1998)
38. Merriam, N., Harrison, M.: Evaluating the interfaces of three theorem proving assistants. In: Bodart, F., Vanderdonckt, J. (eds.) Design, Specification and Verification of Interactive Systems 1996, pp. 330–346. Eurographics, Springer Vienna (1996). http://dx.doi.org/10.1007/978-3-7091-7491-3_17
39. Mitsch, S., Platzer, A.: The KeYmaera X Proof IDE - concepts on usability in hybrid systems theorem proving. In: Dubois, C., Masci, P., Méry, D. (eds.) Proceedings of the Third Workshop on Formal Integrated Development Environment, F-IDE@FM 2016, Limassol, Cyprus, November 8, 2016. EPTCS, vol. 240, pp. 67–81 (2016). https://doi.org/10.4204/EPTCS.240.5
40. Nipkow, T., Wenzel, M., Paulson, L.C. (eds.): Isabelle/HOL. LNCS, vol. 2283. Springer, Heidelberg (2002). https://doi.org/10.1007/3-540-45949-9
41. Ouimet, M., Lundqvist, K.: Formal software verification: model checking and theorem proving. Technical report, March 2007. http://www.es.mdh.se/publications/1215-
42. Owre, S., Rushby, J.M., Shankar, N.: PVS: a prototype verification system. In: Kapur, D. (ed.) CADE 1992. LNCS, vol. 607, pp. 748–752. Springer, Heidelberg (1992). https://doi.org/10.1007/3-540-55602-8_217
43. Platzer, A.: Logical Foundations of Cyber-Physical Systems. Springer, Switzerland (2018). https://doi.org/10.1007/978-3-319-63588-0http://www.springer.com/978-3-319-63587-3
44. Völker, N.: Thoughts on requirements and design issues of user interfaces for proof assistants. Electron. Notes Theor. Comput. Sci. **103**, 139–159 (Nov 2004). https://doi.org/10.1016/j.entcs.2004.05.001, http://dx.doi.org/10.1016/j.entcs.2004.05.001
45. Vujosevic, V., Eleftherakis, G.: Improving formal methods' tools usability. In: Eleftherakis, G. (ed.) 2nd South-East European Workshop on Formal Methods (SEEFM 05), Formal Methods: Challenges in the Business World, Ohrid, 18–19 Nov 2005. South-East European Research Centre (SEERC) (2006)
46. Wenzel, M.: Isar - a generic interpretative approach to readable formal proof documents. In: Proceedings of the 12th International Conference on Theorem Proving in Higher Order Logics, pp. 167–184. TPHOLs 1999, Springer-Verlag, London, UK, UK (1999)

Integration of Verification Techniques

Integration of Static and Dynamic Analysis Techniques for Checking Noninterference

Bernhard Beckert[1], Mihai Herda[1] (ID), Michael Kirsten[1]([✉])(ID), and Shmuel Tyszberowicz[2](ID)

[1] Karlsruhe Institute of Technology (KIT), Karlsruhe, Germany
{beckert,herda,kirsten}@kit.edu
[2] Afeka Academic College of Engineering, Tel Aviv, Israel
tyshbe@tau.ac.il

Abstract. In this article, we present an overview of recent combinations of deductive program verification and automatic test generation on the one hand and static analysis on the other hand, with the goal of checking noninterference. Noninterference is the non-functional property that certain confidential information cannot leak to certain public output, i.e., the confidentiality of that information is always preserved.

We define the noninterference properties that are checked along with the individual approaches that we use in different combinations. In one use case, our framework for checking noninterference employs deductive verification to automatically generate tests for noninterference violations with an improved test coverage. In another use case, the framework provides two combinations of deductive verification with static analysis based on system dependence graphs to prove noninterference, thereby reducing the effort for deductive verification.

Keywords: Information-flow security · Deductive verification · Software testing · Program slicing

1 Introduction

Generally, software developers primarily focus on functional requirements, even though non-functional requirements should also be at the center of attention. One paramount non-functional requirement is confidentiality. In this article, we target the preservation of confidentiality by the requirement that illegal *information flow* shall be avoided, i.e., we want to prevent situations where *high* (confidential) input leaks to *low* (public) output. This property is known as *noninterference* [14]. Intuitively, it requires that high input cannot interfere with low output. Thus, by observing the program's output, one cannot distinguish between different high inputs, i.e., if a program is executed twice with different high inputs but identical low inputs, then an attacker will observe identical behaviors (an attacker can observe low but not high information). Various

© Springer Nature Switzerland AG 2020
W. Ahrendt et al. (Eds.): Deductive Software Verification, LNCS 12345, pp. 287–312, 2020.
https://doi.org/10.1007/978-3-030-64354-6_12

approaches and tools for checking noninterference exist. Some have a high degree of automation, yet produce many false alarms due to an over-approximation of the possible flows of information in the program. Others are more precise, but require more effort and user interaction. Approaches that are based on System Dependence Graphs (SDGs) syntactically compute the dependencies between the program's statements and check whether the low output potentially depends on the high input (see, e.g., Hammer and Snelting [18]). Whereas such approaches scale very well, they over-approximate the actual dependencies in a program, and may yield false alarms. *Logic-based* approaches (see, e.g., Beckert et al. [7] and Greiner and Scheben [32]) have a higher precision (i.e., they produce less false alarms), since they more precisely analyze the concrete semantics of the program statements. However, they have a lower scalability. In these approaches, one tries to formally prove that the terminating states of two arbitrary executions of the same program are low-equivalent (i.e., the low parts of the states have the same values), assuming that the two initial states are low-equivalent. False alarms only occur when the system fails to find a proof in the allotted time even though the proof obligation is valid. Since verifying noninterference using logic-based approaches requires to compare two program executions simultaneously, a quadratic number of program paths must be considered compared to functional verification. Approaches for *test generation* also require a quadratic number of test cases to achieve the same coverage as for a functional property.

In this article, we present an overview of recent combinations [6,21,22] of deductive program verification with automatic test generation on the one hand and static analysis on the other hand, with the goal of checking noninterference. The resulting *Noninterference Framework* can be used both for proving that a given program fulfills a given noninterference property and, also, for finding a counterexample that demonstrates a noninterference violation in case the noninterference property is not fulfilled. For the task of proving noninterference, the framework combines deductive program verification with static analysis, two complementary approaches with respect to precision and scalability, and thereby reduces the effort for the deductive verification. The task of finding counterexamples is achieved by combining deductive program verification with automatic test generation in order to improve the computation of the achieved test coverage. For a more extensive framework description, we refer to Herda [20].

The rest of this article is structured as follows. In Sect. 2, which is based on Herda et al. [21], we define the noninterference properties that are handled with the framework. In Sect. 3, which is based on Ahrendt et al. [4], Beckert et al. [6], and works by Herda et al. [21,22], we present the used approaches. We provide an overview of the framework in Sect. 4, which is based on Herda [20]. Section 5, which is based on Herda et al. [21], presents an approach which uses deductive verification for automatic test generation. In Sects. 6 and 7, which are based on Herda et al. [22] and Beckert et al. [6] respectively, we consider two approaches which combine SDG-based and logic-based approaches for proving noninterference. We discuss implementation aspects of the two combinations in Sect. 8, which is based on previous works [6,20]. In Sect. 9, we present related work. Finally, we conclude in Sect. 10.

2   Information Flow Security

In this section, which is based on Herda et al. [21], we formally define the non-interference properties that can be checked by the Noninterference Framework. In this article, we consider only sequential and terminating programs. We introduce the *low-equivalence* relation $\sim_L$ that characterizes program states that are indistinguishable for an attacker with respect to a set L of low variables, where a program state s is an assignment of values to variables. We assume that the input of a program is included in the program's prestate and that the output of a program is part of the program's poststate. Hence, we define low-equivalence (Definition 1) and thereby noninterference (Definition 2) as follows:

Definition 1 (Low-equivalent states). *Two states s_1, s_2 are low-equivalent with respect to the set L of all low variables if and only if they assign the same values to low variables:*

$$s_1 \sim_L s_2 \Leftrightarrow \forall v \in L \left(v^{s_1} = v^{s_2} \right) \ ,$$

where v^{s_i} denotes the value of the variable v evaluated in state s_i.

Definition 2 (Classical noninterference). *A program P is noninterferent if and only if, for any two initial states s_1 and s_2, the following holds:*

$$s_1 \sim_L s_2 \Rightarrow s_1' \sim_L s_2'$$

where s_1', s_2' are poststates after executing P in s_1 and s_2, respectively.

The classical noninterference property, as presented in Definition 2, requires that any two executions of the program that start in two states which are indistinguishable for the attacker will also terminate in two indistinguishable states. If this holds, then it is guaranteed that the high values of the prestates cannot influence the low values of the poststates.

This property, however, is often too strong for cases where it is acceptable that the attacker sees parts of the high values. A classical example is a login system in which an attacker can try out different combinations of user names and passwords. While the system does not immediately leak the user's password, an attacker can check whether particular combinations are correct, and thus obtain information about sensitive data. To allow such a case, albeit still forbidding cases in which the system outright leaks sensitive information to the attacker, we define (see Definition 3) the notion of noninterference with declassification (i.e., giving the attacker access to parts of the high information). For this, let *expr* be an expression in first order logic describing the high information that an attacker is allowed to know (we denote *expr*'s evaluation in a state s by $expr_s$).

Definition 3 (Noninterference with declassification). *Given a declassification expression expr, a program P is noninterferent if and only if we have for all initial states s_1, s_2 that*

$$s_1 \sim_L s_2 \wedge expr_{s_1} = expr_{s_2} \Rightarrow s_1' \sim_L s_2' \ ,$$

where s_1', s_2' are the final states after executing P in s_1 and s_2, respectively.

For object-oriented programs, it is too restrictive to require that all low variables and heap locations are equal for the final states to be low-equivalent. Consider the case of programs that create new object references: a program will not necessarily create the same reference for different executions, even for exactly the same input. Beckert et al. [7] have developed a variation (Definition 4) of classical noninterference using a semantics that is based on an object isomorphism.

Definition 4 (Low-equivalence with isomorphism). *Two states s_1, s_2 are low-equivalent if and only if*

$$s_1 \sim_L^\pi s_2 \Leftrightarrow \forall v \in L \left(\pi(v^{s_1}) = v^{s_2} \right) \ ,$$

where π is a bijective function on heap locations.

We assume that an attacker cannot see the exact reference address of an object and can compare object references only for equality (e.g., with the Java == operator). Thus, if the object structures in the two poststates are isomorphic, the attacker obtains the same results when comparing the object references for equality. Note that the properties from Definitions 3 and 4 can be combined in order to obtain noninterference with isomorphism and declassification.

3   Approaches of the Noninterference Framework

This section presents the approaches in the Noninterference Framework. We present SDG-based approaches (using Herda et al. [22]) in Sect. 3.1, logic-based approaches (using previous works [6,21]) in Sect. 3.2, and automatic test generation based on symbolic execution (using Herda et al. [21]) in Sect. 3.3.

3.1   SDG-Based Approaches

While the concepts of Program Dependence Graphs (PDG) [13] and System Dependence Graphs (SDG) [23] have been developed during the eighties, their usefulness in the context of information flow security has been first noticed by Snelting [34] in the nineties. Without loss of generality, we use the JOANA tool [18] to explain the functionality of an SDG-based analysis. SDG-based information-flow analyses are purely syntactic, highly scalable, and sound. However, some of the reported noninterference violations may be false alarms. The desired noninterference property (as in Definition 2) is specified by annotating which program parts correspond to high information as well as the parts where low output occurs. JOANA automatically builds an SDG from these annotations.

The resulting SDG is a directed graph consisting of interconnected PDGs, where each PDG represents a single program procedure in the form of a directed graph. Nodes in the SDG represent program statements, conditions, or input parameters, and edges represent dependencies between the nodes (i.e., there is an edge between two nodes if and only if the value or execution of one node may depend on the outcome of the other node). Whether there is an edge between two nodes in the SDG, is determined syntactically by analyzing the control-flow graph of the program. There are three main types of edges in an SDG:

1. data dependency edges, which represent possible direct dependencies,
2. control dependencies, which represent possible indirect dependencies, and
3. interprocedural dependencies, which represent dependencies between nodes in different PDGs.

Formal definitions for the three types of dependencies can be found in Hammer [17, Chapter 2]. In the following, we give informal definitions. A node n' is data-dependent on a node n iff there is a program variable v that is used in n' and defined in n, and there is a path from n to n' in the Control Flow Graph (CFG) such that v is not redefined on any node between n and n' on that path. A node n' is control-dependent on a node n iff the choice of the outgoing edge from n in the CFG determines whether node n' is reached. Note that it is generally undecidable whether a CFG path represents an actual execution path in the program, i.e., some paths in the CFG may represent executions that cannot actually take place. Hence, the CFG is an over-approximation of the actual program behavior. Since the dependencies are defined using CFG paths, they are also an over-approximation of the actual dependencies in the program.

Method calls are represented by special formal-in and formal-out nodes in the SDG. Formal-in nodes represent direct inputs that influence the method execution. These can be input parameters, used fields, other classes called during execution, or the class in which the method is executed. Formal-out nodes represent the influence of the method and can represent the method's return value, global variables, fields in other classes, or exceptions. At each method call site, there are actual-in nodes representing the arguments and actual-out nodes representing the return values. For a given method site, each actual-in node corresponds to a formal-in node of the called method and each actual-out node to a formal-out node. Interprocedural dependencies connect actual-in nodes to the corresponding formal-in nodes, and formal-out nodes to the corresponding actual-out nodes. For every method call, there are also so-called *summary edges* in the SDG from any actual-in to any actual-out node of the method for which the tool finds a possible information flow from the corresponding formal-in to the corresponding formal-out node of the called method.

JOANA detects illegal information-flows through graph analysis, using a special form of conditional reachability analysis, so-called (back- and forward) *slicing* and *chopping*, at the SDG level. A *forward slice* of a node s consists of all SDG-nodes that can be reached from s. Conversely, a *backward slice* of a node s

consists of all nodes on SDG paths ending in s. A *chop* from a node s to a node t consists of all nodes on paths from s to t in the SDG and is commonly computed by first calculating the backward slice for t, and then computing the forward slice for s within the subgraph induced by the backward slice. JOANA reports a security violation whenever there exists a path from a node in the SDG that is annotated as high to a node annotated as low (i.e., when the chop of these two nodes is not empty). Wasserrab and Lohner [36] proved that no potential flow of information is missed, i.e., that JOANA is sound. Since the dependencies modeled in the SDG are in fact over-approximations of actual dependencies in the program, the program is guaranteed to be noninterferent if no SDG path from a high input to a low output is found. However, the program may still be noninterferent, even though there is a path from a high input to a low output.

3.2   Logic-Based Approaches

Logic-based information-flow analysis takes the semantics of the program language into account. The semantics of modern program languages provide a high degree of expressiveness, which becomes important for analysis to deal with sources for illegal information-flow leaks which possibly exploit features of the program semantics. Logic provides a means for formalizing such features, and enables reasoning about their effects on any program variables or locations.

Dynamic logic [8] can express the functional property of *partial correctness* of a program P for a precondition ϕ and a postcondition ψ by the formula $\phi \rightarrow [P]\psi$. This means that ψ holds in all possible states in which P terminates. Since we analyze only deterministic programs, this means that either P terminates and ψ holds afterwards, or the program never terminates. Applying a logical calculus with a deductive theorem prover (e.g., KeY [3]), we can symbolically execute P and attempt to prove this formula. KeY allows for proofs of functional properties specified with the Java Modeling Language (JML) [27]. Furthermore, KeY has been extended to support the verification of noninterference for sequential programs [31,32]. The classical proof obligation (Definition 2) requires that two program runs that start in low-equivalent states will also terminate in low-equivalent states, i.e., given (simplified) in dynamic logic:

$$\left(\underbrace{([P]\, out_l \doteq out_l^A)}_{\text{Execution A}} \wedge \underbrace{([P]\, out_l \doteq out_l^B)}_{\text{Execution B}} \right) \rightarrow \left(\underbrace{(in_l^A \doteq in_l^B) \rightarrow (out_l^A \doteq out_l^B)}_{\substack{\text{Low-equivalent prestates imply} \\ \text{low-equivalent poststates}}} \right)$$

In the above proof obligation, the placeholder out_l represents the low output of program P. On the left hand side of the main implication, the proof obligation contains two executions of P: execution A, after which the low output out_l is equal to out_l^A, and execution B, after which the low output is equal to out_l^B. On the right hand side of the main implication, the proof obligation contains an implication stating that, if the two low inputs in_l^A and in_l^B are equal, then the low outputs out_l^A and out_l^B are equal as well. To support declassification as defined in Definition 3, the second implication of the proof obligation requires additionally that the declassified expressions are equal in the prestates of the two executions. To support object isomorphism as defined in Definition 4, the second implication of the proof obligation is enhanced with the predicate $newObjIso$:

$$(in_l^A \doteq in_l^B) \rightarrow \left(newObjIso(N, h^A, h^B) \wedge (N^A \doteq N^B \rightarrow out_l^A \doteq out_l^B)\right)$$

The predicate $newObjIso$ accepts as parameters a list N of reference type expressions and the two heaps h^A and h^B that represent the two poststates of executions A and B. The predicate holds under the following three conditions:

1. Every reference expression in N is newly created in the poststates of both executions (A and B) of P.
2. Every reference expression in N has the exact same type in the post states of executions A and B.
3. If two reference expressions in N are equal in the poststate of one execution (A or B), then they must be equal in the poststate of the other execution.

These requirements ensure that the reference expressions in N are isomorphic in both poststates. If the reference expressions in N fulfill the $newObjIso$ predicate, the proof obligation no longer requires their equivalence in the two poststates (this relaxation is done with the second implication). Note that the user-provided list N must also be part of the noninterference specification, in addition to the variables that must be low-equivalent before and after both executions.

3.3 Automatic Test Generation

On top of the deductive theorem prover and its calculi for finding functional (or non-functional, see Sect. 3.2) proofs, KeY was extended with an automatical test generation for functional properties [12]. In this section, which is based on [4], we give an overview of KeYTestGen, the current extension of KeY for automatic test generation. KeYTestGen uses symbolic execution and attempts to generate a test suite that achieves a high path coverage. In the following, we present the three steps taken by KeYTestGen to automatically generate tests.

Step 1: Constraint generation. The input to KeYTestGen is a Java method under test (MUT), together with a specified functional property. KeYTestGen loads the proof obligation for the specified MUT and symbolically executes the program. The Java code is transformed into updates, which are a compact representation of the statements' effects. Case distinctions (including implicit ones such as, e.g., whether or not an exception is thrown) in the program are reflected as branches of the proof tree. The symbolic execution is bounded by a number b provided by the user. Hence, loops in the program are unwound a maximum of b times. Each branch in the obtained proof tree represents a b-path (i.e., a path that goes through each cycle at most b times) in the CFG. At the end of the symbolic execution, a model of a leaf of the tree is both a model of the precondition and of the path condition of the b-path that corresponds to that proof tree branch.

Step 2: Test data generation. For generating a test, we first produce a concrete test input *s* which satisfies the test data constraint (i.e., a path condition together with the specification's precondition) obtained from the first step. For finding such models, we use the SMT solver Z3 [29]. The constraints from *step 1* are translated from KeY's Java first order logic [33] into the SMT-LIB 2 language [5] to be processed by Z3. The translation uses bounded data types (i.e., each data type only has a bounded number of instances), so that the SMT solver can find models much faster, but potentially misses some models for too small bounds.

Step 3: Code generation. In the third and final step, the JUnit test cases are generated. Each test case consists of a *test preamble*, a call of the MUT, and a call of the test oracle. The test preamble prepares the inputs for the MUT call, which are taken from the model found in the previous step. The MUT call in the test case is the same as in the proof obligation. The generated test oracle is a boolean method that checks the postcondition after the MUT was executed. Hence, each test suite contains only one oracle method for all test cases.

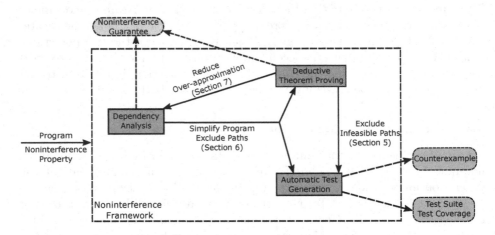

Fig. 1. The noninterference framework

4   The Noninterference Framework

In this section, which is based on Herda [20], we present a framework (illustrated in Fig. 1) for checking noninterference properties. The framework combines multiple contributions (presented in Sects. 5 to 7) to the area of information-flow security. We provide a short overview of the framework and show how its individual approaches are integrated and cooperate. The framework encompasses the following three approaches: (1) *dependency analysis*, (2) *deductive theorem proving*, and (3) *automatic test generation*. Each of these methods has its strengths and weaknesses. By integrating them, the framework uses their strengths to mitigate their weaknesses. The framework handles the following two use cases. In the first one, the analyzed program does not fulfill the specified noninterference property, and the user is looking for a counterexample that showcases the noninterference violation. For this case, the framework provides an approach for automatic test generation, aiming to find noninterference violations. In the second case, the specified noninterference property is fulfilled by the analyzed program, and the user attempts to prove this property. For this case, the framework combines deductive theorem proving with dependency analysis. In the following, we give an overview of the contributions for the two use cases.

4.1 Finding Noninterference Counterexamples

For the case in which the user tries to find a noninterference violation, the framework provides an approach to automatically generate tests for noninterference properties, which is presented in Sect. 5. The approach serves two purposes. First, we can search for counterexamples of the analyzed noninterference property. If such a counterexample is found, the user gets two program inputs that are indistinguishable to the attacker but lead to two different low outputs, thus demonstrating a noninterference violation. Second, we can generate a noninterference test suite that achieves a certain test coverage. This is useful in the event that neither the program could be proved correct nor a counterexample could be found. Then, the user is provided with a test coverage value, which helps to assess the strength of the generated tests. The test generation approach uses deductive program verification to remove infeasible program execution paths from the test generation and from the computation of the achieved coverage. As shown in Sect. 6, the test generation also uses the results provided by the SDG-based analysis for removing parts of the program which are not relevant to the analyzed noninterference property.

4.2 Proving Noninterference

In case a user tries to prove that a given program fulfills a specified noninterference property, the framework combines two existing approaches: (1) dependency analysis (i.e., an SDG-based approach, see Sect. 3.1) and (2) deductive theorem proving (i.e., a logic-based approach, see Sect. 3.2). In order to make use of the advantages of both SDG-based and logic-based approaches, the framework combines these approaches in two ways. In the first combination, as presented in Sect. 6, the SDG-based approach is used to simplify the noninterference proof obligations for the deductive program verification. Those parts of the program that the SDG-method deems irrelevant to the noninterference property are removed before the program is analyzed with the logic-based approach. In the second combination, as shown in Sect. 7, the logic-based approach is used to increase the precision of the SDG-based approach by identifying certain SDG dependencies that are over-approximations and removing their corresponding edges from the SDG. Both combinations can be joined, i.e., the program simplification from Sect. 6 can be applied to simplify the deductive proof obligations for showing that a program dependency is over-approximated.

5   Test Generation for Noninterference Properties

This section presents the part of our Noninterference Framework that handles programs that violate the given noninterference property. We extend the approach for automatic test generation described in Sect. 3.3 to support the properties defined in Sect. 2. For a more extensive description of the automatic test generation, we refer to Herda et al. [21], on which this section is based. In Sect. 5.1, we show how the properties from Sect.2 can be tested. in Sect. 5.2, we explain how such tests are generated automatically. Finally, we extend existing coverage criteria such that they can be used for the generated noninterference test suites in Sect. 5.3.

5.1   Noninterference Tests

We begin by defining noninterference tests suitable for testing classical noninterference from Definition 2 by adapting functional tests from Ahrendt et al. [4].

A *noninterference test* can formally be described as a tuple $\langle s_1, s_2, Or \rangle$, consisting of two prestates representing *test inputs* s_1 and s_2, and an *oracle function* Or. The two prestates s_1 and s_2 are required to be low-equivalent according to either Definition 1 or 4. The oracle function $Or(s_1', s_2') \mapsto \{pass, fail\}$ checks whether the two poststates are low-equivalent. Thus, in order to perform a noninterference test, we execute the MUT twice, with inputs in1 and in2, respectively (see Listing 1). Moreover, for a valid noninterference test, we require the two generated inputs to be low-equivalent. The oracle function then checks whether the two outputs, out1 and out2, are also low-equivalent.

```
1 testMUT() {
2    in1 = generateInput(); // Execution 1 preamble
3    out1 = executeMUT(in1); // MUT call 1
4    in2 = generateLowEqInput(in1); // Execution 2 preamble
5    out2 = executeMUT(in2); // MUT call 2
6    oracle(out1,out2); // Oracle call #
7 }
```

Listing 1. Structure of a noninterference test

In order to check the noninterference properties from Sect. 2, we define the semantics for the functions generateLowEqInput and oracle from Listing 1 as follows: For the noninterference property from Definition 2, the method generateLowEqInput generates a second input that is low-equivalent according to the relation $\sim_L$ from Definition 1. The method oracle checks whether the two outputs are low-equivalent. For the property provided by Definition 3, generateLowEqInput generates a second input such that the two prestates are low-equivalent and, moreover, the results from evaluating the given expression in the two prestates are identical. The oracle function again checks the low-equivalence. Finally, for the property given by Definition 4, generateLowEqInput and oracle use the low-equivalence relation with isomorphism $\sim_L^\pi$.

5.2   Automatic Test Generation

We describe the approach for generating test suites for a given MUT and a specified noninterference property as defined in Sect. 2 by extending the approach for automatic test generation from Sect. 3.3. The main difference to functional properties is that two related program runs are necessary. The test generation approach offers two options that yield the following two scenarios: With the first option, the user searches for noninterference violations. In this case, the constraints that are passed on to the model generator require the two poststates to be non-low-equivalent (i.e., to demonstrate a noninterference violation). This first option is useful in the event that the user has failed to prove that the program is noninterferent and suspects that the program violates the property. With the second option, the user generates a noninterference test suite with a high test coverage. In this case, the constraints do not restrict the poststates in any way. The second option is useful for finding errors given that both verification and counterexample generation have failed. Moreover, generating a high-coverage test suite is useful for finding violations introduced by the operating system or by the compiler. The coverage of the generated test suite can increase the user's confidence in the correctness of the program. The approach for automatic test generation works in three steps as described in the following.

Step 1: Constraint generation. The MUT specified with a noninterference property is loaded into KeY and symbolically executed (Sect. 3.3). At the end of the bounded symbolic execution, we obtain a proof tree where each leaf contains a pair of path conditions, one for each program execution. Thus, a model that satisfies the formulas in a leaf is also a model for the two path conditions represented by the leaf, and for the requirements that the prestates are low-equivalent and the poststates are non-low-equivalent. With the second option, the constraint requiring that the poststates violate the low-equivalence requirement is ignored.

Step 2: Test data generation. For test data generation, we can reuse the SMT-translation used to generate tests for functional properties (see Sect. 3.3). This step can also generate models that fulfill the declassification expressions and thus supports noninterference with declassification (see Definition 3).

Step 3: Code generation. As shown in Listing 1, a noninterference test contains two preambles and two calls of the MUT. For each call, an input configuration is set up and—after the second MUT call—the test oracle is called to decide whether the test was successful or not. For the two preambles, we create two isomorphic input states by duplicating the objects and values from the model. Thereby, we avoid that the second MUT execution affects the first MUT execution's results. The MUT and its surrounding code are taken from the JavaDL modality in the root node of the proof tree. It is important to use the surrounding code—rather than just the MUT's invocation—to ensure semantic equivalence of the actual and the symbolic execution of the code. The surrounding code typically consists of a *try/catch* block which allows the test oracle to decide what to do when an exception is thrown. Each test suite contains only one oracle method that is used for all tests. The oracle checks equality for low variables of primitive type and isomorphism for reference type variables. For references created during the MUT execution, the requirements of *newObjIso* (see Sect. 3.2) are checked. However, for references created in one of the preambles, only the second and third requirements of *newObjIso* are checked.

5.3   Coverage Criteria

We extend existing test coverage definitions in order to make them suitable for measuring the coverage of noninterference test suites, and we discuss the coverage provided by the test suites generated with our approach. Well-established coverage criteria such as *statement*, *branch*, and *path* coverage are defined on the CFG. Full statement coverage of a test suite requires each node in the CFG to be traversed during the execution of the test suite, whereas full branch coverage requires each edge to be traversed, and for full path coverage, each path must be traversed. In order to extend these coverage criteria to the noninterference test suites defined in this paper, we no longer use the standard CFG, but rather the self-composed CFG, to define the notions of *relational* statement, branch and path coverage. The self-composed CFG consists of two copies of the MUT's CFG, with renamed variables and with a directed edge from the end node of the first copy to the start node of the second copy.

Since a CFG may contain loops, the number of paths is possibly infinite. Hence, we only count b-paths (i.e., paths which pass through each cycle at most b times) on the self-composed CFG, and define the *relational bounded path coverage criterion* as #(covered b-paths) / #(b-paths). Our approach explicitly provides the required values for this coverage criterion: the number of generated tests represents the number of covered b-paths, while the number of leaves of the proof tree represents the total number of b-paths in the self-composed CFG. One problem with the relational bounded path coverage criterion is that typically a large portion of the program execution paths in the self-composed CFG are infeasible (i.e., the path condition for that execution path is unsatisfiable). It is generally undecidable whether a path is infeasible or not. Hence, if our test suite has a low coverage, we cannot know whether the paths for which no test was generated are infeasible or whether, given more time, our approach would be able to generate tests for those paths. For noninterference properties, the low-equivalence requirement for the two inputs may cause certain paths in the self-composed CFG to be infeasible. A more useful criterion is therefore the *relational bounded feasible path coverage*, defined as #(covered b-paths) / #(feasible b-paths) on the self-composed CFG. Even though we cannot compute the exact number of feasible b-paths, we can use the theorem prover to show that certain paths are infeasible, and the remaining paths—that could not be proved infeasible—constitute an over-approximation of the feasible b-paths. This over-approximated number is used to compute an under-approximation of the *relational bounded feasible path coverage* for a generated test suite.

An evaluation [21] done on a collection of benchmarks [16] containing both secure and insecure programs shows that relational bounded feasible path-coverage is an appropriate coverage criterion for noninterference properties: for high coverage values, we either find no violations for the secure programs or find at least one violation for most insecure programs.

6   Simplifying Programs for Testing and Verification

This section presents an approach which, given a program and a noninterference property, uses an SDG-based analysis to generate a simplified version of the original program. The simplified program is noninterference-equivalent (with respect to the given property) to the original program, and can be analyzed with a second, more precise approach. We use the logic-based approach (see Sect. 3.2) and automatic test generation (see Sect. 5) as a second approach. Thus, the simplification approach is used by our framework to simplify both searching for counterexamples and proving the property. For a more extensive description of the approach, see Herda et al. [22], on which this section is based. Section 6.1 presents an illustrative example that is also used in Sect. 7, Sect. 6.2 explains how simplified programs are generated, and Sect. 6.3 presents the advantages of the simplified programs for verification and test generation.

6.1   Running Example

Consider the method **secure** in Listing 2 with the parameter **high** as secret input and the method's result value as public output. Since the result value does not depend on the value of **high**, the method is noninterferent—which can be proven using deductive verification.

```
1  int secure(int high, int low) {        13  int identity1(int low, int high) {
2    if (low == 5) {                       14     low = low + high;
3      low = identity2(low, high);         15     low = low - high;
4    } else {                              16     return low;
5      if (low == 2) {                     17  }
6        low = identity1(low, high);       18
7      } else {                            19  int identity2(int low, int high) {
8        low = identity2(low, high);       20     return low;
9      }                                   21  }
10   }
11   return low;
12 }
```

Listing 2. Running example

The corresponding proof must handle nine symbolic execution paths: following Definition 2, we need to analyze two program runs, for each of which we distinguish three different cases, namely that the value of the parameter **low** is (a) 5, (b) 2, or (c) any other value. For this example, SDG-based techniques for checking noninterference will report a possible noninterference violation, as the called method **identity1** contains a *syntactic* dependency between its result value (that is assigned low afterwards) and the parameter high. This dependency, however, only affects the path for which the initial value of low is 2. Hence, the other two execution paths can be guaranteed to be noninterferent by the SDG-based approach.

6.2 Generation of the Simplified Program

In the following, we explain how we can simplify the program from Listing 2 in order to reduce the verification and testing effort. As seen in Sect. 3.1, SDG-based analyses are purely syntactic, highly scalable, and sound, but some of the reported violations may be false positives. However, even if there are false warnings, the SDG-based analysis allows to exclude execution paths and statements that are guaranteed not to affect have any effect on noninterference. A further analysis then only needs to deal with those parts of the program that can potentially lead to an illegal leak according to the SDG-based analysis.

Figure 2 shows the SDG generated by JOANA for the method secure in the running example from Listing 2. The dependencies inside the three calls of the methods identity1 and identity2 are hidden, and only the method call nodes are shown. We use this simplification also in the following for describing paths in the SDG. Therein, node 58 represents the parameter high of the method secure, and node 55 the method's exit node. The two nodes are annotated as high and low, respectively. JOANA reports a security violation that contains an SDG path from the parameter high to the result value of the method secure, but successfully determines that there is no dependency between the parameter high and the result value of the two calls to the method identity2. Since the edges in the SDG represent all syntactical dependencies, JOANA cannot show the same for the call of identity1. Therefore, the SDG path $58 \rightarrow 69 \rightarrow 82 \rightarrow 55$ is reported as possible violation (the numbers correspond to the node ids in Fig. 2). For the two execution paths where identity2 is called, the absence of any illegal information flow is shown, and thus their analysis with the second, more precise, approach can be skipped.

Hence, we create a simplified program by excluding the parts already proved secure by JOANA. A simplified program is based on the backward slice of the low output and excludes some execution paths. We determine which paths to exclude by analyzing both the SDG of the entire program and the chop, to decide whether a branching node (e.g., a node representing an if-statement) must be true or false for an illegal information flow to occur, based on Definition 5.

Definition 5 (Analysis of branching nodes). *Let n_b be a conditional branching node in the backward slice with some node n_l corresponding to the low output. Let N_{true} be the set of successor nodes following the true branch of n_b in the CFG, and let N_{false} be the successor nodes following the false branch in the CFG. We define n_b to be a condition that must be true if the analyzed chop $C(n_h, n_l)$ contains nodes from N_{true} and no nodes from N_{false}. Conversely, n_b is defined as a condition that must be false if the chop contains nodes from N_{false} and no nodes from N_{true}.*

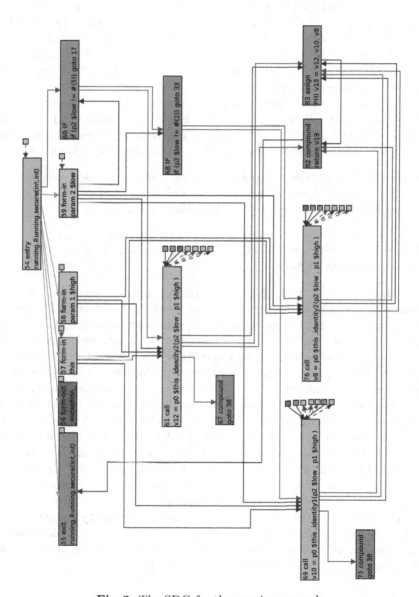

Fig. 2. The SDG for the running example

Consequently, given a high input and a low output corresponding to the SDG nodes n_h and n_l, respectively, and a branching node n_b that must be true (resp. false), any execution path of the original program on the false (true) branch of n_b will not lead to an illegal information flow from n_h to n_l. This allows us to exclude the execution paths that do not lead to an illegal information flow from the further analysis with a second approach. We exclude these paths by adding a special statement that disrupts the symbolic execution at the beginning of a false branch for a branching statement that *must be true* and at the beginning of a true branch for a branching statement that *must be false*. When the program is symbolically executed for verification and we reach a disruptive statement, the proof closes automatically for that branch. The test generation also immediately halts for that path once the symbolic execution reaches a disruptive statement. We can now define the simplified program by Definition 6 as follows.

Definition 6 (Simplified program). *Let n_h and n_l (corresponding to a high input and a low output, respectively) be two nodes in the SDG of a program P. The simplified program P_S consists of the following statements:*

1. *all statements whose SDG-nodes are in the backward slice $S_{bw}(n_l)$,*
2. *disruptive statements on branches that cannot lead to an illegal information flow (according to Definition 5).*

As shown in Herda et al. [22], the simplified program generated according to Definition 6 is noninterference-equivalent to the original program (i.e., the simplified program is noninterferent if the original program is noninterferent, and a counterexample for one program is also a counterexample for other program).

The chop reported by JOANA for the running example contains the nodes 58, 69, 82, and 55 (Fig. 2). In the backward slice of the low output (i.e., of node 55), there are two branching nodes, nodes 60 and 68, corresponding to the two if-statements in the example program. Upon analyzing the two branching nodes, we automatically determine that, if an illegal information flow was possible, the first if-statement would need to take the *false* branch and the second if-statement would need to take the *true* branch. The program in Listing 3 is the simplified program of the running example. While in general the backward slice of the return statement may be much smaller than the original program, it contains the entire program from our example. Nevertheless, our approach determines that the paths which lead to the call of `identity2` cannot lead to an illegal information flow, thereby adding two occurrences of the statement `disruptExecution()`. This statement stops symbolic execution in the event of verifying the running example or generating tests for it.

6.3 Verification and Testing of the Simplified Program

When using KeY to prove noninterference for the running example, we require 771 rule applications. Once the symbolic program execution is finished, there are still nine proof branches, one for each combination of paths in the two program runs as explained in Sect. 6.1, with open goals that remain to be closed.

The verification of the simplified program in Listing 3 still requires 511 rule applications. For other examples, the verification effort may be further reduced by removing program statements through slicing. Therein, the symbolic execution halts when one of the two program runs reaches a path that has already been deemed secure by JOANA, and the open goal of the corresponding proof branch is automatically closed. Thus, of the nine open proof goals remaining after symbolic execution, eight are trivially closed—in some cases even before their symbolic execution is finished.

```
 1 int secure(int high, int low) {
 2   if (low == 5) {
 3     disruptExecution();
 4     low = identity2(low, high);
 5   } else {
 6     if (low == 2) {
 7       low = identity1(low, high);
 8     } else {
 9       disruptExecution();
10       low = identity2(low, high);
11     }
12   }
13   return low;
14 }
```

Listing 3. Simplified program for the running example

The running example showcases how the SDG-based approach can assist verification by excluding both statements and execution paths from the program. The exclusion of execution paths is especially useful when proving noninterference. For an original program with n execution paths, the verification process must prove that the noninterference property holds for n^2 paths. When adding a single disruptive statement, the number of paths that need to be verified in the simplified program drops to a number between $(n-1)^2$ and $n^2/4$ (depending on whether the affected condition is the top level or not). Thus, the number of execution paths that need to be analyzed with the theorem prover can drop to a quarter of those in the original program.

The running example contains three execution paths. Thus, the automatic test generation approach (see Sect. 5) will attempt to generate 3^2 input pairs. However, only three pairs are low-equivalent as the branch that is taken gets determined by the low input. Consequently, the automatic test generation approach generates a test suite with three noninterference tests. When running the automatic test generation approach on the simplified program, only one test will be generated for the case in which both low inputs have the value 2. This is due to the inserted statements in the simplified program that disrupt symbolic execution. For the simplified program, the automatic test generation approach attempts (and succeeds) to generate a noninterference test only once, compared to the above-mentioned nine attempts for the original program. Hence, we have eight test generation attempts (calls to the SMT solver) that cannot lead to a noninterference property violation and are hence soundly skipped.

Besides the exclusion of execution paths as in the case of the running example, using the simplified program reduces the verification and testing effort also due to the removal of program statements from the original program.

7   The Combined Approach

The final part of the Noninterference Framework is the *Combined Approach* (see Beckert et al. [6], on which this section is based, for a more extensive description). The Combined Approach also integrates an SDG-based with a logic-based approach and attempts to prove noninterference. A comparison between the Combined Approach and the approach from Sect. 6 can be found in Sect. 8.

For a given program P, the first step of the Combined Approach is to run the SDG-based analysis in order to check the noninterference property (according to Definition 2) for P. If this step already clears out any illegal information flow for P, we need no further action as noninterference is guaranteed to hold. If, however, the automatic SDG-based approach detects a potential illegal information flow, we continue with the second step of the Combined Approach which checks whether this information flow is a false positive or a genuine leak. Since the SDG-based analysis is the first step, the results provided by our approach are at least as precise as those of the SDG-based analysis. The second and final step of the Combined Approach is to apply a logic-based approach which tries to prove that certain syntactic dependencies in the SDG do not represent actual (semantic) dependencies. If all syntactic dependencies between high inputs and low outputs reported by the SDG-based analysis are proved to not represent semantic dependencies using the logic-based approach, then the analyzed noninterference property is proved to hold for P.

Formally, the Combined Approach (shown in Algorithm 1) works as follows. Let N_h denote the set of all nodes annotated as high, and N_ℓ the set of all nodes annotated as low. Moreover, we define for $n_h \in N_h$ and $n_\ell \in N_\ell$ a *violation* as a pair (n_h, n_ℓ) for which there is a path from n_h to n_ℓ in the SDG of P. We call the set of all nodes on a path from n_h to n_ℓ the *violation chop* $c(n_h, n_\ell)$. The result of the SDG-based approach is hence a set of violations (if this set is empty, noninterference is already guaranteed) for which the Combined Approach validates each violation chop and attempts to prove that it does not represent a semantic dependency in program P. This is done by attempting to show that the chop is interrupted (see Definitons 7 and 8) using a logic-based approach.

Definition 7 (Unnecessary summary edge). *A summary edge $e = (a_i, a_o)$ is called* unnecessary *if and only if there is no potential information flow from the formal-in node f_i to the formal-out node f_o corresponding to the actual-in node a_i and the actual-out node a_o, respectively.*

Definition 8 (Interrupted violation chop). *A violation chop is* interrupted *if we find a non-empty set S of unnecessary summary edges on this chop such that upon deletion of the edges in S from the SDG, no path exists between the source and the sink of the violation chop.*

In order to show that a summary edge $e = (a_i, a_o)$ is unnecessary, a proof obligation is generated for the theorem prover of the logic-based approach. This proof obligation states that there is no information flow from the formal-in node f_i to the formal-out node f_o corresponding to the summary edge e. The proof is

Data: A set S of violation chops
Result: A set T of interrupted violation chops
foreach *Violation chop* $C_V \in S$ **do**
    Build queue Q of summary edges in C_V, ordered by given heuristic;
    while C_V *not interrupted and* Q *not empty* **do**
        Pop summary edge e from Q;
        Generate proof obligation PO for proving that e is unnecessary;
        if PO *proved with theorem prover* **then**
            Delete e from C_V;
        end
    end
    if C_V *interrupted* **then**
        Add C_V to T;
    end
end
return T

Algorithm 1: The Combined Approach

done for all possible contexts of the called method. If the proof is successful, it is guaranteed that the summary edge was only a result of the over-approximation and can thus be soundly deleted.

As described above, the Combined Approach (see Algorithm 1) attempts to prove each violation chop to be interrupted. For each violation chop, we pick a summary edge, generate the appropriate information flow proof obligation for the corresponding program method, and perform a proof attempt with the theorem prover. If the proof succeeds, the summary edge can, by Definition 8, be safely deleted from the SDG. The choice of the summary edge in the violation chop, containing potentially multiple summary edges, is established by a given heuristic. Note that we only need to consider summary edges that belong to a violation chop and it is hence sufficient to regard only a smaller subset of all summary edges. When—upon a successful proof attempt—we delete the corresponding summary edge, we check whether the deletion makes this violation chop interrupted. In this case, we can proceed with the remaining violation chops, attempting to make all of them interrupted. In case either the violation chop is not interrupted after deleting the summary edge or the proof attempt is not successful, we choose the next—following the given heuristic—summary edge from the violation chop. If we are able to interrupt every violation chop by deleting unnecessary edges, the Combined Approach guarantees noninterference.

Note that each violation chop is guaranteed to contain at least one summary edge, namely the one corresponding to the **main** method. Generating a proof obligation for the **main** method, however, is equivalent to verifying noninterference of the entire program with the theorem prover. In practice, however, programs are often inter-procedural, and there are plenty of (different) summary edges for our approach to check. Nevertheless, it may happen in the worst case that we need to verify the **main** method with the theorem prover. This worst-case scenario for our approach occurs in the event that not enough summary edges from inner method calls can be proved to be unnecessary.

For the example in Listing 2, we attempt to show that there is no potential information flow from the parameter `high` to the method's result value `secure`. When applying the SDG-based approach, an illegal information flow is reported, because the method `identity1`'s result value syntactically depends on the parameter `high` of the same method. This reported violation, however, is a false alarm. The violation chop consists of only one path that contains for a summary edge which connects (as explained in Sect. 3.1) the actual-in SDG-node for the parameter `high` and the actual-out SDG-node for `identity1`'s result value. Proceeding with the Combined Approach, we automatically generate a proof obligation for the theorem prover, stating that the result value for `identity1` does not semantically depend on parameter `high`. Upon the attempt to prove the statement, we also prove that the result value of the method `secure` does not depend on the parameter `high` and thus show the noninterference for the method `secure`. This simple example showcases a major advantage of our approach: the logic-based approach does not need to analyze the entire program, but only those parts that cannot be handled by the SDG-based approach.

The evaluation of the Combined Approach [6] shows that noninterference can be proved for programs for which the SDG-based approach—on its own—lacks the necessary precision and the logic-based approach—on its own—does not need to analyze the entire program.

8   Discussion

In Sect. 8.1, which is based on Herda et al. [22], we discuss the challenges of using the logic-based theorem prover KeY and the SDG-based static analysis tool JOANA for implementing the approaches from Sects. 6 and 7. In Sect. 8.2, which is based on Herda [20], we compare the approaches in the Noninterference Framework and show how they can be integrated.

8.1   JOANA and KeY

For JOANA and KeY's challenges in our framework, we identified differing supports of Java features, possibly nonexecutable slices produced by JOANA, and differing program entry points (i.e., modular versus whole-program analysis).

Java Features. While JOANA supports full Java except for reflection, KeY supports sequential Java programs only, as well as only a limited set of Java features. KeY also requires that either the source code or the method contracts of library methods are available. The implementation of the two approaches from Sects. 6 and 7 using JOANA and KeY thus supports the same Java subset that KeY supports. Another challenge lies in the fact that the two tools do not work on the same programming language (respective level). While JOANA works on Java bytecode that is in a single static assignment (SSA) form, KeY works on Java source code. For the soundness of our implementation, we make the (arguably quite reasonable) assumption that the compilation of a Java program into byte-code does not change the noninterference properties of the program. Moreover, this also raises the issue of mapping byte code statements to source code statements. We are able to determine the line in the source code (which can contain more than one source code statement) from which a byte code statement originates. However, a source code statement can be compiled into more than one byte code statement and, due to the SSA form, for some source code statements, we may not even have a corresponding byte code statement. The simplified program from Definition 6 is thus impossible to generate using these tools. Instead, we generate an over-approximation of the simplified program by removing a line in the source code only if (1) the SDG contains a node corresponding to a byte code statement originating from that line and (2) no such node exists in the backward slice of the low output. In order to avoid multiple source code statements on the same line, we first preprocess the source code and transform it so that it contains only one statement per line.

Slice Executability. Another implementation challenge is the fact that SDG-based forward and backward slicing—as done by JOANA—can result in a program that is not executable or may handle jump statements such as goto, break, or continue incorrectly. This is not a problem for JOANA, since it does not need to generate any code for the analysis. For the second step of the approaches from Sect. 6, i.e., verification or test generation, however, having a program that can actually be executed is of great importance. This is a problem when implementing the approach using the slicers provided by JOANA off-the-shelf, but our approach is nevertheless feasible, since (as stated in Hammer [17, Chapter 2]) various solutions have been proposed that enhance SDG-based slicing and enable the generation of executable program slices [1,2,19]. For our implementation, we go about this problem by generating an over-approximation of the simplified program and by restricting ourselves to programs without jump statements. Thus, we obtain executable slices by (a) preserving lines that contain certain types of statements such as constructors or static initializers, and by (b) supporting only programs without jump statements.

Modular and Whole-Program Analysis. Another issue with combining the two tools is the fact that, on the one hand, the analysis performed by KeY is done modularly at method level, and the results hold for any prestate that fulfills the precondition. JOANA, on the other hand, performs a whole-program analysis where the entire program is checked starting from an entry point method—in most cases the main method. If the goal is to verify the whole program, the approaches described in Sects. 6 and 7 do not need any modification regarding this difference. For proving individual program methods, however, the SDG-based approach must analyze the given method without any context information. This is done in our implementation by adding an artificial main method as entry point for JOANA's analysis that only calls the method for which noninterference should be proven. However, this is no problem, as the SDG-based analysis can be implemented in such a way that any other method can serve as entry point.

8.2   Combinations of JOANA and KeY

The Combined Approach from Sect. 7 is well-suited for programs where the part that cannot be handled by the SDG-based approach is concentrated in a called method. If, however, syntactic dependencies between high input and low output are spread throughout the program, the whole program needs to be verified and no simplification is made. In such cases, the approach from Sect. 6 can still benefit from the SDG-based analysis. Using that approach, individual statements that have no effect on a potential noninterference violation can be removed, while the Combined Approach works on method-level granularity.

The Combined Approach and the simplification approach from Sect. 6 are orthogonal. In fact, the program fragment analyzed with the Combined Approach can be further reduced by applying the approach from Sect. 6. By simplifying the program (according to Definition 6), we can remove statements and execution paths that are not relevant with respect to the possible dependency represented by the analyzed summary edge. Since the program that is simplified in this way is noninterference-equivalent to, i.e., conforms to the same noninterference properties as, the original program fragment, the soundness of the Combined Approach is not affected by this simplification.

9   Related Work

A multitude of research has been done on information flow security, dating back to the works by Denning and Denning [9,10] and later by Goguen and Meseguer [14]. A survey on approaches for proving noninterference can be found in works by Sabelfeld and Myers [30]. In the following, we elaborate on some approaches that are similar to ours.

The work by Küsters et al. [25] also aims to achieve the best of both worlds—automatic analysis and interactive techniques for proving noninterference—by combining an automatic SDG-based analysis and a logic-based approach, i.e., a theorem prover. This approach (called *Hybrid Approach*) first attempts to prove noninterference using an SDG-based approach, e.g., an analysis by JOANA. If this attempt fails, the user must identify the cause of a possible false alarm and extend the program such that the affected low output is overwritten with a value that does not depend on the high input. The extended program is then checked by JOANA and, if the modified program is shown to be noninterferent, then—in the next step—a logic-based approach (using, e.g., the theorem prover KeY) is used to show that the extended program is equivalent to the original program (i.e., that the extended program results in the same low output). The Hybrid Approach improves the precision provided by JOANA and reduces the verification with KeY to purely functional proofs. However, the communication between the tools is done completely manually by the user and there is no assistance when searching for the causes of the false alarms. The approach does not utilize the results provided by the SDG-based analysis tool that could both discard those program parts that are irrelevant regarding the analyzed noninterference property and simplify the program to be verified. In fact, applying the program extension above makes the program to be verified in the second step even more complex.

Another combination of SDG-based and logic-based approaches is to check the satisfiability of path conditions for the execution paths that are determined by the reported security violation [17,35]. If a path condition is unsatisfiable, then the respective execution path cannot lead to an illegal information flow. A program input that satisfies the path condition serves as a "witness", and the user can thereby analyze the program execution with that single input (the witness) and check whether an illegal information flow may occur. However, this is a difficult task, especially for indirect dependencies. For our work, the noninterference tests that we generate have two inputs and show the illegal information flow more clearly.

Moreover, there are also other approaches for automatic test generation that check noninterference. However, they do not support all the properties from Sect. 2. Le Guernic [26] proposed a sound information-flow testing mechanism based both on standard testing techniques and on a combination of dynamic and static analysis. Once a path coverage property is achieved, an argumentation regarding noninterference can be established. Furthermore, Milushev et al. present a tool that uses symbolic execution in combination with a form of self-composition for noninterference testing of C programs [28]. A logic-based approach to detect and generate exploits for information flow properties which presents them as JUnit tests is described by Do et al. [11]. Finally, information flow test case generation was also done by Gruska and Hrițcu et al. [15,24].

10 Conclusion

We presented an overview of recent combinations of deductive verification and automatic test generation on the one hand, and static analysis on the other hand, together establishing our *Noninterference Framework*.

In a first use case, we presented an approach that uses deductive verification in order to automatically generate tests with the goal of finding noninterference violations. Deductive verification allows for the systematic generation of noninterference tests for all pairs of program execution paths and can identify pairs of execution paths that may never lead to a counterexample. This combination thus improves the computation of the achieved test coverage for noninterference.

In a second use case, we described two variants of an approach used for proving noninterference properties that combines deductive verification with an SDG-based static analysis. Deductive verification and SDG-based static analysis are complementary approaches. The highly-scalable SDG-based approach is used in a first step to show that large parts of the analyzed program cannot lead to a noninterference violation. In the second step, we apply the precise deductive verification approach for noninterference on the remaining program parts. This combination thus reduces the effort for the deductive verification.

References

1. Abadi, A., Ettinger, R., Feldman, Y.A.: Fine slicing. In: de Lara, J., Zisman, A. (eds.) FASE 2012. LNCS, vol. 7212, pp. 471–485. Springer, Heidelberg (2012). https://doi.org/10.1007/978-3-642-28872-2_32
2. Agrawal, H.: On slicing programs with jump statements. In: Sarkar, V., Ryder, B.G., Soffa, M.L. (eds.) PLDI 1994, pp. 302–312. ACM (1994). https://doi.org/10.1145/178243.178456
3. Ahrendt, W., Beckert, B., Bubel, R., Hähnle, R., Schmitt, P.H., Ulbrich, M. (eds.): Deductive Software Verification - The KeY Book: From Theory to Practice. LNCS, vol. 10001. Springer (2016). https://doi.org/10.1007/978-3-319-49812-6
4. Ahrendt, W., Gladisch, C., Herda, M.: Proof-based test case generation. In: Ahrendt et al. [3], chap. 12, pp. 415–451. https://doi.org/10.1007/978-3-319-49812-6_12
5. Barrett, C., Stump, A., Tinelli, C.: The SMT-LIB standard: Version 2.0. Tech. rep., Department of Computer Science, The University of Iowa (2010), http://smt-lib.org/papers/smt-lib-reference-v2.0-r12.09.09.pdf, www.smt-lib.org
6. Beckert, B., Bischof, S., Herda, M., Kirsten, M., Kleine Büning, M.: Using theorem provers to increase the precision of dependence analysis for information flow control. In: Sun, J., Sun, M. (eds.) ICFEM 2018. LNCS, vol. 11232, pp. 284–300. Springer, Cham (2018). https://doi.org/10.1007/978-3-030-02450-5_17
7. Beckert, B., Bruns, D., Klebanov, V., Scheben, C., Schmitt, P.H., Ulbrich, M.: Information flow in object-oriented software. In: Gupta, G., Peña, R. (eds.) LOPSTR 2013. LNCS, vol. 8901, pp. 19–37. Springer, Cham (2014). https://doi.org/10.1007/978-3-319-14125-1_2
8. Darvas, Á., Hähnle, R., Sands, D.: A theorem proving approach to analysis of secure information flow. In: Hutter, D., Ullmann, M. (eds.) SPC 2005. LNCS, vol. 3450, pp. 193–209. Springer, Heidelberg (2005). https://doi.org/10.1007/978-3-540-32004-3_20
9. Denning, D.E.: A lattice model of secure information flow. Commun. ACM **19**(5), 236–243 (1976). https://doi.org/10.1145/360051.360056
10. Denning, D.E., Denning, P.J.: Certification of programs for secure information flow. Commun. ACM **20**(7), 504–513 (1977). https://doi.org/10.1145/359636.359712
11. Do, Q.H., Bubel, R., Hähnle, R.: Automatic detection and demonstrator generation for information flow leaks in object-oriented programs. Comput. Secur. **67**, 335–349 (2017). https://doi.org/10.1016/j.cose.2016.12.002
12. Engel, C., Hähnle, R.: Generating unit tests from formal proofs. In: Gurevich, Y., Meyer, B. (eds.) TAP 2007. LNCS, vol. 4454, pp. 169–188. Springer, Heidelberg (2007). https://doi.org/10.1007/978-3-540-73770-4_10
13. Ferrante, J., Ottenstein, K.J., Warren, J.D.: The program dependence graph and its use in optimization. Trans. Program. Lang. Syst. **9**(3), 319–349 (1987). https://doi.org/10.1145/24039.24041
14. Goguen, J.A., Meseguer, J.: Security policies and security models. In: Symposium on Security and Privacy (S & P), pp. 11–20. IEEE (1982). https://doi.org/10.1109/SP.1982.10014
15. Gruska, D.P.: Information flow testing. Fundamenta Informaticae **128**(1–2), 81–95 (2013). https://doi.org/10.3233/FI-2013-934
16. Hamann, T., Herda, M., Mantel, H., Mohr, M., Schneider, D., Tasch, M.: A uniform information-flow security benchmark suite for source code and bytecode. In: Gruschka, N. (ed.) NordSec 2018. LNCS, vol. 11252, pp. 437–453. Springer, Cham (2018). https://doi.org/10.1007/978-3-030-03638-6_27

17. Hammer, C.: Information flow control for Java: a comprehensive approach based on path conditions in dependence graphs. Ph.D. thesis, Karlsruhe Institute of Technology (KIT), Germany (2009). https://doi.org/10.5445/KSP/1000012049
18. Hammer, C., Snelting, G.: Flow-sensitive, context-sensitive, and object-sensitive information flow control based on program dependence graphs. Int. J. Inf. Secur. **8**(6), 399–422 (2009). https://doi.org/10.1007/s10207-009-0086-1
19. Harman, M., Lakhotia, A., Binkley, D.: Theory and algorithms for slicing unstructured programs. Inf. Softw. Technol. **48**(7), 549–565 (2006). https://doi.org/10.1016/j.infsof.2005.06.001
20. Herda, M.: Combining Static and Dynamic Program Analysis Techniques for Checking Relational Properties. Ph.D. thesis, Karlsruhe Institute of Technology (KIT), Germany (2020). https://doi.org/10.5445/IR/1000104496
21. Herda, M., Tyszberowicz, S., Müssig, J., Beckert, B.: Verification-based test case generation for information-flow properties. In: SAC 2019, pp. 2231–2238. ACM (2019). https://doi.org/10.1145/3297280.3297500
22. Herda, M., Tyszberowicz, S., Beckert, B.: Using dependence graphs to assist verification and testing of information-flow properties. In: Dubois, C., Wolff, B. (eds.) TAP 2018. LNCS, vol. 10889, pp. 83–102. Springer, Cham (2018). https://doi.org/10.1007/978-3-319-92994-1_5
23. Horwitz, S., Reps, T., Binkley, D.: Interprocedural slicing using dependence graphs. Trans. Program. Lang. Syst. **12**(1), 26–60 (1990). https://doi.org/10.1145/77606.77608
24. Hrițcu, C., et al.: Testing noninterference, quickly. J. Funct. Program. **26**, 1 62 (2016). https://doi.org/10.1017/S0956796816000058
25. Küsters, R., Truderung, T., Beckert, B., Bruns, D., Kirsten, M., Mohr, M.: A hybrid approach for proving noninterference of Java programs. In: CSF 2015, pp. 305–319. IEEE (2015). https://doi.org/10.1109/CSF.2015.28
26. Guernic, G.: Information flow testing. In: Cervesato, I. (ed.) ASIAN 2007. LNCS, vol. 4846, pp. 33–47. Springer, Heidelberg (2007). https://doi.org/10.1007/978-3-540-76929-3_4
27. Leavens, G.T., Baker, A.L., Ruby, C.: Preliminary design of JML: a behavioral interface specification language for Java. SIGSOFT Softw. Eng. Notes **31**(3), 1–38 (2006). https://doi.org/10.1145/1127878.1127884
28. Milushev, D., Beck, W., Clarke, D.: Noninterference via symbolic execution. In: Giese, H., Rosu, G. (eds.) FMOODS/FORTE 2012. LNCS, vol. 7273, pp. 152–168. Springer, Heidelberg (2012). https://doi.org/10.1007/978-3-642-30793-5_10
29. de Moura, L., Bjørner, N.: Z3: An Efficient SMT Solver. In: Ramakrishnan, C.R., Rehof, J. (eds.) TACAS 2008. LNCS, vol. 4963, pp. 337–340. Springer, Heidelberg (2008). https://doi.org/10.1007/978-3-540-78800-3_24
30. Sabelfeld, A., Myers, A.C.: Language-based information-flow security. IEEE J. Sel. Areas Commun. **21**(1), 5–19 (2003). https://doi.org/10.1109/JSAC.2002.806121
31. Scheben, C.: Program-level Specification and Deductive Verification of Security Properties. Ph.D. thesis, Karlsruhe Institute of Technology (KIT), Germany (2014). https://doi.org/10.5445/IR/1000046878
32. Scheben, C., Greiner, S.: Information flow analysis. In: Ahrendt et al. [3], chap. 13, pp. 453–471. https://doi.org/10.1007/978-3-319-49812-6_13
33. Schmitt, P.H.: First-order logic. In: Ahrendt et al. [3], chap. 2, pp. 23–47. https://doi.org/10.1007/978-3-319-49812-6_2
34. Snelting, G.: Combining slicing and constraint solving for validation of measurement software. In: Cousot, R., Schmidt, D.A. (eds.) SAS 1996. LNCS, vol. 1145, pp. 332–348. Springer, Heidelberg (1996). https://doi.org/10.1007/3-540-61739-6_51

35. Snelting, G., Robschink, T., Krinke, J.: Efficient path conditions in dependence graphs for software safety analysis. Trans. Softw. Eng. Methodol. **15**(4), 410–457 (2006). https://doi.org/10.1145/1178625.1178628
36. Wasserrab, D., Lohner, D.: Proving information flow noninterference by reusing a machine-checked correctness proof for slicing. In: Aderhold, M., Autexier, S., Mantel, H. (eds.) VERIFY@IJCAR 2010. EPiC Series in Computing, vol. 3, pp. 141–155. EasyChair (2010). https://doi.org/10.29007/nnzj

SymPaths: Symbolic Execution Meets Partial Order Reduction

Frank S. de Boer[1], Marcello Bonsangue[2] (ID), Einar Broch Johnsen[3]([✉]) (ID),
Violet Ka I Pun[3,4] (ID), S. Lizeth Tapia Tarifa[3] (ID), and Lars Tveito[3]

[1] CWI, Amsterdam, The Netherlands
f.s.de.boer@cwi.nl
[2] Leiden University, Leiden, The Netherlands
m.m.bonsangue@liacs.leidenuniv.nl
[3] Department of Informatics, University of Oslo, Oslo, Norway
{einarj,violet,sltarifa,larstvei}@ifi.uio.no
[4] Western Norway University of Applied Sciences, Bergen, Norway
Violet.Ka.I.Pun@hvl.no

Abstract. Symbolic execution is an important technique for software analysis, which enables systematic model exploration by following all possible execution paths for a given program. For multithreaded shared variable programs, this technique leads to a state space explosion. Partial order reduction is a technique which allows equivalent execution paths to be recognized, reducing the state space explosion problem. This paper provides formal justifications for these techniques in a multithreaded setting by proving the correctness and completeness of symbolic execution for multithreaded shared variable programs, with and without the use of partial order reduction. We then show how these formal justifications carry over to prove the soundness and relative completeness of a proof system for such multithreaded shared variable programs in dynamic logic, such that partial order reduction can be used to simplify the proof construction by mitigating the state space explosion.

1 Introduction

Symbolic execution [1] is an important technique for software analysis. It is especially used for testing, but also for debugging and deductive verification. In fact, the KeY verification system [2] is based on symbolic execution. Symbolic execution is intuitively very appealing, because one symbolic execution may correspond to a large, possibly infinite, class of normal (concrete) executions by representing the input values to a program by logical variables. Symbolic execution has made tremendous progress in recent years; recent surveys [3,4] cover improvements in the effectiveness as well as the achieved code coverage of symbolic execution tools such as, e.g., DART [5], EXE [6], KLEE [7]. As already observed in [8], the formal justification for the technique in terms of correctness has received much less attention. In contrast, [8] formally defines the correctness of symbolic execution by relating a symbolic transition system to a concrete structural operational semantics.

© Springer Nature Switzerland AG 2020
W. Ahrendt et al. (Eds.): Deductive Software Verification, LNCS 12345, pp. 313–338, 2020.
https://doi.org/10.1007/978-3-030-64354-6_13

Symbolic execution has mainly been applied to sequential languages, where different executions can be captured by different path conditions. By considering executions with different path conditions, a tool can systematically explore the entire symbolic execution graph of a sequential program. In contrast, concurrent languages give rise to non-determinism during execution, which is another source of state space explosion when using symbolic execution for such model exploration. In this paper, we study symbolic execution for multithreaded shared variable programs in terms of a symbolic transition system. In order to capture the non-determinism, we combine path conditions with scheduling traces, which reflect the order in which different threads have been selected for execution, into so-called symbolic paths (or *sympaths*). We prove the correctness and completeness of the resulting system by extending the work of [8] to a multithreaded setting. To address the state space explosion resulting from the different possible scheduling decisions, we show how *partial order reduction* (POR) [9] can be introduced into the symbolic execution framework. POR allows symbolic states to be pruned from the overall search space during model exploration, by merging symbolic states with equivalent symbolic paths. We extend the symbolic transition system with a pruning operation for search states by means of POR, and prove the correctness and completeness of the resulting system.

Finally, we consider a proof system for multithreaded shared variable programs using dynamic logic [10], in the spirit of symbolic execution in the KeY system. We show how soundness and relative completeness of this proof system can be obtained by extending the soundness and correctness proofs for the symbolic transition system. We further show how POR can be applied in this setting to reduce the state space explosion during the verification in the proof system, and again prove soundness and relative completeness by extending the corresponding soundness and correctness proofs for the symbolic transition system with POR.

The main contributions of this paper can be summarized as follows:

- A formal model of symbolic execution for multithreaded shared variable programs, with a formal justification in terms of correctness and completeness;
- Pruning techniques for the symbolic execution model using POR, with a formal justification in terms of correctness and completeness;
- A Maude [11] implementation of the two symbolic execution models, allowing their comparison in terms of the number of reduction steps to explore the full state space and the number of final symbolic states; and
- A dynamic logic proof system for multithreaded shared variable programs with pruning techniques using POR, with a formal justification in terms of soundness and relative completeness proofs.

2   Background

2.1   Symbolic Execution

In the development of a formal model of the symbolic execution of multithreaded shared variable programs, we follow the general approach of [8]. We define the symbolic execution of such programs by means of a transition system for generating the atomic computation steps between symbolic configurations. A symbolic configuration consists of the program to be executed, a substitution which symbolically represents the state, i.e., the assignment of symbolic values to the shared program variables, and a path condition. In general, a substitution assigns expressions of the programming language to the program variables.

We then provide a formal justification of this symbolic transition system by relating it to a transition system for generating the atomic computation steps between concrete configurations. A concrete configuration consists of the multi-threaded program that remains to be executed and the assignment of values to the shared program variables. The formal justification involves a proof of correctness and completeness. Correctness establishes that executing the program in any initial state that satisfies the path condition leads to the corresponding execution path. On the other hand, completeness amounts to showing that all concrete executions are covered by the symbolic transition system.

In this paper, we extend the approach of [8] to multithreaded shared variable programs. At the core of this extension lies the symbolic representation of scheduling information in the path condition.

2.2   Partial Order Reduction

Partial order reduction (POR) is a technique to reduce the size of the state space when exploring the different executions of a parallel program by exploiting the commutativity of concurrently executed *independent* transitions [9,12]. This commutativity relation between transitions is lifted to an equivalence relation $\sim$ on traces over these transitions. Given a trace tr reflecting an interleaved execution of a number of parallel threads, the set $[tr]$ of traces equivalent to tr according to the equivalence relation $\sim$, is supposed to preserve the sequential order of transitions for the individual threads. Thus, all equivalent traces have the same length and contain the same events. Let $s \xrightarrow{tr} s'$ denote that the state s' can be reached from a state s by applying the transition steps according to the order given by a trace tr. The pruning of states based on traces is justified during model exploration when the traces are sufficiently expressive to make sure that equivalent traces lead to equal states; i.e., the following must be a theorem [9]:

Theorem 1. *If* $s_0 \xrightarrow{tr_1} s_1$, $s_0 \xrightarrow{tr_2} s_2$ *and* $tr_2 \in [tr_1]$, *then* $s_1 = s_2$.

Observe that, given a trace tr, the elements of $[tr]$ can be enumerated by successively permuting adjacent commuting events. An additional problem is to identify syntactic criteria to approximate this semantic notion of equivalence. This can be done by identifying transitions that correspond to *interference-free* statements [13]; e.g., two transitions are independent if their corresponding statements do not affect each others' program variables.

In program analysis, POR can be used to explore the different equivalence classes of executions, rather than exploring every execution path. Assuming that

$$Pr \in Prog ::= P \ldots P$$
$$P \in Proc ::= \texttt{proc} \ \{s\}$$
$$s \in Stm ::= s; s \mid x := e \mid \texttt{if} \ e \ \{s\} \ \texttt{else} \ \{s\} \mid \texttt{while} \ e \ \{s\}$$
$$e \in Exp ::= x \mid v \mid op(e, \ldots, e)$$
$$op \in Ops ::= == \mid \wedge \mid \vee \mid + \mid - \mid < \mid \leq \mid \ldots$$
$$v \in Val ::= \texttt{True} \mid \texttt{False} \mid 0 \mid 1 \mid 2 \mid \ldots$$

Fig. 1. The syntax of the basic programming language PL.

we can decide whether two traces are in the same equivalence class, we can stop the analysis of the current execution path if we know that its trace is equivalent to the trace of an execution that we have already explored.

3   Combining Symbolic Execution and POR

We formalize how symbolic execution and partial order reduction can be combined in the context of a basic calculus of parallel execution.

3.1   A Basic Calculus of Parallel Processes

To formalize the main concepts of symbolic execution with partial order reduction, we consider a basic programming language PL with a given set of types, including Bool and Int, and a set Var of program variables, with the typical element x. The syntax of PL is defined in Fig. 1, where s denotes a sequence of statements. A program Pr consists of a list of processes P of the form **proc** $\{s\}$, where the statement s of the process will be executed in parallel with the statements of other processes. Statements s contain sequential compositions $s_1; s_2$, assignments $x := e$, conditionals and **while**-statements. Expressions e consist of program variables x, values v, and operators op applied to expressions. The operators include standard operators on the types Bool and Int, and values v the usual values of these types. A *predicate* is an expression of type Bool; the set of predicates is denoted by $BExp$, with typical element b. We assume that programs are well-typed, so operators are recursively applied to the correct number of correctly typed subexpressions.

3.2   Concrete Semantics

A valuation ϵ is a (mathematical) function $Var \rightarrow Val$ which assigns to each program variable $x \in Var$ a value $v \in Val$. For any expression e, let $\epsilon(e)$ denote its value with respect to the valuation ϵ (defined by induction on the structure of e). We now describe a transition system for the concrete execution of PL programs, based on a transition relation between concrete states. These states are given by the grammar in Fig. 2.

Definition 1 (Concrete States). *A concrete state cs is a term $(\!|\epsilon, \Sigma|\!)$, where ϵ denotes a valuation and Σ denotes a thread pool.*

$$cs \in ConState ::= (\!|\epsilon, \Sigma|\!)$$
$$\tau \in Thread ::= \iota(s)$$
$$\epsilon \in Valuation ::= \varepsilon \mid \epsilon[x \mapsto v]$$
$$\Sigma \in ThreadPool ::= \{\tau\} \mid \Sigma \cup \Sigma$$
$$V \in VarSet ::= \{x\} \mid V \cup V$$

Fig. 2. Runtime syntax for the concrete semantics, where ι is a thread identifier, v a value and s a statement.

Figure 3 defines the concrete semantics for PL by means of a transition relation $\rightarrow_c$ between concrete states. The rules CONC-ASSIGN, CONC-COND1, CONC-COND2, CONC-WHILE1 and CONC-WHILE2 respectively describe the concrete executions of assignments, conditional and **while**-statements by a single thread ι. The concrete execution of the assignment in a thread ι, as in rule CONC-ASSIGN, results on an update in ϵ, where the new value for variable x is the value obtained by the valuation $\epsilon(e)$ of the expression e. For a conditional statement in a thread ι, we apply one of the rules CONC-COND1 or CONC-COND2, depending on the valuation $\epsilon(b)$ of Boolean expression b. If the valuation is True, then we reduce the conditional statement to $s1$ by applying rule CONC-COND1, otherwise we reduce it to $s2$ by applying rule CONC-COND2. The **while**-statement is similar to the conditional statement, applying rules CONC-WHILE1 or CONC-WHILE2, respectively. We let $T(\Sigma)$ denote the set of identifiers for the active threads in thread pool Σ (i.e., the threads in the thread pool which have not yet terminated).

$$(\text{CONC-ASSIGN})$$
$$v = \epsilon(e)$$
$$\overline{\quad (\!|\epsilon, \{\iota(x := e; s)\} \cup \Sigma|\!) \quad}$$
$$\rightarrow_c (\!|\epsilon[x \mapsto v], \iota(s)\} \cup \Sigma|\!)$$

$$(\text{CONC-COND1})$$
$$\epsilon(b) = \text{True}$$
$$\overline{\quad (\!|\epsilon, \{\iota(\text{if } b \, \{s_1\} \text{ else } \{s_2\}; s)\} \cup \Sigma|\!) \quad}$$
$$\rightarrow_c (\!|\epsilon, \{\iota(s_1; s)\} \cup \Sigma|\!)$$

$$(\text{CONC-COND2})$$
$$\epsilon(b) = \text{False}$$
$$\overline{\quad (\!|\epsilon, \{\iota(\text{if } b \, \{s_2\} \text{ else } \{s_2\}; s)\} \cup \Sigma|\!) \quad}$$
$$\rightarrow_c (\!|\epsilon, \{\iota(s_2; s)\} \cup \Sigma|\!)$$

$$(\text{CONC-WHILE1})$$
$$\epsilon(b) = \text{True}$$
$$\overline{\quad (\!|\epsilon, \{\iota(\text{while } b \, \{s_1\}; s_2)\} \cup \Sigma|\!) \quad}$$
$$\rightarrow_c (\!|\epsilon, \{\iota(s_1; \text{while } b \, \{s_1\}; s_2)\} \cup \Sigma|\!)$$

$$(\text{CONC-WHILE2})$$
$$\epsilon(b) = \text{False}$$
$$\overline{\quad (\!|\epsilon, \{\iota(\text{while } b \, \{s_1\}; s_2)\}\Sigma|\!) \quad}$$
$$\rightarrow_c (\!|\epsilon, \{\iota(s_2)\} \cup \Sigma|\!)$$

Fig. 3. A concrete semantics for PL.

Initial and Final Concrete States. Given a program $Pr = $ **proc** $\{s_1\} \ldots$ **proc** $\{s_n\}$, let $init(Pr)$ denote the set of threads $\{\iota_1(s_1), \ldots, \iota_n(s_n)\}$ such that

$\iota_1, \ldots, \iota_n$ are distinct thread identifiers. The *initial state* cs_0 for the concrete execution of Pr is given by the concrete state $(\![\epsilon, init(Pr)]\!)$, where ϵ assigns some initial values to the program variables in Pr (i.e., $\epsilon(x) = v_0$, for all $x \in VarSet$). The execution of a program terminates when the concrete state $(\![\epsilon, \Sigma]\!)$ is such that $T(\Sigma) = \emptyset$ (technically, we may add a termination marker as a statement in the runtime syntax). For notational convenience, we denote such final concrete states by $(\![\epsilon, \emptyset]\!)$.

A concrete execution consists of a sequence of concrete states $cs_0, \ldots, cs_n$ such that cs_0 is some initial concrete state of the form $(\![\epsilon, init(Pr)]\!)$, and for $0 \le i < n$ there exist concrete transitions $cs_i \to_c cs_{i+1}$.

Proposition 1 (Reachability for concrete executions). *A concrete state cs is reachable if and only if there exists a concrete execution $cs_0, \ldots, cs_n$ such that $cs_n = cs$.*

This proposition follows by a straightforward induction on the length of the concrete execution.   □

3.3   Symbolic Semantics

We now introduce the machinery for the symbolic execution of PL. Let $vars(e)$ denote an inductively defined function which returns the set of program variables in an expression e. Abstracting from its possible KeY implementation as a sequence of symbolic updates, we define a symbolic substitution σ as a (mathematical) function $Var \to Exp$ which assigns to each program variable $x \in Var$ an expression $e \in Exp$ with the following constructors: ε denotes the empty substitution, and $\sigma[x \mapsto e]$ the substitution mapping x to e and y to $\sigma(y)$ for every other variable y (i.e., $y \ne x$). As usual, composition $\sigma_1 \circ \sigma_2$ is defined recursively over these constructors for substitutions σ_1 and σ_2. By $e\sigma$ we denote the application of the substitution σ to the expression e, defined inductively by

$$x\sigma = \sigma(x)$$
$$op(e_1, \ldots, e_n)\sigma = op(e_1\sigma, \ldots, e_n\sigma) \; . \tag{1}$$

In the sequel, we will also use the alternative function application $\sigma(e)$ which denotes the homeomorphic extension of σ to expressions.

Let sequences ϕ over a set X be constructed from the empty sequence ε, the elements in X as singleton sequences, and by a concatenation operator $\phi_1 \cdot \phi_2$ applied to sequences ϕ_1 and ϕ_2.

We can now define *symbolic paths*, which combine the accumulated Boolean conditions from symbolic execution (Sect. 2.1) with the scheduling traces used for partial order reduction (Sect. 2.2), as follows:

Definition 2 (Symbolic Paths). *A symbolic path ϕ is a sequence of events $\iota\langle e, V_1, V_2\rangle$, where ι is a thread identifier, e a predicate and $V_1, V_2 \subseteq VarSet$.*

$$cn \in Configuration ::= ss \mid cn\ cn$$
$$ss \in SymState ::= (\!|\sigma, \phi, \Sigma|\!)$$
$$\tau \in Thread ::= \iota(s)$$
$$\sigma \in Subst ::= \varepsilon \mid \sigma[x \mapsto e]$$
$$\phi \in SymPath ::= \varepsilon \mid \iota\langle e, V, V \rangle \mid \phi \cdot \phi$$
$$\Sigma \in ThreadPool ::= \{\tau\} \mid \Sigma \cup \Sigma$$
$$V \in VarSet ::= \{x\} \mid V \cup V$$

Fig. 4. Runtime syntax for the symbolic semantics, where ι is a thread identifier, e an expression and s a statement.

The predicates e will be used to capture path conditions, and the sets V_1 and V_2 the write and read effects associated with a program statement. Let $\lceil \phi \rceil$ denote the *path condition* corresponding to a symbolic path ϕ, given as the conjunction of the predicates in the events of ϕ. For a substitution σ and a symbolic path ϕ, let $\sigma(\phi)$ denote the symbolic path obtained by the pointwise application of σ to all expressions in the events of ϕ.

Next we describe a transition system for the symbolic execution of PL based on a transition relation between symbolic configurations, which are *sets* of *symbolic states*. These configurations are given by the grammar in Fig. 4.

Definition 3 (Symbolic state). *A symbolic state ss is a term $(\!|\sigma, \phi, \Sigma|\!)$, where*

- σ *is a symbolic substitution,*
- ϕ *is a symbolic path, and*
- Σ *is a thread pool.*

A configuration cn consists of a set of symbolic states. Given a substitution σ' and a configuration cn, let $\sigma'(cn)$ denote the pointwise application of substitution σ' to each symbolic state in cn, such that $\sigma'((\!|\sigma, \phi, \Sigma|\!)) = (\!|\sigma' \circ \sigma, \sigma'(\phi), \Sigma|\!)$.

Figure 5 defines the symbolic semantics for PL, by means of a (symbolic) transition relation $\rightarrow_s$ between configurations of symbolic states. As usual, $cn \rightarrow_s^* cn'$ denotes that cn' is reachable from cn by a finite number of transitions of $\rightarrow_s$. Transitions may be labelled by the identifier of the thread which is reduced; thus, $\xrightarrow{\iota}_s$ describes an atomic execution step by a specific thread ι. The rules ASSIGN, COND and WHILE respectively describe the symbolic executions of assignments, conditional and **while**-statements by a single thread. An assignment in thread ι is captured by the rule ASSIGN, where the substitution σ is updated with the symbolic value $e\sigma$ for x and the symbolic path ϕ is extended with the event $\iota\langle \text{True}, \{x\}, vars(e)\rangle$, indicating that an assignment has as path condition True, that there is a write to the variable x and there are reads from the variables in the expression e. The symbolic execution of both conditional and **while**-statements generates *two* symbolic states which correspond to the two different outcomes of the evaluation of the Boolean condition. A conditional statement in thread ι is captured by rule COND, which reduces the statement to either s_1 or s_2, depending on the predicates $b\sigma$ and $\neg b\sigma$. This rule abstracts

$$(\textsc{Assign})$$
$$\phi' = \phi \cdot \iota \langle \text{True}, \{x\}, vars(e) \rangle$$
$$\overline{(\!|\sigma, \phi, \{\iota(x := e; s)\} \cup \Sigma|\!)}$$
$$\xrightarrow{\iota}_s (\!|\sigma[x \mapsto e\sigma], \phi', \{\iota(s)\} \cup \Sigma|\!)$$

$$(\textsc{Schedule})$$
$$\{\iota_1, \ldots, \iota_n\} = T(\Sigma)$$
$$\frac{(\!|\sigma, \phi, \Sigma|\!) \xrightarrow{\iota_i}_s cn_i \quad 1 \le i \le n}{(\!|\sigma, \phi, \Sigma|\!) \to_s cn_1 \ldots cn_n}$$

$$(\textsc{Cond})$$
$$\phi_1 = \phi \cdot \iota \langle b\sigma, \emptyset, vars(b) \rangle$$
$$\phi_2 = \phi \cdot \iota \langle \neg b\sigma, \emptyset, vars(b) \rangle$$
$$\overline{(\!|\sigma, \phi, \{\iota(\text{if } b \ \{s_1\} \ \text{else} \ \{s_2\}; s)\} \cup \Sigma|\!)}$$
$$\xrightarrow{\iota}_s (\!|\sigma, \phi_1, \{\iota(s_1; s)\} \cup \Sigma|\!)$$
$$(\!|\sigma, \phi_2, \{\iota(s_2; s)\} \cup \Sigma|\!)$$

$$(\textsc{Context})$$
$$\frac{cn_1 \to_s cn_1'}{cn_1 \ cn_2 \to_s cn_1' \ cn_2}$$

$$(\textsc{While})$$
$$\phi_1 = \phi \cdot \iota \langle b\sigma, \emptyset, vars(b) \rangle$$
$$\phi_2 = \phi \cdot \iota \langle \neg b\sigma, \emptyset, vars(b) \rangle$$
$$\overline{(\!|\sigma, \phi, \{\iota(\text{while } b \ \{s_1\}; s_2)\} \cup \Sigma|\!)}$$
$$\xrightarrow{\iota}_s (\!|\sigma, \phi_1, \{\iota(s_1; \text{while } b \ \{s_1\}; s_2)\} \cup \Sigma|\!)$$
$$(\!|\sigma, \phi_2, \{\iota(s_2)\} \cup \Sigma|\!)$$

Fig. 5. A symbolic semantics for PL with symbolic paths.

the two conditional rules of the concrete semantics by resulting in two possible symbolic states. The **while**-statement is handled analogously in rule WHILE.

The rule SCHEDULE introduces branching by generating *all* symbolic states reachable in one step from a symbolic state with thread pool Σ, by applying a transition rule for each thread ι_i in Σ and by collecting the corresponding resulting configurations cn_i. The rule CONTEXT *lifts* transitions starting from a single symbolic state to transitions between configurations themselves (i.e., configurations should be interpreted modulo the reordering of the states). Remark that the CONTEXT rule introduces branching because different symbolic states can be chosen, but this branching is trivially confluent.

Example 1 (Symbolic execution). This example illustrates the use of the symbolic transition system. Consider a program with two threads:

$$\textbf{proc } \{x := 0; x := y + 1; s\} \qquad \textbf{proc } \{\text{if } (x = 0) \ \{s_1\} \ \text{else} \ \{s_2\}\},$$

where s, s_1 and s_2 are arbitrary statements (possibly sequentially composed and nested). We construct an initial configuration with one symbolic state

$$(\!|\sigma, \varepsilon, \{\iota_1(x := 0; x := y + 1; s), \iota_2(\text{if } (x = 0) \ \{s_1\} \ \text{else} \ \{s_2\})\}|\!),$$

where $\sigma = [x \mapsto x_0, y \mapsto y_0]$ and the two threads are identified by ι_1 and ι_2 respectively. With only one symbolic state, we apply the rule SCHEDULE, which reduces thread ι_1 by means of rule ASSIGN and thread ι_2 by means of rule COND, and obtain a configuration with three symbolic states:

$$(\!|\sigma[x \mapsto 0], \iota_1\langle\text{True}, \{x\}, \emptyset\rangle, \{\iota_1(x := y + 1; s), \iota_2(\textbf{if } (x = 0) \ \{s_1\} \ \textbf{else} \ \{s_2\})\}|\!)$$
$$(\!|\sigma, \iota_2\langle x_0 = 0, \emptyset, \{x\}\rangle, \{\iota_1(x := 0; x := y + 1; s), \iota_2(s_1)\}|\!)$$
$$(\!|\sigma, \iota_2\langle x_0 \neq 0, \emptyset, \{x\}\rangle, \{\iota_1(x := 0; x := y + 1; s), \iota_2(s_2)\}|\!)$$

The execution can now progress in any of the three symbolic states, where one is arbitrarily chosen by the rule CONTEXT. Let us select the first symbolic state. Since there are two threads which can be scheduled in this symbolic state and the COND executes both branches of ι_2, application of the rule SCHEDULE results in a configuration with five symbolic states:

$$(\!|(\sigma[x \mapsto 0])[x \mapsto y_0 + 1], \iota_1\langle\text{True}, \{x\}, \emptyset\rangle \cdot \iota_1\langle\text{True}, \{x\}, \{y\}\rangle,$$
$$\{\iota_1(s), \iota_2(\textbf{if } (x = 0) \ \{s_1\} \ \textbf{else} \ \{s_2\})\}|\!)$$
$$(\!|\sigma[x \mapsto 0], \iota_1\langle\text{True}, \{x\}, \emptyset\rangle \cdot \iota_2\langle x_0 = 0, \emptyset, \{x\}\rangle, \{\iota_1(x := y + 1; s), \iota_2(s_1)\}|\!)$$
$$(\!|\sigma[x \mapsto 0], \iota_1\langle\text{True}, \{x\}, \emptyset\rangle \cdot \iota_2\langle x_0 \neq 0, \emptyset, \{x\}\rangle, \{\iota_1(x := y + 1; s), \iota_2(s_2)\}|\!)$$
$$(\!|\sigma, \iota_2\langle x_0 = 0, \emptyset, \{x\}\rangle, \{\iota_1(x := 0; x := y + 1; s), \iota_2(s_1)\}|\!)$$
$$(\!|\sigma, \iota_2\langle x_0 \neq 0, \emptyset, \{x\}\rangle, \{\iota_1(x := 0; x := y + 1; s), \iota_2(s_2)\}|\!)$$

Thus, the application of the rules CONTEXT and SCHEDULE alternate, the former introduces branching in the execution tree since any symbolic state may be selected and the latter introduces additional symbolic states in a configuration. This alternation continues until the threads identified by ι_1 and ι_2 have both terminated.

Symbolic transitions can be adapted by means of a symbolic substitution:

Proposition 2 (Framing). *For any* $\sigma \in Subst$, $ss \in SymState$, *and* $cn \in Configuration$, *we have that if* $ss \rightarrow_s cn$ *then* $\sigma(ss) \rightarrow_s \sigma(cn)$.

This proposition follows by a straightforward induction on the length of the symbolic execution. $\quad\square$

Initial and final symbolic states. Given a program $Pr = \textbf{proc } \{s_1\} \ldots \textbf{proc } \{s_n\}$, the *initial state* ss_0 for the symbolic execution of Pr is given by a symbolic configuration with a single symbolic state $(\!|\sigma, \varepsilon, init(Pr)|\!)$, where $\sigma(x) = x$, for all $x \in VarSet$. The execution of a program terminates when $T(\Sigma) = \emptyset$ for all symbolic states $(\!|\sigma, \phi, \Sigma|\!)$ in the configuration cn (technically, we may add a termination marker as a statement in the runtime syntax). For notational convenience, we denote such final symbolic states by $(\!|\sigma, \phi, \emptyset|\!)$.

For any computation $ss_0 \rightarrow_s^* cn$, starting from the initial symbolic state ss_0, the symbolic states $ss' \in cn$ represent symbolic states which are *reachable* by a particular scheduling of the threads and a particular symbolic evaluation of the Boolean conditions $\lceil\phi\rceil$ of the conditional and **while**-statements, as recorded by the symbolic path ϕ in ss'. This is captured by the following proposition which relates the above notion of reachability and the following notion of a *symbolic* *execution*: A symbolic execution consists of a sequence $ss_0, \ldots, ss_n$ of symbolic states such that ss_0 denotes the initial symbolic state (as defined above), and for $0 \leq i < n$ there exist symbolic configurations cn_{i+1} and transitions $ss_i \rightarrow_s cn_{i+1}$ such that $ss_{i+1} \in cn_{i+1}$. Note that the reachability of ss_n only states the existence of configurations cn_i, for $0 \leq i \leq n$, such that $cn_0 = ss_0$, $cn_i \rightarrow_s cn_{i+1}$, $0 \leq i < n$, and $ss_n \in cn_n$.

Proposition 3 (Reachability for symbolic executions). *A symbolic state ss is reachable if and only if there exists a symbolic execution $ss_0, \ldots, ss_n$ such that $ss_n = ss$.*

This proposition follows by a straightforward induction on the length of the symbolic execution.   □

3.4   Correctness

We prove correctness with respect to the concrete semantics from Sect. 3.2. Correctness then roughly consists of showing that for every symbolic execution there exists a corresponding concrete execution. We can now introduce the following formulation of the correctness theorem, where the valuation $\epsilon \circ \sigma$, which consists of a composition of the valuation ϵ and the substitution σ, is defined by $\epsilon \circ \sigma(x) = \epsilon(\sigma(x))$.

Theorem 2 (Correctness). *For every symbolic execution $ss_0, \ldots, ss_n$ such that $\epsilon_0(\lceil \phi_n \rceil) = \text{true}$, where ϵ_0 is a valuation and ϕ_n the symbolic path of ss_n, there exists a concrete computation $cs_0, \ldots, cs_n$ such that, for $0 \leq i \leq n$, the states ss_i and cs_i have the same thread pool, and $\epsilon_i = \epsilon_0 \circ \sigma_i$, where ϵ_i denotes the valuation of cs_i and σ_i denotes the substitution recorded by ss_i.*

Proof. The proof proceeds by induction on the length of the symbolic computation and a case analysis of the last transition. As such, it consists of a straightforward extension of the correctness proof of the symbolic execution of the underlying sequential programming language (consisting of assignments, conditional and **while**-statements, and their sequential composition), as given in [8].   □

Corollary 1. *Let $(\!|\sigma_1, \phi_1, \Sigma_1|\!) \rightarrow_s^* (\!|\sigma_n, \phi_n, \Sigma_n|\!)$ cn be a symbolic transition sequence and ϵ a valuation such that $\epsilon(\lceil \phi_n \rceil)$. Then there exists a concrete transition sequence $(\!|\epsilon_1, \Sigma_1|\!) \rightarrow_c^* (\!|\epsilon_n, \Sigma_n|\!)$ such that $\epsilon_i = \epsilon \circ \sigma_i$ for all $1 \leq i \leq n$.*

This corollary follows directly from Theorem 2 and Proposition 2.   □

The converse of Theorem 2 states that for every concrete execution there exists a symbolic one.

Theorem 3 (Completeness). *For any concrete computation $cs_0, \ldots, cs_n$, there exists a symbolic execution $ss_0, \ldots, ss_n$ such that for $0 \leq i \leq n$ the states ss_i and cs_i have the same thread pool, and $\epsilon_i = \epsilon_0 \circ \sigma_i$, where ϵ_i denotes the valuation of cs_i and σ_i denotes the substitution recorded by ss_i.*

The proof of the theorem proceeds by a straightforward induction on the length of the concrete computation and a case analysis of the last transition.   □

Corollary 2. *Let* $(\!|\epsilon_1, \Sigma_1|\!) \rightarrow_c^* (\!|\epsilon_n, \Sigma_n|\!)$ *be a concrete transition sequence and* ϵ *a valuation such that* $\epsilon_1 = \epsilon \circ \sigma_1$. *Then there exists a symbolic transition sequence* $(\!|\sigma_1, \phi_1, \Sigma_1|\!) \rightarrow_s^* (\!|\sigma_n, \phi_n, \Sigma_n|\!)$ *cn such that* $\epsilon_n = \epsilon \circ \sigma_n$ *for all* $1 \leq i \leq n$.

This proposition follows directly from Theorem 3 and Proposition 2.   □

3.5   Partial Order Reduction

In order to provide a syntactic characterization of POR in the transition system of Fig. 5, we first define an equivalence-preserving permutation as an equivalence relation between symbolic paths. For this purpose, we use a syntactic criterion for interference freedom [14,15], based on the disjointness of read-and write-variables between the two events [13].

Definition 4 (Interference Freedom & Path Equivalence). *Given two events* $ev_1 = \iota_1\langle e_1, W_1, R_1\rangle$ *and* $ev_2 = \iota_2\langle e_2, W_2, R_2\rangle$. *The interference freedom of the events* ev_1 *and* ev_2, *denoted* $ev_1 \sim ev_2$, *is defined as follows:*

$$ev_1 \sim ev_2 \iff \iota_1 \neq \iota_2 \text{ and } (R_1 \cap W_2) = (W_1 \cap R_2) = (W_1 \cap W_2) = \emptyset.$$

Let ϕ_1 *and* ϕ_2 *be symbolic paths. Denoted by* $\sim$ *the smallest equivalence relation on symbolic paths such that*

$$ev_1 \sim ev_2 \text{ implies } \phi_1 \cdot ev_1 \cdot ev_2 \cdot \phi_2 \sim \phi_1 \cdot ev_2 \cdot ev_1 \cdot \phi_2$$

We have the following semantical justification of the above definition.

Proposition 4 (Confluence). *Let*

$$(\!|\sigma, \phi, \{\tau_1, \tau_2\} \cup \Sigma|\!) \xrightarrow{\iota_1}_s (\!|\sigma_1, \phi \cdot ev_1, \{\tau_1', \tau_2\} \cup \Sigma|\!) \; cn_1$$

and

$$(\!|\sigma, \phi, \{\tau_1, \tau_2\} \cup \Sigma|\!) \xrightarrow{\iota_2}_s (\!|\sigma_2, \phi \cdot ev_2, \{\tau_1, \tau_2'\} \cup \Sigma|\!) \; cn_2$$

be two symbolic transitions such that $ev_1 \sim ev_2$. *Then there exists a substitution* σ' *such that*

$$(\!|\sigma_1, \phi \cdot ev_1, \{\tau_1', \tau_2\} \cup \Sigma|\!) \xrightarrow{\iota_2}_s (\!|\sigma', \phi \cdot ev_1 \cdot ev_2, \{\tau_1', \tau_2'\} \cup \Sigma|\!) \; cn_2$$

and

$$(\!|\sigma_2, \phi \cdot ev_2, \{\tau_1, \tau_2'\} \cup \Sigma|\!) \xrightarrow{\iota_1}_s (\!|\sigma', \phi \cdot ev_2 \cdot ev_1, \{\tau_1', \tau_2'\} \cup \Sigma|\!) \; cn_1$$

Proof. It suffices to consider the following cases of the events ev_1 and ev_2. The case where $ev_1 = \iota_1\langle b_1\sigma, \emptyset, vars(b_1)\rangle$ and $ev_2 = \iota_2\langle b_2\sigma, \emptyset, vars(b_2)\rangle$ follows immediately from the symbolic semantics of conditional and `while`-statements. Next, let $ev_1 = \iota_1\langle \text{True}, \{x\}, vars(e)\rangle$ and $ev_2 = \iota_2\langle b\sigma, \emptyset, vars(b)\rangle$. By the symbolic semantics of assignments, it follows that $\sigma_1 = \sigma[x \mapsto \sigma(e)]$. Since $ev_1 \sim ev_2$, we have that $x \notin vars(b)$, and thus $b\sigma$ (syntactically) equals $b\sigma_1$. As the last case, let $ev_1 = \iota_1\langle \text{True}, \{x_1\}, vars(e_1)\rangle$ and $ev_2 = \iota_2\langle \text{True}, \{x_2\}, vars(e_2)\rangle$. Furthermore, let $\sigma_1 = \sigma[x_1 \mapsto \sigma(e_1)]$ and $\sigma_2 = \sigma[x_2 \mapsto \sigma(e_2)]$. Since $ev_1 \sim ev_2$, we have that x_1 and x_2 are distinct variables, $x_1 \notin vars(e_2)$, and $x_2 \notin vars(e_1)$. It follows that for $i \neq j \in \{1, 2\}$, $e_i\sigma_j$ equals the expression $e_i\sigma$, and $\sigma_i[x_j \mapsto \sigma_i(e_j)]$ equals the *simultaneous* substitution $\sigma[x_1, x_2 \mapsto e_1\sigma, e_2\sigma]$. □

The following corollary of Proposition 4 states that equivalent symbolic paths uniquely determine the substitution and thread pool of a reachable symbolic state.

Corollary 3 (Determinism). *For any reachable symbolic states $(\!|\sigma, \phi, \Sigma|\!)$ and $(\!|\sigma', \phi', \Sigma'|\!)$, $\phi \sim \phi'$ implies $\sigma = \sigma'$ and $\Sigma = \Sigma'$.*

The equivalence relation $\sim$ is then trivially extended to symbolic states as follows: if $\phi \sim \phi'$ then $(\!|\sigma, \phi, \Sigma|\!) \sim (\!|\sigma, \phi', \Sigma|\!)$. We can now apply a partial order reduction to the symbolic transition system by simply lifting it to the equivalence classes of symbolic states. Let $[cn]$ denote the equivalence classes of the symbolic states of the symbolic configuration cn. In addition, let γ be a selection function such that $[cn]_\gamma$ denotes the symbolic configuration which results from selecting from each of the equivalence classes of the symbolic states of the symbolic configuration cn a (canonical) representative. We then have the following partial order reduction rule.

$$(\text{POR}_\gamma)$$

$$\frac{[cn]_\gamma \to_s cn'}{cn \to_{por_\gamma} cn'}$$

Correctness and completeness of the partial order reduction rule with respect to the symbolic transition system follows from the above corollary which ensures that the partial order reduction rule is independent of the choice of the representatives of the equivalence classes of symbolic states. This is formalized by the following proposition.

Proposition 5 (Bisimulation). *The transition systems $\to_s$ and $\to_{por_\gamma}$ are bisimilar with respect to the equivalence relation $\sim$: Let cn_1 and cn_2 be two symbolic configurations such that $[cn_1] = [cn_2]$. Then for any transition $cn_1 \to_s cn_1'$, there exists a transition $cn_2 \to_{por_\gamma} cn_2'$ such that $[cn_1'] = [cn_2']$, and vice versa.*

Proof. It suffices to prove that $ss \sim ss'$ and $ss \xrightarrow{\ell}_s cn$ implies that there exists a cn' such that $ss' \xrightarrow{\ell}_s cn'$ and $[cn] = [cn']$, which follows from a straightforward case analysis of the transition $ss \xrightarrow{\ell}_s cn$. □

A symbolic state ss is POR_γ reachable if there exists a symbolic configuration cn such that $ss_0 \rightarrow^*_{por_\gamma} cn$ and $ss \in cn$ (where ss_0 denotes the initial symbolic state, as defined above).

Corollary 4 (Correctness of POR). *For any symbolic state ss that is POR_γ reachable, there exists an equivalent symbolic state $ss' \sim ss$ which is $\rightarrow_s$ reachable (i.e., there exists a symbolic configuration cn such that $ss_0 \rightarrow^*_s cn$ and $ss' \in cn$).*

Proof. Induction on the length of the computation $ss_0 \rightarrow^*_{por_\gamma} cn$, where $ss' \in cn$, using the above proposition.   □

Corollary 5. *For any POR computation $(\!|\sigma, \phi, \Sigma|\!) \rightarrow^*_{por_\gamma} (\!|\sigma', \phi', \Sigma'|\!)$ cn, there exists a symbolic computation $(\!|\sigma, \phi, \Sigma|\!) \rightarrow^*_s (\!|\sigma', \phi', \Sigma'|\!)$ cn.*

Proof. The proof follows directly from Corollary 4 and Proposition 2.   □

Corollary 6 (Completeness of POR). *For any symbolic state ss that is $\rightarrow_s$ reachable, there exists an equivalent symbolic state $ss' \sim ss$ which is POR_γ reachable.*

Proof. Induction on the length of the computation $ss_0 \rightarrow^*_s cn$, where $ss' \in cn$, using the above proposition.   □

Corollary 7. *For any symbolic computation $(\!|\sigma, \phi, \Sigma|\!) \rightarrow^*_s (\!|\sigma', \phi', \Sigma'|\!)$ cn, there exists a POR computation $(\!|\sigma, \phi, \Sigma|\!) \rightarrow^*_{por_\gamma} (\!|\sigma', \phi', \Sigma'|\!)$ cn.*

Proof. The proof follows directly from Corollary 6 and Proposition 2.   □

Note that Corollary 7 holds because we are free in the choice of γ. In Sect. 5, we fix a particular selection function, meaning all symbolic *states*, but not all symbolic *computations*, will be reachable.

4   Dynamic Logic for Multithreaded Programs

This section demonstrates how the integration of symbolic execution and partial order reduction presented in Sect. 3 can be put to use to define a dynamic logic proof system for multithreaded programs.

4.1   Dynamic Logic

The formulas of dynamic logic are defined inductively, starting from the set $BExp$ of Boolean expressions.

Definition 5 (DL Formulas). *Given a set $BExp$ of Boolean expressions over variables $x \in VarSet$, symbolic substitutions $\sigma \in Subst$ and thread pools $\Sigma \in ThreadPool$, the dynamic logic formulas are defined inductively as the smallest set **DL** such that*

1. $\Psi \in \mathbf{DL}$ if $\Psi \in BExp$
2. $\neg\Psi_1, \Psi_1 \wedge \Psi_2, \Psi_1 \vee \Psi_2, \Psi_1 \rightarrow \Psi_2, \Psi_1 \leftrightarrow \Psi_2 \in \mathbf{DL}$ if $\Psi_1, \Psi_2 \in \mathbf{DL}$
3. $\exists x \cdot \Psi, \forall x \cdot \Psi \in \mathbf{DL}$ if $x \in VarSet$ and $\Psi \in \mathbf{DL}$
4. $[\Sigma]\Psi \in \mathbf{DL}$ if $\Psi \in \mathbf{DL}$
5. $\{\sigma\}\Psi \in \mathbf{DL}$ if $\sigma \in Subst$ and $\Psi \in \mathbf{DL}$

The set $\mathbf{DL}$ extends the set $\mathbf{FOL}$ of first-order logic formulas with two *modalities* $[\Sigma]\Psi$ and $\{\sigma\}\Psi$, which we refer to as the box-modality and the update-modality, respectively. (Note that the update modality here features a symbolic substitution σ, which differs slightly from the symbolic updates in KeY. Symbolic substitutions may be implemented using symbolic updates.) A formula $\Psi \in \mathbf{DL}$ is called *first-order* if it does not contain any modality (i.e., $\Psi \in \mathbf{FOL}$). For simplicity, we may write $[Pr]\Psi$ to express $[init(Pr)]\Psi$, where $Pr \in Prog$.

We write $\epsilon \models \Psi$ to denote that a formula Ψ is valid in a valuation ϵ (or that ϵ satisfies Ψ). The satisfiability of a DL formula can be defined as follows (e.g., [10]):

Definition 6 (Satisfiability of DL Formulas). *Let $\Psi \in \mathbf{DL}$, $e \in BExp$ and ϵ a valuation. Satisfiability is defined inductively as follows:*

$$\epsilon \models e \iff \epsilon(e) = \top$$
$$\epsilon \models \neg\Psi \iff \epsilon \not\models \Psi$$
$$\epsilon \models \Psi_1 \wedge \Psi_2 \iff \epsilon \models \Psi_1 \text{ and } \epsilon \models \Psi_2$$
$$\epsilon \models \Psi_1 \vee \Psi_2 \iff \epsilon \models \Psi_1 \text{ or } \epsilon \models \Psi_2$$
$$\epsilon \models \exists x \cdot \Psi \iff \epsilon[x \mapsto \epsilon(e)] \models \Psi \text{ for some } e \in Exp$$
$$\epsilon \models \forall x \cdot \Psi \iff \epsilon[x \mapsto \epsilon(e)] \models \Psi \text{ for all } e \in Exp$$
$$\epsilon \models [\Sigma]\Psi \iff \epsilon' \models \Psi \text{ for all } \epsilon' \text{ such that } (\!|\epsilon, \Sigma|\!) \rightarrow_c^* (\!|\epsilon', \emptyset|\!)$$
$$\epsilon \models \{\sigma\}\Psi \iff \epsilon' \models \Psi \text{ and } \epsilon' = \epsilon \circ \sigma$$

Operators for implication and equivalence can be defined as usual in terms of negation and disjunction. This definition of the box-modality $[\Sigma]\Psi$ corresponds to *partial correctness* in the sense that the formula only needs to hold for all execution paths that lead to a final state; in particular, $[\Sigma]\Psi$ is true if the execution of Σ never terminates. The update modality $\{\sigma\}\Psi$ corresponds to executing a sequence of assignments. Observe that $\{\sigma\}\{\sigma'\}\Psi \leftrightarrow \{\sigma \circ \sigma'\}\Psi$.

4.2 A DL Sequent Calculus for Multithreaded Programs

We first define a sequent calculus for proving DL formulas over multithreaded Pr programs, and then transform it into a transition system similar to $\rightarrow_s$.

A *sequent* of the form $\Gamma \Rightarrow \Psi$, where Γ and Ψ are sets of formulas, expresses that the conjunction of the formulas in the antecedent Γ implies the disjunction of the formulas in the succedent Ψ; a sequent $\Gamma \Rightarrow \Psi$ is valid, denoted $\models \Gamma \Rightarrow \Psi$ if and only if its corresponding implication is valid.

The sequent calculus is given by the rules in Fig. 6. To prove a sequent, one constructs a proof tree with the sequent as an open goal at the root by repeatedly applying rules to open proof goals until all open goals have been closed. The application of a rule to an open goal closes the goal and extends the tree with new open goals corresponding to the premises of the rule. An axiom closes an open goal. A particular feature of this calculus is that sequents are labelled, such that the thread which is symbolically executed in the rules DL-ASSIGN, DL-COND and DL-WHILE is determined by the label. Rule DL-SCHEDULE forces all threads to be explored in the construction of the proof tree. We omit standard rules for first-order logic (e.g., [2, Ch. 2]), and assume that we can determine whether sequents of the form $\Gamma \Rightarrow \Psi$ hold, when Γ, Ψ consist of formulas in **FOL**. Consequently, we can decide whether a branch can be closed by checking if the formulas in the antecedent Γ are inconsistent or by means of the rule DL-REDUCE, which reduces the sequent to first-order formulas by applying the substitution σ to Ψ (assuming Ψ consists of formulas in **FOL**, otherwise one of the presented rules applies).

To show that a DL formula Ψ is true for a program Pr, we need to construct a proof by applying the rules of the sequent calculus, starting from the sequent $\Gamma \Rightarrow \{\sigma\}[init(Pr)]\Psi$, where $x\sigma = x$ for all $x \in VarSet$. Observe that due to the interleaving of threads, we may need to prove many equivalent sequents in different nodes of the proof tree. These sequents differ only in the order in which steps from different non-interfering threads have been selected in the branches leading to the nodes.

In order to eliminate such redundant nodes during the proof construction, we now consider a path-sensitive reformulation of this calculus. For this purpose, we introduce *path-sensitive sequents*, a variation of the sequents above, in the form $\Gamma, \phi \Rightarrow \Psi$, where ϕ is a symbolic path as defined in Sect. 3. The correspondence with the standard sequents is obtained by lifting the symbolic path to, e.g., $\Gamma, \lceil \phi \rceil \Rightarrow \Psi$ for the sequent above. We consider a transition relation $\rightarrow_{dl}$ between sets Ω of path-sensitive sequents that need to be proven, corresponding to the open leaf nodes of the proof tree constructed by the sequent calculus above. The rules of the transition relation $\rightarrow_{dl}$ are presented in Fig. 7. Each transition in the proof system takes a sequent from Ω and replaces it with some new sequents. As before, we omit the standard rules for first-order logic; we remove sequents that correspond to closed leaf nodes in the proof trees, such that a closed proof tree in the proof calculus here corresponds to an empty set of sequents. Thus, a sequent $\Gamma, \phi \Rightarrow \Psi$ has a proof if $\Gamma, \phi \Rightarrow \Psi \rightarrow_{dl}^* \emptyset$ (or if the formulas in $\Gamma, \lceil \phi \rceil$ are inconsistent). Observe that as a consequence of the representation, we have a linear sequence of proof steps rather than a proof tree.

The rules of the transition system in Fig. 7 correspond closely to the sequent calculus of Fig. 6. For each rule of the sequent calculus, the corresponding transition rule is obtained by letting the left-hand-side of the transition be the conclusion of the proof rule and the right-hand-side its set of premises. The remaining transition rule DLT-CONTEXT corresponds in the transition system to the selection of open nodes in the proof tree for the next construction step (this step is not formalized in the sequent calculus). Observe that the transition system $\rightarrow_{dl}$ is *locally confluent* as the result of applying DLT-CONTEXT to different sequents in a set Ω is unaffected by the order of these rule applications.

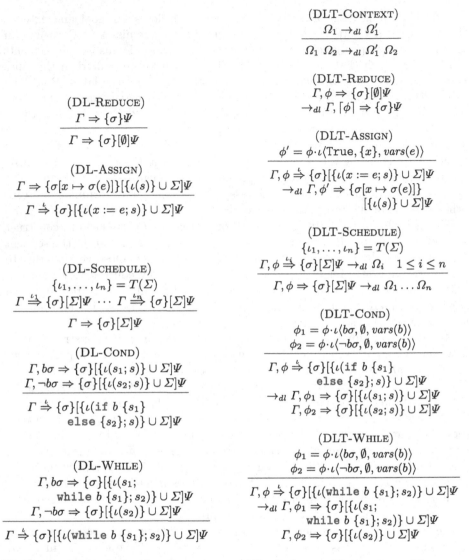

Fig. 6. A proof calculus for dynamic logic.

Fig. 7. A transition system with symbolic paths for dynamic logic.

4.3 Soundness and Relative Completeness for the DL Proof System

Our goal is to establish that the DL proof system for multithreaded programs is sound and relative complete. For this purpose, we take the formulation as a transition system (Fig. 7) as our starting point, and connect it to the symbolic execution framework defined in Sect. 3. In fact, the symbolic execution achieved by the transition relation $\rightarrow_{dl}$ corresponds exactly to that achieved by the transition relation $\rightarrow_s$, as expressed by the following lemma.

Lemma 1. $\Gamma, \phi \Rightarrow \{\sigma\}[\Sigma]\Psi \to_{dl} \{\Gamma, \phi' \Rightarrow \{\sigma'\}[\Sigma']\Psi\} \cup \Omega$ *if and only if* $(\!|\{\sigma, \phi, \Sigma|\}) \to_s (\!|\{\sigma', \phi', \Sigma'|\})$ *cn.*

Proof. Follows by induction over the transition rules. For each rule in the transition system (Fig. 7), select the corresponding rule for symbolic execution, and vice versa. □

Lemma 1 allows soundness to be shown in terms of the soundness of the symbolic execution framework and the soundness of the underlying proof system for FOL.

Theorem 4 (Soundness). *Let* $\Sigma \in ThreadPool$, $\sigma \in Subst$, $\phi \in SymPath$ *and* $\Gamma, \Psi \in \mathbf{DL}$. *If* $\Gamma, \phi \Rightarrow \{\sigma\}[\Sigma]\Psi \to_{dl}^* \emptyset$, *then* $\vdash \Gamma, \phi \Rightarrow \{\sigma\}[\Sigma]\Psi$.

Proof. Without loss of generality, we may assume that Ψ consists of first-order formulas. Assume $\Gamma, \phi \Rightarrow \{\sigma\}[\Sigma]\Psi \to_{dl}^* \emptyset$. Then, due to the confluence of the transition system $\to_{dl}$, there is a derivation $\Gamma, \phi \Rightarrow \{\sigma\}[\Sigma]\Psi \to_{dl}^* \Omega$ such that $\Sigma' = \emptyset$ for all $\Gamma, \phi' \Rightarrow \{\sigma'\}[\Sigma']\Psi \in \Omega$. Then by applying DLT-REDUCE, we get $\Gamma, \lceil\phi'\rceil \Rightarrow \{\sigma'\}\Psi \to_{dl}^* \emptyset$. This last reduction uses the proof system for FOL, which by assumption gives $\models \Gamma, \lceil\phi'\rceil \Rightarrow \{\sigma'\}\Psi$ for any concrete valuation.
Let ϵ be a valuation such that $\epsilon \models \Gamma, \lceil\phi'\rceil$, and by Def. 6, we have $\epsilon \models \{\sigma'\}\Psi$. By Def. 6 again, we have $\epsilon_2 \models \Psi$ where $\epsilon_2 = \epsilon \circ \sigma'$.
By Lemma 1 and the assumption $\Gamma, \phi \Rightarrow \{\sigma\}[\Sigma]\Psi \to_{dl}^* \emptyset$, we get $(\!|\{\sigma, \phi, \Sigma|\}) \to_s^* (\!|\{\sigma', \phi', \emptyset|\})$ cn. Given this and $\epsilon \models \lceil\phi'\rceil$ (implied by $\epsilon \models \Gamma, \lceil\phi'\rceil$), then by Corollary 1 we get $(\!|\{\epsilon_1, \Sigma|\}) \to_c^* (\!|\{\epsilon_2, \emptyset|\})$ such that $\epsilon_1 = \epsilon \circ \sigma$ and $\epsilon_2 = \epsilon \circ \sigma'$. This together with $\epsilon_2 \models \Psi$ and Def. 6 gives $\epsilon_1 \models [\Sigma]\Psi$; consequently by Def. 6 again, we get $\epsilon \models \{\sigma\}[\Sigma]\Psi$. Finally, $\lceil\phi'\rceil$ implying $\lceil\phi\rceil$ gives $\epsilon \models \Gamma, \phi \Rightarrow \{\sigma\}[\Sigma]\Psi$. □

The relative completeness of the proof system can be shown in terms of the correctness of the symbolic execution framework and the relative completeness of the underlying proof system for FOL in a similar way.

Theorem 5 (Relative Completeness). *Let* $\Sigma \in ThreadPool$, $\sigma \in Subst$, $\phi \in SymPath$ *and* $\Gamma, \Psi \in \mathbf{DL}$. *If* $\models \Gamma, \phi \Rightarrow \{\sigma\}[\Sigma]\Psi$, *then* $\Gamma, \phi \Rightarrow \{\sigma\}[\Sigma]\Psi \to_{dl}^* \emptyset$.

Proof. Since we aim to show *relative completeness*, we assume the completeness of the underlying first-order logic proof system; i.e., $\models \psi$ implies $\psi \to_{dl}^* \emptyset$ for any first-order formula ψ. Moreover, without loss of generality, we may assume that Ψ consists of only first-order formulas.
Assume $\epsilon \models \Gamma, \phi \Rightarrow \{\sigma\}[\Sigma]\Psi$ for some ϵ, and assume further $\epsilon \models \Gamma \wedge \lceil\phi\rceil$. This gives $\epsilon \models \{\sigma\}[\Sigma]\Psi$. By Def. 6, we have $\epsilon' \models [\Sigma]\Psi$ where $\epsilon' = \epsilon \circ \sigma$. Then by Def. 6 again, we have $\epsilon'' \models \Psi$ for all valuations ϵ'' such that $(\!|\{\epsilon', \Sigma|\}) \to_c^* (\!|\{\epsilon'', \emptyset|\})$. Given this together with $\epsilon' = \epsilon \circ \sigma$ and by Corollary 2, there exist a symbolic computation $(\!|\{\sigma, \phi, \Sigma|\}) \to_s^* (\!|\{\sigma', \phi', \emptyset|\})$ cn for some σ' and ϕ' such that $\epsilon'' = \epsilon \circ \sigma'$.
Since $\epsilon'' \models \epsilon \circ \sigma'$ gives $\epsilon \models \{\sigma'\}\Psi$, then by assuming $\epsilon \models \Gamma \wedge \lceil\phi'\rceil$, we get $\models \Gamma \wedge \lceil\phi'\rceil \Rightarrow \{\sigma'\}\Psi$. By Lemma 1, we have $\Gamma, \phi \Rightarrow \{\sigma\}[\Sigma]\Psi \to_{dl}^* \{\Gamma, \phi' \Rightarrow \{\sigma'\}[\emptyset]\Psi\} \cup \Omega$, where $\Gamma, \phi' \Rightarrow \{\sigma'\}[\emptyset]\Psi$ can be reduced to $\Gamma, \lceil\phi'\rceil \Rightarrow \{\sigma'\}\Psi$ by rule DLT-REDUCE. Finally by the completeness of FOL that gives us $\Gamma, \phi' \Rightarrow \{\sigma'\}\Psi \to_{dl}^* \emptyset$, the theorem follows. □

Remark that the rule DLT-WHILE here is based on unfolding the **while**-loop to emphasize its similarity with the rule WHILE of Sect. 3.3. The rule could be lifted to reasoning about infinite unfoldings of the **while**-loop using a loop-invariant in the usual way; the proof of relative completeness would then require an assumption about a sufficiently strong invariant to prove reachability for all finite approximations of the infinite unfoldings.

4.4 Partial Order Reduction in Proof Search

We now lift the equivalence relation $\sim$ of Def. 4 to DL sequents as follows: if $\phi \sim \phi'$ then $\Gamma, \phi \Rightarrow \{\sigma\}[\Sigma]\Psi \sim \Gamma, \phi' \Rightarrow \{\sigma\}[\Sigma]\Psi$. Let $[\Omega]$ denote the equivalence classes of sets Ω of path-sensitive sequents. Let γ be a selection function such that $[\Omega]_\gamma$ denotes the path-sensitive sequent which results from selecting from each of the equivalence classes of path-sensitive sequents of the set Ω a (canonical) representative. This allows us to define the following partial order reduction rule for the proof construction in DL:

$$\text{(DL-POR)}$$
$$\frac{[\Omega]_\gamma \to_{dl} \Omega'}{[\Omega] \to_{dlpor_\gamma} [\Omega']} \tag{2}$$

The transition system $\to_{dlpor_\gamma}$ is locally confluent as the result of applying (DLT-Context) to different sequents in a set $[\Omega]_\gamma$ is not affected by the order of these rule applications.

Remark that in the proof system we have formalized as $\to_{dlpor_\gamma}$, the state of the proof search is represented as a set Ω of open proof goals. The same ideas could also be formulated in a proof system which represents the proof using a more standard graph-like proof structure, in which each sequent in Ω corresponds to an open proof goal in a leaf node of the graph. If the symbolic paths are kept on a canonical form in the sequents (see Sect. 5), the rule DL-POR would correspond to a rule which merges nodes with different occurrences of the same proof goal, turning the proof into a directed acyclic graph.

Correctness and relative completeness of $\to_{dlpor_\gamma}$ can be shown following the proofs for Theorems 4 and 5 above. In fact, the symbolic execution achieved by the transition relation $\to_{dlpor_\gamma}$ corresponds exactly to that of the transition relation $\to_{por_{\gamma'}}$, as expressed by the following lemma.

Lemma 2. $\Gamma, \phi \Rightarrow \{\sigma\}[\Sigma]\Psi \to_{dlpor_\gamma} \{\Gamma, \phi' \Rightarrow \{\sigma'\}[\Sigma']\Psi\} \cup \Omega$ *if and only if* $(\!|\{\sigma, \phi, \Sigma\}\!) \to_{por_{\gamma'}} (\!|\{\sigma', \phi', \Sigma'\}\!)$ cn.

Proof. Follows by induction over the transition rules. For each rule in the transition system for $\to_{dlpor_\gamma}$, select the corresponding rule for $\to_{por_{\gamma'}}$, and vice versa. □

Lemma 2 allows soundness and relative completeness to be shown for $\to_{dlpor_\gamma}$, following the proof structure of Theorems 4 and 5 above.

Theorem 6 (Soundness). *Let $\Sigma \in$ ThreadPool, $\sigma \in$ Subst, $\phi \in$ SymPath and $\Gamma, \Psi \in \boldsymbol{DL}$. If $\Gamma, \phi \Rightarrow \{\sigma\}[\Sigma]\Psi \rightarrow^{*}_{dlpor_\gamma} \emptyset$, then $\models \Gamma, \phi \Rightarrow \{\sigma\}[\Sigma]\Psi$.*

Proof (Sketch). Since $\rightarrow_{dlpor_\gamma}$ is locally confluent, we can adapt the proof structure of Theorem 4. The proof then follows from Corollary 5 and Lemma 2. $\quad\square$

Theorem 7 (Relative Completeness). *Let $\Sigma \in$ ThreadPool, $\sigma \in$ Subst, $\phi \in$ SymPath and $\Gamma, \Psi \in \boldsymbol{DL}$. If $\models \Gamma, \phi \Rightarrow \{\sigma\}[\Sigma]\Psi$, then $\Gamma, \phi \Rightarrow \{\sigma\}[\Sigma]\Psi \rightarrow^{*}_{dlpor_\gamma} \emptyset$.*

Proof (Sketch). We adapt the proof structure of Theorem 5. The proof then follows from Corollary 7 and Lemma 2. $\quad\square$

5 Implementation

We have developed a prototype implementation of the transition systems $\rightarrow_s$ and $\rightarrow_{por_\gamma}$ from Sect. 3, in order to report on experimental results and validate the approach. The prototype is developed in Maude [11], which allows writing executable models in rewriting logic [16]. We do not cover the full details of the implementation[1] here, but focus on how it differs from the transition system presented in Sect. 3.

Given a program Pr, our implementation executes the program symbolically. The program terminates when all threads have terminated, resulting in a configuration of final symbolic states. In addition, we output statistics about how many symbolic states are in a configuration and the number of applications of the rule SCHEDULE needed to reach a configuration from the initial configuration, in order to compare the two systems $\rightarrow_s$ and $\rightarrow_{por_\gamma}$.

The implementation stays very close to the transition systems defined in Sect. 3. One notable difference is that while the rule POR$_\gamma$ achieves partial order reduction by lifting the symbolic transition system to equivalence classes and by fixing a selection function γ to obtain the canonical representative, the implementation transforms all symbolic states to a canonical form. We achieve this by defining an ordering between *interference-free* events, and by choosing the smallest lexicographic representative. The ordering of interference-free events depends on the thread identifiers, which we assume to have a total order; in the implementation, these are represented as natural numbers.

Another difference is that the while statement in Sect. 3 is possibly unbounded, which can lead to an infinite number of paths in a symbolic setting. In order to get terminating executions for the examples in the prototype, the **while**-loop has been given an optional bound.

Example 2. The following is a very simple program with three threads, all of which perform a single assignment.

$$\texttt{proc } \{y := x\} \qquad \texttt{proc } \{z := x\} \qquad \texttt{proc } \{x := 2\}$$

---

[1] The implementation is available at https://github.com/larstvei/sympaths.

There are six final search states for this program in $\rightarrow_s$, with the following symbolic paths:

$$\iota_0\langle\text{True}, \{y\}, \{x\}\rangle \cdot \iota_1\langle\text{True}, \{z\}, \{x\}\rangle \cdot \iota_2\langle\text{True}, \{x\}, \emptyset\rangle$$
$$\iota_1\langle\text{True}, \{z\}, \{x\}\rangle \cdot \iota_0\langle\text{True}, \{y\}, \{x\}\rangle \cdot \iota_2\langle\text{True}, \{x\}, \emptyset\rangle$$
$$\iota_0\langle\text{True}, \{y\}, \{x\}\rangle \cdot \iota_2\langle\text{True}, \{x\}, \emptyset\rangle \quad \cdot \iota_1\langle\text{True}, \{z\}, \{x\}\rangle$$
$$\iota_1\langle\text{True}, \{z\}, \{x\}\rangle \cdot \iota_2\langle\text{True}, \{x\}, \emptyset\rangle \quad \cdot \iota_0\langle\text{True}, \{y\}, \{x\}\rangle$$
$$\iota_2\langle\text{True}, \{x\}, \emptyset\rangle \quad \cdot \iota_0\langle\text{True}, \{y\}, \{x\}\rangle \cdot \iota_1\langle\text{True}, \{z\}, \{x\}\rangle$$
$$\iota_2\langle\text{True}, \{x\}, \emptyset\rangle \quad \cdot \iota_1\langle\text{True}, \{z\}, \{x\}\rangle \cdot \iota_0\langle\text{True}, \{y\}, \{x\}\rangle$$

According to Definition 4, we have $\iota_1\langle\text{True}, \{z\}, \{x\}\rangle \sim \iota_0\langle\text{True}, \{y\}, \{x\}\rangle$. With partial order reduction in $\rightarrow_{por_\gamma}$, symbolic states that contain symbolic paths that only differ in the order of independent events can be *pruned* from the search. Executing the program in our implementation of in $\rightarrow_{por_\gamma}$ gives the following four symbolic paths, which cannot be reduced further.

$$\iota_0\langle\text{True}, \{y\}, \{x\}\rangle \cdot \iota_1\langle\text{True}, \{z\}, \{x\}\rangle \cdot \iota_2\langle\text{True}, \{x\}, \emptyset\rangle$$
$$\iota_0\langle\text{True}, \{y\}, \{x\}\rangle \cdot \iota_2\langle\text{True}, \{x\}, \emptyset\rangle \quad \cdot \iota_1\langle\text{True}, \{z\}, \{x\}\rangle$$
$$\iota_1\langle\text{True}, \{z\}, \{x\}\rangle \cdot \iota_2\langle\text{True}, \{x\}, \emptyset\rangle \quad \cdot \iota_0\langle\text{True}, \{y\}, \{x\}\rangle$$
$$\iota_2\langle\text{True}, \{x\}, \emptyset\rangle \quad \cdot \iota_0\langle\text{True}, \{y\}, \{x\}\rangle \cdot \iota_1\langle\text{True}, \{z\}, \{x\}\rangle$$

Example 3. The program in Fig. 8 consists of three threads, where the first two threads iterate in a **while**-loop, and the last thread assigns a variable to p, depending on the values of i, m, j and n. In the program, the variables x and y are shared between two out of three threads, while the other variables are local to a thread. To make the program terminating, we use *bounded* **while**-loops to specify the number of iterations of the loops that should be performed. Since there is no synchronization, the program has a high number of concurrent interleavings.

```
proc {                   proc {                   proc {
  while (i < m)[1] {       while (j < n)[1] {       if (i == m and j == n) {
    x := x * i;              y := y * j;              p := x * y
    i := i + 1              j := j + 1            } else {
  }                       }                          p := -1
}                       }                          }
                                                 }
```

Fig. 8. A concurrent program

The search space for this program grows very quickly. If we consider two instances of the program, with bounds $1, 1$ and $2, 1$ for the two **while**-loops, respectively, the following table shows the number of symbolic search *states* upon termination and the number of *steps* in terms of applications of the scheduling rule for executions with and without partial order reduction. In the table, the leftmost column shows the bounds of the two **while**-loops.

Figure 9 shows how many symbolic search states are visited during the search. As expected, when no partial order reduction is applied, the number of states

	$\rightarrow_s$		$\rightarrow por_\gamma$	
Bounds	States	Steps	States	Steps
1,1	6744	14495	35	596
2,1	58944	132884	97	1562

grows monotonically. However, with partial order reduction, the number of states peaks at 110 states in the middle of the search, but many of these are later found to be equivalent, leading to a final number of 35 states.

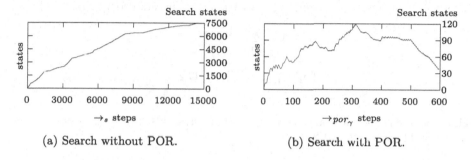

(a) Search without POR.   (b) Search with POR.

Fig. 9. The number of symbolic search states for the program with bounds $1, 1$.

6 Language Extensions

In this section, we briefly describe some possible extensions to the programming language.

6.1 Aliasing

In this paper, we considered a multithreaded shared variable programming language that only includes assignments to simple variables. Assignments involving arrays or fields of objects give rise to aliasing. In [8], a formal model is described for the symbolic execution of such assignments in a sequential context. Extending this model to multithreaded programs further requires a definition of the equivalence relation between symbolic paths that takes aliasing into account, in order to apply partial order reduction. More specifically, the commutativity of two events will depend on the aliasing information encoded by the symbolic path preceding these two events.

6.2   Dynamically Spawned Threads

It is straightforward to extend the language and the symbolic transition system $\to_s$ with dynamic thread creation. A new thread can be introduced by adding a syntactic construct **new**(s) to Pr. Since threads in the symbolic states are represented by a thread pool, the dynamically created thread needs to both be inserted into the thread pool and maintain the uniqueness of thread identifiers. Let a predicate fresh(ι, Σ) express that a thread identifier ι does not occur among the identifiers of the threads already in the thread pool Σ. It should be noted that the thread identifies are only generated at run-time and cannot be manipulated by the program. As such they are different from the object identities in KeY. The introduction of dynamically created threads can be handled by extending the symbolic transition system $\to_s$ with the following additional rule:

$$(\text{NewThread})$$
$$\frac{\text{fresh}(\iota', \Sigma)}{\begin{array}{c}(\!|\sigma, \phi, \{\iota(\textbf{new}(s'); s)\} \cup \Sigma|\!) \\ \xrightarrow{\iota}_s (\!|\sigma, \phi, \{\iota(s), \iota'(s')\} \cup \Sigma|\!)\end{array}}$$

The proofs of correctness and completeness are straightforward extensions of the proofs of Theorems 2 and 3.

6.3   Synchronization

The programming language discussed in this paper has no means of synchronization between threads. Synchronization can be achieved through simple mechanisms like locks or channels, or the more general mechanism of guarding statements with a condition on shared memory (e.g., **await** $(x < 5)$ in the syntax of ABS [17]). We can extend the language with guards by adding an event with the condition of the guard to the symbolic path whenever a guarded thread is scheduled. In the context of partial order reduction, equivalence between paths remains the same, as the conditions imposed by guards are no different than the conditions of conditional or **while**-statements.

6.4   Object Orientation

Above we already discussed the symbolic execution of assignments to fields of objects. In [8] a formal model of the symbolic execution of a basic sequential objet-oriented language is given which includes method calls. Of particular interest here is that the underlying symbolic representation of the heap abstracts from concrete object identifiers (or "locations"). In contrast, in the KeY system the symbolic execution of field assignments is defined with respect to an explicit heap variable. Such an explicit heap variable introduces a mismatch between the abstraction level of the programming language and its symbolic execution. On the other hand, in [18] we already formalized symbolic execution for abstract object creation in dynamic logic which, as in [8], does not involve an explicit heap variable. As such this formalization provides a promising basis for further extensions to object-oriented multithreaded programs, using the partial order reduction techniques as described in this paper.

7 Related Work

Symbolic execution of concurrent programs is limited by the state space explosion due to all possible interleavings of concurrent events [19]. As such, the number of execution paths and of branching points where path conditions need to be evaluated, grows exponentially in the number of concurrent events within each thread. Many techniques have been proposed to mitigate state explosion [3], for example by using heuristics [20], abstractions [21], or by either merging [22,23] or pruning states [9,24,25]. We studied the latter approach in this paper.

Similar to [24,26,27], we assume the execution of a program symbolically on a virtual machine that dynamically computes a dependency relation between states. Executions that have the same causal structure can be pruned, as they are equivalent with respect to finding errors in the given program. Our approach differs from prior works on combining partial order reduction techniques with symbolic execution. The main difference is that we provide a formal framework for studying the correctness and completeness of the symbolic and the reduced semantics with respect to that with concrete values. In this respect, we extend the work in [8] to concurrency.

Although it does not play a role in the programming language we considered in this paper, in general, the computation of the dependency relation may involve alias analysis. To avoid imprecision and extra computational burden, it could be interesting to investigate the combination of the current results with the syntax-based method proposed in [8] for checking aliases.

Our second contribution is a sound and relative complete dynamic logic for concurrent programs using partial order reduction. Several variations of dynamic logic exist for sequential programs, but only few calculi extend dynamic logic to concurrency. Most notably, concurrent dynamic trace logic [28] extends dynamic logic with symbolic execution rules for concurrent interleavings and dynamic thread creation based on the rely/guarantee methodology, the dynamic logic for concurrent Java [29] has been implemented in the KeY system [2], and the dynamic logic for Creol [30] supports compositional verification of an object-oriented modeling language for concurrent distributed applications [31]. The latter is very similar to our dynamic logic, because its semantics is based on traces, reformulating the work in [32] in the context of dynamic logic. The main difference with our approach is in the use of partial order reduction, so that verification is not only compositional but also effective. Other related dynamic logics for concurrency are Peleg's Concurrent Dynamic Logic [33], its extension with channels and shared variable communication [34], and the dynamic logic for communicating concurrent systems [35]. The former can only treat concurrent systems with no communication, while the latter can describe communications and concurrency using a CCS-based language with Kleene-star for recursion. Neither of these logics, however, focus on partial order reduction.

8 Conclusion

The use of symbolic execution for multithreaded languages may lead to a state space explosion during model exploration. In this paper, we have studied how symbolic execution can be combined with partial order reduction, a technique for pruning symbolic states during model exploration by pruning states with equivalent symbolic paths. Our study is *foundational*: we develop a formal model of symbolic execution for multithreaded programs and provide a formal justification for the correctness of this model. We show how the formal model can be extended to incorporate partial order reduction, and provide a formal justification of correctness for the extended model. We then show how a proof system in dynamic logic for the considered multithreaded programming language corresponds to the formal model of symbolic execution such that correctness proofs for the latter carry over to prove soundness and relative completeness for the proof system. These proofs, which curiously establish the soundness and relative completeness of the proof system with partial order reduction by means of bisimulation, provide a formal justification for pruning nodes during proof construction, thereby simplifying the proof construction for multithreaded programs.

In this paper, our focus has been on the formal justification of the basic mechanisms of symbolic execution combined with partial order reduction for multithreaded programs. This work leaves many possible extensions unexplored. The current formulation of symbolic execution (and the corresponding proof system) will generate many unfeasible paths. One interesting extension of our work is the further pruning of search states by evaluating the consistency of symbolic paths, which opens for many different evaluation strategies (e.g., [3]). Another interesting extension is the treatment of aliases for the dependency relation underlying partial order reduction, which leads to imprecision and extra computational burden. It would also be interesting to investigate the formal justification of more aggressive pruning techniques, such as prefix-pruning over the equivalence relation of the partial order reduction.

Acknowledgement. We thank the reviewers for their valuable comments.

References

1. King, J.C.: Symbolic execution and program testing. Commun. ACM **19**(7), 385–394 (1976)
2. Ahrendt, W., Beckert, B., Bubel, R., Hähnle, R., Schmitt, P.H., Ulbrich, M. (eds.).: Deductive Software Verification - The KeY Book - From Theory to Practice, LNCS, vol. 10001. Springer, Heidelberg (2016)
3. Baldoni, R., Coppa, E., D'Elia, D.C., Demetrescu, C., Finocchi, I.: A survey of symbolic execution techniques. ACM Comput. Surv. **51**(3), 50:1–50:39 (2018)
4. Cadar, C., Sen, K.: Symbolic execution for software testing: three decades later. Commun. ACM **56**(2), 82–90 (2013)
5. Godefroid, P., Klarlund, N., Sen, K.: DART: directed automated random testing. In: Sarkar, V., Hall, M.W. (eds.) Proceedings ACM SIGPLAN Conference on Programming Language Design and Implementation (PLDI'2005), pp. 213–223. ACM (2005)

6. Cadar, C., Ganesh, V., Pawlowski, P.M., Dill, D.L., Engler, D.R.: EXE: automatically generating inputs of death. In: Juels, A., Wright, R.N., di Vimercati, S.D.C. (eds.) Proceedings 13th ACM Conference on Computer and Communications Security (CCS'2006), pp. 322–335. ACM (2006)

7. Cadar, C., Dunbar, D., Engler, D.R.: KLEE: unassisted and automatic generation of high-coverage tests for complex systems programs. In: Draves, R., van Renesse, R. (eds.) Proceedings 8th USENIX Symposium on Operating Systems Design and Implementation (OSDI 2008), pp. 209–224. USENIX Association (2008)

8. de Boer, F.S., Bonsangue, M.M.: On the nature of symbolic execution. In: ter Beek, M.H., McIver, A., Oliveira, J.N. (eds.) FM 2019. LNCS, vol. 11800, pp. 64–80. Springer, Cham (2019). https://doi.org/10.1007/978-3-030-30942-8_6

9. Godefroid, P. (ed.): Partial-Order Methods for the Verification of Concurrent Systems. LNCS, vol. 1032. Springer, Heidelberg (1996). https://doi.org/10.1007/3-540-60761-7

10. Harel, D., Kozen, D., Tiuryn, J.: Dynamic Logic. MIT Press (October Foundations of Computing), Cambridge (2000)

11. Clavel, M., et al.: All About Maude - A High-Performance Logical Framework. LNCS, vol. 4350. Springer, Heidelberg (2007). https://doi.org/10.1007/978-3-540-71999-1

12. Clarke, E.M., Grumberg, O., Peled, D.A.: Model Checking. MIT Press, Cambridge (2011)

13. Andrews, G.R.: Concurrent Programming - Principles and Practice. Benjamin/Cummings, San Francisco (1991)

14. Owicki, S.S., Gries, D.: An axiomatic proof technique for parallel programs I. Acta Inf. 6, 319–340 (1976)

15. Apt, K.R., de Boer, F.S., Olderog, E.: Verification of Sequential and Concurrent Programs. Texts in Computer Science. Springer, Heidelberg (2009)

16. Meseguer, J., Rosu, G.: The rewriting logic semantics project: a progress report. Inf. Comput. 231, 38–69 (2013)

17. Johnsen, E.B., Hähnle, R., Schäfer, J., Schlatte, R., Steffen, M.: ABS: a core language for abstract behavioral specification. In: Aichernig, B.K., de Boer, F.S., Bonsangue, M.M. (eds.) FMCO 2010. LNCS, vol. 6957, pp. 142–164. Springer, Heidelberg (2011). https://doi.org/10.1007/978-3-642-25271-6_8

18. de Gouw, S., de Boer, F.S., Ahrendt, W., Bubel, R.: Integrating deductive verification and symbolic execution for abstract object creation in dynamic logic. Softw. Syst. Modeling 15(4), 1117–1140 (2016)

19. Steele, G.L.: Making asynchronous parallelism safe for the world. In: Proceedings of the 17th ACM SIGPLAN-SIGACT Symposium on Principles of Programming Languages (POPL 1990), pp. 218–231. ACM (1989)

20. Li, Y., Su, Z., Wang, L., Li, X.: Steering symbolic execution to less traveled paths. In: Proceedings of the 2013 ACM SIGPLAN International Conference on Object Oriented Programming Systems Languages and Applications (OOPSLA 2013), pp. 19–32. ACM (2013)

21. Guo, S., Kusano, M., Wang, C., Yang, Z., Gupta, A.: Assertion guided symbolic execution of multithreaded programs. In: Proceedings of the 2015 10th Joint Meeting on Foundations of Software Engineering (ESEC/FSE 2015), pp. 854–865. ACM (2015)

22. Kuznetsov, V., Kinder, J., Bucur, S., Candea, G.: Efficient state merging in symbolic execution. In Vitek, J., Lin, H., Tip, F. (eds.) Proceedings ACM SIGPLAN Conference on Programming Language Design and Implementation (PLDI'2012), pp. 193–204. ACM (2012)

23. Scheurer, D., Hähnle, R., Bubel, R.: A general lattice model for merging symbolic execution branches. In: Ogata, K., Lawford, M., Liu, S. (eds.) ICFEM 2016. LNCS, vol. 10009, pp. 57–73. Springer, Cham (2016). https://doi.org/10.1007/978-3-319-47846-3_5

24. Boonstoppel, P., Cadar, C., Engler, D.: RWset: attacking path explosion in constraint-based test generation. In: Ramakrishnan, C.R., Rehof, J. (eds.) TACAS 2008. LNCS, vol. 4963, pp. 351–366. Springer, Heidelberg (2008). https://doi.org/10.1007/978-3-540-78800-3_27

25. Flanagan, C., Godefroid, P.: Dynamic partial-order reduction for model checking software. In: Proceedings of the 32nd ACM SIGPLAN-SIGACT Symposium on Principles of Programming Languages (POPL 2005), pp. 110–121. ACM (2005)

26. Khurshid, S., Pasareanu, C.S., Visser, W.: Generalized symbolic execution for model checking and testing. In: Garavel, H., Hatcliff, J. (eds.) TACAS 2003. LNCS, vol. 2619, pp. 553–568. Springer, Heidelberg (2003). https://doi.org/10.1007/3-540-36577-X_40

27. Visser, W., Pasareanu, C.S., Khurshid, S.: Test input generation with Java PathFinder. SIGSOFT Softw. Eng. Notes **29**(4), 97–107 (2004)

28. Bruns, D.: Deductive verification of concurrent programs. Technical Report 3, Karlsruher Institut für Technologie (KIT) (2015)

29. Beckert, B., Klebanov, V.: A dynamic logic for deductive verification of concurrent programs. In: Proceedings Fifth IEEE International Conference on Software Engineering and Formal Methods (SEFM 2007), pp. 141–150. IEEE Computer Society (2007)

30. Ahrendt, W., Dylla, M.: A system for compositional verification of asynchronous objects. Sci. Comput. Program. **77**(12), 1289–1309 (2012)

31. Johnsen, E.B., Owe, O., Yu, I.C.: Creol: a type-safe object-oriented model for distributed concurrent systems. Theoretical Comput. Sci. **365**(1), 23–66 (2006)

32. Dovland, J., Johnsen, E.B., Owe, O.: Observable behavior of dynamic systems: component reasoning for concurrent objects. Electr. Notes Theor. Comput. Sci. **203**(3), 19–34 (2008)

33. Peleg, D.: Concurrent dynamic logic. In: Proceedings of the Seventeenth Annual ACM Symposium on Theory of Computing (STOC 1985), pp. 232–239. ACM (1985)

34. Peleg, D.: Communication in concurrent dynamic logic. J. Comput. Syst. Sci. **35**(1), 23–58 (1987)

35. Benevides, M.R.F., Schechter, L.M.: Propositional dynamic logics for communicating concurrent programs with CCS's parallel operator. J. Log. Comput. **24**(4), 919–951 (2014)

Author Index

Printed in the United States
By Bookmasters

Printed in the United States
By Bookmasters